CONTENDING FOR THE **FAITH**

Dear friends, although I was very eager to write to you about the salvation we share, I felt I had to write and urge you to contend for the faith that was once for all entrusted to the Saints (Jude 3).

'With customary thoroughness and exacting exegesis, Professor Reymond leads us through a maze of theological topics which call out for a clear biblical perspective in our day. The doctrine of creation, the nature of the new covenant, the continuing authority of the fourth commandment, and the real nature of Roman Catholicism are a few among the important subjects covered. Those who are lost in a fog of modern uncertainty about the unity of Scripture, religious inclusivism and the nature of the Christian life will find Reymond a sure and clear guide. His guiding principle is that God can be glorified in our theological reflection only as we listen to the teaching of his authoritative Word. Reymond is a much needed prophetic voice in our day, calling us to pay attention to 'Thus says the Lord.'

Iain D. Campbell
Free Church of Scotland, Back, Isle of Lewis

CONTENDING FOR THE **FAITH**

LINES IN THE SAND THAT STRENGTHEN THE CHURCH

ROBERT L. REYMOND

MENTOR

To my two colleagues in the
Department of Systematic Theology
at Covenant Theological Seminary
St. Louis, Missouri

Dr. J. Oliver Buswell, Jr.
and
Dr. David Clyde Jones

who taught me through my association with them
more theology than either of them ever realised,
I dedicate this book
with profound gratitude.

Copyright © Robert L. Reymond 2005

ISBN 1-84550-045-8

10 9 8 7 6 5 4 3 2 1

Published in 2005
in the
Mentor imprint
by
Christian Focus Publications, Geanies House,
Fearn, Ross-shire, IV20 1TW, Scotland.

www.christianfocus.com

Cover design by Alister MacInnes

Printed and bound by
WS Bookwell, Finland

Contents

	Preface	7
1.	The Justification of Theology with Special Application to Contemporary Christology	9
2.	The Historical Integrity of Genesis 1–11	29
3.	"In the Space of Six Days"	39
4.	The Theological Significance of the Biblical Doctrine of Creation	53
5.	The Angels of God	65
6.	The Contributions of Ugaritic Study to Old Testament Study	77
7.	Salvation Principles Governing the Genesis Patriarchs and the Exodus Redemption	87
8.	An *Amicus* Brief for Unconditional Election	103
9.	My Vision of the Department of Systematic Theology in a Reformed Seminary	113
10.	Revisiting How We Should Support the Doctrine of the Trinity	117
11.	The Trinitarianism of the Westminster Confession of Faith: Nicene or Reformed?	125
12.	Why Must Jesus Be God and Man?	129
13.	The Sanders/Dunn "Fork in the Road" in the Current Controversy Over the Pauline Doctrine of Justification by Faith	145

14. Lord's Day Observance: Mankind's Proper
    Response to the Fourth Commandment   165

15. Children in the Covenant   187

16. Brunner's Dialectical Encounter   209

17. Barth's Doctrine of Election and Reconciliation   237

18 Bultmann's Demythologized Kerygma   277

19. Dr. John H. Gerstner on Thomas Aquinas
    as a Protestant   307

20. Dr. Robert H. Schuller's Self-Esteem:
    The New Reformation   319

21. Dr. John Stott on Hell   339

22. Review of Walter C. Kaiser's *Toward an
    Exegetical Theology: Biblical Exegesis for
    Preaching and Teaching*   363

23. The "Very Pernicious and Detestable" Doctrine of
    Inclusivism   367

24. Why the Roman Catholic Church Is a Threat Only
    to Roman Catholics and a Non-Threat to Everyone
    Else   389

25. What's Wrong with Islam?   401

    Subject Index   423
    Persons Index   427
    Bible Characters Index   431
    Scripture Index – Old Testament   433
                        New Testament   437

Preface

When I began my formal teaching at Covenant Theological Seminary in St. Louis, Missouri in 1968 my professorial title was assistant professor of systematic theology and apologetics, which title I took seriously until I was granted full professorship at which time my title was shortened to professor of systematic theology. As a professional apologist I felt the keen responsibility to "contend for the faith that was once for all entrusted to the saints" (Jude 3) in those areas where I thought I had acquired some competency.

The articles in this book, for the most part, are a selection from around two hundred papers in the areas of systematic theology and apologetics that I wrote originally for the seminary classroom. Over the years I distributed them, even those that had been written originally as addresses, to my classes for student discussion during a single class period at Covenant Seminary and now at Knox Theological Seminary in Fort Lauderdale, Florida. Some class discussions spilled over to a second or third class period. The one thing these articles generally have in common is their apologetic flavor, that is to say, each in its own way contends for the biblical and Reformed faith as I understand that faith. Several have been published before; some are seeing public light of day for the first time.

I offer them now to a broader readership because, in my opinion, they address topics that generally are being debated within the church at large today. The article, "The Contributions of Ugaritic Study to Old Testament Study" is the one exception here, but I opted to include it because of its apologetic value for demonstrating what I regard to be the proper approach to Old Testament study. It is my hope that these papers will generate more light than heat, but if any of them should generate some heat, which may well occur, so be it. But the reader may be assured that it was never my intention when I wrote these articles merely to generate heat; my intention was and always has been to defend the Faith that was once for all entrusted to the saints.

Robert L. Reymond
July 2004

Chapter One

The Justification of Theology with Special Application to Contemporary Christology

The highly esteemed American philosopher-theologian of revered memory, Dr. Gordon Haddon Clark, begins his 1984 book, *In Defense of Theology,* with the following statement:

> Theology, once acclaimed "the Queen of Sciences," today hardly rises to the rank of a scullery maid; it is often held in contempt, regarded with suspicion, or just ignored.[1]

If Professor Clark is correct in his assessment, that is to say, if there is today this widespread disregard bordering on contempt for theology, one might at first blush be excused if he should feel it entirely proper to be done with theology altogether and to devote his time and energies to some intellectual pursuit holding out promise of higher esteem among men. One might even wonder wherein resides the justification for such a gathering as this, called for the express purpose of advancing the cause of theology. The issue can be pointedly framed in the form of a question: How is theology,[2] as an intellectual discipline deserving today of the church's highest interest and of the occupation of men's mind, to be justified?

If this conference were a conference in philosophical theology, to this question I would respond with one very simple basic sentence: God has revealed the truth about himself, about us, and about the

---

Note: I read this paper at the Edinburgh Conference in Christian Dogmatics sponsored by Rutherford House, Edinburgh, Scotland, August 26-31, 1985.

[1]Gordon Haddon Clark, *In Defense of Theology* (Milford, Michigan: Mott Media, 1984), 3.

[2]The term "theology" is used in this paper in the somewhat restricted but still fairly broad sense for the disciplines of the classical divinity curriculum with its departments of exegetical, historical, systematic, and practical theology, or for what is practically the same thing, namely, the intelligent effort which seeks to understand the Bible, viewed as revealed truth, as a coherent whole.

relationship between himself and us in Holy Scripture; therefore, we should study Holy Scripture. The product of such study would be theology. Or we might say this another way: If there is a God, he must be someone we should know; and if he has spoken to us in and by the Scriptures of the Old and New Testaments, that very fact is sufficient warrant in itself to justify our study of the Scriptures. Indeed, it mandates the study of the Scripture, or what amounts to the same thing, the engagement of men's minds in the theological enterprise. We would even urge that not to study Scripture, *if God has revealed himself therein*, is the height of folly and the clearest evidence of a certain kind of insanity!

This particular ground or justification for the study of theology is so overwhelming that all other reasons, from an apologetic perspective, would be unnecessary. And I say again, if this were a conference in philosophical theology or apologetics, that this would be the justification I would offer for doing theology. Then the remainder of this paper would be devoted to the task of stating the case for what has often been called the first principle of the Christian faith, namely, that God is "really there" and that he has spoken to us, rationally, authoritatively, and univocally, in and by the inspired Scriptures of his prophets and apostles. This I have already attempted to do in my book on apologetic method, entitled *The Justification of Knowledge*,[3] so I see no need to restate the entire case now. Suffice it to say simply at this point that, for me, the Scriptures of the Old and New Testaments are self-attestingly, self-authenticatingly of divine origin as to content and message, the Word of the self-attesting Christ of Scripture, carrying inherently within them their own divine *indicia*, such as

> the heavenliness of the matter, the efficacy of the doctrine, the majesty of the style, the consent of all the parts, the scope [goal] of the whole (which is to give all glory to God), the full discovery [disclosure] it makes of the only way of man's salvation, the many other incomparable excellencies, and the entire perfection thereof *(Westminster Confession of Faith,* I.V),

which properties, the *Confession of Faith* reminds us, are arguments whereby the Holy Scripture "doth *abundantly evidence* itself to be

---

[3]Robert L. Reymond, *The Justification of Knowledge* (Third printing; Phillipsburg, New Jersey, Presbyterian and Reformed, 1984).

the Word of God" (I.V; emphasis supplied). If my concern today, may I say again, were purely and strictly an apologetic one, it would be Augustinian/Anselmic/Calvinistic fideism, expressed in the phrase "*credo ut intelligam*" ("I believe in order that I may understand"), whereby the child of God through *believing* study seeks an ever-fuller *understanding*[4] of the self-authenticating truths of God in Scripture, that I would urge and defend.

The nature of this conference, it seems to me, however, calls for the explication of a different kind of rationale for engaging in the theological enterprise, and this I would suggest should be done along lines more biblical than apologetical.

The Biblical Justification for Theology

When we inquire into the issue before this dogmatics conference on the justification of theology, if I understand its intended import, what we are asking is simply this: Why should we engage ourselves in intellectual and scholarly reflection on the message and content of the Holy Scripture? And a related question is this: Why do we do this, as Christians, the particular way that we do? To these questions, I would suggest, the New Testament offers at least the following four reasons:[5] (1) Christ's own theological method, (2) Christ's mandate to teach in the Great Commission, (3) the apostolic model, and (4) the apostolically-approved example and activity of the New Testament church. Consider each of these briefly with me.

Christ's own theological method
It is Christ himself, by his example and method of interpretation, who established for his church both the prerogative and the pattern to exegete the Scriptures of the Old and New Testaments in the special way that it does, and to derive from those Scriptures, by theological deduction, their special application to his person and work. This is clear from the New Testament itself. For in addition to those specific occasions when he applied the Old Testament to himself (see, for

---

[4]*Fides quaerens intellectum.*

[5]I wish to express my indebtedness to conversations with Professor David C. Jones, my friend and colleague in the Systematics Department at Covenant Theological Seminary for some of the thoughts I am expressing here.

example, Matt. 22:41-45; Luke 4:14-21; John 5:46), we are informed in Luke 24:25-27 that "beginning with Moses and all the prophets, [the glorified Christ] *explained [diermēneusen]* to them in all the Scriptures the things concerning himself" (emphasis supplied). Beyond all controversy, such an exhaustive engagement in Scripture exposition involved our Lord in theological activity in the most heightened sense.

In his small book, *According to the Scriptures,* with sensitivity and depth of insight, C. H. Dodd develops the point I am making here. Let us listen to this eminent biblical scholar for a few moments:

At the earliest period of Church history to which we can gain access, we find in being the rudiments of an original, coherent and flexible method of biblical exegesis which was already beginning to yield results.

...Very diverse scriptures are brought together so that they interpret one another in hitherto unsuspected ways. To have brought together, for example, the Son of Man who is the people of the saints of the Most High, the Man of God's right hand, who is also the vine of Israel, the Son of Man who after humiliation is crowned with glory and honour, and the victorious priest-king at the right hand of God, is an achievement of interpretative imagination which results in the creation of an entirely new figure. It involves an original, and far-reaching, resolution of the tension between the individual and the collective aspects of several of these figures, which in turn makes it possible to bring into a single focus the "plot" of the Servant poems..., of the psalms of the righteous sufferer, and of the prophecies of the fall and recovery (death and resurrection) of the people of God, and finally offers a fresh understanding of the mysterious imagery of apocalyptic eschatology.

This is a piece of genuinely creative thinking. Who was responsible for it? The early Church, we are accustomed to say.... But creative thinking is rarely done by committees, as useful as they may be for systematizing the fresh ideas of individual thinkers, and for stimulating them to further thought. It is individual minds that originate. Whose was the originating mind here?

Among Christian thinkers of the first age known to us there are three of genuinely creative power: Paul, the author to the Hebrews, and the Fourth Evangelist. We are precluded from proposing any one of them for the honour of having originated the process, since even Paul, greatly as he contributed to its development, demonstrably did not originate it.... The New Testament itself avers that it was Jesus Christ Himself who first directed the minds of His followers to certain parts of the scriptures as those in which they might find illumination upon the meaning of His mission and destiny.... I can see no reasonable ground for rejecting the statements of the Gospels that (for example) He pointed to Psalm cx as a better guide to the truth about His mission and destiny than the popular beliefs about the Son of David, or that He made that connection of the "Lord" at God's right hand with the Son of Man in Daniel which proved so momentous for Christian thought, or that He associated with the Son of Man language which had been used of the Servant of the Lord, and employed it to hint at the meaning, and the issue, of His own approaching death. To account for the beginning of this most original and fruitful process of rethinking the Old Testament we found need to postulate a creative mind. The Gospels offer us one.[6]

Beyond dispute the four Gospels depict Jesus of Nazareth as entering deeply into the engagement of the mind with Scripture and drawing out original and fascinating theological deductions therefrom. And it is he who establishes for us the pattern and end of our own theologizing: If we would be his disciples, we must follow him in making the interpretation of Scripture the basis and norm of our theology, and we must arrive finally at him in all of our theological labors.

The mandate in the Great Commission
Theology is a task of the church; of this there can be no doubt. For after setting for us the example and establishing for us the pattern and end of all theology, the glorified Christ commissioned his church to *teach* (*didaskontes*) all nations (Matt. 28:18-20). And theology, essential to this teaching, serves in carrying out the Great Commission as it seeks to set forth in a logical and coherent manner the truth God has revealed in Holy Scripture about himself and the world he has created.

The divine Commission to the church to disciple, to baptize, and

---

[6]C. H. Dodd, *According to the Scriptures* (London: James Nisbet, 1952), 108-10. Two caveats are in order here, however. First, while we obviously appreciate Dodd's granting to Jesus alone the creative genius to bring these several Old Testament themes together to enhance understanding of his person and work, it is extremely important to insist that, in so doing, Jesus did not bring a meaning to the Old Testament that was not intrinsic to the Old Testament itself. Second, I believe that the "Son of Man" in Daniel 7:13-14 is properly to be interpreted individually as applying to Christ rather than collectively as Dodd suggests.

to teach all nations clearly places upon the church, indwelt and empowered by the Holy Spirit, certain *intellectual* demands. There is the *evangelistic* demand to address the gospel to the needs of every generation, for the Commission is to disciple all the nations, with no restriction as to time and place. There is the *didactic* (or catechetical) demand "to correlate the manifold data of revelation in our understanding and the more effectively apply this knowledge to all phases of our thinking and conduct."[7] Finally, there is, as we have already noted, the *apologetic* (or polemic) demand ultimately to justify the existence of Christianity and to protect the message of Christianity from adulteration and distortion (see Tit. 1:9). Theology has risen, and properly so, in the life of the church in response to these concrete demands in fulfilling the Great Commission.

The apostolic model
Such activity as eventually led to the church's engagement in theology is found not only in the teaching of Jesus Christ but also in the rest of the New Testament. Paul wastes no time after his baptism in his effort to "prove" (*sumbibazein*) to his fellow Jews that Jesus is the Christ (Acts 9:22). Later, as a seasoned missionary, he enters the synagogue in Thessalonica "and on three Sabbath days he *reasoned* [*dielexato,* "dialogued"] with them *from the Scriptures, explaining* [*dianoigōn*] and *proving* [*paratithemenos*] that the Christ had to suffer and rise from the dead" (Acts 17:2-3; emphasis supplied). The learned Apollos "vigorously *refuted* [*diakatēlegcheto*] the Jews in public debate, *proving* [*epideiknus*] *from the Scriptures* that Jesus was the Christ" (Acts 18:28; emphasis supplied).

Nor is Paul's evangelistic "theologizing" limited to the synagogue. While waiting for Silas and Timothy in Athens Paul "*reasoned* [*dielegeto*] not only in the synagogue with Jews and the God-fearing Greeks but also *in the marketplace* day by day *with those who happened to be there*" (Acts 17:17; emphasis supplied). This got him an invitation to address the Aeropagus, which he did in terms that could be understood by the Epicurean and Stoic philosophers gathered there (see his quotation from the Greek poets in 17:27) without, however, any accommodation of his message to what they were

---

[7]John Murray, "Systematic Theology," *Westminster Theological Journal,* XXV (May 1963), 138.

prepared to believe. In a masterful theological summary presented with evangelistic and apologetic sensitivity, Paul carefully presented the great truths of revelation concerning the Creator, man created in his image, and man's need to come to God through the Judge and Savior he has provided, even Jesus Christ.

But Paul's "theologizing" was not exclusively evangelistic. In addition to that three-month period at Ephesus during which he spoke boldly in the synagogue, arguing persuasively (*dialegomenos kai peithōn*) about the Kingdom of God (Acts 19:8), Paul had discussions (*dialegomenos*) daily in the lecture hall of Tyrannus over a two-year period, not hesitating, as he would say later (see Acts 20:17-35), "to preach anything that would be helpful to you but have taught [*didaxai*] you publicly and from house to house," declaring to both Jews and Greeks that they must turn to God in repentance and have faith in Jesus Christ (Acts 20:20-21). In a word, he declares: "I have not hesitated to proclaim the *whole will of God*" (Acts 20:27; emphasis supplied).

No doubt we see in Paul's letter to the Romans, his major exposition of the message entrusted to him – not only the broad outline and essential content of the gospel he preached but also the theologizing method he employed. Notice should be taken here of the theological flow of the letter: how Paul moves logically and systematically from the plight of the human condition to God's provision of salvation in Christ, then, in turn, on to the results of justification, objections to the doctrine, and finally to the Christian ethic that flows from God's justifying mercies toward us. It detracts in no way from Paul's "inspiredness" (1 Thess. 2:13; 2 Pet. 3:15-16; 2 Tim. 3:16) to acknowledge, as he set forth this theological flow of thought under the Spirit's superintendence, that he reflected upon and deduced theological conclusions from (1) earlier inspired conclusions, (2) biblical history, and (3) even his own personal position in Christ. Indeed, one finds these "theologizing reflections and deductions" embedded in the very heart of some of the Apostle's most radical assertions. For example, after stating certain propositions, at least ten times Paul asks: "What shall we say [conclude] then?" and proceeds to "deduce by good and necessary consequence" the conclusion he desires his reader to reach (see 3:5, 9; 4:1; 6:1, 15; 7:7; 8:31; 9:14, 30; 11:7). In the fourth chapter the Apostle draws the theological conclusion both that circumcision is unnecessary to the blessing of justification (!)

and that Abraham is the spiritual father of the uncircumcised Gentile believer (!) from the simple observation based on Old Testament history that "Abraham believed the Lord, and he credited it to him for righteousness" (Gen. 15:6) some fourteen years *before* he was circumcised (Gen. 17:24), striking theological deductions to draw, to say the least, in his particular religious and cultural milieu simply from the "before and after" relationship between two historical events! Later, to prove that "at the present time there is a remnant chosen by grace" (Rom. 11:5), Paul simply appeals to his own status as a Christian Jew (Rom. 11:2), again a striking assertion to derive from the simple fact of his own faith in Jesus.

The activity of the New Testament church

Finally, our engagement in the task and formation of theology as an intellectual discipline based upon and derived from Scripture gains additional support from the obvious activity of the New Testament church itself,[8] for our attention is already called in the New Testament to a body of saving truth, as in Jude 3 ("the faith once delivered to the saints"), 1 Timothy 6:20 ("the deposit"), 2 Thessalonians 2:15 ("the traditions"), Romans 6:17 ("the pattern of doctrine"), and the "faithful sayings" of the pastoral letters of Paul (1 Tim. 1:15; 3:1; 4:8-9; 2 Tim. 2:11-13; Tit. 3:3-8).[9] These descriptive terms and phrases unmistakably and incontestably indicate that in the days of the Apostles the theologizing process of reflecting upon and comparing Scripture with Scripture, collating, deducing, and framing doctrinal statements into creedal formulae approaching the character of church confessions had already begun (see, for example, Rom. 10:9; 1 Cor. 12:3; 1 Tim. 3:16). And all of this was done with the full knowledge and approval of the Apostles, indeed, with the full and personal engagement and involvement of the Apostles themselves in the theologizing process (see, for example, in Acts 15:1-16:5 the activity of the Apostles in the Jerusalem assembly, laboring not as Apostles but as elders in the deliberative activity of preparing a conciliar theological response to the issue being considered then for the

---

[8]See J. N. D. Kelly, "Credal Elements in the New Testament," *Early Christian Creeds* (London: Longmans, 1950, 1960).

[9]See George W. Knight, III, *The Faithful Sayings in the Pastoral Letters* (Kampen: J. H. Kok, 1968), for an exposition of these "faithful sayings."

church's guidance).

Hence, when we today, under the guidance of the Spirit of God and in faith, come to Holy Scripture and with all the best intellectual tools make an effort to explicate it, trace its workings in the world, systematize its teachings, and propagate its message, thus hard won, to the world, we are standing squarely in the theologizing process present in and witnessed and mandated by the New Testament itself!

Surely herein resides the biblical justification for the theological enterprise in our own time and our personal engagement in it. Indeed, so clear is the scriptural mandate for theology that one is not speaking to excess were he to suggest that our concern should not be one primarily of *whether* we should engage ourselves in theology or not – the Lord of the church and his Apostles leave us no other option here (see Matt. 28:20; 2 Tim. 2:2; Tit. 1:9; 2:1); we have to be engaged in it if we are going to be faithful to him. Rather, what should be of primary concern to us is whether, in our engagement in it, we are *listening* as intently and submissively as we should to Christ's voice speaking to his church in Holy Scripture. In short, our primary concern should be: Is our theology correct? Or perhaps better: Is our theology *orthodox*?

A Case in Point: Two Modern Christologies

An illustration of what, for me, highlights this greater concern is what is being written today in the area of Christology. Such writing in its own way justifies in a powerful way the Evangelical's continuing engagement in orthodox theology. Just as the central issue of the church's theology in the Book of Acts was christological (see 9:2; 17:2-3; 18:28), so also today Christ's own questions, "What do you think about the Christ? Whose son is he?" (Matt. 22:42), continue to occupy center stage in current theological debate. While the conciliar Definition of Chalcedon in AD 451 espousing a two-natured Christ has generally satisfied Christian orthodoxy, that Definition has fallen upon hard times in the church of our day (see, for example, an extreme example of this in *The Myth of God Incarnate*). The church dogma that this one Lord Jesus Christ is very God and very man and is both of these in the full unabridged sense of these terms and is both of these simultaneously has been increasingly rejected not only, it is alleged, on biblical grounds but also as a contradiction, an impossibility, indeed, a rank absurdity. As a result, it is widely affirmed today that Christology in a way heretofore unparalleled in the church is simply "up for grabs." It constitutes "a whole new ball game."

The Johannine phrase, *ho logos sarx egeneto* ("the Word became flesh") is at the center of the modern debate and in its own way, as a point of departure, crystallizes the major issue of the current controversy: Is Christology to be a Christology "from below," that is, is it to take its departure from a human Jesus (*sarx*, "flesh"), or is it to be a Christology "from above," that is, is it to begin with the Son of God (*ho logos*, "the Word") come to us from heaven? And in either case, what precisely is the import of John's choice of verb: the *egeneto*? Faced with such questions, is it not clear that never has the need been greater for careful, biblically-governed, hermeneutically-meticulous theologizing as the church addresses the perennial question: *Who is Jesus of Nazareth*?

Any response to this question would be well-advised to recall at the outset that the ultimate aim of the early Fathers throughout the decades of controversy over this matter (AD 325–451) was simply to describe and to defend the verbal picture which the Gospels and the rest of the New Testament draw of Jesus of Nazareth. Certainly, inter-necine party strife and rancor between some individuals made complete objectivity in the debate extremely difficult at times. But a faithful reading of the Nicene and Post-Nicene Fathers must lead one to the conclusion that it was neither the concern just to "have it one's own way" nor the desire to contrive a doctrinal formula so intellectually preposterous that it would be a stumbling block to all but the most gullible of men that led them to speak as they did of Jesus Christ as a two-natured single Person. Rather, what ultimately underlay their entire effort, we may affirm without fear of correction, was simply the faithful (that is, "full of faith") resolve to set forth as accurately as words available to them could do what the New Testament said about Jesus. If their creedal terms were sometimes expressed in the terms of earlier and current philosophy, those terms nonetheless served the church well then (were they not simply "contextualizing" the truths of Scripture about Christ?) and still do in most quarters of the Christian community in communicating who the Bible declares him to be. If the "four great negative Chalcedonian adverbs" (*asunkutōs* ["without confusion"], *atreptōs* [without transmutation"], *adiairetōs* ["without division"], *achōristōs* ["without separation"]) describe not so much how the two natures –

the human and the divine – *are* to be related in the unity of the one Person of Christ as how they are *not* to be related, still it can and should be said that these adverbs served to protect both what the Fathers believed the Scriptures clearly taught about Jesus and, at the same time, the *mystery* of his person as well. My own deep longing is that the church today might be as faithful and perceptive in assessing the picture of Jesus in the Gospels for our time as these spiritual forebears were for theirs.

I fear, however, that it is not just a modern dissatisfaction with their usage of Greek philosophical terminology or the belief that the early Fathers simply failed to read the Bible as accurately as they might have that lies behind the totally new and different reconstructions of Jesus presently being produced by some doctors in the church. Rather, it is a new and foreign manner of reading the New Testament, brought in as the result of the "assured results" of "Enlightenment criticism" – a new hermeneutic reflecting canons of interpretation neither derived from Scripture nor sensitive to grammatical/historical rules of reading an ancient text – that is leading men to draw totally new portraits of Christ. But along with these new portraits of Christ, a Christ also emerges whose purpose is no longer to reverse the effects of a space/time fall from an original state of integrity and to bring men into the supernatural Kingdom of God and eternal life but rather to shock the modern somehow into an existentially-conceived "authentic existence," or into any number of other religio-psychological responses to him.

Now I believe that it is quite in order to ask, over against the creators of these "new Christs": Is the mindset of modern man really such that he is incapable of believing in the Christ and the so-called "mythological kerygma" (Bultmann) of the New Testament? Is it so that modern science compels the necessity of "demythologizing" the church's proclamation and to reinterpret it existentially? I believe not. In fact, what *I* find truly amazing is just how many truly impossible things (more than Lewis Carroll's seven, I assure you) that modern man is able to believe every day – such as the view that asserts that this present universe is the result of an impersonal beginning out of nothing plus time plus chance, or that man is the result of forces latent within nature itself, or that man is essentially good and morally perfectible through education and social manipulation, or that morals need not be grounded in unchanging ethical absolutes.

It is also still in order to ask: Who has better read and more carefully handled the Biblical material – the ancient or the new Christologist – with reference to both the person and purpose of Jesus Christ?

Bultmann's existential Jesus

Consider Bultmann, the exegete, for a moment as a case in point. When, in his commentary on John, he comes to John 1:14, he writes: "The Logos became flesh! It is the *language of mythology* that is here employed,"[10] specifically "the mythological language of Gnosticism."[11] For Bultmann, all the emphasis in this statement falls on *sarx* ("flesh") and its meaning, so that "the Revealer is nothing but a man."[12] Morever, the Revealer's *doxa* ("glory") "is not to be seen...*through* the *sarx*...; it is to be seen in the *sarx* and nowhere else."[13]

When one takes exception to this and observes, however, that this statement cannot mean that the Word became flesh and thus ceased to be the Word (who earlier was said to be in the beginning with God and who was God [1:1]), both because the Word is still the subject of the phrase that follows, "and dwelt among us," and because John's sequel to this latter phrase is "and we beheld his glory *as* [the *hōs* here denotes not only comparison but also identification][14] of the unique Son of the Father" whom John then further describes as "the unique one, God [himself; so F. F. Bruce], who is in the bosom of the Father" (1:18), one has just reason to wonder at the exegesis behind Bultmann's response that John's assertions are reflecting the perspective of *faith* that has understood that the revelation of *God* is located precisely in the *humanity* of Jesus,[15] and that they are not statements about the divine *being* of Jesus but rather the later church's

---

[10]Rudolf Bultmann, *The Gospel of John: A Commentary*, translated by G.R. Beasley-Murray from *Das Evangelium des Johannes* (Oxford: Basil Blackwell, 1971), 61.

[11]Bultmann, *The Gospel of John: A Commentary*, 61.

[12]Bultmann, *The Gospel of John: A Commentary*, 62; see too his statement: "It is in his sheer humanity that he is the Revealer" (63).

[13]Bultmann, *The Gospel of John: A Commentary*, 63.

[14]See F. Büschel, "*monogenēs*," *Theological Dictionary of the New Testament*, IV, 740 (fn. 15).

[15]Bultmann, *The Gospel of John: A Commentary*, 62f., 60.

mythological shaping of the *meaning* of Jesus for faith!

Can the exegete who is not a follower of the highly personalized, individualistic, existential school of Bultmann be blamed if he politely demurs from this perspective? For here there remains not even a kenotic Christ who once was God and who divested himself of his deity but only an existential Christ who in *being* never was or is God but is only the Revealer of God to *faith*. But of course the "faith" here is purely subjective and existential, devoid of any historical facticity.

The questions must be squarely faced: Is Bultmann's interpretation preferable to that of Chalcedon? Is it in any sense exegetically sustainable? Is not the language of John 1:14 clearly the language of an *eyewitness* (see "we beheld" and the commentary on this phrase in 1 John 1:1-3)? And does not the Evangelist imply in his "*we* beheld" that *others* as well as he "beheld his glory" (see John 21:24), which glory he identifies *as* (*hōs*) the glory of his divine being as "unique Son of the Father"? And just how observable Jesus' divine glory was is evident on nearly every page of the Gospels, in every sign-miracle he performed, a glory which neither bystander could overlook nor enemy deny (see 2:11; 3:2; 9:16; 11:45-48; 12:10-12, 37-41; see Acts 2:22: "as you yourselves know"; see too, Acts 4:16: "...and we cannot deny it").[16] Later, when doubting Thomas eventually came to faith in Jesus and cried out, "My Lord and my God" (20:28), he did so, not because an existential flash bringing new pistic appreciation of the meaning of the human Jesus for human existence overpowered him, but because his demand to see the print of the nails with his own eyes was graciously met (see John 20:25, 27, 29), and because the only possible implication of Christ's resurrection appearance for the nature of his *being* (see Rom. 1:4) impacted inescapably upon him in terms of his exclamation: "[You are] my Lord and my God!"

Bultmann's Christology, only one of many examples of a Christology "from below," represents one extreme to which faulty theologizing can lead the church – the extreme of portraying the Christ as to his being as a mere man and only a man. But this conclusion not

---

[16]It is directly germane to our point here to observe in connection with Christ's first sign-miracle (John 2:1-11) that John does not say that the disciples' faith was the pathway to the beholding of Jesus' glory but, to the contrary, his miracle manifested his glory, and his disciples believed on him *as a consequence*.

only the Fourth Gospel but also the New Testament as a whole finds intolerable. A careful consideration of each context will show that *theos* ("God") is employed as a christological title at least eight times in the New Testament (John 1:1, 18; 20:28; 1 John 5:20; Rom. 9:5; Tit. 2:13; Heb. 1:8, 2 Pet. 1:1; see also Col. 2:9). Hundreds of times Jesus is called *kurios*, "Lord," the Greek word employed by the LXX to translate the Hebrew Tetragrammaton (see, for example, Matt. 7:21; 25:37, 44; Rom. 10:9-13; 1 Cor. 2:8; 12:3; 2 Cor. 4:5; Phil. 2:11; 2 Thess. 1:7-10). Old Testament statements spoken by or describing Yahweh, the Old Testament God of the covenant, are applied to Christ in the New (see, for example, Ps. 102:25-27 and Heb. 1:10-12; Isa. 6:1-10 and John 12:40-41; Isa. 8:12-13 and 1 Pet. 3:14-15; Isa. 45:22 and Matt. 11:28; Joel 2:32 and Rom. 10:13). Divine attributes and actions are ascribed to him (Mark 2:5, 8; Matt. 18:20; John 8:58; Matt. 24:30). Then there is Jesus' own self-consciousness of his divine nature (see John 3:13; 6:38, 46, 62; 8:23, 42; 17:6, 24; and the famous so-called "embryonic Fourth Gospel" in Matt. 11:25-28 and Luke 10:21-22). Finally, the weight of testimony that flows from his miracles and his resurrection (Rom. 1:4) must be faced without evasion. It carries one beyond the bounds of credulity to be asked to believe that the several New Testament writers, living and writing under such varying circumstances, places, and times, were nonetheless all seduced by the same mythology of Gnosticism. All the more is this conclusion highly doubtful in light of the fact that the very presence of a pre-Christian Gnosticism has been seriously challenged by much recent scholarship.[17]

---

[17]See Edwin M. Yamauchi, *Pre-Christian Gnosticism: A Survey of the Proposed Evidence* (Updated edition; Grand Rapids: Baker, 1983), particularly Chapter 12; see also C.H. Dodd, *The Interpretation of the Fourth Gospel* (CUP, 1955); the Dodd *Festschrift*, *The Background of the New Testament and its Eschatology*, edited by W. D. Davies and D. Daube (CUP, 1956), especially the articles by W. F. Albright and R. P. Casey; and Raymond E. Brown, *The Gospel According to John I-XII* (Garden City, NY: Doubleday, 1966), LVI.

Käsemann's docetic Christ

Now, very interestingly, it is by one of Bultmann's students, Ernst Käsemann, that we find argued the other extreme in current Christology, a Christology "from above."[18] In his *The Testament of Jesus*, Käsemann also deals at some length with the meaning of John 1:14; only he argues, to use Ridderbos' words, that the Evangelist intends by *sarx* here "not the means to veil the glory of God in the Man Jesus, but just the opposite, to reveal that glory before every eye. The flesh is the medium of the glory."[19]

According to Käsemann, John's Jesus, far from being a man, is rather the portrayal of a god walking across the face of the earth. Commenting on "the Word became flesh," Käsemann queries: "Is not this statement totally overshadowed by the confession, 'We beheld his glory,' so that it receives its meaning from it?"[20] Thinking it to be so, Käsemann contends that the Fourth Gospel uses the earthly life of Jesus "merely as a backdrop for the Son of God proceeding through the world...."[21] Furthermore, he urges: "...the glory of Jesus determines [the Evangelist's] whole presentation so thoroughly from the very outset that the incorporation and position of the passion narrative of necessity becomes problematical,"[22] so problematical, in fact, Käsemann believes, that "one is tempted to regard it as being a mere postscript [*Nachklappt*] which had to be included because John could not ignore this tradition nor yet could he fit it organically into his work."[23] So great is John's emphasis on the divine glory of Jesus that, according to Käsemann, the Fourth Gospel has slipped into a "naive docetism":

---

[18]I am indebted to Herman N. Ridderbos for calling my attention to this contrast between teacher and student. See Ridderbos, "The Word Became Flesh," *Through Christ's Word*, translated by Richard B. Gaffin, Jr. and edited by W. Robert Godfrey and Jesse L. Boyd, III (Phillipsburg, New Jersey: Presbyterian and Reformed, 1985), 3-22, especially 5.

[19]Ridderbos, "The Word Became Flesh," *Through Christ's Word*, 6.

[20]Ernst Käsemann, *The Testament of Jesus: A Study of the Gospel of John In the Light of Chapter 17*, translated by Gerhard Krodel from *Jesu letzter Wille nach Johannes 17* (Philadelphia: Fortress, 1968), 9-10.

[21]Käsemann, *The Testament of Jesus*, 13.

[22]Käsemann, *The Testament of Jesus*, 7.

[23]Käsemann, *The Testament of Jesus*, 7.

John [formulated who Jesus was and is] in his own manner. In so doing he exposed himself to dangers.... One can hardly fail to recognize the danger of his Christology of glory, namely, the danger of docetism. It is present in a still naive, unreflected form....[24]

In sum, John "was able to give an answer [to the question of the center of the Christian message] only in the form of a naive docetism,"[25] Jesus' humanity really playing no role as it stands "entirely in the shadow" of Jesus' glory as "something quite non-essential."[26] "In what sense," Käsemann asks, "is he flesh, who walks on the water and through closed doors, who cannot be captured by his enemies, who at the well of Samaria is tired and desires a drink, yet has no need of drink and has food different from that which his disciples seek.... How does all this agree with the understanding of a realistic incarnation?"[27] He seriously doubts whether "the 'true man' of later incarnational theology becomes believable" in John's Christology.[28]

What is one to say about Käsemann's opposite extreme to that of Bultmann? One can only applaud Käsemann's emphasis here on the "very God" character of Jesus, but surely Ridderbos is right when, commenting on John 1:14, he writes:

Egeneto, 'became,' is not there for nothing. It is surely a matter of a new mode of existence. Also, not accidental is the presence of *sarx*, 'flesh,' which...indicates man in his weakness, vulnerability, and transiency. Therefore, it has been said, not incorrectly, that this statement...certainly approximates the opposite of what one would expect if it were spoken of a docetic...world of thought.[29]

---

[24]Käsemann, *The Testament of Jesus,* 26, 77; see his statement. "The assertion, quite generally accepted today, that the Fourth Gospel is anti-docetic is completely unproven" (26, fn. 41).

[25]Käsemann, *The Testament of Jesus*, 26.

[26]Ridderbos, "The Word Became Flesh," *Through Christ's Word*, 9.

[27]Käsemann, *The Testament of Jesus*, 9.

[28]Käsemann, *The Testament of Jesus*, 10.

[29]Ridderbos, "The Word Became Flesh," *Through Christ's Word*, 10. Ridderbos' reference here in his "it has been said" is to the opinions of R. Schnackenburg, *Das Johannesevangelium*, 244, and Raymond E. Brown, *The Gospel According to John*, I-XII, 24. But one could add almost indefi-

Moreover, nowhere is Jesus' humanity more apparent in a natural and unforced way than in John's Gospel. Our Lord can grow weary from a journey, sit down at a well for a moment of respite, and ask for water. He calls himself (8:40) and is called by others a man (*anthrōpos*) many times (4:29; 5:12; 7:46; 9:11, 16, 24; 10:33; 11:47; 18:17, 29; 19:5). People know his father and mother (6:42; 7:27; 1:45). He can spit on the ground and make mud with his saliva (9:6). He can weep over the sorrow Lazarus' death brings to Mary and Martha (11:35). He can be troubled (*hē psuchē mou tetaraktai*) as he contemplates his impending death on the cross (12:27). Here is clearly a *man*, for whom death was no friend, who could instinctively recoil against it as a powerful enemy to be feared and resisted. He can have a crown of thorns pressed down on his head (19:2) and be struck in the face (19:3). At his crucifixion (note: he can die!) a special point[30] is made of the spear thrust into his side (see also *sōma*, that is, "body" in 19:38, 40), from which wound blood and water flowed forth (19:34). And after his resurrection on at least two occasions he showed his disciples his hands and feet, and even ate breakfast with them by the Sea of Galilee. Here is no docetic Christ! Clearly, in John's Christology we have to do with *sarx*, "flesh," a man in weakness and vulnerability, a "true man." In Käsemann's interpretation of John's Jesus, while we certainly have to do with a Christology "from above," the Christ therein is so "wholly other" that his humanity is only a "costume" and no part of a genuine Incarnation.

Where precisely does the biblical material in John lead us, however (and here I turn to my own "theologizing")? Does not a fair reading of John's testimony in its entirety yield up a Jesus who is a true man, and yet at the same time One who is *more than* (*not* other than) true man? And in what direction are we instructed to look for the meaning of this "more than" save just the "more than" of the deity of the Son of God, the One who was with God the Father in the beginning and

---

nitely to this list the names of scholars who view John as self-consciously opposing docetism by his statement in 1:14; for example, Leon Morris, *The Gospel According to John* (Grand Rapids: Eerdmans, 1971), 102, and F. F. Bruce, *The Gospel of John* (Grand Rapids: Eerdmans, 1983), 39-40.

[30]See John 19:35: "The man who saw it has given testimony, and his teaching is true."

who himself was and is God (John 1:1-3), who "for us men and for our salvation," without ceasing to be what he is, took into union with himself by means of the virginal conception what he was not and became a man, and as God-incarnate entered the world from the body of a woman (see Gal. 4:4)?

And what about Käsemann's suggestion that the Fourth Gospel's *theologia gloriae* so overpowers everything in its path that there is really no room in it for a *theologia crucis*, that John brings it in simply because he cannot ignore the tradition? I respectfully submit that such a perspective emanates from his theological system rather than from exegesis and objective analysis. The *theologia crucis* fits as comfortably in John's Gospel as it does in the Synoptics or elsewhere. It is introduced at the outset in the Forerunner's "Behold the Lamb" (1:29, 36) and continues throughout as an integral aspect of John's Christology, for example, in the several references to the "hour" that was to come upon Jesus (2:4; 7:30; 8:20; 12:23; 13:1; 17:1), in Jesus' Good Shepherd discourse where he reveals that he would lay down his life for the sheep (10:11, 15), and in his teaching of the grain of seed which must die (12:24).

It must be clearly seen that the implication in Käsemann's intimation that the dogma of a *divine* Savior does violence to a theology of the *cross* mortally wounds Christianity as the redemptive religion of God at its very heart. Both Christ's deity and Christ's cross are essential to our salvation. But the implication of Käsemann's point is just to the opposite effect: that one can have a theology of glory or a theology of the cross, but one cannot have both simultaneously. But, I ask, do not these two theologies stand as friends side by side throughout the New Testament? Paul, for example, whose theology is specifically a theology of the cross can, even as John, see precisely *in the cross* Christ's glory and triumph over the kingdom of darkness (Col. 2:15). The author of Hebrews can affirm that it is precisely *by his death* that Jesus destroyed the devil and liberated those enslaved by the fear of death (2:14-15). Clearly, Käsemann's construction cannot be permitted to stand unchallenged for it plays one scriptural theme off over against a second equally scriptural theme that is in no way intrinsically contradictory to it.

Is there a sense, then, in light of all of this, in which we may legitimately speak of both kinds of Christologies – "from above" and "from below" – in the Gospels? I believe there is, but in the sense clarified by the great Princeton theologian, Benjamin B. Warfield, now over seventy-five years ago:

> John's Gospel does not differ from the other Gospels as the Gospel of the divine Christ in contradistinction to the Gospels of the human Christ. All the Gospels are Gospels of the divine Christ...But John's Gospel differs from the other Gospels in taking from the divine Christ its starting point. The others begin on the plane of human life. John begins in the interrelations of the divine persons in eternity.
>
> [The Synoptic Gospels] all begin with the man Jesus, whom they set forth as the Messiah in whom God has visited his people; or rather, as himself, God come to his people, according to his promise. The movement in them is from below upward.... The movement in John, on the contrary, is from above downward. He takes his start from the Divine Word, and descends from him to the human Jesus in whom he was incarnated. This Jesus, says the others, is God. This God, says John, became Jesus.[31]

* * * * *

By these last paragraphs I have illustrated what I think the theological task is and how it is to be fulfilled. Our task as theologians is simply to listen to and to seek to understand and to explicate what we hear in the Holy Scriptures in their entirety for the health and benefit of the church and in order to enhance the faithful propagation of the true gospel. With a humble spirit and the best use of grammatical/historical tools of exegesis we should draw out of Scripture, always being sensitive to all of its well-balanced nuances, the truth of God revealed therein. If we are to emulate our Lord, his Apostles, and the New Testament church, that and that alone is our task. As we do so, we are to wage a tireless war against any and every effort of the many hostile existentialistic and humanistic philosophies that abound around us to influence the results of our labors.

Have we solved all of the problems inherent in the church dogma of a two-natured Christ by this method? No, obviously not. Problems remain, for example, in the doctrine of the eternal generation of the

---

[31]Benjamin B. Warfield, "John's First Word," *The Westminster Teacher,* January, 1908; cited in *Selected Shorter Writings of Benjamin B. Warfield,* edited by John E. Meeter (Nutley, New Jersey: Presbyterian and Reformed, 1970), I:148-9.

Son,[32] in the doctrine of the *anhypostasia*, and how, for example the same Person simultaneously can be ignorant (Mark 13:32; Luke 2:52) and yet know all things (Matt. 9:4; John 1:47; 2:25; 11:11, 14). And there is always a place for theological refinement. But the fact that problems remain for him as he carries out the task incumbent upon him gives the theologian no warrant to play one Scripture truth off over against another (for example, Christ's deity off over against his humanity, or a theology of glory off over against a theology of the cross) and to reject one clear emphasis in Scripture out of deference for another of equal prominence that he may happen to prefer. And it is right here – in his willingness to submit his mind to *all* of Scripture, *pasa graphē* (2 Tim. 3:16) – that the theologian as a student of the Word most faithfully emulates the example of his Lord (see Matt. 4:4, 7, 10; 5:17-18; Luke 24:27 [notice the reference to "all the Scriptures"]; John 10:35). Simply put, it is in submission to Scripture that the theologian, as he goes about his task, best reflects that disciple character to which he has by grace been called.

---

[32]See, for example, the writings of such men as John Calvin, Charles Hodge, Benjamin Warfield, John Murray, J. Oliver Buswell, Jr. and Donald Macleod where Christ's implicit subordinationism "in modes of subsistence as well as of operation" in the Nicene formula is called into question, and where the case is made for Christ as *autotheos* ("God of himself").

Chapter Two

The Historical Integrity of Genesis 1–11

The historical integrity of Genesis 1–11 is only one aspect, though a very important aspect, of the larger question: Is the Pentateuch, of which it is a significant part, reliable history? Can the Pentateuchal history be trusted? So before I address directly the announced topic, I want to say something first about the reliability of the Pentateuch as a whole.

The church's historic position on this larger issue is that the Pentateuch or "Law of Moses" as the first section of the Old Testament, along with the Old Testament as a whole, is the divinely inspired Word of God (see Num. 12:6-8; Deut. 18:14-21; Hab. 2:2-3; Jer. 36; Luke 16:17; John 10:35; 1 Cor. 2:6-7; 1 Thess. 2:13; 2 Tim. 3:16; 2 Pet. 1:20-21; 2 Tim. 3:15-16).[1] And until the appearance of the higher critical documentary theories of Eichhorn (1823), Hupfeld (1853), Graf (1865), and Wellhausen (1878), both Jews and Christians alike held this historic position including specifically the Mosaic authorship of virtually the whole Pentateuch. This time-honored latter position – the Mosaic authorship of the Pentateuch – is supported by

1. the Pentateuch itself (see Exod. 17:14; 24:4; 34:27; Num. 33:2; Deut. 31:9, 24);
2. the rest of the Old Testament (see Josh. 23:6; Judg. 3:4; Mal. 4:4);
3. Jesus' teaching (see John 5:46-47); and
4. the rest of the New Testament (see Acts 28:23; Rom. 10:19; 1 Cor. 9:9).

Of course, post-Mosaic anachronisms of the nature of editorial modernizations of old place-names and archaic word endings may possibly be present here and there in the Pentateuch. And almost certainly Deuteronomy 34 (the account of Moses' death) is post-Mosaic, written very likely by Joshua. Nevertheless, Moses, the

---

[1]See my *A New Systematic Theology of the Christian Faith* (Nashville, Tennessee: Thomas Nelson, 1998), chapter two.

fifteenth-century BC lawgiver, had been viewed as the primary author of the Pentateuchal literature until the several documentary theories were advanced in the eighteenth and nineteenth centuries.

But with the rise and subsequent refinements of the several documentary hypotheses, the Mosaic authorship of the first five books of the Old Testament has come more and more into disrepute, calling into question as a result the testimonies of the rest of Scripture and of Christ himself. This is serious enough but if the documentary hypotheses were to prevail it would make it impossible to write a biblical theology that presumes the historical progressiveness of revelation. Nevertheless, in spite of these problems, today through the influence of Martin Noth and Gerhard von Rad, it is widely believed that the Pentateuch is an elaborate composite of several ancient circles of tradition reflecting Israel's religious pilgrimage from Abrahamic times to the post-exilic period.

The four most prominent strands of tradition believed to be discoverable within the Pentateuch are designated by Old Testament scholars by the letters J, E, D, and P. Each strand of tradition is thought to be extractable from the others on the basis of certain clues reflecting the specific interests of each. The J (Yahwistic) tradition is supposed to have arisen in Judah around 850 BC. Around 750 BC the E (Elohim) tradition supposedly arose in Northern Israel or Ephraim. These two traditions were then editorially woven together sometime in the seventh century (JE). Sometime later, in the same century but before 621 BC (the time of Josiah's reform), Deuteronomy (D) was allegedly published to assist him in his reform effort. Finally, during and after the exile, priestly writers are reputed to have rounded out the expanding literary corpus with priestly legislation (P). Again and again the criteria that have been employed to partition the Pentateuchal material in this manner have themselves come under scholarly scrutiny and have been shown to be highly speculative and artificial. Cyrus Gordon, for example, claims that "newly discovered texts show that much of the material ascribed to 'P' is very early, even pre-Mosaic," and he goes on to charge the advocates of the several documentary theories of "giving hypothetical dates to hypothetical strata (documents) and calling this 'historical criticism'."[2] Recent

---

[2]Elmer B. Smick, "Numbers", *Wycliffe Bible Commentary* (1972), edited by Charles F. Pfeiffer and Everett F. Harrison, Moody Press, 112.

scholarship, furthermore, has demonstrated the similarity between the pattern of Deuteronomy and the suzerainty treaties of the mid-second millennium BC.[3] But always the higher critics have simply made what they regard to be the necessary adjustments to their theories in light of these criticisms and have continued to espouse and propagate the same general JEDP theory. For instance, recent trends in Pentateuchal criticism now acknowledge that each of the traditions rests upon a much older tradition than the written tradition itself, some blocks of this oral and fragmentary tradition even going back to Mosaic times, but the actual production of these traditions as literary pieces is still said to have followed a historical process such as that outlined above.[4]

A more viable and reasonable response to the questions surrounding the issue of the authorship of the Pentateuch – and one in keeping with the testimony of Scripture itself – is that suggested by J. Barton Payne.[5] Payne believes that Scripture itself distinguishes three levels of Mosaicity within the Pentateuchal books:

1. parts actually written by Moses (for example, Numbers 33:3-49; see particularly 33:12), which level "may well include considerably more material, where the work of his immediate hand simply has not [been] recorded within the OT text";

2. parts composed by Moses, though not necessarily written down by him (for example, Deuteronomy 33:2-29), which "include all his quoted statements and, for all practical purposes, remain equivalent to the previous level"; and

3. parts historically authentic and springing from the Mosaic period and incorporated under Mosaic instruction (for example, Numbers 12:3; Deuteronomy 34).

Agreeing with this general approach, Kenneth A. Kitchen also speaks of

---

[3]See Meredith G. Kline, *Treaty of the Great King* (1963), Eerdmans.

[4]See, for example, Bernhard Anderson, "The Pentateuch," in *The Oxford Annotated Bible* (1962), eds. Herbert G. May and Bruce M. Metzger, Oxford University Press, xxiv.

[5]J. Barton Payne, *Encyclopedia of Biblical Prophecy* (1973), Harper and Row 172-73.

1. the necessity of granting "an utter minimum" to Mosaic authority;

2. the possibility beyond this minimum of Moses causing to be written by dictation "considerably more"; with

3. nearly the whole Pentateuch in its present form coming as early as Joshua! Kitchen speaks only of orthographic and linguistic revisions coming after this time.[6]

Once these levels are recognized, it is possible to affirm Mosaic superintendence over the Pentateuch as a whole, while explaining at the same time the fact that portions of the Pentateuch are written in the third person about Moses.

The authorship of the Pentateuch, in the final analysis, turns on the question of trust in the testimony of Christ himself regarding its Mosaicity. For those who believe that Christ is God manifest in the flesh with all the attributes of deity intact within him, his testimony to the effect that "Moses wrote about me" (John 5:46) in his "writings" (John 5:47) is decisive and final. Incidentally, there is indication in John 5:43 – compare it with the "in my name" phrase of Deuteronomy 18:19 – that Jesus had in mind the great passage in Deuteronomy 18:15-18 concerning the prophet like unto Moses, that for the higher critic is D, a seventh-century document. This appeal to Christ's testimony should not be interpreted to mean that evangelical scholarship cannot meet scholarly denial by scholarly counter-affirmation. Indeed, the various documentary theories that call into question the Mosaic authorship of the Pentateuch, as we have already implied, have themselves been called into question in our day by solid evangelical scholarship. Hence, the Bible believer does not need to feel for a moment that he must deny the substantially Mosaic authorship of the Pentateuch on scholarly grounds while at the same time affirming it on "faith" grounds. But the suggestion above that the question of the authorship of the Pentateuch impinges ultimately on the question of Christ's testimony simply faces forthrightly the implications both for Christ's person and ministry and for the Christian faith as a whole that are implicit in the denial of Mosaic authorship by the higher critical documentary hypotheses. It is as simple as this:

---

[6]Kenneth A. Kitchen, "Moses," in *New Bible Dictionary*, edited by J. D. Douglas (Grand Rapids: Eerdmans, 1962), 849-50.

If Christ was in error when he said that *Moses* wrote, he could be equally in error when he said that Moses wrote about *him*. I would judge that this is too high a price to pay. Those who affirm the deity of Christ and confess him as their Savior, if they are loyal to him, will out of that loyalty gladly submit to his opinion in the matter and rest their case on his infallible declaration that Moses wrote about him.

Assuming then for very good reason that Moses wrote the Pentateuch under the Holy Spirit's inspiration we will turn directly to a consideration of the historical reliability of Genesis 1–11. It should come as no surprise to the initiate to Old Testament studies, in light of what we have just discussed, that modern critical Old Testament thought regards the early chapters of Genesis as at best aetiological legend or religious *Saga*, that is, as mythological stories that respectively, while not actually historical, intend either to offer an explanation for some sociological characteristic such as mankind's native abhorrence of snakes or to convey some religious truth such as man's inhumanity to man. Simply put, the problem in these chapters for modern man is the distinctly supernatural character of the events that they report, such as

1. the creation of the universe *ex nihilo* in the space of six days and more specifically as a special aspect of that general creation the creation of man by a direct act of God (because of the supposed "pre-scientific" nature of the events that Genesis 1 and 2 record, the trend in modern secularistic intellectual life, influenced as it is by modern scientism's unfounded dogmatic dictum of cosmic and biological evolution, is to regard the so-called "two accounts of creation" in Genesis 1 and 2 as ancient Hebrew cosmogonies comparable in nature to the mythological *Enuma elish* of ancient Babylon);
2. God's covenant arrangement with Adam;
3. Adam's fall into sin with his lapse's resultant effects on the race (in connection with this event we read of a talking serpent, two trees the fruit of which impart life or death respectively, and cherubim who guard the tree of life with a flaming sword);
4. the extraordinary longevity of the antediluvian patriarchs;
5. the universal flood; and
6. the tower of Babel incident.

For the following exegetical reasons, I believe that the church must resist the current secularistic trend and continue to hold, as it has historically done, to the historical integrity of the first eleven chapters of Genesis:

1. The character of the Hebrew itself, employing as it does the *waw* consecutive verb to describe sequential historical events, the frequent use of the sign of the accusative and the relative pronoun, as well as the stylistic and syntactical rules of Hebrew narrative rather than Hebrew poetry, gives every indication that the author (Moses) intended these chapters to be construed as straightforward historical narration of early earth and human history. If one wants a sample in this section of Scripture of what the author's poetry – with its parallelism of thought and fixed pairs – would look like, he can consider Genesis 4:23-24.

2. In Genesis 12–50 the author uses the phrase "These are the generations of…" five times to introduce a new patriarch's history, the general history of whom is not doubted by contemporary scholarship (see 25:12, 19; 36:1, 9; 37:2). But he also employs the same phrase six times in Genesis 1–11 to introduce new blocks of material (see 2:4; 5:1; 6:9; 10:1; 11:10, 27), the last one of these six containing the story of Abraham whose historicity is no longer questioned by most Old Testament scholars. Hence, the last six occurrences of this phrase introduce acknowledged "generally reliable" historical data. Does this not suggest that Moses intended the first five occurrences of the phrase also to introduce blocks of early historical data? And does this not suggest that he intended the entirety of Genesis to be viewed under the literary genre of history?

3. In Genesis 1–11 there are sixty-four geographical terms, eighty-eight personal names, forty-eight generic names, and at least twenty-one identifiable cultural terms (for example, gold, bdellium, onyx, brass, bitumen, mortar, brick, stone, harp, pipe, cities, towers), all suggesting that Moses was describing the world that we know and not a world belonging to another level of reality of mental conception.

4. It should be noted that each divine judgment in Genesis 1–11 is followed by an expression of divine grace: God's covering of our first parents after he had pronounced judgment upon them; his protection for Cain after he had judged him; and his establishing his covenant with Noah after the judgment of the Flood. But where is

God's expression of grace after his dispersing of the race into nations after the tower of Babel incident in Genesis 11? Does not God's call of Abraham in Genesis 12, in whom the dispersed nations of the earth would be blessed, answer to the character of the Babel judgment and thus complete the judgment/grace pattern? It would seem so. Apparently, Moses was unaware of the break between Genesis 1–11 and Genesis 12–50 brought about by the alleged shift in literary genre between the two sections (Gen 1–11, myth; Gen 12–50, history) that many Old Testament scholars see.

5. Scripture in its entirety regards the Genesis account of man's early beginnings and doings as reliable history. The Genesis account of creation is referred to many times elsewhere in the Old and New Testaments. We could with little trouble cite two-dozen passages that do so. For example, direct references and allusions to the Genesis creation may be found in Exodus 20:11, 31:17, Deuteronomy 4:32, Psalms 33:6, 90:2, 136:5-9, 148:2-5, Isaiah 40:25-26, 42:5, 44:24, 45:12, 48:13, 51:13, Amos 4:13, Jeremiah 10:12, Zechariah 12:1, Matthew 19:4-5, John 1:2-3, Ephesians 3:9, Colossians 1:16, 1 Timothy 2:13, Hebrews 1:2, 11:3, and Revelation 4:11, 10:6-7. This is only a partial list. In every instance the Genesis account of creation lies behind these later references and is assumed by them to be a reliable record of what occurred "in the beginning" of the cosmos. To call into question the historical reliability of Genesis 1–2 is to call into question the trustworthiness and authenticity of the entirety of Scripture testimony on the issue of origins. The fall of man (Gen. 3) is referred to in Job 31:33, perhaps Isaiah 43:27, Hosea 6:7, Romans 5:12-19, 2 Corinthians 11:3, and 1 Timothy 2:14. Cain's murder of Abel (Gen. 4) is referred to in Matthew 23:35, Luke 11:51, Hebrews 11:4, 1 John 3:12, and Jude 11. Finally, the Genesis flood (Gen 6–9) is referred to in Isaiah 54:9, Matthew 24:37-39, Luke 17:26-27, Hebrews 11:7, 1 Peter 3:20, and 2 Peter 2:5, 3:6.[7] To call into question

---

[7]Henry Morris and John Whitcomb in their *The Genesis Flood* (Baker, 1976) argue that the universality of the Genesis flood is evident from the (1) the stated depth of the flood-waters (Gen. 7:19-20); (2) the duration of the flood (40 days of rain, 110 days of water continuing to rise, making 150 days in all of "prevailing" [Gen. 7:24], 74 days of decreasing [Gen. 8:5], 40 days before Noah sent out the raven [Gen. 8:6-7], 7 more days before Noah sent out the dove for the first time [Gen. 8:10], 7 more days before he sent

the historicity of Genesis 3–11, then, is again to call into question the trustworthiness and authenticity of a great deal of later Scripture testimony.

6. The genealogies in 1 Chronicles 1 and Luke 3 regard Adam as the divinely created first human being, both mentioning him in their genealogical listings. Neither genealogy gives the slightest impression that one should realize that he is on reliable historical ground as he moves back by them to the time of Abraham but that the names of Abraham's ancestors, given in Genesis 5 and 11, are historically shaky and untrustworthy. These early genealogies, in fact, are treated by the Chronicler and Luke as being as reliable as the later Genesis genealogy in Genesis 12 through 50 of Abraham, Isaac, and Jacob, or the genealogy of David in Ruth 4:18-20.

7. Finally, again the integrity of our Lord's teaching is at stake, for in Matthew 19:4-5 and Mark 10:6-8 he refers to the creation of man in such a way that it is beyond question that he had Genesis 1:27 and Genesis 2:24 in mind and that he viewed these so-called "two diverse accounts of creation" as a trustworthy record of what took place at the beginning of human history. He also refers to the "blood of Abel" (Matt. 23:35) and to the Genesis flood (Matt. 24:37-39). To question the basic historical trustworthiness, authenticity, and integrity of Genesis 1–11 is to assault the integrity of Christ's own teaching.

---

out the dove for the second time [Gen. 8:10], 29 more days elapse [Gen. 8:13], and 57 more days elapse [Gen. 8:14], making a total of 371 days for the entire period; (3) the size of the ark (437.5 feet long, 72.92 feet wide, and 43.75 feet high; for Noah to have built a vessel of such size simply for the purpose of escaping a local flood is beyond belief; (4) the whole process of constructing such a vessel, involving over a century of planning and building, simply to escape a local flood would have been foolish; in such a period of time Noah could have moved just about anywhere in the world he chose in order to escape a local flood regardless of its extremities; (5) Peter bears testimony to the destruction that the Genesis flood brought to the ancient world (2 Pet. 3:3-7); (6) the total destruction, with the exception of eight people, of a widely distributed race (Luke 17:26-30); and (7) God's later covenant promise not to destroy every living thing again by the waters of a flood (8:21); such a promise makes it impossible to accept the view that only a part of the race was destroyed by the flood, for many lesser floods have occurred in human history that have wreaked death and destruction upon multitudes of people.

For these seven reasons I submit that the church not only may but also must regard these early chapters of Genesis in general as reliable history and the Genesis account of creation in particular as a reliable record of the origin of the universe, a record preserved without error by the superintending oversight of the Holy Spirit (2 Pet. 1:20-21; 2 Tim. 3:15-17). We may encounter difficulties in interpreting some of the details of Genesis 1–11 simply because we are working exegetically and hermeneutically with highly circumscribed, greatly compressed, non-technical narrative accounts of the beginning of the cosmos and all things in it, but these difficulties are infinitely to be preferred to the scientific and philosophical difficulties that confront modern interpreters who propound non-theistic responses to the issues of the origin of the universe, the presence of evil in the world, and man's spiritual and moral ills.

Chapter Three

"In the Space of Six Days"

With the words, "in the space of six days," the *Westminster Confession of Faith*, IV.1, and the *Westminster Catechisms, Larger,* Question 15, and *Shorter,* Question 9, describe the *length of time* (for that is what the word "space" means in these contexts) that God took (1) to create the original uninhabitable earth out of nothing (*ex nihilo*), (2) to bring this uninhabitable earth to a well-ordered, habitable state for plant, animal, and human life, and (3) to create the first man and woman and to place them in the Garden of Eden.

Much has been written about the length of these days of creation, whether they were (1) ordinary days of around twenty-fours hours duration ("the prevailing view," writes Berkhof [1]), or (2) long ages, or (3) some combination of days and ages, or (4) ordinary days in which God simply revealed over a time span of six days what he had done at creation over a much longer period of time (Bernard Ramm), or (5) simply a non-historical framework intended to serve as the literary device whereby information about the divine activity in creation might be presented in an aesthetically pleasing and helpful fashion and at the same time specifically highlight the Sabbath rest as man's eternal destiny.[2] So much has been written about this matter, in fact, that I hesitated to write even this short essay about it. But since many PCA (Presbyterian Church in America) churches are concerned about this matter at the present time, I became emboldened to voice my opinion on this topic with the hope that it will generate at least some light and no heat.

---

[1]Louis Berkhof, *Systematic Theology* (Grand Rapids: Eerdmans, 1949), 153.

[2]Arie Noordtzij of the University of Utrecht pioneered the "framework hypothesis" around 1930. It has been advanced since then by Herman H. Ridderbos, Meredith Kline, D. F. Payne, J. A. Thompson, Henri Blocher, Ronald Youngblood, Tremper Longman, and Mark E. Ross. For a brief but insightful rebuttal of this view see Kenneth L. Gentry, Jr.'s "Exegetical and Theological Observations on the Framework Hypothesis" (A Report of the the Minority regarding the Framework Hypothesis in his PCA presbytery).

The main exegetical argument behind these non-literal-day views is that the Hebrew word for "day" *(yôm)* is allegedly employed in the Genesis account of creation itself (Genesis 1 and 2) with a variety of nuances. For example, their advocates contend that (1) in Genesis 1:5 God designates the light he had created as *yôm* in distinction from the darkness which he designates as *(layᵉlâh)*, (2) in Genesis 1:14-18 *yôm* occurs three times to denote "daylight" (that is, the twelve-hour "morning" half of the ordinary day) over against night-time[3]; (3) in Genesis 2:4b the entire account of creation, that is, the activity of all six days, is described as "the day [*yôm*] that the LORD God made the earth and the heavens"; and finally, (4) throughout the Genesis 1 account each successively numbered *yôm* (six in all – 1:5, 8, 13, 19, 23, 31) is said to be comprised of an "evening" and a "morning."[4] Accordingly, because *yôm* may not mean ordinary days in Genesis 1, long- or age-day advocates urge, because it would have, for example, required a great amount of time (1) for the plants of the field created on day three to grow after they had been watered by a mist from the earth (Gen. 2:5), (2) for light from distant stars created on day four to reach the earth, and (3) for Adam on day six to study the nature of and, in light of his research, to give names to all the cattle, fowl, and other beasts of the earth (Gen. 2:19-20), that the days of Genesis 1 were much more likely long ages than ordinary days. But given the fact that it does not follow, just because *yôm may* have a variety of meanings, that its most likely meaning in a given context *should* be set aside for another meaning without sufficient warrant, is the fact itself that *yôm may* be employed in diverse ways really all that significant? Does not this fact simply alert the biblical exegete that he must be careful to assess the meaning of each separate occurrence of *yôm* in its own specific context? *Is not the length of*

---

[3]The meaning of *yôm* here is very likely the same meaning as #1. Moreover, it should be noted that in the phrase "for days and years" in Genesis 1:14 the plural *yāmîm* ("days") cleary intends to refer to normal twenty-four-hour days that make up the mentioned years. Here is one indisputable occurrence of *yôm* as a designation of an ordinary twenty-four-hour day in Genesis 1, and there may well be more such occurrences in the account. Only solid exegesis can determine if this is the case.

[4]The meaning of these occurrences of *yôm* are the very occurrences that are in dispute. Therefore, their meaning may not legitimately be used to support the long-day theory.

the days of Genesis 1, then, finally to be determined by the exegetical/
theological question of what was most likely Moses' intended meaning
of yôm in Genesis 1 derived from a broad consideration of the entirety
*of Scripture teaching (*analogia Scripturae*) on the matter?*

    I do not believe that another (or a lengthy) discussion on my part
will settle the issue, but for my part I can discern no reason, either
from Scripture or from the physical sciences, for departing from the
commonly held view that the days of Genesis were ordinary days of
around twenty-four hours in length.[5] For it may be observed with
reference to the first example above that God describes the entire
first day of creation in the very terms ("light" and "darkness" and

---

    [5]One tires of hearing it said, as does Hugh Ross in *The Fingerprint of
God*, 2nd edition (Orange, Calif.: Promise, 1991) that "many of the early
church fathers and other biblical scholars interpreted the creation days of
Genesis 1 as long periods of time. The list includes...Augustine, and
later Aquinas to name a few" (141). Andrew Dickson White is much closer
to the truth when he states in his older work, A *History of the Warfare of
Science with Theology* (New York: D. Appleton, 1896), that "down to a
period almost within living memory [1896], it was held, virtually 'always,
everywhere, and by all,' that the universe, as we now see it, was created
literally and directly by the voice or hands of the Almighty, or by both – out
of nothing – in an instant or in six days" (60). In fact, Augustine did not
hesitate to say repeatedly that God created the universe *ex nihilo* and that
the "days" of Genesis, as Ernan McMullin summarizes Augustine's view in
his *Evolution and Creation* (Notre Dame: University Press, 1985), were
"stages in the angelic knowledge of creation," the "days" themselves
occurring in "an indivisible instant, so that all the kinds of things mentioned
in Genesis were really made simultaneously" (11-12). Augustine was also
willing to say that "from Adam to the flood there were 2,262 years according
to the calculation data in our versions of the Scripture" *(The City of God,*
Book 15, Chapter 20) – hardly a chronology in keeping with an
evolutionary view of the origin of the universe. As for Aquinas, suffice
it to say that nowhere does he explicitly declare for the days as being ages.
To the contrary, he states: "The words *one day* are used when day is first
instituted, to denote that one day is made up of twenty-four hours" *(Summa
Theologica,* Question 74, Article 3).
    While the Protestant Magisterial Reformers, Martin Luther and John Calvin,
espoused a literal creation *ex nihilo* and the days of Genesis as ordinary
days, it is true, regrettably, that later stalwarts of the faith such as Charles
Hodge and Benjamin B. Warfield and Princeton Seminary in general were

their equivalent terms, "morning and evening") that we use today to describe an ordinary twenty-four-hour day; with reference to the second example it may be noted that *yôm* clearly intends primarily the "daylight" of an ordinary twenty-four day; and with reference to the third example (the occurrence of *yôm* in Genesis 2:4), it may be that, while the singular *yôm* appears to denote the entire six-day period of Genesis 1, it *may* refer, in Moses' more detailed and topically-arranged Genesis 2 account of God's creative activity pertaining specifically to man, *only* to the original divine act of bringing the earth and heaven into existence out of nothing (which occurred on

---

willing to allow for an interpretation of the days of Genesis 1 as periods of indefinite duration in light of alleged scientific evidence and even to adjust the teaching of Scripture to conform to the "geological ages."

I say "Princeton Seminary in general" because Francis Landey Patton, President of the Seminary, declared in his May, 1912 sermon, "Princeton Seminary and the Faith," in *The Centennial Celebration of the Theological Seminary of the Presbyterian Church in the United States of America* (Reprint; Eugene, OR: Wipf and Stock, 2001):

> The theological position of Princeton Seminary is exactly the same today that it was a hundred years ago. This may seem like a strange statement to make about a living institution in this very progressive age. *We have of course put a new interpretation on the "days" of Genesis; and in other particulars have used the results of science to help us in the interpretation of the Scriptures"* (350).

This admission on Patton's part is quite significant for it means that the Princeton men (1) knew that the traditional view of the days of Genesis were ordinary days, (2) knew that the confessional phrase, "in the space of six days," intended six ordinary days, and (3) knew that they were self-consciously departing from their own confessional tradition in this matter. And because Princeton Seminary's influence was so widespread among the American clergy the current prevalence of this view within the Presbyterian ministry today must be traced back to Princeton Seminary's departure from its confessional tradition.

What is so sad about all this is that ministers who espouse the "day-age" view today, unaware of Princeton's self-conscious shift away from the ordinary-day view, very likely believe that the *Westminster Confession of Faith* intended no one particular view of the days and that they are therefore not out of accord with the intent of the *Confession* when they teach their divergent view.

day one) inasmuch as the word "generations" (*tôl^edhôth*) implies that a "history" will follow it and then several other creative acts of God are actually topically noted in Genesis 2 (see 2:5, 7, 9, 22).[6] Accordingly, I believe the following fourteen reasons warrant Christians to continue to espouse what Berkhof labeled the "prevailing view" of the days as literal days:

1.Because there was no man around at the time of the creation of the universe to observe its creation, God had to reveal the data of Genesis 1 to Moses who recorded it as God revealed it. And in light of the fact that God declared in Numbers 12:6-8 that when he spoke to Moses, unlike the manner in which he would speak to the prophets who would follow him, he would "speak to him mouth to mouth, *clearly* [*mar'eh*] and not in enigmas [*hidhôth*]," I would suggest that we may and should assume at the outset of our argument that the creation account in Genesis 1 describes "clearly and not in enigmas" the divine activity during the creation week, that is to say, we may assume that we will not need to discover the subtly hidden true meaning of the text that lies beneath and is something other than the ordinary meaning of the words of the text.

2. The word "day" (*yôm*), in the singular, dual, and plural, occurs some 2,225 times in the Old Testament with the overwhelming preponderance of these occurrences designating the ordinary daily cycle. Normally, the preponderate meaning of a term should be maintained unless contextual considerations force one to another view.

I would refer the reader to Jack P. Lewis, "The Days of Creation: An Historical Survey of Interpretation," *JETS* 32/4 (December 1989) 433-55, for a brief but thorough survey of what the church fathers said throughout the church age about the days of Genesis 1.

[6] Literally translated, Genesis 2:4 reads: "These are [the] generations of the heavens and the earth in their being created [that is, "when they were created"], in the day of the making of Yahweh God [that is, "when Yahweh God made"] earth and heavens." It is entirely possible that this verse is intended as a grand summary statement of all that follows it in chapter 2. My suggestion here, however, is that, given the two facts that "generations" (*tôl^edhôth*) implies that a "history" will follow it and that some creative activity on God's part is later actually alluded to, it may be that *yôm* in 2:4b should be viewed as referring only to God's original creation of heaven and earth out of nothing on (ordinary) day one of Genesis 1.

As Robert Lewis Dabney states with respect to the meaning of *yôm* in Genesis 1:

> The narrative [of Genesis 1] seems historical, and not symbolical; and hence the strong initial presumption is, that all its parts are to be taken in their obvious sense.... The natural day is [*yôm*'s] literal and primary meaning. Now, it is apprehended that in construing any document, while we are ready to adopt, at the demand of the context, the derived or tropical meaning, we revert to the ordinary one, when no such demand exists in the context.[7]

Louis Berkhof also writes:

> In its primary meaning the word *yôm* denotes a natural day; and it is a good rule of exegesis, not to depart from the primary meaning of a word, unless this is required by the context.[8]

I agree with this assessment and concur with Dabney and Berkhof that no such contextual demand to depart from the preponderate and primary meaning of *yôm* exists in Genesis 1.

3. The recurring phrase, "and there was evening and there was morning, the first day," etc. (1:5, 8, 13, 19, 23, 31), suggests as much. For if God, as I believe, conducted his creative activity during the "daylight" hours of the first six days, then the phrase, "and there was evening and there was morning," describes the recurring "night/light" phases of each creation-day. Moreover, these qualifying words, "evening" and "morning" attached here to each of the first six days, occur together outside of Genesis by my reckoning in 30 verses,[9] and in each instance are employed as descriptions of parts of an ordinary day.

4. Genesis attaches a numeral to each of the days of creation (1:5, 8, 13, 19, 23, 31; 2:2-3). In the 119 instances elsewhere in the

---

[7] Robert Lewis Dabney, *Lectures in Systematic Theology* (Grand Rapids: Zondervan, 1972 reprint), 254-55.

[8] Louis Berkhof, *Systematic Theology*, 154.

[9] Gen. 49:27; Exod. 16:8, 13; 18:13-14; 27:21; Lev. 6:20; 24:3; Num. 9:15, 21; Deut. 16:4; 28:67; 1 Sam. 17:16; 1 Kgs. 17:6; 2 Kgs. 16:15; 1 Chr. 16:40; 23:30; 2 Chr. 2:4; 13:11; 31:3; Ezra 3:3; Esth. 2:14; Job 4:20; Pss. 55:17; 90:6; Eccl. 11:6; Isa. 5:11; 17:14; Ezek. 24:18; 33:22; Zeph. 3:3.

Pentateuch and the 357 instances outside the Pentateuch where *yôm* stands in conjunction with the cardinals (one, two, three, etc.) or ordinals (first, second, third, etc.), it never means anything other than a normal, literal day (see, for example, Ex. 12:15; 24:16; Lev. 12:3).

5. With the creation of the sun "to rule the day" and the moon "to rule the night" occurring on the fourth day (Gen. 1:16-18), days four through six would almost certainly have been ordinary days. This would suggest that the seventh would also have been an ordinary day.[10] This would suggest in turn, if we may assume that the earth was rotating on its axis at that time, that days one through three would have been ordinary days as well for there is no exegetical reason to assert that with the creation of the sun and moon on day four God

---

[10] An oft-repeated argument for the days of Genesis 1 to be construed as long periods of time is that, since the Biblical account does not employ for the seventh day (the Sabbath) the concluding phrase, "and the evening and the morning were the seventh day," the seventh day Sabbath must still be continuing, and as God's Sabbath rest it will continue forever. This observation is then used to suggest that the first six days may also have been long periods of time as well.

I would suggest in response that because the divine activity on the Sabbath day differed in character from that on the first six days (rest over against work), a different concluding formula was appended to indicate not only the end of the seventh day but also the conclusion of the creation week, namely, "and by the seventh day God ended his work which he had made; and he rested on the seventh day from all his work which he had made" (my translation). These words suggest an end of the seventh day as surely as do the words, "and the evening and the morning were the first day."

Moreover, since Adam's fall had to occur after day six since at the end of day six God declared that everything that he had made was "very good [*tôbh m^eʾôdh*]," (Gen. 1:31), it is difficult to see, first, how God's activity could have been described as one of "rest" on the seventh day, that is, the "rest" or "peace" expressed in the "joy and satisfaction attendant upon" the consummation of his work (Geerhardus Vos, *Biblical Theology* [Grand Rapids: Eerdmans, 1988 reprint of 1948 edition], 139-40), (1) if on that seventh "long day" Adam fell sometime before he became 130 years old (Gen. 5:3), bringing the entire race under divine condemnation, (2) if God had to search for Adam and then judged him (Gen. 3), and (3) if God is "always at his work to this very day" (John 5:17), and second, how God could have declared day seven in any sense a "blessed" and "holy" day if all of man's

sped up the rotation of the earth on its axis, thereby shortening the days to twenty-four hour periods.

6. In the 858 occurrences of the plural "days" (*yāmîm*) in the Old Testament (see particularly Exodus 20:11), their referents are always ordinary days. The plural "ages" are never expressed by the plural word *yāmîm*.

7. Had Moses intended to express the idea of seven "ages" in Genesis 1, there was a term ready at hand which he could have employed – the term *'ôlām* which means "age" or "period of indeterminate duration." Furthermore, if Moses intended "age" by the term "day," one must conclude that the terms "evening" and "morning" are unnatural terms to describe the halves of an age.

8. The overall impression left by the expressions, "God said, 'Let there be light,' and there was light" (1:3); "God said, 'Let there be an expanse....' So God made the expanse.... And it was so" (1:6-7); "God said, 'Let the water...be gathered to one place, and let dry land appear.' And it was so" (1:9); "God said, 'Let the land produce vegetation....' And it was so" (1:11); "God said, "Let there be lights in the expanse....' And it was so" (1:14-15); "God said, 'Let the land produce living creatures....' And it was so" (1:24); and "God said, 'Let us make man....' So God created man" (1:26-27), is that these results of God's creative fiats were immediate and direct. As Psalm 33:6 and 9 declare: "By the word of the LORD were the heavens made, their starry host by the breath of his mouth.... For he spoke, and it came to be; he commanded, and it stood firm."

---

history of sinning has occurred on it. But if day seven came to an end just like the six days before it, with the fall of Adam following day seven, and if the work to which Jesus refers in John 5:17 commenced after the Sabbath day of Genesis 2:1-3 then everything falls into place.

The argument which urges that the seventh day of Genesis 2:1-3 is represented in Psalm 95:7-11 and Hebrews 4:3-6 as an open-ended (but finite) day of rest has, to say the least, a tenuous base inasmuch as these passages may just as easily have a different interpretation placed upon them, namely, that the "rest" spoken of in them refers to the believer's *eschatological* rest of which the Sabbath day rest is the type (which latter fact, incidentally, is the reason why Christians should observe the fourth commandment today: the Sabbath is the type of the rest yet awaiting the people of God).

9. If we follow the *analogia Scripturae* principle of hermeneutics enunciated in the *Westminster Confession of Faith,* I.9, to the effect that "the infallible rule of interpretation of Scripture is the Scripture itself: and therefore, when there is a question about the true and full sense of any Scripture (which is not manifold, but one), it must be searched and known by other places that speak more clearly," I would submit that the "ordinary day" view has most to commend it since Moses grounds the commandment regarding seventh day Sabbath observance in the divine Exemplar's creative activity and rest: "In six days the LORD made the heavens and the earth, the sea, and all that is in them, but he rested on the seventh day. Therefore the LORD blessed the Sabbath day and made it holy" (Exod. 20:11; see also Exod. 31:15-17 which asserts the same thing).

10. In Matthew 19:4-5 Jesus connects both the creation of the world and the marriage of Adam and Eve in Genesis 1:27 and 2:24 respectively back to the "in the beginning" declaration of Genesis 1:1: "...at the beginning [*ap archēs*] the Creator 'made them male and female,' and said, 'For this reason a man will leave his father and mother and be united to his wife, and the two will become one flesh.'" Mark's citation of Jesus' statement makes Jesus' meaning even more explicit if that is possible for he reports that Jesus said: "...at the beginning *of creation* [*apo de archēs ktiseōs*] he made them male and female" (Mark 10:6). If Jesus believed that between the "beginning" to which he referred – surely an allusion to Genesis 1:1 – and the creation of Adam in Genesis 1:27 long intervening ages covering millions, if not billions, of years had occurred, would not the meaning of his simple statement that the first pair's creation was "at the beginning of creation" be either grossly inaccurate or reduced in sense virtually to zero? But he could have said these things quite meaningfully if only a matter of six ordinary days separated the "beginning" of Genesis 1:1 from the creation of our first parents and if Adam and Eve were at that time creatures only a matter of hours old.

11. In light of *Westminster Confession of Faith,* XXI.vii, where it declares: "He hath particularly appointed one day in seven, for a Sabbath, to be kept holy unto him: which *from the beginning of the world* to the resurrection of Christ, was the last day of the week" (emphasis supplied), it seems quite appropriate to conclude that when

WCF, IV.1 speaks of God creating all things "in the space of six days," it intends by its phrase, "the space of six days," six ordinary days of approximately twenty-four hours each.

12. According to Rev. David W. Hall (PCA), based on his research of their sermons and extra-confessional writings, the men of the Westminster Assembly uniformly held, and intended to teach by their confessional expression, "in the space [time span] of six days," that the days of Genesis 1 were six ordinary days of approximately twenty-four hours each. If Hall's conclusion is correct (and he has publicly asked on the floor of the PCA General Assembly for any evidence that would prove his conclusion to be wrong, but to date very little has been forthcoming), then any other understanding of the creation days, on a strict interpretation of the *Westminster Confession of Faith,* would clearly be an exception to the teaching of the *Confession.*

13. In my opinion, the "long age" advocate has no real explanation or reason to offer for the necessity or desirability of his long ages. But one cannot help but wonder whether the main impulse behind the postulation of the days of Genesis as long ages by some biblical scholars is their concern to bring the Genesis account of creation into conformity with the pronouncements of the physical sciences, specifically, to the insistence of Lyellian geologists and Darwinian evolutionists that the earth's geological strata and its fossil evidence clearly show that the earth has experienced long ages of animal death *before* man ever appeared on the planet. If so, then a clash immediately occurs over the issue as to whether death was present in the world prior to Adam's sin. For according to Scripture, in the beginning the diet of both animals and man was vegetarian (Gen. 1:29-30; 9:3), and it was only later that Adam's sin introduced not only death into the human race but also – as a result of God's curse upon the world for that sin (Rom. 8:20-23) – the currently-existing "red in tooth and claw" condition in the animal world. Thus the deaths of all the animal fossils would have occurred *after* Adam's fall. Therefore, the biblical scholar who maintains on the one hand that he is a Bible believer but on the other that the fossil evidence indicates that animal death was in the world long before Adam's fall and that therefore the days of Genesis have to be long ages is walking a precarious path indeed and should think long and hard about the implications of his endorsement of the evolutionary interpretation of the fossil evidence before he

subscribes to it, for the two positions, quite frankly, are irreconcilably contradictory.

14. With regard to the framework hypothesis (two parallel triads of "days" that are not intended to be periods of time at all that culminate in the Sabbath), I am reminded of J. Oliver Buswell, Jr.'s comment that the alleged parallels between days one and four, two and five, and three and six are like seeing faces in clouds: they are there only in the eyes of the beholder and not plainly there at that; and whether Moses intended these parallels is entirely another matter.[11] Moreover, the clear consecution of the six days evident, first, in the simple fact of their consecutive numbering and, second, in the fact that events that occur on days four through six necessarily presuppose the events of days one through three fly in the face of the proposed parallels. Furthermore, one might be excused were he to conclude that a view that took the church over nineteen hundred years to discover is surely suspect.

While the framework hypothesis offers some interesting insights, I think the character of the Hebrew of Genesis 1:1–2:3 disallows it, employing as it does the *waw* consecutive verb some fifty-five times throughout the record to describe narrational sequential events, the sign of the accusative twenty-six times, and the relative pronoun twelve times, as well as the stylistic, syntactical, and accent rules of Hebrew narrative rather than Hebrew poetry. In sum, the Hebrew gives every indication that Moses intended Genesis 1 and 2 to be taken as straightforward historical narration of early earth history. (If one wants a sample in this early part of Scripture of what Moses' poetry – with its parallelism of thought and fixed pairs – would look like, he can consider Genesis 4:23-24.)

But what about the examples given above of alleged activities of the creation week that, it is alleged, would have required a great deal more time than twenty-four hours to accomplish, namely, the need for sufficient time (1) for the plants of the field created on day three to grow after their watering by the mist that went up from the earth (Gen. 2:5-6), (2) for light traveling 186,000 miles per second to reach

---

[11] J. Oliver Buswell, Jr., *A Systematic Theology of the Christian Religion* (Grand Rapids: Zondervan, 1962), 1:143. See also Edward J. Young, *Studies in Genesis One* (Philadelphia: Presbyterian and Reformed, 1964), 44-105.

the earth from the distant stars created on day four, and (3) for Adam's study of the nature of and his giving of names to all the cattle, fowl, and other beasts of the earth (Gen. 2:19-20)? Do they not create major problems for the ordinary-day view?

I don't think so. I could say more in response but it is enough to say *about the first example* that Genesis 2:5-6 appears to describe the situation pertaining to the region of the Garden of Eden and not to the earth at large; the vegetation created on day three was already present and flourishing; *about the second example*, that God not only created the distant stars of the heavens but doubtless also created the light between the earth and any star he would have deemed it necessary for Adam to see; and *about the third example*, that Adam did not have to go on a safari to hunt down and trap the creatures he was to name (quite likely to be restricted also to the creatures in the Eden area), for we are expressly informed that God brought them to Adam (2:19). And Adam could have named them not individually but according to physical categories, *as God himself did*. That is to say, with very little research or expenditure of time he could have said, if the language he then spoke was Hebrew (which, of course, it was not): "I will name the large four-footed creatures $b^e h\bar{e}m\hat{a}h$ [lit. "a large four-footed creature"], the creatures that fly in the air *'ôph* [lit. "a flying thing"], the creatures that swarm in the water *shêretz* [lit. "a swarming thing"], the creatures that crawl in the field *remes* [lit. "a crawling thing"], etc." And, I say again, he could have done all this with little expenditure of time. After all, the divine purpose behind this exercise was not to make Adam the "world's leading scientist" in these matters; it was to bring home to him forcefully from his analysis of their physical appearances that the "helper corresponding to him" was not to be found among any of these categories of "lesser" creatures since he and he alone was *'ādhām*, a "man" created in the image of God.

Moreover, it needs to be asserted, if we take the very idea of divine creation seriously, that God would have originally created many, if not all, living things in a state of maturity, that is, with the *appearance* of age beyond their *actual* age, which created entities certainly included Adam and Eve. In conclusion, I would urge that no creature created during the creation week would have *necessarily* required long ages to make its appearance on earth. All living things, including man, could have been created within the time span of six ordinary days just as Genesis 1 strongly implies. And apart from such a necessity, Christian prudence would dictate that we uphold and espouse what has always been the "prevailing view" (Berkhof), namely, that the days of Genesis 1 were ordinary literal days.

Chapter Four

The Theological Significance of the
Biblical Doctrine of Creation

The Bible teaches that God created the heavens and the earth *ex nihilo* and all things in them. It is this doctrine in a unique and profound way that defines who we are – *personal* beings, *significant* beings created in God's image – unlike God, true enough, in that we are *created*, but like him in that we are created *in his image*. It is this doctrine too that grounds the creature's responsibility to serve and to glorify the Creator God.

Modern secular thought, however, regards the early chapters of Genesis as at best religious *Saga*, that is, as mythological stories that, while not actually historical, nevertheless intend either to offer an explanation for some sociological characteristic such as mankind's native abhorrence of snakes or the reason human beings wear clothing or to convey some religious truth such as man's inhumanity to man. For reasons offered elsewhere in this volume[1] I submit that the church not only may but also *must* regard the Genesis account of creation as a reliable record of the origin of the universe, a record preserved from error by the superintending oversight of the Holy Spirit (2 Pet. 1:20-21; 2 Tim. 3:15-17).

The "Vanity" of the Modern Cosmologists

We believe in this seminary that "it pleased God the Father, Son, and Holy Ghost, for the manifestation of the glory of his eternal power, wisdom and goodness, in the beginning, to create or make of nothing the world, and all things therein, whether visible or invisible, in the space of six days; and all very good" (*Westminster Confession of*

Note: I gave this article first as an address in Rayburn Chapel, Covenant Theological Seminary, November 6, 1989 as part of a special weeklong lecture series on "Creation, Evolution, and the Spiritual Life." It then appeared in *Presbyterion: Covenant Seminary Review* (Fall 1989), Vol. XV, Num. 2, 16-26.
[1]See Chapter Two: "The Historical Integrity of Genesis 1–11."

Faith, IV.1). The Bible neither knows nor allows for another explanation for the "thatness" of the universe. But today most modern scientific cosmologists (or theoretical physicists) would have men believe that all that is, is the result – to employ Dr. Francis Schaeffer's expression – of "an impersonal beginning plus time plus chance." When they assert this, they are declaring, of course, that they and all other existing things are the products ultimately of chance. But then this means that they have no intelligible ground for asserting any significance for themselves and no intelligible base for their morals. Everything becomes "chaos and old night." For them to continue to insist on their personal worth and the necessity of morals under such a condition is simply to leap to an unfounded dogmatic assertion, for if we are only products of chance why shouldn't the law of the jungle – only the fit should survive, might makes right – prevail?

Modern man has found basically only two ways to live without the one living and true God as the base for his sciences and morality. Though still insisting for no justifiable reason really on the sanctity of his personal rights, he either entirely refuses to face the implications of his practical atheism, becoming thereby a mere "technician" in his daily labors, and then leaping to anything that will even temporarily make him *feel* significant, such as the acquisition of money and material things, love of the arts, sexual promiscuity, drugs, or therapy (these things having become his "gods") – however irrational such a leap is (and it is irrational: remember the "meaninglessness" theme of the Teacher of Ecclesiastes?), even though the "leap" may actually destroy him physically. Or he makes a studied effort to argue by means of his physical and biological sciences that no God created the universe out of nothing, but to the contrary the universe spontaneously "created" (and is continuing to "create") itself and everything in it. Accordingly, there is no infinite, personal Creator. That is, capitalizing now the "c" of the word "cosmos," he makes it the cause and end both of itself and of all things in it – including himself, and without acknowledging that he is doing so offers up to the now-"deified" cosmos the worship and service he as "religious man" (*homo religiosus*) should reserve for the Creator. Tragically, in both cases modern man, in his flight from God and right reason, destroys himself as a person who makes truly significant and meaningful decisions, for he has abandoned the only base for justifying, first, what he believes in his heart of heart is true about himself, namely, that he is individually and personally significant, and, second, his conclusions in science and personal and social ethics.

I must say more about this second path that modern man follows since it gives the appearance of being the more "learned" and thereby the more "respectable" of the two, since more and more men of science are giving it credence by calling it "scientific fact" and since what is man's "scientific fact" today becomes mankind's "religion" tomorrow.

Let me begin by reminding you that there has always been one non-negotiable, absolutely necessary idea for science. It is the *sine qua non* – the "without which nothing" – of all scientific inquiry. This controlling idea is expressed by the Latin dictum, *ex nihilo nihil fit* – "Out of nothing nothing comes." This axiom is universally accepted and everywhere assumed. What is it that Maria sang in the *Sound of Music* upon learning that Captain Trapp loved her? "Nothing comes from nothing, nothing ever could; so somewhere in my youth or childhood, I must have done something good." Well, her *non sequitur* theology is wretched, but her logic is impeccable – "Nothing comes from nothing; nothing ever could." All science is hemophiliac at this point. Simply scratch this absolute axiom and modern science will bleed to death since all experimental science will then have to reckon with the real possibility, regardless of the controls erected around its experiments, that at any moment a totally "new beginning" may spontaneously intrude itself into the control area. Indeed, it can never be certain that a totally "new beginning" has not intruded itself undetected into its results and skewed its conclusions. Nevertheless, to avoid what they refer to as the "God-hypothesis," modern cosmologists are increasingly willing to ignore this self-evident *sine qua non* and to espouse some form of spontaneous generation out of nothing as the explanation for the universe.

The June 13, 1988 issue of *Newsweek* magazine documented this ever-widening trend in an article entitled "Where the Wild Things Are." Reflect upon the following quotations from this article: "Cosmologists are no longer content to invoke the deity" as the ultimate explanation behind the universe (60). To what do they now look? "For better or for worse [they] have cast their lot with the laws of physics and not with Einstein's friend, the Old One, the Creator" (65). "…in the greatest leap of imagination, *most [!] cosmologists now believe that the universe arose from nothing, and that nothing is as certain to give rise to something as the night is to sire the dawn*"

(60). Alan Guth, a brilliant M.I.T. cosmologist, flying in the face of the popular adage, declares that the universe is, after all, a "free lunch," that is that it came from nothing – that there was nothing, not God, not energy, not matter, simply nothing (But wait, Guth says, there was "possibility"!) – and then suddenly and spontaneously the void of nothing "gave rise to?", no, "decayed" into all the matter and energy the universe now has. He contends that the universe, "not with a bang so much as with a pfft,…ballooned *accidentally* out of the endless void of eternity, from a stillness so deep that there was no 'there' or 'then,' only possibility" (Guth, of course, is fudging here; there couldn't even be "possibility," a mathematical concept, if there was nothing).[2] More technically, Guth has proposed (with refinements from others) that an *infinitely* dense, *infinitely* hot point (note the use of the term "infinite" that is traditionally used as a description of the infinite, personal God of Scripture) called a "singularity" (he does not explain why or how this "singularity" got "there"; apparently, it spontaneously "decayed" from nothing) spontaneously exploded, that within a ten-millionth of a quadrillionth of a sextillionth (that's a 1 preceded by "point 43 zeroes") of a second later the universe was about the size of a grain of dust, that one-hundred thousandth of a quadrillionth of a quadrillionth (that's a 1 preceded by "point 34 zeroes") of a second later it had doubled in size, that – well, you get the point – it has been expanding and forming "quarks" and "leptons" (the building blocks of matter), then (possibly) cosmic "strings" (the seeds for galaxies), then protons and neutrons (the building blocks of atomic nuclei), then atoms and galaxies (in that order) ever since. All this supposedly began about fifteen billion years ago, with our own sun and solar system emerging from all this about five billion years ago.

Edward P. Tryon, professor of physics at the City University of New York, proposes that the universe created itself "spontaneously from nothing (*ex nihilo*) as a result of established principles of physics."[3] Alex Vilenkin, a Tufts University cosmologist, explains all this this way: "The universe as a young bubble had tunneled like a metaphysical mole from somewhere else to arrive in space and

---

[2]See Dennis Overbye, "The Universe According to Guth," in *Discover* (June 1983), 93, emphasis supplied.

[3]Edward P. Tryon, "What Made the World?" in *New Scientist* 101 (8 March 1984), 14.

time. That someplace else was 'nothing.'"[4] Edward Kolb of the Fermi National Accelerator Laboratory near Chicago explains this by informing us that "even when you have nothing, there's something going on."[5] These descriptive explanations of the universe, I think you will agree, sound like something written, if not by some college freshman in an English composition class who flunked his introductory course in logic, perhaps by romantic poets (and I hope that romantic poets will forgive me for saying that), rather than deliverances issued by straight-faced, deadly serious scientists.

Carl Sagan, the late David Duncan professor of astronomy and space sciences and director of the Laboratory for Planetary Studies at Cornell University, uses different words, but his view is no more scientifically demonstrable or logically respectable. "The cosmos," he pontificates "prophet-like" in his best-seller, *Cosmos*, "is all that is or ever was or ever will be" – an assertion on the face of it that goes far beyond *scientific* statement and that enters deeply into metaphysics, speculative philosophy, religion, even eschatology. Apparently, he believes that the material cosmos, if it has not existed forever in some form (a *credo* by the way, that is not without its philosophical difficulties and ambiguities), "created" and is continuing to "create" itself. He explains what he calls the "beauty and diversity of the biological world," the "music of life" – that's poetic, and it's about you and me that he's talking here – by the concept of evolution brought about through "natural [that is, impersonal nature's] selection." For Sagan, this conception, over against the so-called "personal God-hypothesis" is "equally appealing, equally human, and far more compelling."[6]

But wait. Is it? How can one speak meaningfully or intelligently of impersonal matter "selecting" anything"? Selection suggests intelligent choice of one end or course of action rather than another end or course of action. But what makes Sagan's "natural selection" work? Said another way, what are the "causal powers" within the evolutionary process upon which he suspends the origin of all things? Does Sagan believe that intelligence governs the power of nature? No, he does not. So I ask again, what then are the "causal powers"

---

[4]Overbye, "The Universe According to Guth," in *Discover*, 99.

[5]"Where the Wild Things Are," in *Newsweek* (June 13, 1988), 62.

[6]Carl Sagan (1980), *Cosmos*, Random House, 15-19.

within the evolutionary process that "created" you and me? Sagan's response? *Accident, randomness, fate, chance!* But what are these? All are synonyms for the last word – chance. And what is chance? Chance is a word we use to describe mathematical possibilities, but *chance cannot be a cause of anything because chance is not a being, not energy, not mass, not power, not intelligence, not an entity.* It is only a mathematical concept. Once we see this, it becomes clear that Sagan too is asking us to believe that "nothing" selected something – including you and me – to be, that out of non-intelligence we arose, that out of an impersonal beginning we emerged! But how can we, on these grounds, argue that we are significant persons, or continue to think of ourselves as meaningful beings? Why isn't it now, on these grounds, just as appropriate to think of ourselves as a mere "accident of nature" as did Sir James Jeans in his *The Mysterious Universe* or as "the gruesome result of nature's failure to take antiseptic precautions" as did Sir Arthur Eddington in his *New Pathways in Science*? And why isn't it just as appropriate to regard the elephant as a more advanced state of the evolutionary process since it has a thicker skin than man? Or the dog since it has a keener sense of smell? Or the horse since it can run at greater speeds? And why isn't it just as appropriate to conclude, since man seeks to prey upon, tame, imprison, and put to his own use all the other creatures on earth, that he among all the living species is the *greatest* predator of them all and therefore the *lowest* stage of evolutionary development to date?

These views of the new cosmologists, I insist, are not "equally appealing, equally human, and far more compelling" than the "personal God view." To prefer the frivolous notion that "nothing" is the final reality behind everything to the majestic concept in the opening words of Genesis, "In the beginning God created," represents the nadir of theoretical thought. This preference reflects the depth to which men are willing to descend into the abyss of the rationally absurd to avoid the religiously obvious. As statements of science, the science these views represent can sink no lower since these views leap over reason into the sea of absurdity. To paraphrase the Apostle Paul:

> Although [such men] claim to be wise, they [have] become fools and [have] exchanged the glory of the immortal God for the unfathomable mysteries of the created universe.... They have exchanged the truth of

God for a lie and worship and serve created things rather than the Creator who is to be praised forever. Amen (Rom. 1:21-23, 25).

They do this, of course, as Paul also says, in their ungodliness and unrighteousness in order to suppress their innate awareness of the Creator. For to become truly God-conscious is to become truly creature-conscious, and to become creature-conscious is to become covenant-conscious and to become covenant-conscious is to become sin-conscious. And this situation they want to avoid at all costs, even to their own hurt. For in their denial of God as the final Reality behind all things, they also destroy their own significance as persons who make really significant decisions.

What is ironic, of course, in all this is that the creationist view of origins cannot be taught in the public school systems of our land and is not tolerated in the physics, geology, and biology departments of our great state universities because it is judged a purely religious concept even though it best conforms to the *ex nihilo nihil fit* foundation principle of modern science and answers the two ultimate philosophical questions of being: "Why is there something instead of nothing?" And, "Why is there cosmos (order) instead of chaos (disorder)?" R. C. Sproul quite correctly observes in this connection:

> Nature cries for a sufficient cause for being. Reason demands that…if something now exists, then something has always existed. To postulate that something comes from nothing is to substitute mythology for science.
>
> Classical Christianity asserts the doctrine of creation *ex nihilo*. That means creation out of nothing. This, however, does not mean that once there was nothing and now there is something. *Ex nihilo* creation means that the eternal self-existent God (who is *something*) brought the universe into existence by the power of creation.[7]

Thinking people will judge the views of these new cosmologists for what they are – rank mysticism and sheer intellectual madness. For this reason, I trust that judicious scientists – not just theologians and philosophers – will eventually step forward and correct them. And they do need correcting, for when educated men make absurd statements, they are no less absurd than when uneducated people make them.

What then is the theological significance of biblical creationism?

---

[7]R. C. Sproul, "Cosmos or Chaos," *Table Talk* (25 August 1988), 7.

Not only does it address and satisfy the screaming intellectual need that we all have as thinking persons for a rational explanation of the universe and ourselves that will preserve significance for us at the same time, but it also defines who we are as men and leaves us, so defined, with great worth and dignity. It also provides the theistic context necessary for moral absolutes. Without the biblical doctrine of creation we are left with non-answers in these areas.

Two Men Named Francis

I would call your attention as we begin to bring this address to its conclusion to two men named Francis who saw quite clearly the futility of the world's non-answers and the vacuousness and meaningless of a universe without God as its final Reality, and who accordingly described the threat to human personal significance intrinsic to the two basic paths that modern man has followed to avoid God. The first, an English poet of the Victorian Age, is Francis Thompson (1859-1907), who immortalized the futility of life without God in his stirring poem, *The Hound of Heaven*. Poetically cataloging his own flight from God and his search for an alternative refuge in human love, in a careless life of indolent leisure, even in the innocent smile of children, at line 61 he begins to elaborate what he discovered from his attempt to find lasting fulfillment and happiness in the study and mastery of the mysteries of the material universe:

> "Come then, ye other children, Nature's – share
> With me" (said I) "your delicate fellowship;
>   Let me greet you lip to lip,
>   Let me twine with you caresses,
>   Wantoning
>   With our Lady-Mother's vagrant tresses,
>   Banqueting
>   With her in her wind-walled palace,
>   Underneath her azured daïs,
>   Quaffing, as your taintless way is,
>   From a chalice
> Lucent-weeping out of the dayspring."
>   So it was done:
> *I* in their delicate fellowship was one –
> Drew the bolt of Nature's secrecies,
> *I* knew all the swift importings
>   On the wilful face of skies;

I knew how the clouds arise
  Spuméd of the wild sea-snortings;
    All that's born or dies
Rose and drooped with – made them shapers
  Of mine own moods, or wailful or divine –
  With them joyed and was bereaven,
  I was heavy with the even,
  When she lit her glimmering tapers
  Round the day's dead sanctities.
  I laughed in the morning's eyes.
I triumphed and I saddened with all weather,
  Heaven and I wept together,
And its sweet tears were salt with mortal mine;
Against the red throb of its sun-set heart
  I laid my own to beat,
  And share commingling heat;
But not by that, by that, was eased my human smart.
In vain my tears were wet on Heaven's grey cheek.
For ah! we know not what each other says,
  These things and I; in sound *I* speak –
Their sound is but their stir, they speak in silences.
Nature, poor stepdame, cannot slake my drouth;
  Let her, if she would owe me,
Drop yon blue bosom-veil of sky, and show me
  The breasts o' her tenderness:
Never did any milk of hers once bless
  My thirsting mouth.
  Nigh and nigh draws the chase,
  With unperturbéd pace,
Deliberate speed, majestic instancy;
  And past those noised Feet
  A voice comes yet more fleet –
  "Lo! Naught contents thee, who content'st not Me."

To live life and to try to understand oneself and the material universe about one without the God who made all things, Francis Thompson learned, is indeed to live futilely. He learned, as the Preacher of Ecclesiastes declared, "Vanity of vanity! All such life is vanity!"

The second Francis is our own beloved Francis Schaeffer of late and revered memory. No man proved to be more perceptive and expressed himself more profoundly than did Dr. Schaeffer about these matters. The entire ministry of L'Abri Fellowship that he founded was committed to exposing the hollowness of modern man's atheistic world and life view. The following words he dictated to his wife Edith from his hospital bed a few days before his death May 15, 1984. Edith tells us that they were to become his "last written page, ending the books he had written, set[ting] forth once again the basic foundation he felt so important as a base for life, a world view."[8] We would be well advised to listen to his last dictated words:

> For a long time now, it has been held, and universally accepted, that the final reality is energy which has existed forever in some form and energy which has its form by pure chance. In other words, intelligence has no basic place in the structure of the universe from the Enlightenment onward. Therefore, we are to accept totally the basic structure of the universe as impersonal.
>
> This means, therefore, that neither religion nor intelligence are in the universe. The personality issue does not enter into *what* the universe is, nor into *who* people are in this theory. Under this theory, there is no place for morals, nor for there being any meaning to the universe. And the problem here is that [this description of things] is simply not what we observe about the universe – nor especially about man himself. In spite of this, modern man continues to press on, saying that this is what the universe is, and especially what the individual is. In other words, we have been told that in faith we must insist blindly on what the universe is and what man is. In other words, man is simply a mathematical thing – or formula – even though it brings him sorrow.
>
> This is simply mysticism in its worst form, and the final denial of rationality. With understanding, one sees the proud egotism of holding this basic philosophic concept against what comes to man from every side.
>
> What would we do with any other theory that postulated such a theorem? Certainly it would be put aside. Why do we continue to hold this theorem as to what reality is, when in any other area we would simply throw it out?
>
> The answer is clear that it is simply a mystical acceptance. In other words, man is so proud that he goes on blindly accepting that which is not only intellectually inviable, but that which no one can live with in government or personal life, and in which civic life cannot live.
>
> To go back and accept that which is the completely opposite – that

---

[8]Edith Schaeffer, *Forever Music* (Nashville, Tenn.: Thomas Nelson, 1986), 62.

the final reality is an Infinite Personal God who created the world – is rational, and returns us to intelligent answers, and suddenly opens the door. It not only gives answers, but puts us once more in a cosmos in which people can live, breathe, and rejoice.

If modern man would only be honest, he would say that it is his theory which is in collapse.[9]

Surely Dr. Schaeffer is correct. The Bible and right reason roundly condemn as willful moral perversity both the practical atheism of the modern "Yuppy" and the atheistic affirmations of the modern cosmologists, the Bible insisting to the contrary that the one living and true God alone has eternally existed and that the universe began as the result of his creative activity. Only the biblical response to the question of origins makes sense, and only the theistic reality behind it (1) defines us in such a way that we possess genuine worth and dignity as men created in God's image, (2) provides our human sciences with an intelligent base for predication and our morality systems with the necessary base for just decisions, and (3) saves us as individuals from becoming pieces of flotsam scattered on the ocean of "chaos and old night" by the whim of an impersonal, a-rational "cosmic litterbug," meaningless ciphers drowning in an equally meaningless universal sea of ciphers. Genesis 1 and 2 are the bedrock of this saving teaching. The church has traditionally understood Genesis as teaching a divine creation *ex nihilo*, and more particularly, the creation of man in his own image by a direct act of God. The church cannot afford to abandon these absolutely fundamental articles of faith, and it will do so only at great cost to itself and to the people it seeks to win to faith and to a home in heaven, because only as men are God's creatures do they have personal significance and only as they are his creatures are they responsible moral beings answerable finally, of course, to him.

---

[9]Edith Schaeffer, *Forever Music*, 61-2.

Chapter Five

The Angels of God

Because of the TV series, "Touched by an Angel," in which a trio of "angels" – one black female angel (Tess), one white female angel (Monica) and a white male angel (Andrew)[1] – spew forth New Age Pantheism and a steady stream of legalistic teaching (that is, salvation by works) to the people to whom God sends them, there is a great deal of unbiblical, muddle-headed thinking on the part of Americans today about God's angels and their relationship to mankind. I have written this short study in order to set the record straight on this vital biblical topic.

The Biblical Terminology

The Hebrew word translated "angel" is מַלְאָךְ, *mal'āk*; the Greek word is ἄγγελος, *angelos*, from which we derive by transliteration our English word "angel." The two words, occurring almost 300 times in the Bible, literally mean "messenger" and therefore are at times

---

[1] In real life Della Reese (Tess) is a minister in her church that lists on its website as its first teaching that "everything that exists, or ever will exist, is pressed out of the body of God (God substance) in different forms of manifestation. Since the nature of God is Absolute Good and everything is God substance, there can be no evil in reality." This is New Age Pantheism: we are all good pieces of God. Reese, married three times and living out her declared philosophy of life – "Do what you wanna do. Allow yourself to be as wonderful as you really already are" – became involved with her third husband before his divorce and brags in her autobiography about the great time they had in a hotel room: "I now knew he was THE ONE...the man God had chosen for me, an angel. I didn't feel I owed anything to [his wife]. Watching the lengths to which she went in order to oppose the divorce, I couldn't see her point of view or her perspective or her condition or anything EXCEPT her in my way." Reese officiated at the second marriage of Roma Downey (Monica) that ended in a painful split. John Dye (Andrew), whose role is the angel of death in the series, opines that it doesn't matter whether "you're a Buddhist or a Christian...gay or straight or whatever; it's about coming to find out through yourself who God is." Hardly what the Bible or Christians would regard as model angels.

employed to designate (1) angels as such, (2) human beings, (3) "disembodied souls," as we shall see at the end of this study, and (4) even impersonal things such as Paul's "thorn in the flesh" (2 Cor. 12:7), a physical malady that he calls "Satan's messenger." With respect to the angels, the terms intend that they should be understood as *God's* messengers or ambassadors to men.

They are also called "holy ones" (Job 5:1), "heavenly beings" (Ps 29:1), and "sons of God" (Job 1:6; 38:7).

Their Creation

Angels are a unique class of created beings (Ps. 148:2, 5; Col. 1:16) as are humans a unique class of created beings. Human children are not "little angels" (there are no "little" angels since angels are sizeless), and human beings do not become angels when they die; indeed, they never will become angels. In fact, though God created mankind "a little lower than the angels" (Ps. 8:5), the godly portion of mankind will someday judge the evil angels (1 Cor. 6:3). Unlike human beings who are corporeal, angels are non-corporeal spirit beings (Matt. 8:16; 12:45; Luke 7:21; 8:2; 11:26; Acts 19:12; Eph. 6:12). Holy Scripture regularly speaks of them in the masculine gender, but this is not to suggest that they possess the human male genitalia.

Because Scripture tells us nothing about the precise time when they were created, we must infer that God created them during the creation week, perhaps on the first day of creation inasmuch as Scripture informs us that the "sons of God" (a biblical synonym for angels) sang together and shouted for joy when God "laid the foundation of the earth" (Job 38:7; see 1:6). We know nothing regarding their precise number, but they comprise a very great though finite host (Deut. 33:2; 1 Kgs. 22:19; Dan. 7:10; Ps. 68:17; Rev. 5:11).

Their Nature

As non-corporeal spirit beings angels have neither flesh nor bones (Luke 24:39). They can be present in great numbers in a very limited area (Luke 8:30); indeed, one could speculate that inasmuch as no material attribute can be applied to them, an infinite number of them, if there were such, could occupy a single point in created space. They are also invisible to the human eye (Col. 1:16) unless for special purposes (2 Kgs. 6:15-17) and for limited periods of time they assume in God's providence a body-like, always adult male, appearance in order to converse with human beings (Gen. 18-19; Luke 1:11). Also, as spirit beings they do not marry (Matt. 22:30) and they do not and cannot reproduce themselves.[2] Though they are neither omniscient nor omnipotent inasmuch as they, like humankind, are creatures of God, they are nonetheless highly intelligent and exceedingly powerful beings (2 Sam. 24:16; Ps. 103:20; 2 Thess. 1:7; 2 Pet. 2:11).

The fact that the Bible speaks of "the voice of an archangel" (1 Thess. 4:16) and of "Michael the archangel" who with "his angels" war against Satan and his angels (Jude 9; Rev. 12:7) and names two angels specifically, Michael and Gabriel, the latter of whom describes himself as "Gabriel, who stands in the presence of God" (Luke 1:19),[3] suggests that the good angels may be divided into two companies in heaven under the command of these two archangels,[4] their two companies comprising in their totality the sinless angelic host of heaven over which God rules today in his role as "Yahweh, God of hosts."

Angels are rational, moral beings (2 Sam. 14:20; Matt. 24:36; Eph. 3:10; 1 Pet. 1:12; 2 Pet. 2:11). As originally created, all of the angels were morally good (Gen. 1:31), but apparently only two-thirds of them – the elect angels (1 Tim. 5:21) – remained in their created state of integrity, specifically, those under the command of the archangels Gabriel (meaning "God's mighty hero," Dan. 8:16; 9:21; Luke 1:9; 26) and Michael (meaning "Who is like God? No one [implied]!," Dan.

---

[2]Since angels as non-material beings are incapable of sexual activity, the interpretation of Genesis 6:2-4 that would make the "sons of Gods" fallen angels who married "the daughters of men" and produced "mighty men, men of renown" is far-fetched, not to mention unimaginable. The "sons of God" expression, while it may in some contexts refer to angels, refers here either to "godly men" viewed indiscriminately who married unbelieving women, (2) the godly line of mankind who intermingled with the ungodly line, or (3) the royal offspring of earthly kings (considered in ancient times as "gods"), that is, pagan princes, who married as many wives as they wanted, thereby contributing to the breakdown of the divinely-ordained originally monogamous marriage relationship.

[3]The apocryphal writings name three more – Raphael, Uriel, and Jeremiel – but these writings are not inspired and therefore should not be used as trustworthy sources for doctrine.

[4]Admittedly, there could be more than two archangels because Daniel 10:13 refers to Michael as "one of the chief princes," "princes," הַשָּׂרִים, *hassārîm*, here being in the plural, not the dual.

10:13, 21; 12:1; Jude 9; Rev. 12:7). One-third of them, under the command of their archangel (we do not know what his name was originally;[5] we know him now as Satan, "Adversary"), by an act of will kept not their original state and fell with him (John 8:44; 2 Pet. 2:4; Jude 6). We do not know precisely what their sin entailed – it was doubtless some act of willful rebellion against God – or precisely when they lapsed into sin, but at the end of Genesis 2, the events of which come within the sixth day of Genesis 1, God pronounced that all that he had made was "very good" (Gen. 1:31); therefore, it would seem that the angelic fall had not yet occurred. But at the beginning of Genesis 3 we find the Tempter enticing Eve to sin against God. So apparently Satan and his angels fell at some point in the period of time between Genesis 2 and Genesis 3.

Of course, the angels who did not fall – the elect angels – were kept from falling according to God's eternal plan by his preserving power. Their election, because God did not elect them out of a totality of a fallen angelic order inasmuch as these elect angels never fell, can only be understood along supralapsarian lines.[6] For reasons sufficient to himself, God simply by decree granted to these angels perseverance in their created integrity and denied it to Satan and his angels.

The Elect Angels' Holy Service for God

Different titles are used to describe the elect angels. In general, they are called "principalities, powers, thrones, and dominions" (Eph. 3:10; Col. 1:16), which titles underscore their dignity and authority and very probably refer to different ranks among them. Some are called "cherubs" (כְּרֻבִים, *kᵉrubhîm*), and in this role are represented as

---

[5]"Lucifer" (Isa. 14:12, KJV) was not his name originally. The Hebrew word, הֵילֵל, *hêlēl*, translated "Lucifer" in the KJV, means "shining one" and refers in the context of Isaiah 14 to the planet Venus, the "morning star" (so ASV, RSV, NASV, NEB, NIV, NLT, ESV). It is not Satan who is poetically called Venus here but the king of Babylon (Isa. 14:4, 16 [see אִישׁ, *îsh*, meaning "man," in this verse]) who has his moment of glory on the world stage but whose empire the Medo-Persian Empire then replaces.

[6]"Supralapsarian" means here that God's discriminating decree – that determines that some are elect; others are not – concerning the angels as a created order occurred "prior to" his decree concerning their fall.

special guardians of God's holiness (Gen. 3:24; Exod. 25:18; 1 Kgs. 6:23-32; Pss. 80:1; 99:1; Isa. 37:16; Ezek. 1:26-28; Heb. 9:5). One time four of the angels are called "seraphs" (שְׂרָפִים, *s^erāphîm*, Isa. 6:2; see Rev. 4:6-9). Berkhof distinguishes between these two orders of angels:

> In distinction from the Cherubim, [the Seraphim] stand as servants round about the throne of the heavenly King, sing his praises, and are ready to do his bidding. While the Cherubim are the mighty ones, [the Seraphim] might be called the nobles among the angels. While the former guard the holiness of God, [the Seraphim] serve the purpose of reconciliation [note that one of them mediately touches Isaiah's lips with a coal from the heavenly altar] and thus prepare men for the proper approach to God.[7]

Speaking generally, the elect angels' ordinary service seems to consist in praising God night and day (Job 38:7; Pss. 103:20; 148:2; Rev. 5:11) and *as ministering spirits* to serve those who are to inherit salvation (Heb. 1:14; see Ps. 104:4). They sang to the glory of God at the birth of Christ (Luke 2:14), and they rejoice over the conversion of sinners (Luke 15:10). More specifically, they are present in the church (1 Cor. 11:10; 1 Tim. 5:21), and *as stewards* they watch over believers at God's command (Ps. 91:11: Heb. 1:14), providing for them in time of need (1 Kgs. 19:5-7); *as soldiers* they guard and keep believers safe from danger (Ps. 34:7; see 2 Kgs. 6:16); *as consolers* they comfort believers in their fears (Gen. 21:17; Isa. 6:6-7); *as protectors* they stand beside believers against Satan (Zech. 3:1; Jude 9); *as correctors* they afflict believers for their sins that they might be roused out of their sins and brought to repentance (2 Sam. 24:16), and *as tender nurses* they bear believers to heaven at death (Ps. 91:11-12; Luke 16:22).

As aspects of their extraordinary work in redemptive history, *as agents* they mediated the law from God to Moses (Acts 7:53; Gal. 3:19a; Heb. 2:2), *as oracles* they announced Christ's virginal conception (Matt. 1:20-21; Luke 1:14, 15, 34-35), his resurrection from

---

[7]Louis Berkhof, *Systematic Theology* (Fourth revised edition; Grand Rapids: Eerdmans, 1981), 146. It is striking that the Seraphim, though absolutely holy in their created integrity, still feel it essential to cover themselves with four of their six wings as they fly about the throne of the transcendentally holy God who in Isaiah 6:1 is the preincarnate Son/Word of God.

the dead (Matt. 28:6), and his second coming (Acts 1:11) as well as instructed the saints of God (see Dan. 8:16-17; 9:22). *As executers* they presently carry out God's judgments on his enemies (Acts 12:23; see 2 Sam. 24:16; 2 Kgs. 19:35; 1 Chron. 21:16) and will return with Christ (Matt. 24:31) and take part in the final judgment, separating at Christ's command the saved from the lost and gathering God's elect unto him (Matt. 13:41, 49), and *as witnesses* they will hear Christ the judge either acknowledge or deny men at the final judgment (Luke 12:8-9; Rev. 3:5; 14:11).

The Lapsed Angels' Evil Service for Satan

Regarding Satan himself, the Holy Scripture clearly teaches that he is a real personal spirit. They refer to him by the names Abaddon and Apollyon (Rev. 9:11), both meaning "destroyer," Beelzebub (Matt. 12:24; Luke 11:15), meaning "Lord of flies," and Belial or Beliar (2 Cor. 6:15), meaning "worthlessness." They represent Satan as the accuser of the brotherhood (Rev. 12:10; see Job 1-2; Zech. 3:1), the ancient serpent (Rev. 12:9; see Gen. 3:1), the angel of the abyss (Rev 9:11), the devil (Rev. 12:9), our enemy (Matt. 13:25, 28, 39; 1 Pet. 5:8), the evil one (Matt. 5:37; 6:13; 13:19, 38; Eph. 6:16; 2 Thess. 3:3; 1 John 2:13-14; 3:12; 5:18-19), the father of lies and a murderer of men's souls (John 8:44), the prince of demons (Matt. 9:34; 12:24; Mark 3:22; Luke 11:15), the prince of this world (John 12:31; 14:30; 16:11), the ruler of the kingdom of the air (Eph. 2:2), and the tempter (Matt. 4:3; 1 Thess. 3:5).

The Scriptures teach regarding Satan's deeds generally that, while he does not exercise totally free rein over mankind because of divinely-imposed limitations and restraints (see Job 1:12; 2:6; Matt. 12:29; Rev. 20:2-3), he nonetheless is said to rage against men (Rev. 12:12), to prowl around like a roaring lion looking to devour the sons of men (1 Pet. 5:8), to work in the sons of disobedience (Eph. 2:2), to blind the minds of unbelievers so that they cannot see the light of the gospel of the glory of Christ (2 Cor. 4:4), to turn men away from God to serve him (1 Tim. 5:15), to take men captive to do his will (2 Tim. 2:26), to deceive the nations (Rev. 12:9; 20:3, 7), to sow tares in the field of the world (Matt. 13:25), to obstruct world missions (1 Thess. 2:18), to masquerade as an angel of light (2 Cor. 11:14), to make war against the saints (Rev. 12:17), to throw Christians into prison (Rev. 2:10), to oppress people with physical and mental illness (Acts 10:38), to lie and to murder (John 8:44), and to hold (under God) the power of death (Heb. 2:14). Specifically, the Bible teaches that it was he who tempted Adam to sin (Gen. 3:1-5), who accused Job of serving God for profit (Job 1-2) and who then afflicted him (with God's permission) with physical and mental anguish (Job 2:7), who desired the body of Moses (Jude 9), who incited David to sin (1 Chr. 21:1), who accused Joshua the high priest of sin (Zech. 3:1), who tempted Jesus to sin (Matt. 4:11), who crippled a woman for eighteen years (Luke 13:11, 16), who incited Peter to oppose Jesus' approaching death (Matt. 16:23; Mark 8:33), who requested permission to sift Peter as wheat (Luke 22:31), who put it into the heart of Judas to betray Christ (John 13:2) and who then entered into Judas (John 13:27), who filled Ananias' heart to lie against the Holy Spirit (Acts 5:3), and who tormented Paul with a "thorn in the flesh" (2 Cor. 12:7). So there can be no question that the Bible portrays Satan as a very real and very evil spiritual being.

The Scriptures also speak, with regard to his governance of the entire demonic world, of definite "power aspects" of Satan's kingdom of evil, for it refers to the "reign of darkness" (Luke 22:53; see Luke 4:6; Acts 26:18; Col. 1:13) and to the "hour of darkness" (Luke 22:52), to "principalities and powers" (Eph. 6:12; Col. 2:15), to "powers of this dark world" (Eph. 6:12), and to "spiritual forces of evil in the heavenly realm" against which the person who lacks the spiritual armor of God cannot possibly stand (Eph. 6:12-13). Satan devises schemes (Eph. 6:11) and traps (2 Tim. 2:26), appoints demonic underlings to oversee his interests among the nations (Dan. 10:11-11:1), is the spiritual "father" of many human beings who are his "children" (John 8:44; Acts 13:10), and inspires all the false religions of this world (1 Cor. 10:20) as well as the many anti-Christian religious organizations and false worshipers that are arrayed against the people of God (Rev. 2:9; 3:9).

Christ defeated Satan at his temptation (Matt. 12:29; Luke 11:18-22) and his kingdom of evil at and by his cross (Col. 2:15), and he will finally cast the devil and his angels into "the eternal fire prepared" for them (Matt. 25:41).

Unlike the good angels who "perennially praise God, fight His battles, and serve Him faithfully" (Berkhof), Satan's underlings, the lapsed third of God's angelic host, are the personal agents of Satan, the Supreme Power of darkness. Particularly in the Gospels one finds many references to demonic spirits. These are fallen angels who would prefer, if they are not allowed to possess a human being, to possess even swine because they are, though regarded as "unclean" in the Levitical legislation, at least still creatures of the God they despise. From their speech we learn that their theology is quite orthodox: they know that Jesus is the Holy Son of God, that he is their judge, and that their destiny is perdition in the bottomless pit that is the eternal lake of fire (Matt. 8:29; 25:41; Mark 1:24). But because of their sinful nature their theological orthodoxy does not help them in the slightest, for as Christ's sworn enemies they hate him and

are bent on cursing God, battling against Him and His anointed, and destroying His work. They are in constant revolt against God, seek to blind and mislead the elect, and encourage sinners in their evil.[8]

The Special Question of Guardian Angels

Does each human being have a guardian angel who is assigned to him at his birth or baptism? No, writes John Calvin: "We ought to hold as a fact that the care of each one of us is not the task of one angel only, but all with one consent watch over our salvation" (*Institutes*, I.14.7; see also his comment on Mark 5:9 in his *Harmony of the Gospels*: "Every man has many angels to acts as his guardians."). That is to say, the care of each of us is not the task of one angel only. Apparently, if Calvin is correct, it takes a lot of angels to watch over each one of us!

Some Fathers in the church, virtually from the beginning of the church age, have held to the contrary that two verses in particular – Matthew 18:10 and Acts 12:15 – teach that each individual human being is assigned a specific angel at his birth or baptism as his guardian angel, who then guides him through life, assisting him in his struggles against evil, and protecting him from physical harm. The two verses read as follows:

Matthew 18:10: See that you do not look down on one of these little ones. For I tell you their angels in heaven always see the face of my Father in heaven.

Acts 12:15: When she kept insisting that it was [Peter], they said, "It must be his angel."

---

[8]Berkhof, *Systematic Theology*, 149.

With regard to the Matthean statement, it is entirely possible, however, since Christ uses the plural number ("their angels"), that he intended to teach that not one but many angels watch over each and every believer (see Gen. 32:1; Acts 5:19), carrying out God's will on their behalf. And with regard to the Acts statement, it is entirely possible that either the people within the house intended to refer to a *human* messenger that they presumed Peter had sent to them from prison in his stead or they were simply voicing a common notion of the time that may in fact have been an erroneous notion. In either case the verse is eliminated as ground for the proposed doctrine that each of us has a guardian angel.

Benjamin B. Warfield has argued against the notion that the "angels" in these verses refer to guardian angels,[9] contending that the phrase, "these little ones," in the Matthew passage speak not of children as such but more properly of his disciples in general and that their "angels" in this context seem more appropriately to refer to these disciples' disembodied souls considered as a class.[10] He declares that

> the real difficulty of explaining these passages by the aid of the notion of "guardian angels" is that this notion does not in the least fit their requirements. Where should a "guardian angel" be, except with his ward? That is the essential idea of a "guardian angel"; he is supposed to be in unbroken attendance upon the saint committed to his charge. But neither in Matt. xviii. 10, nor in Acts xii. 15 are the angels spoken of found with their wards; but distinctly elsewhere.[11]

After cogently arguing for the translation of "disembodied soul" for the Greek ἄγγελος, *angelos*, in these two passages, Warfield asserts:

---

[9]Benjamin B. Warfield, "The Angels of God's 'Little Ones,'" *Selected Shorter Writings of Benjamin B. Warfield*, edited by John E. Meeter (Nutley, New Jersey: Presbyterian and Reformed, 1970), I:253-66.

[10]D. A. Carson, *Matthew* in *The Expositor's Bible Commentary*, edited by Frank E. Gaebelein (Grand Rapids: Zondervan, 1984), 8:401, declares: "The most likely explanation is the one Warfield defends."

[11]Warfield, "The Angels of God's 'Little Ones,'" I:256. And must it not be also said that too many infants in the womb and little children have come to serious physical harm and even physical death through wanton abortions and accidents? Where were their guardians angels when these things occurred?

What could so enhance the reverence with which "these little ones"...should be treated than the assurance that it is specifically their souls [as a class] which in heaven stand closest to the Father's throne?...Surely nothing could so heighten the sense of the real dignity that belongs to these little ones, whether the specially humble or the specially young be intended, than such a declaration.[11]

And he concludes:

There has been suggested no explanation of these two unique phrases—"the angels of these little ones" and "Peter's angel"—which has not difficulties in its way. Possibly it may be found, however, that the interpretation which sees in them designations of disembodied souls, despite the scorn with which this suggestion has ordinarily been treated, has more to say for itself and fewer difficulties to face than any other. It satisfies all the conditions of the passages themselves—which cannot be said of any of its rivals. It is rooted in a natural extension of the common meaning of the term employed. And it presupposes no conceptions which cannot be shown to have existed in circles out of which Christianity arose—which again cannot be said of its rivals. Perhaps that is as much as we should ask before we give it our preference.[12]

This much can be said with certainty: the angels are "ministering spirits sent out to serve for the sake of those who are to inherit salvation" (Heb. 1:14). But even this verse does not stipulate that each Christian has a guardian angel; rather, it simply implies that the angelic order as a class of created beings finds rendering corporate service to the redeemed people of God a major reason for its very existence.

And oh yes, one last point in defense of the good angels in light of the fuzzy thinking about them today: We may be sure that they do not teach New Age Pantheism or soteric legalism. They do not avoid using the name "Jesus", the only name that saves, as do the angels Tess, Monica, and Andrew in the TV series. They embrace and rejoice in the saving grace that God exhibits in Jesus Christ toward fallen mankind (Luke 15:10; Rev. 5:11-12) and "long to look" into our salvation and its trophies of grace (1 Pet. 1:12).

---

[12]Warfield, "The Angels of God's 'Little Ones'" I:264.

And can it be that I should gain
An int'rest in the Savior's blood?
Died he for me, who caused his pain?
For me, who him to death pursued?
Amazing love! How can it be
that thou, my God, shouldst die for me?

'Tis myst'ry all! Th'Immortal dies:
who can explore his strange design?
In vain the firstborn seraph tries
to sound the depths of love divine.
'Tis mercy all! Let earth adore,
let angel minds inquire no more.

                                    Charles Wesley

Chapter Six

The Contributions of Ugaritic Study
to Old Testament Study

In the spring of 1928 a Syrian peasant, plowing a field near the inlet known as Minet al Beida ("White Harbor"), uncovered the upper part of a stairway that, upon further digging, led to a sepulcher. The discovery was reported to the Department of Antiquities that launched a preliminary investigation during which some Cypro-Micenaen potsherds were discovered. The department then determined that the site was worthy of a more detailed investigation. A few months later, in 1929, a French expedition under the leadership of Claude F. A. Schaeffer began the excavation and uncovered at what is known today as Ras esh Shamra ("Fennel Head"), the ancient city of Ugarit.

Named probably after *ugr*, a messenger god of Ba'l,[1] and located twenty-five miles south of the present Turkish border in the cove Minet al Beida (referring no doubt to the white chalk cliffs at the end of the cove), Ugarit was apparently an influential capital port of the fifteen and fourteenth centuries BC. The Amarna Letters found in Egypt show that Ugarit was a well-known but small kingdom. One letter refers to fire damage at Ugarit. Another contains evidence of international commerce conducted by Ugarit – Byblos was refused the right of import of prize logs from Ugarit. The excavation revealed that barbarians invaded Ugarit from time to time, forcing the city to fortify itself. It came under the control of Egypt's Eighteenth Dynasty, at which time it enjoyed its "golden age." The city was finally destroyed about 1250 BC (Charles Schultz). Sabatino Moscati dates its end about a century earlier.[2]

Note: I wrote this lecture for delivery at the quarterly meeting of the Southeastern Section of the Evangelical Theological Society meeting at Covenant College, Chattanooga, Tennessee, 1967.

[1]See Cyrus Gordon, *Ugaritic Handbook* (Roma: Pontificum Institum Biblicum, 1947), glossary number 48.

[2]Sabatino Moscati, *Ancient Semitic Civilizations* (New York: Putnam's Sons, 1960), 99-123. Moscati also provides a brief but worthwhile discussion of Ugarit and its literature.

The city of Ugarit is important for Old Testament studies because of extensive literature found there. Owing to its international character, the ancient city yielded up letters of every description. There are ritual and mythological texts. A veterinarian's manual prescribing, for example, a fig preparation for some fevers (see 2 Kings 20:7) was found. It also recommended a Babylonian treatment for the toothache: smashing a certain type of caterpillar on the gum. Incantation texts and word lists for school purposes were discovered. Such information as this was not as easily won as one might at first conclude, however. Most of the writing was in an unknown cuneiform script. It was not until scholars, Bauer and Virolleaud to mention two, had painstakingly deciphered the wedge-shaped writing that the new Semitic language known today as Ugaritic came into its own as a modern Semitic study and as a vehicle for shedding new light on Old Testament times.

A word should be said about the process of decipherment. Because the characters were relatively few in number, these scholars assumed that they were dealing with an alphabetic script, and because of its geographic locality, they assumed that it was related to the Semitic family of languages. Their work proved that both assumptions were correct. Ugaritic was found to be a sister language of Hebrew. Because of this fact and because the ciphered content of the texts revealed vast amounts of information on Canaanite custom and religious practice, Ugaritic deserves serious study by the student of the Old Testament. The purpose of this paper is to demonstrate by example and illustration how Old Testament study can be enhanced and illuminated through a knowledge of and study of the Ugaritic texts.

1. Ugaritic grants fresh insights into Hebrew etymology, morphology, and syntax

A. The meaning of the Hebrew word עַלְמָה, *'almāh*, has long plagued the Hebrew student. Beside the question whether it was derived from a root meaning "to conceal," hence, when applied to a female, "one who is concealed," that is, a virgin, or from a root meaning "to be mature [sexually]," hence, when applied to a female, a young woman of marriageable age, it has been generally observed that בְּתוּלָה, *bᵉthûlāh* is clearly a designation for "virgin" and had Isaiah meant "virgin" in Isaiah 7:14, he would surely have employed this latter word. In Text 77 of the Ugaritic literature, however, a text very much of the nature of Semitic poetry, *btlt* is found in line 5 and *glmt* is found in parallelism to it in line 7, both words having reference to the same female. From this it is apparent that both words, at least in Ugaritic, imbibed of something of the same meaning. More will be said on this point later in 4.B.

B. It is apparent from Ugaritic that the uniliteral prefix *k* might not always be intended as the preposition "as," "like," or "according to" as in Hebrew, but rather it may upon occasion be related to the asseverative *ky* meaning "indeed," "surely," or "certainly." Thus instead of "With what shall a young man cleanse his way? By taking heed thereto *according to* your word," perhaps a better rendering of Psalm 119:9 would be "By observing *indeed* your word." Instead of "...for he was like a man of faith," the literal rendering of Nehemiah 7:2, perhaps "...for he was certainly a man of faith" would be closer to the intended meaning.

C. In matters of syntax Ugaritic vindicates certain unusual phenomena of biblical Hebrew. Ellipsis is quite common,[3] the plural may have several uses,[4] parataxis is employed,[5] the idea of purpose is shown by the *l* plus the infinite,[6] the infinite has two forms, the absolute and the construct, the former often substituting for the finite verb as in Hebrew, and the aspect of the verb does not refer to time but rather to state of action. Many other similarities between Ugaritic and Hebrew might be cited.

Ugaritic, then, is a powerful aid in cementing in one's mind the phenomena of the Hebrew language. Moreover, it might explain a syntactical problem of Hebrew.

2. Ugaritic dispels liberal efforts in the field of higher criticism

A. Liberals have long advanced the presence of Aramaisms in the books of Jonah, Proverbs, Ruth, Ecclesiastes, Daniel, Ezra, certain of the Davidic Psalms (for example, Psalm 139) and the speech of Elihu as proof of the late date of the composition of these reputedly

---

[3]Gordon, *Ugaritic Handbook*, paragraph 13.96.
[4]Gordon, *Ugaritic Handbook*, paragraphs 6.13; 13.16.
[5]Gordon, *Ugaritic Handbook*, paragraph 13.54.
[6]Gordon, *Ugaritic Handbook*, paragraph 13.60.

much older material. A study of Ugaritic, however, will reveal the presence of Aramaisms in this fifteenth century BC Ugaritic material. For example, the Aramaic $d^e bak$ of Ezra 6:3 (Hebrew, $z^e bak$) is found in the Ugaritic texts 1:17, 19:13, 1 *Aqht*, 185 and elsewhere.[7] Thus E. J. Young is absolutely right when he avers: "...it must be stressed that the presence of Aramaisms in the Old Testament is no indication of the date of the document in question."[8] Ugaritic supports this conservative position.

B. Liberals in the past have wanted to emend the poetry of the Old Testament in places to make a passage fit into a perceived poetic meter. Conservatives just as loudly have contended that such a basis for emendation is arbitrary and unjustified. G. Douglas Young examined the vast amount of poetry from Ugarit and concluded: "That regular metre can be found in such poetry is an illusion."[9] The conservative contention that Semitic poetry aims primarily to achieve parallelism of thought and not a prescribed metric pattern receives strong support from the Ugaritic literature.

C. Julius Wellhausen in his article "Pentateuch" in the *Encyclopedia Britannica* writes:

> The Priestly Code gives us an hierarchy fully developed, such as existed after the exile. Aaron stands above his sons as the sons of Aaron stand above the Levites. He has not only the highest place, but a place quite unique like that of the Roman pontiff; his sons minister under his superintendence (Num. 3:4), he himself is the only priest with full rights; as such he wears the Urim and Thummim, and the golden ephod; and none but he can enter the holy of holies and offer incense there. Before the exile there were, of course, differences of rank among the priests, but the chief priest was only *primus inter pares*; even Ezekiel knows no high priest in the sense of the Priestly Code.[10]

---

[7]Gordon, *Ugaritic Handbook*, glossary term 513.

[8]E. J. Young, *An Introduction to the Old Testament* (Grand Rapids: Eerdmans, 1949), 330.

[9]G. Douglas Young, "Ugaritic Prosody," *Journal of Near Eastern Studies* IX (1950) 124-33.

[10]Julius Wellhausen, "Pentateuch" in *Encyclopedia Britannica* (9th edition), XVIII:510.

He also writes in the same source:

> It is absurd to speak as if Graf's hypothesis meant that the whole ritual [of the Torah] is the invention of the Priestly Code, first put into practice after the exile; all that is affirmed by the advocates of that hypothesis is that in earlier times the ritual was not the substucture of an hierarchy, that there was in fact no hierarchy before the exile.[11]

The inscriptions found on two bronze adzes, however, fly in the face of the Graf-Kuenen-Wellhausen hypothesis at this juncture for one makes reference to the "chief of the priests" and the other actually names Khersonni as the "high priest." Here is evidence from Ugarit of a priestly hierarchy as early as the fifteen-fourteenth centuries. Furthermore, Text 1 implies an elaborate ritual as it mentions "burnt offering" (line 4), "peace offering" (line 8), "birds" (line 21), and numerous other large and small animal sacrifices throughout, all to be offered to the Canaanite pantheon. Certainly, the Hebrews could have had at least a similar religious system in the fifteen-fourteenth centuries. Of course, the Bible believer maintains that Israel did have one, and that a God-given one.

D. Following Robert Pfeiffer's *Introduction to the Old Testament* (79), Merrill F. Unger writes:

> Division of the Hebrew text into words apparently took place in the interval between the completion of the Septuagint translation (ca. 150 BC), which indicates that the Hebrew from which it was translated contained no such word divisions, and the presumable date of the Isaiah Scrolls (125—100 BC) which contain such word divisions.[12]

If this is true – that Hebrew originally had no word divisions – then there is the possibility of error in the division of the words. P. Kahle suggests such an error, for example, in the apparatus of Kittel's *Biblica Hebraica* at Genesis 4:7. But I would contend that such was not the case. On the contrary, the Moabite Stone (9th century BC) and the Siloam Inscription (8th century BC), both written in Old Hebrew,

---

[11]Wellhausen, "Pentateuch," 513.

[12]Merrill F. Unger, *Introductory Guide to the Old Testament* (Grand Rapids: Zondervan, 1951), 129.

clearly mark word division with a dot. But more significant, practically all of the Ugaritic material of the fifteen-fourteenth centuries BC indicates word division by a special wedge set aside for that purpose alone. I would contend that the original writers of the Hebrew Bible could well have followed the same procedure.

Thus Ugaritic supports many conservative claims in the field of higher criticism.

3. Ugaritic literature elucidates Old Testament events

The largest composition found at Ugarit is known as "The Great Ba'l Epic," or "The Epic of Ba'l and Anat." Ba'l was the god who gave fertility by providing rain to sustain life and to promote growth. In the epic Ba'l meets Mot, the god of aridity and death. Mot slays Ba'l and, of course, with his death rain ceases to fall. Anat, Ba'l's sister and mistress, discovering that Mot has slain Ba'l, meets the god of death and defeats him. Somehow, not explained in the texts, Ba'l is then revived. Of course, with his resuscitation the rains come again. Thus the Ba'l worshiper relates the agricultural season in Palestine with the death and resuscitation of Ba'l. Ba'l worship was introduced into the religious life of Israel through the marriage of Ahab and Jezebel. The prophets of Yahweh, however, strongly argued that Yahweh alone was both Creator and Sustainer of life, and that the recognition of Ba'l as the god who sustained life by the gift of rain was apostasy. Gerald A. Larue provides the following explanation of how the Ba'l Epic from Ugarit eludicates the conflict between Elijah and the prophets of Ba'l:

> Perhaps the most dramatic biblical portrayal of the struggle between the religion of Yahweh and the religion of Ba'al is found in I Kings 17-19. According to 17:1 and 18:1-7 a severe drought, extending over several years, threatened the nation with starvation. Ba'al worshipers would naturally explain the lack of rain by references to the death of Ba'al. Elijah knew that the lack of rain was punishment resulting from the forsaking of Yahweh by his people (17:1). The contest on Mount Carmel was to determine which deity provided the rain. The ritual acts of the prophets of Ba'al are similar to those recorded in the myth of Ba'al. As El gashed himself in mourning for the dead Ba'al, so did the prophets of Ba'al gash themselves (I Kings 18:28). At noon, when the sun was at its zenith and the heat was most severe, Elijah taunted the Ba'alists with their mythology. Perhaps Ba'al was on a journey? According to the myth

Elijah was correct, for Ba'al was in the underworld of death with Mot. Perhaps Ba'al was asleep? Again accurate, for according to the myth Ba'al was asleep in death. In spite of their efforts the prophets of Ba'al failed. Ba'al was still dead. After Elijah performed his ritual and Yahweh had answered by fire, the rains came (cf. I Kings 18:41-46). The point had been made. Yahweh, not Ba'al, sustained life, and gave or withheld the rains.[13]

By referring to the Ba'l myth of Ugarit the Bible student has elucidated this Old Testament event. The same could be done many times over. Indeed, a comparison and contrast of Hebrew and Canaanite religious practices will go far in establishing the sublimity of the former over the latter, and thus establish the divine origin of the religion of the Old Testament.

4. Ugaritic throws light on theological quandaries

A. Liberal theologians have often questioned on moral grounds Yahweh's command to Israel to destroy the Canaanites. They charge that such an order demonstrates an extremely low stage of morality in Israel's God. On this point Unger writes:

> The Ugaritic epic literature has helped to reveal the depth of depravity which characterized Canaanite religion. Being a polytheism of an extremely debased type, Canaanite cultic practice was barbarous and thoroughly licentious.[14]

William F. Albright concurs:

> ...the decimation of the Canaanites prevented the complete fusion of the two kindred folk which would almost inevitably have depressed Yahwistic standards to a point where recovery was impossible. Thus the Canaanites, with their orgiastic nature worship, their cult of fertility in the form of serpent symbols and sensuous nudity, and their gross mythology, were replaced by Israel, with its nomadic simplicity and purity of life, its lofty monotheism, and its severe code of ethics. In a not altogether dissimilar

---

[13]Gerald A. Larue, "Prophets and Canaanites," *Christianity Today* (June 6, 1960), 10.

[14]Merrill F. Unger, *Archeology and the Old Testament* (Grand Rapids: Zondervan, 1954), 175.

way, a millennium later, the African Canaanites, as they still call themselves, or the Carthaginians, as we call them, with the gross Phoenician mythology which we know from Ugarit and Philo Byblius, with human sacrifice and the cult of sex, were crushed by the immensely superior Romans, whose stern code of morals and singularly elevated paganism remind us in many ways of early Israel.[15]

The literature from Ugarit clearly reveals a thoroughly immoral Canaanite religion. "Compromise between Israel's God and the degraded deities of Canaanite religion was unthinkable. Jehovah and Baal were poles apart. There could be no compromise without catastrophe."[16] Thus the Ugaritic literature provides a major clue to the reason behind the divine command to Israel to exterminate the Canaanites.

B. We noted earlier that the Bible student who contends that עַלְמָה, *'almāh,* means "virgin" in Isaiah 7:14, receives support from the Ugaritic Text 77. There its Ugaritic cognate stands in parallel with the Ugaritic cognate of בְּתוּלָה, *b^ethûlah*, the latter quite clearly meaning "virgin." Hence Matthew guided by the Holy Spirit was correct, not only theologically but etymologically, when he applied Isaiah 7:14 to the virginal conception of Jesus Christ. The Bible believer can and must believe, therefore, that עַלְמָה, *'almāh,* in Isaiah 7:14 means "virgin" because Matthew interprets the word παρθένος, *parthenos,* in Matthew 1:18 and 1:25 in this way.

* * * * *

In the foregoing pages I have attempted to demonstrate by example some of the contributions that a study of Ugaritic can make to Old Testament studies. I noted (1) that Ugaritic can aid in the mastery of its cognate language Hebrew, (2) that Ugaritic has upon occasion embarrassed the liberal scholar concerning his claims in the field of higher criticism, (3) that a study of the Ugaritic texts can illuminate events of the Old Testament, especially the words and acts of Israel's prophets as they denounced Ba'lism, and (4) that Ugaritic provides new material to augment theological debate.

---

[15]William F. Albright, *From the Stone Age to Christianity* (Baltimore: Johns Hopkins, 1940), 214.

[16]Merrill J. Unger (1954), *Archeology and the Old Testament,* Zondervan, 177.

Ugaritic, of course, is no panacea for all theological ills, not by a long shot. Indeed, biblical scholarship, having survived the pan-Babylonian and pan-Egyptian eras of Old Testament study, should be extremely cautious to avoid a pan-Ugaritic interpretation of the Old Testament. But if this study has awakened the budding Old Testament student's interest in the ancient culture of Ugarit and a desire to learn more about the literary corpus found there, I feel certain that a more scholarly approach to Old Testament studies will be the result. Furthermore, the mind that has been regenerated by God's Holy Spirit will not fail to be impressed from his study of Ugaritic with the superiority of the Word of God as revealed in Holy Scripture over the word of man from Ugarit.

Chapter Seven

Salvation Principles Governing the Genesis Patriarchs and the Exodus Redemption

Just as "everything that was *written* in the past was written to teach us, so that through endurance and the encouragement of the Scriptures we might have hope" (Rom. 15:4), so also God intended that everything that *happened* in Old Testament times should also be our instructors – "These things happened to them as examples and were written down as warnings for us, on whom the fulfillment of the ages has come" (1 Cor. 10:11). In keeping with these statements of Paul, long have competent Old Testament scholars recognized in the recorded histories of both the Genesis patriarchs and Moses' exodus redemption living embodiments of vital biblical doctrines and salvation principles. Although the search for such truths upon occasion has carried some over-zealous students of the Bible to excess in their affirmations, no less an authority than C. F. Keil was willing to write: "The patriarchs were types of faith for all the families that should spring from them, and be blessed through them."[1] So too is the exodus redemption. In this brief article I would like to highlight several salvific principles that clearly governed the salvation histories of the Genesis patriarchs and the exodus redemption effected by Moses. These principles provided the rationale behind God's orchestrating all the historical details of these segments of Old Testament history the way he did.

---

[1]C. F. Keil, *The Pentateuch* (Reprint; Grand Rapids: Eerdmans, [n.d.]), I:183. Geerhardus Vos would agree with Keil's assessment, for in a magnificent chapter in his *Biblical Theology* (Grand Rapids: Eerdmans, 1948), 79-114, he draws from the revelation of the patriarchal period (Gen. 12-50) the several soteric principles discussed here that have universal applicability to every Christian today.

Salvation Principles in the Patriarchal History

Abraham – faith that obeys (Genesis 12:1-25:11)
At least five great principles of redemptive revelation are exhibited in God's relationship with Abraham and his consequent spiritual development that apply to and are reflected in the experience of every believer.[2]

1. Election
With God's choice of and command to Abraham to leave his country, his kindred, and his father's house, the covenant of grace, inaugurated in Genesis 3:15, assumed a covenantal form that became definitive for all time to come. All recorded Biblical history prior to Genesis 12 seems to stand only as introduction to God's election of Abraham while all that follows Abraham's election is simply the outworking of God's promises covenantally given to him and to his seed. That God's election of Abraham was totally gracious is obvious since he and his family had doubtless been idolaters in Ur (Josh. 24:2). Nothing about him was meritorious; Paul, in fact, portrays him in Romans 4:4-5 as the archetype of the "ungodly" man who worked not but believed God for his justification. To him God came, and by a confident faith generated only by God's gracious quickening, Abraham believed and obeyed God

> and went, even though he did not know where he was going. By faith he made his home in the promised land like a stranger in a foreign country; he lived in tents, as did Isaac and Jacob, who were heirs with him of the same promise. For he was looking forward to the city with foundations, whose architect and builder is God. (Heb 11:8-10)

God's promise that in Abraham *all* the families of the earth would be blessed indicates, however, that his election must be viewed as a *particularistic* means to a glorious universalistic end – the salvation of an elect seed out of every kindred, nation, and tongue.

2. The historical objective facticity of God's interposition into the affairs of men
The character of God's promises to Abraham – to make his

---

[2]See Vos, *Biblical Theology*, 89-105.

biological family (that at that time was non-existent) great, to give to his family the *land* of Canaan, and to make him a blessing to *all the families* of the earth, thereby making him the heir of the *world* (Rom. 4:13) – points up the historical objective facticity of God's intervention in the affairs of men on their behalf. The emphasis throughout the Abraham material, rather than on being on what Abraham was to do for God, is on what God would objectively do for Abraham. The very concreteness of these gifts gave assurance to Abraham that the covenant God was real and concerned in an immediately tangible way for him.[3]

3. *The divine monergism behind the covenant promise and the fulfillment-process*

Abraham was not allowed to introduce the synergistic principle at the point of the "cutting" of the Abrahamic covenant in Genesis 15. While he was in a deep sleep, God *alone* passed between the pieces of the covenant sacrifice, binding only himself to its promises (Gen. 15:12-21). Nor was he allowed to intrude the synergistic principle into the fulfillment process by attaining through his own efforts the divine promises though he tried to in the case of the Hagar incident and the birth of Ishmael (see Gen. 16; 17:18-19). For quite intentionally God in his character as El Shaddai (אֵל שַׁדַּי, *êl shadday*) – the God who governs nature for supernature ends (Gen. 17:1; 28:3; 35:11; 43:14; 49:25; Exod. 6:3) – waited until Abraham was "as good as dead" before he gave to him the seed of promise, clearly bringing out the absolute monergism of the divine power in accomplishing the things he promises (Gen. 21:1-7; see Rom. 4:19-21). Abraham was taught thereby that salvation belongs to God *alone*, that God *alone* works to fulfill his soteric promises to mankind.

4. *Faith as the subjective response to objective supernaturalism*

Abraham's subjective response to the objectivity of the divine monergism was faith (*sola fide*), whereupon God "credited his faith

---

[3]So today the historical nature of Christ's objective work of redemption – his incarnation, his active obedience, his cross-work, and his bodily resurrection from the dead – yields assurance to the believer that his faith is not based on "sophisticated myths [σεσοφισμένοις μύθοις]" (2 Pet. 1:16) but on historical events vouched for by divine testimony.

to him as righteousness" (Gen. 15:6) to highlight the concomitant truth that his promises are born of and received by grace alone (see Romans 4:16 – ἵνα κατὰ χάριν, *hina kata charin*, "in order that it may be according to grace"). Abraham's entire life experience following upon God's call that came in Ur was a "school of faith in which the divine training developed this grace from step to step."[4] Every event of his life reflected either a passing (p) or failing (f) grade with regard to his faith experience: at the time of his call (Gen. 12, p), in the hardships of famine and the pilgrim life (Gen. 13, p), in the temptation of riches (Gen. 13, p) in his heart for the just war and the potential for pride that could result from military victory (Gen. 14, p), in the prospect of childishness (Gen. 15, p), in the delay in attaining the divine promise (Gen. 16, f), in seeking a place for Ishmael in the fulfillment-process (Gen. 17, f), in his response to the needs of others (Gen. 18, p), in his fear of men's faces (Gen. 20, f) in his permanent separation from Ishmael (Gen. 21, p), in the prospect of the death of his special love, Isaac, through whom the Abrahamic blessing was to come to the nations (Gen. 22, p), in the purchase of the cave of Machpelah for Sarah (Gen. 23, p), in the selection of a bride for Isaac (Gen. 24, p), and in leaving his possessions at death to Isaac rather than to Ishmael (Gen. 25, p). In some of these times of testing, as we just noted, he showed himself faithless. But with unwavering, gracious patience God continued to enroll Abraham year after year in the school of faith until his training reached its climax in the test of Genesis 22 in which he was asked to sacrifice "his only son, whom you love, even Isaac" to God. In his willingness to offer up the seed through whom all of the divine promises were to be realized, believing that God would raise Isaac from the dead (see Gen. 22:5: "we will come again," Heb. 11:17-19), Abraham exhibited both a willingness to submit his life's plan fully to God's plan for him and an unwavering confidence in God's covenant faithfulness to take care of his future.

In Abraham's mature faith are found the ingredients of a true faith: a complete resting in God, a renunciation of all purely human resources for securing the divine promises, a reverential awe of God, and a reliance upon God alone.

---

[4]Vos, *Biblical Theology*, 97.

5. The high ethic of the patriarchal religion

Though true morality will inevitably spring from the redemptive base and be inspired by the faith principle, in many ways Abraham had to learn, as every believer must, that "the religious favor of God cannot continue except accompanied by ethical living."[5] This is just to say that Abraham, though justified by faith alone (Gen. 15:6), was not justified by a faith that was alone (Gen. 22:15-18; see Jam. 2:21-23). God taught him that the ethical righteousness commensurate with the faith that justifies is the outcome and result only of a constant "walking before him" (Gen. 17: 1). God stressed that it is necessary to the fulfillment-process (as a determined-upon means to a determined-upon end) that Abraham instruct his children to keep the way of the Lord to do righteousness and justice (Gen. 18:17-19). Abraham evidenced his awareness that ethical righteousness was important to God when he acknowledged the necessity of the presence of at least some righteous men in Sodom if the city was to be spared (Gen. 18:23-32).

For Abraham and the covenant family miraculously springing from his loins through faith, circumcision – the covenant sign and seal of a righteousness that comes through faith apart from circumcision (viewed as a symbol of works) (Rom. 4:11), though circumcision has value if one keeps covenant with God (Rom. 2:25) – became the outward sign of this high patriarchal ethic because it spoke of the removal of uncleanness and moral impurity at the very source of life.

Isaac – faith that submits (Genesis 25:19-35:29)

In his allotment of the chapters of Genesis to the great patriarchal triad of Abraham, Isaac, and Jacob, C. F. Keil, following the "generations" framework of the book itself, places Abraham within the history of Terah (see Gen. 11:27), the early life of Jacob within the history of Isaac, and Joseph's life within the later history of Jacob. Such a division, though true to the Genesis framework provided by the "These are the generations of" expression, tends, however, to obscure the disparity between the amount of information we are given to Abraham and Jacob on the one hand and Isaac on the other. No careful reader of Genesis can fail to notice that Isaac, the middle member of the triad, receives scant notice in comparison to the first

---

[5]Vos, *Biblical Theology*, 102.

and third members. Moreover, what is recorded about Isaac is deeply rooted in and highly repetitious of events in the life of his father. For example, Isaac is blessed for Abraham's sake and in turn he blesses Jacob with the blessing of Abraham. Like his father's wife, his own wife experiences protracted barrenness before the birth of her two sons. Like his father, he thinks himself to be in danger in Gerar, proposes the same solution, and receives essentially the same reaction from Abimelech. Like his father's two sons, so his two sons possess dissimilar characters, God choosing to convey his covenantal blessing through the younger son in both cases. Even the wells he digs were originally his father's wells, and the names he gives them were names that his father had originally named them. Such similarity, opines Vos, "is too striking to be regarded as accidental…. If, therefore, there be such a scarcity of the new, such a lack of assertive originality, in the story of Isaac, the reason for this must lie in the need of thus expressing some important revelation principle."[6]

What was the divine intent behind the orchestration of such similar histories for Abraham and Isaac, with redemptive revelation exhibiting such little newness in and by the life of Isaac? Franz Delitzsch believes that the pattern so evident in the narrative's handling of the patriarchal triad expresses an important characteristic of the historical process:

> Isaac is the middle, the entirely secondary and rather passive than active member of the patriarchal triad. The usual course of the historical process is, that the middle is weaker than the beginning and the end, the fundamental figure of its rhythmic movement being the amphimacer ' o '.[7]

Applying Delitzsch's insight to the patriarchal history, Vos draws the following conclusion:

> The redeeming work of God passes by its very nature through three stages. Its beginnings are marked by a high degree of energy and productivity; they are creative beginnings. The middle stage is a stage of suffering and

---

[6]Vos, *Biblical Theology*, 105-6.

[7]Franz Delitzsch, *A New Commentary on Genesis* (Edinburgh: T. & T. Clark, 1894), II:131. An amphimacer is a metrical foot consisting of a short syllable between two long syllables in quantitative verse or of an unstressed syllable between two stressed syllables in accentual verse, such as in the words, "runaway" or "twenty-two."

self-surrender, and is therefore passive in its aspect. This in turn is followed by the resumed energy of the subjective transformation, characterizing the third stage.[8]

It is particularly in his self-surrender to Abraham at Moriah that Isaac displays the principle of submission, but everything about his history underscores the *submission* that is characteristic of true covenant sonship: he was born of God's grace and promise, was in a special (that is, covenantal) sense his father's heir, experienced at Moriah a "dying to self" and a "resurrection to newness of life," and in faith prayed, worshiped, provided his contemporaries with life-giving water from his father's wells, and blessed his children in accordance with God's will concerning things to come (see Gen. 17:16; 22; 25:5; 26:17-22; Heb. 11:20). His problems were similar to those of the present sons of faith; in his conflict with his sons he foreshadowed the believer's struggle with the flesh and the spirit. He survived lapses of faith and knew the persecution of an alien society.[9]

Jacob – faith that transforms (Genesis 37:1–50:13)

When the Bible student applies the pattern within the patriarchal triad to the applicational side (the *ordo salutis*) of God's soteric plan on man's behalf, Abraham's experience corresponds to the creative, regenerative, and justifying stage, Isaac's to the repentance/faith and surrender (or conversion) stage that follows upon God's initiating act of effectual calling through regeneration, and Jacob's to the resumed energy stage of the divine monergism in the subjective transformation of the human soul from its natural baseness to God-wrought goodness (sanctification).[10] Throughout the Genesis

---

[8]Vos, *Biblical Theology*, 106.

[9]As a revelational depiction of Christ's mediatorial sonship, Isaac, as his father's "only son," was "obedient to death" in his father's design to sacrifice him to God. From Abraham's perspective, he was, "in a figure," raised from the dead. As a reward for his submission to his father's will he received and loved as his bride and wife, Rebekah, his father's gift to him (see Heb. 5:8; 11:17-19; John 17:2, 6, 9, 11, 12, 24).

[10]Later recorded biblical history, looking back to Genesis, invariably portrays the patriarchal age as dominated by Abraham, Isaac, and Jacob, with Joseph's history being included within Jacob's history. This later biblical representation of the matter is only being sensitive to the organic process of

treatment of Jacob's life the theme of progressive revelation is "grace overcoming human sin and transforming human nature."[11]

1. Undeserved election

Of the three patriarchs Jacob's character is depicted as the least ideal. Hence, since the main principle to be seen in his life is the subjective transformational side of the redemptive process, lest this transformation should be attributed in any sense and to any degree to a mere "growing ethical consciousness" in him, the first soteric principle placed in the foreground of his life is God's underserved election of Jacob. Vos writes:

> Election is intended to bring out the *gratuitous* character of grace. With regard to the objective part of the work of redemption there is scarcely any need of stressing this. That man himself has made no contribution towards accomplishing the atonement is obvious in itself. But no sooner does the redeeming work enter into the subjectivity of man that the obviousness ceases, although the reality of the principle is not, of course, in the least abated. The semblance easily results, that in receiving and working out the subjective benefits of grace for his transformation, the individual man has to some extent been the decisive factor. And to affirm this, to however small a degree, would be to detract in the same proportion from the monergism of the divine grace and from the glory of God. Hence

---

special revelation itself (see Gen. 37:2), and reflects the fact that Joseph, unlike his patriarchal ancestry, did not "live in tents" in the promised land during his majority years. Nevertheless, in Joseph's life a certain principle clearly stands out that is worthy of mention. The principle that the believer's exaltation (glorification) follows upon suffering and overcoming the world is revealed in the events of Joseph's life (see Rev. 2:26, 31). Wronged by his brothers, falsely accused of immorality by the licentious wife of Potiphar and unjustly imprisoned for it, and forgotten by an ungrateful beneficiary of his wisdom, Joseph nevertheless remains faithful to God and in the end God elevated him to a position in Egypt second only to Pharaoh himself (see Gen. 39:2-6, 20-23; 45:8-9). By faith Joseph chose for himself the life of overcoming! In all of his tests, he manifested faith in God, humility, holiness, and a sense of divine providence guiding his life (Gen. 45:5; 50:20). As a result of his trust, God providentially exalted him to his position of authority whereby he proved to be the salvation not only of his father's entire family but also a blessing to all the earth (Gen. 41:57).

[11]Vos, *Biblical Theology*, 108.

at this point by an explicit declaration [Gen 25:23; see Rom 9:11-13] the principle [of grace] is rendered forever secure.[12]

Was not the principle of election already operative earlier in the lives of Abraham and Isaac? Most assuredly it was, as we have already noted in connection with Abraham. But in the case of Jacob it is most important that the principle of election be spelled out in even greater and clearer terms.

In Abraham's case, someone might erroneously argue that God chose him because of some moral worth intrinsic to him such as his capacity for faith or obedience. In this case his election would have been based upon human merit. So a clearer illustration in Isaac is proffered to underscore the truth that all true inward human goodness is exclusively the fruit of the divine choice: "In Isaac shall thy seed be called" (Gen. 21:12). Someone might reply: "But Isaac was chosen rather than Ishmael because he was the son of Sarah, Abraham's wife, while Ishmael was the son of Hagar, the bondwoman. So yet again, a clearer illustration of gratuitous election is provided.

Jacob's election points up in the clearest imaginable way that election is grounded in the sovereign decision alone, completely apart from any consideration of human merit. Note the following facts: Both Esau and Jacob had the same father and the same mother. Esau was actually the firstborn, though both were born at the same birth period, and yet God preferred the younger over the older. Finally, the election could not possibly have been grounded in superior human merit in Jacob for it was announced to his mother before either was born, before either had any opportunity to do good or evil. In fact, a comparison of Esau and Jacob will suggest that in many respects Esau natively possessed the more noble character of the two. Paul argues precisely these points in Romans 9, maintaining that Jacob is the classic example of divine election. He mentions Isaac, true enough, but hurries on to Jacob, for here clearly no human merit can be advanced as the reason for the divine choice.

2. *The divine overture of grace*
In Genesis 28 God initially draws near to Jacob in a personal way by the vision of the ladder reaching to heaven. Jacob was fleeing for his life from Esau from whom, with the aid of his mother, he had stolen

---

[12]Vos, *Biblical Theology*, 108.

his paternal blessing of the firstborn and was heading for a branch of the family in Haran that was infected with idolatry and worldliness. Jacob's own nature would predispose him toward the imitation of Haran's sins. Thus God in his grace drew near to Jacob in personal communication and repeated his promises that he had made to Abraham and Isaac, thereby bringing Jacob, directly and personally, within the purview of the Abrahamic covenant and the hope of the covenant promises. God emphasized in Genesis 28:15 that he would constantly be with Jacob: "I am with you and will watch over you wherever you go, and I will bring you back to this land. I will not leave you until I have done what I have promised you." Certainly such a statement could never cease to serve as a basis of hope for the fleeing patriarch. But Jacob seems not yet to have understood divine grace, for while he vows that Yahweh will be his God, he does so only on the condition that God should always go with him, take care of him, and supply his physical needs (Gen. 28:20-21; see the "if" in verse 20).

3. Spiritual conversion

On many occasions in Haran, though always under Yahweh's providential care (see Gen. 30:30), Jacob exhibited the craftiness and worldliness of his character, apparently persuaded that through the instrumentality of his native powers he could secure both the divine favor and earthly blessing. Many years later, while returning to Canaan and being still fearful of Esau, Jacob found himself engaged in the strange experience of wrestling with a mysterious stranger, an event that worked a permanent change not only in his physique but also in his character (Gen. 32:22-32).

The bodily nature of this wrestling left a permanent physical mark upon Jacob, symbolizing *externally*, I would submit, the permanent *internal* change that God worked in his heart. For the very terms in which the event is couched – plus the changing of Jacob's name to Israel and Jacob's determined insistence upon receiving the stranger's blessing – indicate that the physical wrestling hardly exhausts the import of the struggle. Side by side with the physical struggle ran the inner spiritual conflict between God and the soul desperately in need of him.

Hosea 12:4-5 states that Jacob was fighting God on this occasion. Jacob doubtless realized that the "man" was no ordinary mortal, particularly after the stranger's crippling touch to his thigh. Jacob's refusal to be overcome before he received the stranger's blessing, even with his apparently insurmountable physical disqualification, symbolizes the yearning of his now-regenerate part to secure the divine blessing.

Hosea also states that Jacob wept and made supplication to the stranger. What is the significance of this supplication, accompanied as it was with weeping? When we note that not only was Jacob wrestling the stranger (Gen. 32:28) but that the stranger (the Angel of the Lord) was also wrestling with Jacob (Gen. 32:24), even inflicting upon him a permanent physical wound, it is clear that God was showing his displeasure with Jacob's "life in the flesh." This realization undoubtedly governed the frame of mind with which the patriarch prayed. Hence we may conclude that Jacob supplicated God for pardon. We may also be certain that the stranger's changing Jacob's name to Israel meant that God had granted Jacob the grace of forgiveness and the restoration to a right relationship with him.

Martyn Lloyd-Jones notes that this incident teaches several things about all genuine conversion: First, it is always an intensely personal experience. Second, it always brings us into a personal relationship with God. Third, it brings us to a place where we recognize it as the most important thing in all of life. Fourth, it always leads to a permanent change. Fifth, it is always surprising. Sixth, it is always God's doing. Seventh, it reveals that the problems to which we gave so much of our time and attention before (in Jacob's case he feared facing Esau) were never the vital problems; the vital problems are our relationship to God and the danger we face without him.

4. Continual Spiritual warfare

The Genesis narrative continues, even after its report of Jacob's name-change, to employ both of his names – Jacob and Israel – side by side (see, for example, Gen. 45:25–46:2; 48:2; 49:2), a most interesting fact in itself but all the more so when one takes into account the fact that in Abraham's case, once God changed his name from Abram to Abraham, never again does the Genesis narrative refer to him by his former name. Vos explains this phenomenon this way:

> Abraham was a new name given to express the change in the objective sphere, a destiny assigned by God, exempt from relapse or imperfection.

In a subjective transformation, on the other hand, the old is never entirely done away with. As before, side by side with Jacob's perversity [before and in Haran], there had been an element of spirituality, so also afterwards, side by side with the now matured spirituality, there remained traces of the old nature. Hence God continued to subject the patriarch to discipline of affliction even to his old age.[13]

Jacob's life portends the subjective change that the believer on his pilgrim walk to Glory normally undergoes as his "flesh wars against the Spirit and the Spirit against the flesh" throughout his days on earth (Gal. 5:17). While his justification is complete (Abraham's life reflects this), his subjective transformation is never completed here. Only after he takes leave of his house of clay in death and flies to the God who created and redeemed him is he made perfect in holiness. This spiritual struggle is what we see vividly portrayed in Jacob/Israel's life.

* * * * *

Rich lessons are in store for the Christian who studies the lives of the three great Genesis patriarchs. Their lives exhibit Holy Scripture's central truth that salvation is by grace through faith, as well as many auxiliary truths applicable to the present-day believer. Abraham's was a faith that justifies and obeys; Isaac's was a faith that submits and blesses; and Jacob's was a faith that wrestles with sin and perseveres to the end. These are not three kinds of faith but characteristics of the one true faith that every child of God possesses – made his by grace – that alone finally saves. It is *this* faith that is at work in the life of every believer and it is *this* faith that will carry him to Glory.

Salvation Principles in the Redemptive Event of the Exodus

As a major feature of the Old Testament ground for the truth later enunciated by Paul that "everything that was written in the past was written to teach us" (Rom. 15:4; see 1 Cor. 10:1-11 where Paul employs the exodus and certain subsequent wilderness events for this pastoral purpose), the great exodus redemption of the people of

---

[13]Vos, *Biblical Theology*, 114.

God from Egypt (and Moses' inspired record of it) communicated God's redemptive ways to his Old Testament people as it would later do to us, his New Testament people.

That it is not reading too much into the event of the exodus to characterize it as a redemptive event is borne out by the fact that the biblical text represents it by precisely this term:

Exodus 6:6: "I will free you from being slaves to them, and I will *redeem* [גָּאַל] you with an outstretched arm and with mighty acts of judgment."

Exodus 15:13: "In your unfailing love you will lead the people you have *redeemed* [גָּאַל]"

Deuteronomy 7:8: "But it was because the LORD loved you...that he brought you out with a mighty hand and *redeemed* [פָּדָה] you from the land of slavery.

Deuteronomy 9:26: "O Sovereign LORD, do not destroy your people, your own inheritance, that you *redeemed* [פָּדָה] by your great power and brought out of Egypt with a mighty hand."

The exodus event is also described as Yahweh's "salvation (Exod. 14:13), Moses also writing: "That day the LORD saved Israel from the hands of the Egyptians" (Exod. 14:30). Later, Stephen applied the title "redeemer" to Moses, a type of Christ (Acts 7:35).

Far from their becoming after Sinai a nation living under divinely-imposed constraints of *legalism*, the people of the Mosaic theocracy, having been delivered from their slavery precisely as the result of the great redemptive activity of God in the exodus event (this event becoming for the rest of the Old Testament the redemptive event *par excellence* of the Old Testament), became God's "treasured possession," "a kingdom of priests and a holy nation" (Exod. 19:5-6; Deut. 7:6) in order to "declare the praises of him who brought them out of darkness into his marvelous light" (1 Pet. 2:9). In the exodus God revealed the following four salvific principles that regulate all true salvation and that bind the "soteriologies" of the Old and New Testaments indissolubly together into one "great salvation."

1. The origin of the exodus redemption in purpose and execution
The exodus redemption, in both purpose and execution, originated in the sovereign, loving, electing grace of God. This bedrock principle is expressly affirmed in Deuteronomy 7:6-8:

> You are a people holy to the LORD your God. The LORD your God has chosen you out of all the peoples on the face of the earth to be his people, his treasured possession. The LORD did not set his affection on you and choose you because you were more numerous than other peoples, for you were the fewest of all peoples. But it was because the LORD loved you and kept the oath he swore to your forefathers [which oath itself was grounded in sovereign electing grace, Heb. 6:13-18] that he brought you out and with a mighty hand and redeemed you from the land of slavery, from the power of Pharaoh king of Egypt.

And it is implied in God's description of the nation as his "firstborn son" in Exodus 4:22-23 (see also Deut. 14:1; Isa. 1:2-3; 43:6; 63:16; 64:8; Jer. 3:4; 31:9; Hos. 11:1; Mal. 1:6; 2:10) – sonship being from the very nature of the case non-meritorious and all the more so since Israel's sonship was not sonship by nature but by adoption (Rom. 9:4).

In actual execution of the exodus it is highly significant that there was no religious or moral difference between the nation of Egypt or the descendants of Jacob in Egypt: both peoples were *idolatrous* (Exod. 12:12; Josh. 24:14; Ezek. 23:8, 19, 21) and *sinful* (Deut. 9:6-7). Egypt was judged *because of* its sin; Israel was delivered *in spite of* its sin. Accordingly, it was God who had to "make a difference" between the Egyptians and the Israelites (Exod. 8:22-23; 9:4, 25-26; 10:22-23; 11:7).

2. The power that accomplished the exodus redemption
The exodus redemption was accomplished by God's almighty power and not by the strength of man (Exod. 3:19-20). Every detail of the event was divinely arranged to highlight the great salvific truth that it is God who must save his people because they are incapable of saving themselves. God permitted Moses to attempt Israel's deliverance at first by his own strategy and in his own strength, and allowed him to fail (Exod. 2:11-15; Acts 7:23-29). Then he sent Moses back to Egypt with the staff of God in his hand to "perform miraculous signs with it" (Exod. 4:17). God himself promised, precisely in order

to "multiply" his signs in order that he might place his power in the boldest possible relief and this in order that both Egypt and Israel would learn that he is God, that he would harden Pharaoh's heart throughout the course of the plagues, and he did so (Exod. 7:3; 10:1-2; 11:9; see Rom. 9:17). And the Song of Moses in Exodus 15 has as its single theme the extolling of God for his mighty power that saved Israel.

3. The expiation present in the exodus redemption

The exodus redemption, notwithstanding the two previous facts that it sprang from God's gracious elective purpose and was accomplished by God almighty power, actually delivered only those who availed themselves of the expiation of sin afforded by the efficacious covering of the blood of the paschal lamb (Exod. 12:12-13, 21-23, 24-27). This truth underscores the fact that biblical redemption is not simply deliverance by power but deliverance by price as well.

That the paschal lamb was a "sacrifice" is expressly declared in Exodus 12:27, 34:25, and 1 Corinthians 5:7. As a biblical principle, wherever the blood of a sacrifice is shed and applied as God has directed so that he withholds his judgment, the expiation or "covering" of sin is effected. Accordingly, the exodus redemption came to its climax precisely in terms of a divinely required substitutionary atonement in which the people had to place their confidence if they were to be redeemed.

4. The results of the exodus redemption

The exodus redemption resulted in the creation of a new theocratic community liberated from slavery to the hostile powers of its previous master in order to serve its gracious new Redeemer and Lord.

Again and again throughout Egypt's ordeal of the plagues God ordered Pharaoh: "Let my people go that they may serve me" (Exod. 3:18; 4:23; 5:1; 7:16; 8:1, 20; 9:1, 13; 10:3). The Bible knows nothing of a people of God springing into existence as the result of his redemptive activity who then continue to remain or who are allowed to continue to remain under the hostile power of their former master (see Rom. 6:6, 17-22; 7:4-6, 23-25; 8:2-4; 2 Cor. 5:15, 17). Though Pharaoh suggested compromises that would have resulted in something less than complete liberation for Israel (Exod. 8:25, 28; 10:11, 24), Moses, the prophet of God (Hos. 12:13), would have none of them. Accordingly, Israel left Egypt *completely* (Exod. 12:37; 13:20), becoming as the redeemed community that it was a *guided* people (Exod. 13:21-22) and a *singing* people (Exod. 15) who had their sacraments (Exod. 14:21-23; 16:4, 13-15; 17:1-6; see 1 Cor. 10:2-4) and whose perseverance in their pilgrim struggles was dependent ultimately on the intercession by the "man on top of the hill" and not on their own strength and stratagems (Exod. 17:8-16). And far from Israel "rashly accepting the law" at Sinai and thereby "falling from grace" when the nation promised its obedience to God's law (as the dispensational school alleges) since the very preface of the ten commandments (Exod. 20:1-2) places these "ten words" within the context of and represents them as the anticipated outcome of the redemption that they had just experienced, it was to be through Israel's very obedience to these commandments that the nation was to evidence before the surrounding nations that it was God's "treasured possession," his "kingdom of priests," and "a holy nation" – precisely the same way, it should be pointed out that the church of Jesus Christ today evidences before the watching world the gracious relationship that it sustains to God. Peter informs Christians that they, just as Israel in Old Testament times, are a "chosen people, a royal priesthood, a holy nation, a people belonging to God, in order that you may declare the praises of him who called you out of darkness into his wonderful light" (1 Pet. 2:9). And Christians, just as Israel was to do through its obedience to God's laws, are to show forth his praises before a watching world as "aliens and strangers in the world" by "living such good lives among the pagans that…they may see your good deeds and glorify God on the day he visits us" (1 Pet. 2:11-12).

* * * * *

Reflection on these four salvific principles will make clear that they govern not only Old Testament redemption but New Testament redemption as well. All biblical redemption is of one piece: it originates in God, it is effected by God, it expiates by sacrifice the sins of the redeemed, and it creates a new people whose purpose it is to worship and to serve him. If the Christian's understanding of redemption does not coincide with any one of these basic principles, so evident in the exodus redemption, his understanding of redemption is defective, and he needs to retool it until it encompasses all four of these vital redemptive principles.

Chapter Eight

An *Amicus* Brief for Unconditonal Election

Behind every other reason that can be given for a person's salvation ultimately stands God's sovereign, unconditional election. Without this feature of biblical salvation all of the other reasons that might be advanced for one's salvation lack any final ground, certainty, and assurance. This truth is so patent on the face of biblical teaching that it is not too much to say that the person who rejects it as being inimical to human freedom perceived as the real ultimate and distinguishing cause of salvation has not yet learned the ABCs of biblical soteriology. In this article I intend to demonstrate the foundational, essential character of unconditional election for salvation from a consideration of two themes in the biblical material in the books of Exodus and Romans that treat Israel's exodus from Egypt.

The Divine Rejection of Pharaoh and Egypt

God arranged every detail of the exodus event in order to highlight the great salvific truth that it is he who would have to take the initiative and deliver his chosen people if they were to be delivered at all because they neither desired Moses to deliver them nor were they capable of delivering themselves.[1] During his conversation with Moses leading up to Israel's exodus from Egypt God declared that he would harden Pharaoh's heart throughout the course of the ten plagues precisely *in order to* (see לְמַעַן, *le͏ma'an* in Exodus 10:1; 11:9) "multiply" his signs and wonders and thereby to place his sovereign power in the boldest possible relief and this in order that both Egypt and Israel would learn that it was his power that effected their deliverance (see the Song of Moses in Exodus 15). This signal demonstration of his sovereign power, the text of Exodus 3–14 informs us, God

---

[1]God ordained that Moses would unsuccessfully attempt to deliver his people from Egypt by his own prowess and leadership (see Exodus 2:11-15; Acts 7:23-29) before he sent him to Pharaoh with the rod of God in his hand.

accomplished through the means of repeatedly hardening Pharaoh's heart.

In order to claim that God's hardening activity in this story is to be viewed only as a reactionary, conditional and judicial hardening rather than a more ultimate, discriminating and distinguishing hardening, some Bible students have urged that God hardened Pharaoh's heart only after Pharaoh had already hardened his own heart. A careful assessment of the biblical data will show, however, that there is nothing in the entire context of Exodus to suggest that this is the proper approach to this *crux interpretum*.[2] It is true, of course, that Pharaoh would have already had a sinner's heart prior to the event, and it is also true that three times the Exodus material informs us that Pharaoh hardened his heart,[3] but these facts alone do not require that we must say that Pharaoh would necessarily have hardened his heart against Israel after the first confrontation (Exod. 7:6-13). He might just as readily, in God's providence, have become convinced by the first plague that the better part of wisdom dictated letting Israel go. A careful examination of the biblical text will reveal not only that ten times is it said that God hardened Pharaoh's heart,[4] but also that God twice declared to Moses, even before the series of confrontations between Moses and Pharaoh began, that he would harden Pharaoh's heart "and [thereby] multiply my signs and wonders in the land of Egypt" (Exod. 4:21; 7:3). The first time then that it is said that Pharaoh's heart was hard, the text expressly declares that it occurred "just as the LORD had spoken" (Exod. 7:13), clearly indicating that Pharaoh's hardness of heart came about as the result of God previous promise that he would harden it. And the first time it is said

---

[2]See G. K. Beale, "An Exegetical and Theological Consideration of the Hardening of Pharaoh's Heart in Exodus 4-14 and Romans 9," *TrinJ* 5 NS (1984): 129-54.

[3]Exodus 8:15 (MT 8:11), 32 (MT 8:28); 9:34. The other verses that are cited as evidence that Pharaoh hardened his heart (Exod. 7:13, 14, 22; 8:19 [MT 8:15]; 9:7, 35) simply state that Pharaoh's heart "was hard," leaving the question of who did the hardening unanswered. So three Old Testament verses tell us that Pharaoh hardened his heart, six state neutrally that his heart was hard, while ten verses in Exodus alone inform us that the sovereign God hardened Pharaoh's heart.

[4]Exodus 4:21; 7:3; 9:12; 10:1, 20, 27; 11:10; 14:4, 8, 17 (see also Deuteronomy 2:30; Joshua 11:20; Psalm 105:25; Romans 9:18).

that Pharaoh "made his heart hard," again we are informed that it was so "just as the Lord had spoken" (Exod. 8:15; see also 8:19; 9:12, 35). Paul will later declare in Romans 9, as we shall shortly see, that in his hardening activity God was merely exercising his sovereign right as the potter over the clay to do with his own as he pleased (Rom. 9:17-18, 21). In the Exodus context God, in fact, declared that the reason behind his raising Pharaoh up and placing him on the throne of Egypt (or "preserving" him on the throne as some translators construe the Hebrew) was in order to show Pharaoh his power and in order to proclaim *his* name throughout the earth (Exod. 9:16; Rom. 9:17). It is evident from both Exodus and Romans that Pharaoh and Egypt were at the disposition of an absolute Sovereign.

The Divine Election of Moses and Israel

In Romans 9, in view of Israel's high privileges as the Old Testament people of God and the lengths to which God had gone to prepare them for the coming of their Messiah, Paul addresses the naked anomaly of Israel's official rejection of Christ. He addresses this issue at this point in Romans for two reasons: first, he is aware, if justification is by faith alone as he had argued earlier, with the racial connection of a person accordingly being irrelevant to his justification (see Rom. 2:28-29), that one could ask: "What then becomes of all of God's promises made to Israel as a nation? Haven't they proven to be ineffectual?" Paul knows that, unless he can answer this inquiry, the integrity of the Word of God would be in doubt, at least in the minds of some. This in turn raises the second question: "If the promises of God to Israel proved ineffectual, what assurance does the Christian have that those divine promises implicit in the great theology laid out in Romans 3–8 won't also prove to be finally ineffectual for him?" Accordingly, Paul addresses the issue of Israel's unbelief head-on. His explanation in one sentence is this: God's promises to Israel have not failed simply because God never promised to save every Israelite; rather, he promised to save the elect (true) "Israel" within the nation of Israel (Rom. 9:6). He proves this by underscoring the fact that from the beginning of God's dealings with Abraham and his seed not all the natural seed of Abraham were accounted by God as "children of Abraham" – Ishmael, Abraham's firstborn, was excluded from being a "child of promise" by sovereign reprobative divine arrangement (Rom. 9:7-9).

Now few Jews in Paul's day would have had any difficulty with the exclusion of Ishmael from God's gracious covenant. But someone might have argued that Ishmael's rejection as a "child" of Abraham was due, first, to the fact that, though he was Abraham's biological seed, he was also the son of Hagar the servant woman and not the son of Sarah, and second, to the fact that God foresaw that Ishmael would "persecute him that was born after the Spirit" (Gal. 4:29; see Gen. 21:9; Ps. 83:5-6). In other words, someone might argue that God drew the distinction that he did between Isaac and Ishmael, not because of a sovereign divine election of the former alone, but because they had two different earthly mothers and because of Ishmael's foreseen subsequent hostility to Isaac. The fact of the two mothers is true enough, and indeed this fact is not without *figurative* significance, as Paul himself argues in Galatians 4:21-31. But Paul clearly perceives that the principle that is operative in Isaac's selection over Ishmael is one of sovereign, unconditional discrimination and not one grounded in any way in human circumstances. Lest this elective principle that governed the choice of Isaac (and all the rest of the saved) be lost on his readers, Paul moved to a consideration of Jacob and Esau. Here there were not two mothers. In their case there was one father (Isaac) and one mother (Rebeccah). Moreover, in their case the two boys were twins, Esau – as Ishmael before him – even being the older and thus the person who normally would be shown the preferential treatment reserved for the firstborn son. Moreover, the divine discrimination, Paul reminds his reader, was made *prior* to their birth, *before* either had done anything good or bad. Paul explicitly states in Romans 9:11-13:

> ...before the twins were born or had done anything good or bad – in order that God's purpose according to election might stand: not by works but by him who calls – she was told, "The older will serve the younger." Just as it is written[5] : "Jacob I loved, but Esau I hated."[5]

---

[5]Because Romans 9:13 is a quotation from Malachi 1:2, 3 that was written at the end of Old Testament canonical history, Arminian theologians contend that God's election of Jacob and his rejection of Esau are to be traced to God's prescience of Edom's sinful existence and despicable historical treatment of Israel (Ezek. 35:5). But for the following reasons this

Clearly, for Paul both election ("Jacob I loved") and reprobation ("Esau I hated") are to be traced to God's sovereign discrimination between them.

We also learn from Romans 9:11-13 that the elective principle in God's eternal purpose serves and alone comports with the grace principle that governs all true salvation. Note Paul's statement again, "...in order that *God's purpose according to election* might stand: *not according to works but according to him who calls* – she was told...." Here we see the connection between God's grace and his elective purpose dramatically exhibited in his discrimination between

---

interpretation intrudes the "works" element into Romans 9 that is foreign to Paul's entire argument and totally distorts his point:

(a) The Malachi context is against it. The very point the prophet is concerned to make is that after his election of Jacob over Esau God continued to love Jacob *in spite of* Jacob's (Israel's) similar history to that of Esau (Edom) as far as covenant faithfulness is concerned and to reject Esau *because of* his wickedness.

(b) To inject into Paul's thought here to the slightest degree the notion of human merit or demerit as the ground for God's dealings with the twins is to ignore the plain statement of Paul: "...*before the twins were born or had done anything good or bad* – in order that God's purpose according to election might stand, *not by works* but by him who calls – she was told...."

(c) To inject into Paul's thought here the notion of human merit or demerit as the ground for God's dealings with the twins is also to make superfluous and irrelevant the following anticipated objection to Paul's position captured in the question: "Is God unjust?" No one would even think of accusing God of injustice if he had related himself to Jacob and Esau on the basis of human merit or demerit. But it is precisely because Paul had declared that God related himself to the twins, not on the basis of human merit but solely in accordance with his own elective purpose, that he anticipated the question: "Why does this not make God arbitrarily authoritarian and unjust?" It is doubtful whether any Arminian will ever be faced with the question that Paul anticipated here simply because the Arminian doctrine of election is grounded in God's prescience of people's faith and good works. It is only the Calvinist, insisting as he does that God relates himself to the elect "out of his mere free grace and love, without any foresight of faith or good works, or perseverance in either of them, or any other thing in the creature, as conditions, or causes moving him thereunto; and all to the praise of his glorious grace" (*Westminster Confession of Faith*, III.5) who will face this specific charge that God is unjust.

So much for the Arminian understanding of Romans 9:13.

Jacob and Esau, which discrimination, Paul points out, occurred "*before* [μήπω, *mēpō*] the twins were born, before either had done anything good or bad" (see Gen. 25:22-23). Paul elucidates the *ratio* standing behind and governing the divine discrimination signalized in his phrase, "in order that God's 'according to [κατά, *kata*] election purpose' might stand [that is, might remain immutable]," in terms of the following phrase, "not according to [ἐκ, *ek*] works but according to [ἐκ, *ek*] him who calls [unto salvation]."[6] This is equivalent to saying: "not according to works but according to grace." Paul is teaching here that God's elective purpose is not, as in paganism, "a blind unreadable fate" that "hangs, an impersonal mystery, even above the gods," but rather that his elective purpose serves the intelligible purpose of "bringing out the *gratuitous* character of grace."[7] In fact, Paul refers later to "the election of grace [ἐκλογὴν χάριτος, *eklogēn charitos*]" (Rom. 11:5), that is, "the election *governed by* grace." The upshot of all this is just to say: "If unconditional election; then grace; if conditional election, then no grace!" To say "sovereign grace" is really to utter a redundancy, for to be gracious at all toward the creature undeserving of it *requires* God to be sovereign in his distributive exhibition of it.

In Romans 9:15-18 and 9:20-23 Paul then responds to two objections to his teaching on divine election, both of which he frames in question form: first, "What then shall we say? 'Is God unjust?'" (Rom. 9:14) – the question of divine justice or fairness, and second, "One of you will say to me: 'Then why does God still blame us? For who resists his will?'" (Rom. 9:19) – the question of human freedom. In response to both objections, as we shall see, Paul simply appeals to God's absolute, sovereign right to do with the human race as he pleases in order to accomplish his own holy ends.

In Romans 9:15-18, in response to the first question (the question of divine justice or fairness), contrasting Moses – Paul's example of the elect man in whose behalf God had sovereignly determined to display his mercy (Rom. 9:15; see also 9:23) – and Pharaoh – his

---

[6]See Bauer, Arndt, Gingrich, Danker (1979), *A Greek-English Lexicon of the New Testament and Other Early Christian Literature*, The University of Chicago Press, 235, 3, i, for support for this rendering of ἐκ, *ek*.

[7]Geerhardus Vos, *Biblical Theology* (Grand Rapids: Eerdmans, 1954), 108, 110 (emphasis original).

example of the non-elect man – whom God had sovereignly determined to raise up *in order to* [ὅπως, *hopōs*] show by him his power and to publish his name in all the earth (Rom. 9:17; see also 9:22), Paul first declares: "[Salvific mercy] does not depend on man's will or effort but on God who shows mercy…" (Rom. 9:16). By this remark Paul removes completely and forever the human will as the determining factor in salvation and makes it abundantly clear that God's dealings with mankind are grounded in decretive, elective considerations within himself that brook no recourse to human willing or human working. Then Paul concludes: "Therefore God has mercy on whom he wants to have mercy, and he hardens whom he wants to harden" (Rom. 9:18), finally answering the question concerning the justice of God in view of his elective and reprobative activity, as we said earlier, by a straightforward appeal to God's sovereign right to do with people as he pleases in order that he might exhibit the truth that any and all spiritual good in them is the fruit of his grace alone.

Then in Romans 9:20-23, in response to the second question (the question of human freedom), after his indignant, stinging rebuke: "Who are you, O man, to talk back to God?" Paul employs the familiar Old Testament metaphor of the potter and the clay (see Isa. 29:16; 45:9; 64:8; Jer. 18:6) and asks: "Does not the potter have the right to make out of the same lump of clay some pottery for noble purposes and some for common use?" Here is Paul's entire response:

> …who are you, O man, to talk back to God? Shall what is formed say to him who formed it, "Why did you make me like this?" Does not the potter have the right to make out of the same lump of clay some vessels for honor and some for dishonor." [Surely God has the right, does he not], if, determining to show his wrath and to make his power known [see the same verbs used earlier of Pharaoh in Romans 9:17], he endured with much long-suffering vessels of wrath prepared for destruction [as he did with Pharaoh throughout the period of the plagues], *even in order to* [καὶ ἵνα, *kai hina*[8]] make the riches of his glory [that is, his grace[9]] known to vessels of mercy prepared in advance for glory?

---

[8]Paul's καὶ ἵνα, *kai hina*, at the beginning of Romans 9:23 teaches that God's reprobation of the vessels of wrath serves the divine end of making known to the vessels of mercy the riches of his grace.

[9]See Ephesians 1:6, 7, 12, 14. God's "glory" is just the inescapable "weight" (כָּבוֹד, *kabōdh*, "weight") of the sheer "godness" of the triune God,

He, of course, expects an affirmative response to his rhetorical questions. Hence Paul teaches here, first, that the potter sovereignly makes both kinds of vessels, and second, that he makes both out of the same lump of clay. The metaphor clearly implies that the determination of a given vessel's nature and purpose – whether for noble or for common use – is the potter's sovereign right to make, *apart from any consideration of the clay's prior condition*. This suggests in turn that God sovereignly determined the nature and purpose of both the elect and the non-elect in order to accomplish his own holy ends, *apart from a consideration of any prior condition that may or may not have been resident within them*. Proverbs 16:4, in my opinion, aptly expresses the intention of Paul's metaphor: "The LORD has made everything for his own purpose, even the wicked for the day of evil." So here, as earlier, Paul simply appeals again to God's sovereign right to do with people as he pleases in order to accomplish his own holy ends. And he registers his appeal to God's sovereignty without qualification even though he fully understands that the "man who does not understand the depths of divine wisdom, nor the riches of election, can see only arbitrariness in the sovereign freedom of God."[10] This feature of the potter metaphor then lays stress on the divine will as the sole, ultimate determinative cause for the distinction between elect and non-elect.

God's promises had not failed regarding Israel, Paul argues in sum, because God's dealings with mankind, including Israel, are not determined ultimately by anything they do but rather are determined by his own sovereign elective purpose. Therefore, Christians too may be assured that, God having set his love upon them from all eternity by his sovereign purposing arrangement, nothing will be able to separate them from the love of God that is in Christ Jesus our Lord (see Rom. 8:28-39).

---

the sum total of all that he is, that is, of all of his attributes. The word "glory" is also used in Scripture to refer to single attributes of God as well, precisely which one to be inferred from the context (see, for example, Romans 3:23 where "glory" intends his righteousness, Romans 6:4 where "glory" refers to his power). In Romans 9:23 I would suggest that God's "glory" refers to his grace or mercy.

[10] G. C. Berkouwer, *Divine Election* (Grand Rapids: Eerdmans, 1960), 79.

An Arbitrary or Purposive God?

For many Christians the teaching of unconditional election raises the question of arbitrariness in God. Even Geerhardus Vos, commenting on Romans 9:11-13, acknowledges "the risk of exposing the divine sovereignty to the charge of arbitrariness"[11] that Paul was willing to run in order to underscore the fact that the *gracious* election of Jacob (and the corresponding reprobation of Esau) was decided before (indeed, *eternally* before) the birth of the brothers, before either had done anything good or bad. Arminian theologians, of course, would spare their readers Vos's words "risk of exposing" and simply charge that the Reformed understanding of election does in fact expose God to the charge of arbitrariness in his dealings with mankind. What may be said in response to this charge? Does the Reformed doctrine of unconditional election (that we are insisting is the Pauline understanding of election as well) impute arbitrariness to God when it affirms that God discriminated between man and man before they were born, completely apart from a consideration of any conditions or causes (or the absence of these) in them?

With Paul (Rom. 9:14) we respond to these questions simply and tersely: "Not at all, and for two reasons!" First, does not Paul affirm precisely what these criticisms are intended to call into question? Does he not declare that God discriminated between Esau and Jacob before they were born? Does he not assert that God's discrimination was made completely apart from a consideration of the moral conditions present within Esau and Jacob (see his "before either had done good or bad" and his "not by works")? Second, whether God's dealings with people are arbitrary depends entirely on the meaning of the word "arbitrary" that one is employing. If Arminians mean by the word to choose or to act this way at one time and that way at another with no rhyme or reason, that is to say, willy-nilly or inconsistently, or to choose or to act without regard to any norm or reason, in other words, capriciously, such choosing or acting Reformed thinkers steadfastly deny that they impute to God. They insist that God always acts in a fashion consistent with his prior, settled discrimination, and that his prior, settled discrimination among mankind, as Paul informs us, was wisely determined – now note – *in*

---

[11]Vos, *Biblical Theology*, 109.

the interests of the grace principle (see Rom. 9:11-12; 11:5). As Vos states, because Paul recognized that the degree, however small, to which an individual is allowed to intrude himself as the decisive factor in receiving and working out the objective benefits of grace for his transformation "detract[s] in the same proportion from the monergism of the divine grace and from the glory of God,"[12] he calls his readers' attention to God's "sovereign discrimination between man and man, to place the proper emphasis upon the truth, that *His grace alone* is the source of all spiritual good to be found in man."[13] This is just to say that if God chose the way he did, out of the infinite depths of the riches of his wisdom and knowledge (Rom. 11:33), *in order to manifest his grace* (Rom. 9:11), that is to say, if he did so *for a purpose*, then *he did not choose arbitrarily or capriciously*. One may not approve of his purpose, but if God acted *purposively*, then he did not act arbitrarily. In other words, the condition governing the reason for his choosing certain men to salvation the way he did – namely, the exhibition of his grace – did not, and cannot, lie in the creature *if grace is to be exhibited*. If it did, the creature would be the determining agent in salvation and would become thereby, for all intents and purpose, his own savior (which is rank Pelagianism). And if there was a wise reason in God for choosing the way he did (and there was: that he might make room for the exhibition of his grace as alone the source of all spiritual good in men), then he did not discriminate between man and man arbitrarily or capriciously. Of course, "there may be many other grounds [that is, reasons] for election, unknown and unknowable to us," it is true. But, as Vos reminds us, "this one reason we *do* know, and in knowing it we at the same time know that, whatever other reasons exist, they can have nothing to do with any meritorious ethical condition of the objects of God's choice."[14]

---

[12]Vos, *Biblical Theology*, 108.

[13]Vos, *Biblical Theology*, 110 (emphasis supplied).

[14]Vos, *Biblical Theology*, 110.

Chapter Nine

My Vision of the Department of Systematic Theology in a Reformed Seminary

Systematic Theology is that methodological study of the Bible that views the Holy Scriptures as a *completed* revelation in distinction from the discipline of Biblical Theology that approaches Scripture as an *unfolding* revelation. In general, the systematic theologian, viewing the Scriptures as he does, seeks to understand the plan, purpose, and didactic intention of the divine mind revealed in Sacred Scripture holistically, and to arrange that plan, purpose, and didactic intention in orderly and coherent fashion as articles of the Christian faith. Of course, the systematician who teaches students for ministry in Reformed churches such as the Presbyterian Church in America (PCA) has additional responsibilities.[1] I will elaborate on what I mean.

A Reformed seminary that intends to prepare men for ordination in the PCA should make sure that its course offerings will help the ministerial candidate meet the requirements of the PCA Uniform Curriculum. Students intending to serve in the evangelical church at large will, of course, be greatly helped by the same curriculum standards. Accordingly, the department of systematic theology in such a seminary should offer courses that cover, as integral parts of Holy Scripture's body of sacred truth, the following theological *loci* of Scripture itself: Scripture (including hermeneutics), God, Man, Christ, Salvation, the Church, and Last Things. Also falling within the department's province are articulation of the Christian's pattern of life (Personal and Social Ethics) and the Christian presentation of truth to those outside the church (Apologetics). All of the course offerings of the department should proceed from a deep, unwavering commitment to the Holy Scriptures as the inspired and inerrant Word

---

[1] I wrote this vision statement, with input from Dr. David C. Jones, my colleague at the time in the department, as part of my responsibilities as chairman of the systematic theology department at Covenant Theological Seminary, St. Louis, Missouri, which seminary is the national seminary of the Presbyterian Church in America (PCA).

of God, the only infallible Rule of faith and life, and to the *Westminster Confession of Faith* and the *Larger and Shorter Catechisms* as the most accurate extra-biblical creedal summation, interpretation, exposition, and exhibition to date of the system of doctrine and teachings of the Sacred Scriptures. With this base underlying them, the courses of the department should be designed to provide the student with opportunities for growth and development in the following areas of understanding, skills, and attitudes:

Understanding

The course offerings of the department of systematic theology should be designed to provide the student with an understanding of the following theological areas:

A. The major *loci* and cardinal doctrines of Christian theology as set forth in Holy Scripture. This means that the student should receive in the classroom, with no change in content (only in manner of presentation), *preachable* and *teachable* material.

B. The historic faith of the early church and the manner in which the church articulated and expressed its faith in such symbols and creeds as the Apostles' Creed, the Nicene Creed, the Niceno-Constantinopolitan Creed, the Definition of Chalcedon, and the so-called Athanasian Creed.

C. The distinctive nature, richness, and beauty of the Reformed faith as the teaching of Holy Scripture, as interpreted, expounded, and exhibited in John Calvin's *Institutes of the Christian Religion* and the great Reformed confessions, particularly the *Westminster Confession of Faith* and the *Larger* and *Shorter Catechism*.

D. Reformed orthodoxy and its validity as the only fully viable contemporary expression of biblical orthodoxy.

E. The dominant motifs of contemporary theology from the posture of Reformed confessionalism.

F. The philosophical, ideological, and religious themes of contemporary thought where they affect the content of the Christian gospel (the εὐαγγελιον, *euangelion*), Christian proclamation of the gospel (the κηρυγμα, *kērugma*), and Christian teaching about the gospel (the διδαχη, *didachē*).

Skills

The course offerings of the department should also be designed to provide the student with opportunities to cultivate the following skills:

A. The ability to derive, through the hermeneutical art of the grammatical/historical exegetical method, of the teaching of Holy Scripture and the synthesis of the several parts of the whole of Scripture teaching on any given subject.

B. The ability to view the individual articles of the Christian faith systematically, both as distinct in themselves and also in relation to the entire body of Christian doctrine.

C. The ability to analyze theological treatises of every era of the church's history from the perspective of Holy Scripture and the Reformed faith.

D. The ability to recognize and to evaluate contemporary trends in theology from the perspective of Holy Scripture and the Reformed faith.

E. The ability to address the assertions and concerns of contemporary philosophical, ideological, and religious thought with both a scripturally-based Christian apologetic and a relevant expression of the Christian proclamation.

F. The ability to apply his doctrinal insights winsomely and practically to Christian living and to a world in great need.

Attitudes

The course offerings of the department should be designed to provide the students with opportunities for growth and development in the following heart attitudes:

A. Reverence for the Holy Scriptures as God's Word to us from another world and as the final instructional source and norm for faith and life.

B. Constant readiness to see God's kingdom and covenants as the hermeneutical key to the understanding of Holy Scripture.

C. Appreciation for his Reformed heritage.

D. Perseverance in his effort to grow as a systematic theologian.

E. Respect for the works of others who have addressed themselves to the systematic task, such as Augustine, John Calvin, Francis Turretin, Charles and A. A. Hodge, William G. T. Shedd, James Henley Thornwell, Robert Lewis Dabney, Herman Bavinck, Benjamin B. Warfield, and John Murray.

F. Awe as one who has been granted the great privilege to study the "unsearchable riches of Christ" revealed in Holy Scripture.

G. Soberness as one who has been called to preach God's word of judgment as a dying man to dying men.

H. Joy as one who has been called to proclaim God's Word of grace to all people.

I. Meekness as one who recognizes that he too must live by and under the Word that he studies and applies to the lives of others.

J. Humble reliance upon God for all of these things, with the perpetual prayer that the "favor of the LORD will rest upon him and establish the work of his hands" (Ps. 90:17).

To implement successfully this vision of the department of systematic theology, professors in the department should be role models for their students in these areas. If possible, in addition to their academic achievements, they should have acquired some pastoral experience.

By their personal exhibition of the fruit of the Spirit before all men, by their love for and careful handling of Holy Scripture in the classroom and in the pulpit, by their own continuing scholarly development, by their personal and professional relationship with their colleagues, by their unfeigned concern for Christ's church and for the lost, and by reliance upon the Lord in all things, professors in the department should challenge their students to become men and women who will be able to train others to walk with God, to interpret and communicate God's Word, and to lead God's people through the twenty-first century or until Christ returns in great power and glory.

Chapter Ten

Revisiting How We Should Support
the Doctrine of the Trinity

Recently Dr. Robert Letham used my *A New Systematic Theology of the Christian Faith* as a foil for his theologizing on the *filioque*. Even though he has to acknowledge that "much New Testament scholarship[1] argues that the procession [of the Spirit from the Father referred to in John 15:26] refers to economic activity only…and not at all to eternal antecedent realities in God himself," in a lecture delivered at Mid-America Reformed Seminary on November 10, 1999 entitled "East is East and West is West? Another Look at the *Filioque*,"[2] Dr. Letham, citing my *A New Systematic Theology of the Christian Faith*, stated: "Robert L. Reymond thinks that referring this to immanent realities in God is to go beyond the bounds of Scripture," and then he opposed my position by citing as his rebuttal witness the Jesuit scholar, Bertrand de Margerie, who declares that this restriction of John 15:26 to the Spirit's temporal mission is

> a simplistic exegesis that lacks a theological background and is the work of exegetes who fail to reflect on the logical and metaphysical presuppositions of the scriptural texts.[3]

---

[1]See my *A New Systematic Theology of the Christian Faith* (Second edition; Nashville, Tennessee: Thomas Nelson, 1998), 337-40, where I provide the evidence for this assertion.

[2]Robert Letham, "East is East and West is West? Another Look at the Filioque," in *Mid-America Journal of Theology* (2002), Vol. 13:73.

[3]Bertrand de Margerie, *The Christian Trinity in History* (Petersham, Massachusetts: St. Bede's Publications, 1982), 169. To assert as de Margerie and Letham do here, because one refuses to "logicize" and philosophize "metaphysically" about John 15:26 and other similar biblical texts in order to arrive at *their* conclusions, that his is "simplistic exegesis that lacks a theological background" is pretty pompous, to say the least. Such a one must find his consolation against this pomposity, I would suggest, in the fact that this puts him in the company of John Calvin who, according to Charles Hodge (*Systematic Theology* [Grand Rapids: Eerdmans, n.d.], I:466), was

What Letham and de Margerie mean here is that if I, as well as "much New Testament scholarship," would reflect rightly on 'the logical and metaphysical presuppositions" behind the simple statement in John 15:26 (that occurs, by the way, only this one time in the entire New Testament), ὃ παρὰ τοῦ πατρός ἐκπορεύεται, *ho para tou patros ekporeuetai*, to be translated "who from[4] the Father is coming forth," as well as upon the teaching of John 14:16, 26; 16:7, 13-15; and 20:22, we would conclude with them that the statement implies that in the infinite depths of the divine being itself an "always continuing yet ever complete" and necessary act of the first and second persons in the Trinity is occurring whereby "they ...become the ground of the personal subsistence of the Holy Spirit, and put the third person in possession of the whole divine essence, without any division, alienation or change" (Berkhof's definition of the Spirit's eternal procession, with which definition the reader should know Letham would agree).[5]

I think any fair-minded reader would conclude that such an involved conclusion is quite a stretch, to say the least. One might even be pardoned for wondering if the Apostle John, who wrote these words, had even an inkling that his words were reflecting such a "timeless act" that is "always continuing and yet ever complete,"[6] an act that makes the Father and the Son the ground of the personal subsistence of the Holy Spirit and that puts the Holy Spirit "in possession of the whole divine essence, without any division, alienation or change." In my opinion, to claim that such an interpretation was present to his mind would be to import into the Gospel the doctrinal conclusions from the controversies of the fourth century. I, for one, doubt that John intended such an act, but this is only my opinion and no weight one way or the other should be placed upon this opinion of mine in the present context.

What concerns Dr. Letham primarily is this: that our (I am

"little inclined to enter into these speculations" and was "opposed to going beyond the *simple* statement of the Scriptures" (emphasis supplied).

[4]Benjamin B. Warfield, "The Biblical Doctrine of the Trinity" in *Biblical and Theological Studies* (Philadelphia: Presbyterian and Reformed, 1952), 40, supplies the words "fellowship with" after the word "from."

[5]Louis Berkhof, *Systematic Theology* (New combined edition; Grand Rapids: Eerdmans, 1996), 97.

[6]Berkhof, *Systematic Theology*, 93.

including in my "our" here his acknowledged "much New Testament scholarship") not reflecting on the "logical and metaphysical presuppositions" of such a statement "has the effect of undermining the reality and truthfulness of God's revelation by positing the idea that what God does economically does not necessarily indicate who he is."[7] That is to say, according to Dr. Letham we must and should be willing to deduce what God is *in se* as the *ontological* Trinity from what the Bible represents the three Persons of the Godhead as doing *economically* in history.[8]

I have no problem with this general sentiment, of course, as long as we do not overreach ourselves and arrive at conclusions that are based more on speculation than on clear biblical testimony and then declare these conclusions "orthodoxy," which is what has too often occurred in the history of dogma.[9] I think a similar concern is what led John Calvin, after citing Augustine's explanation of the relation between the Father and the Son in his *Institutes of the Christian Religion*, 1.13.19, first to declare: "…it is far safer to stop with that relation which Augustine sets forth [in the fifth book of *On the Trinity*] than by too subtly penetrating into the sublime mystery to wander through evanescent speculations," and then to state later in the *Institutes*, 1.13.29:

---

[7]Letham, "East is East…," *Mid-America Journal of Theology*, 73.

[8]Dr. Letham apparently holds this view even though he declares in a second lecture ("The Holy Trinity and Christian Worship", *Mid-America Journal of Theology*, 97) delivered at the same institution: "We haven't got a clue what goes on in the ontological Trinity – it is completely beyond us…we don't know the inner workings of the Trinity and can never know, and it may even border on sacrilege to talk about it." We haven't got a clue? Now Dr. Letham has confused me. I thought that he believes that the Trinity's economical activities are just that: clues to what "goes on" in the ontological Trinity. Are not the Son's "eternal generation" and the Spirit's "eternal procession" acts that Letham contends "go on" in the ontological Trinity and that he believes that one who does not "lack a theological background" (de Margerie) may and ought to infer from the Trinity's economical activities?

[9]A case in point is the doctrine of the *filioque* itself. Does the Spirit eternally process from the Father alone or from the Father and the Son (*filioque*)? Eastern Christendom maintains the former is correct; Western Christendom maintains the latter is correct. Both think the other is unorthodox. And the *filioque* clause has continued to this day to be a major bone of contention between Western Christendom and the Eastern churches.

Certainly I have not shrewdly omitted anything [from my discussion of the relation between the Father and the Son] that I might think to be against me: but while I am zealous for the edification of the church, I felt that I would be better advised not to touch upon many things that would profit but little, and would burden my readers with useless trouble. For what is the point in disputing whether the Father always begets? Indeed, it is foolish to imagine a continuous act of begetting, since it is clear that three persons have subsisted in God from eternity.

But if the economical activities of the Persons of the Godhead do not *necessarily* reflect eternally continuing activities going on in the infinite depths of the ontological Trinity, what may we say with some degree of certainty that they do reflect? In response to this question I would suggest that they reflect the division of redemptive labor eternally determined upon in the pre-creation Covenant of Redemption. Benjamin B. Warfield expands upon my answer somewhat, writing:

There is, of course, no question that in "modes of operation," as it is technically called – that is to say, in the functions ascribed to the several persons of the Trinity in the redemptive process, and, more broadly, in the entire dealing of God with the world – *the principle of subordination is clearly expressed.* The Father is first, the Son is second, and the Spirit is third, in the operations of God as revealed to us in general, and very especially in those operations by which redemption is accomplished. Whatever the Father does, He does through the Son...by the Spirit. The Son is sent by the Father and does His Father's will...; the Spirit is sent by the Son and does not speak from Himself, but only takes of Christ's and shows it unto His people...; and we have Our Lord's own word for it that "one that is sent is not greater than he that sent him" (Jn. xiii. 16). In crisp decisiveness, Our Lord even declares, indeed: "My Father is greater than I" (Jn. xiv. 28); and Paul tells us that Christ is God's, even as we are Christ's (I Cor. iii. 23), and that as Christ is "the head of every man," so God is "the head of Christ" (I Cor. xi. 3). *But it is not so clear that the principle of subordination rules also in "modes of subsistence," as it is technically phrased; that is to say, in the necessary relation of the Persons of the Trinity to one another.* The very richness and variety of the expression of their subordination, the one to the other, in modes of operation, create a difficulty in attaining certainty whether they are represented as also subordinate the one to the other in modes of subsistence. Question is raised in each case of apparent intimation of subordination in modes of subsistence, whether it may not, after all, be explicable as only another expression in modes of operation. It may be natural to assume that a subordination in modes of operation rests on a subordination in modes of subsistence; that the reason why it is the Father that sends the Son and the Son that sends the Spirit is the Son is subordinate to the Father and the Spirit to the Son [in modes of subsistence]. But we are bound to bear in mind that *these relations of subordination in modes of operation may just as well be due to a convention, an agreement, between the Persons of the Trinity – a "Covenant" as it is technically called, by virtue of which a distinct function in the work of redemption is voluntarily assumed by each.* It is eminently desirable, therefore, at the least, that some definite evidence of subordination in modes of subsistence should be discoverable before it is assumed. …the fact of the humiliation of the Son of God for His earthly work does introduce a factor into the interpretation of the passages which import his subordination to the Father, which throws doubt upon the inference from [the terms "Father" and "Son"] of an eternal relation of subordination in the Trinity itself. It must at least be said that in the presence of the great New Testament doctrines of the Covenant of Redemption on the one hand, and of the Humiliation of the Son of God for His work's sake and of the Two Natures in the constitution of His Person as incarnated, on the other, the difficulty of interpreting subordinationist passages of eternal relations between the Father and the Son becomes extreme. The question continually obtrudes itself, whether they do not rather find their full explanation in the facts embodied in the doctrines of the Covenant, the Humiliation of Christ, and the Two Natures of His incarnated Person (emphases supplied).[10]

I noted in the first edition of my *A New Systematic Theology* that the subordination in modes of operation on the part of the Persons of the Godhead may well rest on the eternal Covenant of Redemption, for which there is a large amount of biblical support and thus requires no speculation[11] – within which Covenant, as I have already said, the order of relational (*not* essential) subordination between the Father and the Son and between the Father and the Son on the one hand and the Spirit on the other doubtless dictated the three Persons' division of redemptive labors – and I would have asserted this in the second edition of my *A New Systematic Theology* had it not been for the fact that my publisher placed me under rather strict space limitations in

---

[10]Warfield, "The Biblical Doctrine of the Trinity," in *Biblical and Theological Studies*, 53-5.

[11]See my *A New Systematic Theology of the Christian Faith* (First edition; Nashville, Tennessee: Thomas Nelson, 1998), 337-8.

the rewriting of any chapter and therefore this suggestion was omitted due to lack of space. I also stated in the first edition that

> to look elsewhere for the warrant for these proposed ontological relational subordinations within the Godhead, that is to say, to press back behind the eternal covenant of redemption and to attempt to think about the ontological Trinity "behind" and "apart from" all redemptive considerations, is to think about the Trinity bereft of all content save for only its barren existence. But the covenant of redemption, properly construed, will not permit even Genesis 1 and the doctrine of God as Creator to be considered apart from redemptive considerations [because even God's creative activity was initiated with redemptive considerations in mind according to Ephesians 3:9-10]. It is eminently desirable, therefore, that definite exegetical evidence for [any] proposed eternal subordinationism within the Godhead in modes of subsistence be offered before the church is asked to accept them.[12]

For myself, therefore, I think that the doctrine of the Trinity should be argued and supported biblically, with a *minimum* of theological or philosophical speculation on the church's part.[13] Confessing that there is only one living and true God who is eternally and immutably indivisible, I believe that the two great objective redemptive events of the Incarnation of God the Son and the outpouring of God the Holy Spirit at Pentecost, together with the clear biblical implicates of each, provide sufficient impetus to understand the Christian God in Trinitarian terms. The evidence for the Trinity is just the biblical evidence, of whatever kind, for the deity of Jesus Christ and the distinct personal subsistence of God the Holy Spirit. Said another way, whatever biblical evidence, wherever expressed in Holy Scripture, which can be adduced in support of the deity of Jesus Christ and the personal subsistence of the Holy Spirit is evidence for the Christian doctrine of the Trinity. This method, I submit, is the proper way to support and explicate this central doctrine of the Christian faith.

---

[12]Reymond, *A New Systematic Theology of the Christian Faith* (First edition), 338.

[13]John Calvin, *Institutes*, 1.13.5, even states: "I could wish [such terms as "Trinity," "Person," etc.] were buried, if only among all men this faith were agreed on: that Father and Son and Spirit are one God, yet the Son is not the Father, nor the Spirit the Son, but that they are differentiated by a peculiar property."

In closing, I must say that what is truly amazing to me is how glibly most followers, including Dr. Letham, of John Calvin who argued in his day, against the speculations of the ancient fathers, for the autotheotism ("God of himself") of the Son and the Spirit, still speak today, primarily because it is ancient church "tradition," of the Father as alone, by his act of eternally generating the Son, the "beginning" (ἀρχή, *archē*), the "fountain" (πηγή, *pēgē*), and the "cause" (αἰτία, *aitia*) of the Son's essential deity (θεότης, *theotēs*), and together with the Son, by their mutual act of eternally processing the Spirit, as the "beginning" (ἀρχή, *archē*), the "fountain" (πηγή, *pēgē*), and the "cause" (αἰτία, *aitia*) of the Spirit's essential deity (θεότης, *theotēs*) – all highly charged speculative theology and language[14] – without any apparent concern that such teaching denies to the Son and the Spirit the attribute of self-existence which is necessarily theirs as Yahweh God.[15]

As I have asked many times before on many occasions, I ask again: should not our primary concern be to assure ourselves that our faith *first of all* passes biblical muster, employing the faith and creeds of the ancient fathers, while we revere their creedal labors, only as

---

[14]In his *Systematic Theology* (Greenville, SC: Greenville Seminary Press, 1994), 1:152, Morton H. Smith correctly states that the Nicene theologians taught that "the Father is the beginning, the fountain, the cause, the principle of the being of the Son" and that "the Son derives his essence from the Father by eternal and indefinable generation of divine essence from the Father to the Son." He then correctly notes: "Calvin was the first one to challenge these…two speculations. He taught that the Son was *a se ipso* with regard to his deity. He did not derive his essence from the Father. There is no warrant in the Scripture for the subordination of the Son in his essence to the Father. The same may be said of the Holy Spirit. He is *a se ipso* as regards his essence." If there were such a derivation of essence, then the *same* essence would be both unbegotten and begotten, both unbegotten and processing, depending upon the Person under consideration – a quagmire of contradictions.

See my *A New Systematic Theology of the Christian Faith* (Second edition), 329-40, for additional support from Charles Hodge, Benjamin B. Warfield, John Murray, and others for the non-speculative "Calvinistic" understanding of the Trinity.

[15]Charles Hodge in his *Systematic Theology*, I:467, declares Calvin's argument that the Son's autotheotism is proven by the fact that the Scriptures call him Yahweh to be "conclusive."

secondary aids and helps as we seek to learn and to enunciate the truth of the infallible Scriptures? I certainly think so. And I could wish that more Reformed theologians and pastors were less concerned to be "creedally correct" and more concerned to be biblically governed in their Trinitarian beliefs and pronouncements.

Chapter Eleven

The Trinitarianism of the *Westminster Confession of Faith*: Nicene or Reformed?

In the Fall 2000 (Vol. 62. No. 2) issue of *The Westminster Theological Journal* Dr. Robert Letham reviewed my *A New Systematic Theology of the Christian Faith* (First Edition). One of his criticisms had to do with my question regarding whether the Trinitarianism of the *Westminster Confession of Faith*, II.3, is "Nicene" or "Reformed" – by "Reformed" here I simply mean the *non-speculative* view of "eternal generation" and "eternal procession" espoused by John Calvin and his followers – a question that I do not regard as inappropriate or out of bounds to raise. I had suggested that the view of the *Confession* is the latter but not in any totally new or radical way, of course; indeed, I acknowledge that the language of the *Confession* is that of the earlier Nicene and Niceno-Constantinopolitan Creeds. Dr. Letham argued in rebuttal that by so doing I had severed the Reformation cause away from the ancient church – a breech that Calvin himself had employed every fiber of his being to avoid – and in so doing had virtually committed the unpardonable theological sin.

Dr. Letham contends that I arrived at my conclusion by "building an unprovable hypothesis on an insupportable theory." But have I? When we learn that Calvin's Trinitarianism, along with other tenets of his faith, "created a party," even the Reformed churches (B. B. Warfield), whose view of God was *"fundamentally* different"[1] from the past in the belief that "the persons of the Trinity are equal to one another in every respect" (G. Bray), why should we not at least consider whether or not the *Westminster Confession of Faith*, the high-water mark of Reformed confessional writing, just might have intended by its very brief statement on the Trinity in II.3 to side with Calvin's non-speculative understanding of the Trinity over against the Nicene Fathers' sometimes speculative understanding of the

---

[1]Gerald Bray's "fundamentally different" is probably a bit strong. "Different in some respects" would be truer as a description, I believe.

doctrine? Particularly pressing does this question become when we recall that

> when during the first weeks of its sessions, the Westminster Assembly was engaged on the revision of the Thirty-nine Articles, and Article viii on the Three Creeds came up for discussion, objection was made to the ἐκ θεοῦ [*ek theou*] clauses. It does not appear that there was any pleading for the subordinationist position: the advocates for retaining the Creeds rather expended their strength in *voiding the credal statement of any subordinationist implications*.[2]

Why should we not conclude, then, when these same men, their earlier debates on Article viii having prepared the way for a more summary mode of procedure, turned to the task of writing a new confession of faith – the confession that we now know as the *Westminster Confession of Faith* – that they would have had the same opposition to any and all subordinationist implications in this new confessional expression of their Trinitarianism? In fact, as Alex F. Mitchell observes, "the so-called Athanasian Creed is shrunk up into the single sentence"[3] of II.3, concerning which reduction John Murray states:

> [Chapter II, Article 3's] brevity is striking and its simplicity is matched only by its brevity. Both surprise and gratification are evoked by the restraint in defining the distinguishing properties of the persons of the Godhead. It had been Nicene tradition to embellish the doctrine, especially that of Christ's Sonship, with formulae beyond the warrant of Scripture. The Confession does not indulge in such attempts at definition. Later generations lie under a great debt to Westminster for the studied reserve that saved the Confession from being burdened with such speculative notions as commended themselves to theologians for more than a thousand years, but to which Scripture did not lend support. Hence all we find on this subject is the brief statement: 'the Father is of none, neither begotten nor proceeding; the Son is eternally begotten of the Father; the Spirit eternal proceeding from the Father and the Son.'[4]

---

[2]Benjamin B. Warfield, "Calvin's Doctrine of the Trinity," *Calvin and Calvinism* (Reprint; Grand Rapids: Baker, 1991), V:279, fn. 137, italics supplied.

[3]Alex F. Mitchell, *Minutes of the Sessions of the Westminster Assembly Divines* (Edinburgh: William Blackwood and Sons, 1874), li.

Does not this collocation of data suggest that a difference does exist between Nicene Trinitarianism and what I would characterize as the non-speculative Trinitarianism of the Westminster Assembly? I think so, but while I do not want to dogmatize, I will say this: while it is just possible that the Westminster divines intended to stand by the earlier creeds uncritically and to affirm the early church's particular doctrines of the Father's *continuing* generation of the Son out of himself and the Spirit's *continuing* procession out of the Father and the Son with respect to their *essential* being as God, I would suggest that much more likely they intended their Trinititarian statement – clearly shorn of virtually all of the Nicene verbiage and thus its non-biblical speculations – to be understood, in keeping with Calvin's more scriptural insights, as an expression denoting the eternal "order" in the Godhead.

It is true that certain English churchman of the period, such as George Bull and John Perkins, wrote defenses of the Trinitarianism of the Nicene Creed, but I find it difficult to believe that the framers of the *Confession* simply leaped back over Calvin's treatment of the Trinity as if it were non-existent and returned uncritically to the theology of Nicea with its speculative subordinationism in essential subsistence of the Son to the Father (and later of the Spirit to the Father and the Son). American orthodox Presbyterian theologians, such as Charles Hodge, Benjamin B. Warfield, John Murray, J. Oliver Buswell, Jr., Loraine Boettner, and Morton H. Smith, have generally followed the sixteenth-century Reformers' insistence that the second and third Persons of the Godhead are both autotheotic, that is, God of themselves, and thus are both self-existent Persons.

Dr. Letham's criticism arises from a very proper concern, namely, the implication in my question as I posed it that Reformed Trinitarianism is different from the Trinitarianism of the ancient church, thus severing the Reformation cause away from the ancient church at a strategically vital nexus. He contends, as we have already noted, that Calvin himself, solicitous to maintain catholic unity with the ancient church as evidenced by his frequent favorable citations of the early fathers, particularly Augustine, would have opposed such a severing with every ounce of strength in his being. While Dr.

---

[4]John Murray, "The Theology of the Westminster Confession of Faith," *Collected Writings of John Murray* (Edinburgh: Banner of Truth, 1982), 4:248.

Letham's concern is appropriate since it is certainly true that we should not sever the Magisterial Reformation away from the teaching of the ancient church where it is not necessary to do so, I believe that this is one among several instances in which it is necessary to do so. Moreover, I believe that Dr. Letham has too high a view of the ancient church's stature as a church authority. This becomes evident when he concludes his review by posing Colin Gunton's question:

> …if we can no longer…appropriate for ourselves the language of the past – for example, the affirmations of the Nicene Creed – then on what grounds are we able to judge whether we share the faith of the Fathers who formulated the Creed?

But Gunton's question (and indirectly, Dr. Letham's) begs the whole point of our difference. Is our primary concern to be to assure ourselves that we "share the faith of the Fathers who formulated the Creed"? I think not. Is our primary concern to be to "appropriate for ourselves the language of the past"? I think not. Is not our primary concern to be to assure ourselves that our faith *first of all* passes biblical muster, employing the faith and creeds of the ancient fathers as secondary aids and helps as we seek to learn and to enunciate the truth of the infallible Scriptures? I certainly think so, and I believe that Dr. Letham thinks so as well. And is not the faith of the ancient fathers, while we revere their creedal labors, to be considered by us as a secondary authority to the teaching of Scripture itself? I certainly think so, and again I believe that Dr. Letham thinks so as well. Therefore, I do not think that it is essential to the contemporary Reformed church's commitment to the "faith of the fathers" as set forth in the early ecumenical councils that it must accept their creedal pronouncements uncritically with no qualifications. And neither did John Calvin.

Chapter Twelve

Why Must Jesus Be God and Man?

When Pastor Geoffrey Thomas asked me last Fall to address the Grace Baptist Assembly today, you may be assured that I felt both greatly honored and highly privileged by his invitation. I am still trying to understand why he would extend this gracious invitation to me when it is just a plain fact that the United Kingdom has many of the world's most gifted pastor/theologians dwelling within its borders, any one of whom could do a far better job of fulfilling the task which he assigned me. Nevertheless, Pastor Thomas, in his letter of invitation, asked me to speak on the subject "Why Must Jesus Be God and Man?" and this is the title of my address that has been published in your assembly notices, a question that raises the issue of the necessity of the Atonement.

I will begin with a historical note: In 1098 Anselm (1033-1109), Archbishop of Canterbury, completed the greatest of his works, *Cur Deus Homo – Why [Did] God [Become] Man?* – not a volume *per se* on the two natures of Christ in which one would expect to find the evidence being set forth for the full unabridged deity and the full unabridged humanity of Christ and the nature of their hypostatic union in the one Person of Christ. Rather, it is a treatise on the Atonement in which he rejected the ancient (also medieval) theory that the death of Christ was a ransom paid to the devil: "As God owed nothing to the devil but punishment, so...whatever was demanded of man, he owed to God and not to the devil,"[1] and interpreted Christ's death rather, in light of the justice and mercy of God, as a vicarious satisfaction offered to God the Father as the legal representative of the Trinity for the sins of the world. In a word, Anselm argued that man's sin, as failure to render to God that conformity to his will that the creature owes him, insults the honor of God and makes the offender

---

Note: I delivered this address to the Grace Baptist Assembly at Child's Hill Baptist Church, London, England on May 16, 1997.

[1]Anselm, *Cur Deus Homo* (Reprint: La Salle, Illinois: Open Court, 1959), Bk. II, Ch. 19:285-86.

liable to render satisfaction. Since dishonoring the infinite God is worse than destroying countless worlds, even the smallest sin has infinite disvalue for which no created good can compensate by way of satisfaction. Though God's nature forbade that his purposes should be or would be thwarted by created resistance, his justice required that he not overlook such a great offence against him. Therefore, Anselm reasoned, first, because only God can do that which is immeasurably undeserving, second, because humans (unlike the fallen angels) come in biological families, and, third, because justice permits an offense of one family member to be compensated by another – if, given these circumstances, God then became a human family member, he could discharge man's debt for him. Hence, for Anselm the necessity of the atonement.

In this matter I am persuaded that in general Anselm got it right. God owed the devil and his minions nothing. It was God's offended honor that required redress. So, you see, I am convinced that Anselm placed the fact of the Incarnation and the cross work of Christ in the only context in which they have, or can have, any meaning – the exigencies arising from man's sin. It is this conviction that I believe my assignment would have me explicate for you this morning.

Since time will not allow a discussion of Adam's prelapsarian state of integrity (*status integritatis*) I must presume it for the purpose of this address. But suffice it to say that Adam, our first parent, was created in God's image and as such was the crowning act of God's creative activity. Man is accordingly *homo religiosus* as soon as he is *homo sapiens* or *homo* in any sense at all. With Adam God entered into covenant, obliging Adam to live obediently before him. Here let me simply note that Adam, though God created him upright (Eccl. 7:29), fell from the "golden age" of innocence in which he was created by "transgressing covenant" (Hos. 6:7). And according to the representative principle of that original covenant his first sin with its guilt and corruption was imputed to all those descending from him by ordinary generation (see here Rom. 5:12-19), which means in a sentence that all those descending from him by ordinary generation sinned in him and fell with him in his first transgression.

It is this state of affairs that is the biblical-theological backdrop for the Incarnation and the cross work of Christ. For from the one original race sin and its corruption, imputed to every son and daughter of Adam (with the exception of Christ who being virginally conceived did not descend from Adam by ordinary generation) whereby we are rendered utterly indisposed, disabled, and made opposite to all good and wholly inclined to all evil, do proceed all of our actual transgressions. To summarize, we are not sinners because we sin, but we sin because we are sinners, born with a nature enslaved to sin.

Now it will not be a waste of time if we spend sometime descriptively summarizing the natural state in which fallen mankind now resides (*status corruptionis*) under the following three heads: total depravity, total inability, and real guilt before God.

Total Depravity

Mankind, collectively and individually, is totally depraved. Man in his raw, natural state as he comes from the womb is morally and spiritually corrupt in disposition and character. Every part of his being – his mind, his will, his emotions, his affections, his conscience, his body – has been affected by sin. His understanding is darkened, his mind is at enmity with God, his will to act is slave to his darkened understanding and rebellious mind, his heart is corrupt, his emotions are perverted, his affections naturally gravitate to that which is evil and ungodly, his conscience is untrustworthy, and his body is subject to mortality. The Scriptures are replete with such representations of the condition of mankind:

Genesis 6:5-6: "The LORD saw that…every inclination of the thoughts of [man's] heart was only evil all the time."

Genesis 8:21: "The LORD…said in his heart: '…the inclination of [man's] heart is evil from childhood."

1 Kings 8:46: Solomon declared that "…there is no one who does not sin" against God.

Psalm 14:1-3: "The fool [this term denotes the spiritually and morally deficient man, and is thus descriptive of every man outside of Christ] says in his heart, 'There is no God.' They are corrupt, their deeds are vile; there is no one who does good. The LORD looked down from heaven on the sons of men to see if there are any who understand, any who seek God. All have turned aside, they have together become corrupt; there is no one who does good, not even one."

Psalm 51:5 [MT 51:7]: David declared: "Surely I have been a sinner from birth, sinful from the time my mother conceived me."

Psalm 58:3: Again, he declared: "Even from birth the wicked go astray; from the womb and they are wayward and speak lies."

Psalm 130:3: "If you, O LORD, kept a record of sins, O Lord, who could stand?"

Psalm 143:2: David again affirmed: "…no one living is righteous before you."

Ecclesiastes 7:20: "There is not a righteous man on earth who does what is right and never sins."

Ecclesiastes 9:3: "The hearts of men…are full of evil and there is madness in their hearts while they live."

Isaiah 53:6: "We all [the elect], like sheep, have gone astray, each of us has turned to his own way."

Isaiah 64:6 [MT 64:5]: "All of us have become like one who is unclean and all our righteous acts are like filthy rags."

Jeremiah 17:9: "The heart is deceitful above all things and beyond [human] cure. Who can understand it?"

Luke 11:13: Jesus declared of his disciples: "…you are evil."

Romans 1:29-32 (see also 1:18-28): Of the Gentiles Paul asserts that they "have become filled with every kind of wickedness, evil, greed and depravity. They are full of envy, murder, strife, deceit, and malice. They are gossips, slanderers, God-haters, insolent, arrogant and boastful; they invent ways of doing evil; they disobey their parents; they are senseless, faithless, heartless, ruthless. Although they know God's righteous ordinance that those who do such things deserve death, they not only continue to do these very things but also approve of those who practice them."

Romans 3:9-23: Two chapters later Paul declares: "Jews and Gentiles alike are all under sin. As it is written [and now follows his fourteen-point indictment against the entire human race – each indictment drawn from an Old Testament Psalm with one exception]:

'There is no one righteous, not even one;
there is no one who understands,
no one who seeks God.
All have turned away,
they have together become worthless;
there is no one who does good,
not even one. [Psalm 14:1-3]
Their throats are open graves;
their tongues practice deceit. [Psalm 5:9]

132

The poison of vipers is on their lips. [Psalm 140:3]
Their mouths are full of cursing and bitterness. [Psalm 10:7]
Their feet are swift to shed blood;
ruin and misery mark their ways,
and the way of peace they do not know. [Isaiah 59:7-8]
There is no fear of God before their eyes.' [Psalm 36:1]
...for all have sinned [in Adam] and are continually falling short of the glory [righteousness] of God."

Galatians 3:22: "...the Scripture 'shuts up in prison' under sin the whole world."

Ephesians 2:1-3: To the Ephesians believers, Paul writes: "As for you, you were dead in your trespasses and sins, in which you used to live when you followed the ways of this world and of the ruler of the kingdom of the air, of the spirit which is now at work in those who are disobedient. All of us also lived among them at one time, gratifying the cravings of our sinful nature and following its desires and thoughts. Like the rest, we were by nature objects of wrath."

Ephesians 4:17-19: Paul also states categorically that Gentiles live "in the futility of their thinking. They are darkened in their under-standing and separated from the life of God because of the ignorance that is in them due to the hardness of their hearts. Having lost all sensitivity, they have given themselves over to sensuality so as to indulge in every kind of impurity, with a continual lust for more."

1 John 1:8, 10: John the beloved disciple affirms: "If we claim to be without sin, we deceive ourselves and the truth is not in us.... If we claim we have not sinned, we make him out to be a liar and his word has no place in our lives."

1 John 5:19: Finally, we may cite John again: "...the whole world lies in the power of the evil one."

From such passages it is clear that the one who disputes the universality of sin's dominion is not arguing with the Christian who asserts as much but with Scripture itself. Also, from such passages, as well as many others that could be cited, it is clear that the Bible affirms of fallen mankind total, that is, pervasive, depravity. By "pervasive depravity" I do not mean that people act as bad as they actually are by nature since they are prevented from doing so by God's common restraining grace both within and outside of them, such as (1) their innate awareness of both the living God and his righteous ordinance that sinners deserve death (Rom. 1:19-21, 32), (2) the works of the law written on their hearts, their consciences – the "lamp of the LORD" (Prov. 20:27) within them – bearing witness by accusing or excusing them (Rom. 2:15), and (3) civil government's threatened sanctions against wrongdoers (Rom. 13:1-5). By "pervasive depravity" I mean rather that all mankind is corrupt through the totality of their being, with every part, power, and faculty and of their nature – mind, intellect, emotions, will, conscience, body – being affected by the Fall.[2]

With respect specifically to the noetic effects of sin, none of the above is intended to say or to imply that Adam's fall brought him or his progeny to a perpetual state of irrationality, that is, the inability ever to reason correctly. But it is my opinion that it is *only* because of God's common grace extended to them that fallen men are still able at all to follow or to mount a logical argument. Except for the illumination of the divine Logos that he gives to every man coming into the world (John 1:9), the Fall would have had the effect of bringing men to a perpetual state of illogicality that, since recognition and belief of the truth is essential to salvation (see John 4:24; 8:32; Rom. 1:25; 2:8; 2 Thess. 2:10-12; 1 Tim. 2:4; 2 Tim. 2:25; 4:4), would have placed them beyond the reach of redemption. But even with this divine gift of rationality, because of the noetic effects of sin men must still face the fact, as they mount their arguments and construct their sciences, that falsehood, unintentional mistakes, lapses in logic, self-delusion and self-deception, the intrusion of fantasy into the

---

[2]The Bible clearly affirms that God has shown and continues to show a measure of favor or undeserved kindness to his creatures in general. He provides the sustenance they need for their physical survival and well-being. He restrains the effects of sin in both individuals and society and enables the unregenerate to perform civic good, that is, to accomplish things that promote the welfare of others. Not the least evidence by any means of his common goodness to them is his sustaining of men in their scientific enterprises and their search for truth about themselves and the physical universe, enabling them to make many very useful discoveries about the world and the universe. Of course, the knowledgeable Christian will recognize that the efforts of the unregenerate scientist are only successful because he is unwittingly "borrowing capital" from the Christian-theistic understanding of the universe in which uniformity in nature and the orderly meaning of facts are guaranteed by God and his eternal plan.

imagination, the influence of the negative reasoning of other men's minds, physical weakness influencing the total human psyche, the disorganizing relationships of life, the effect of misinformation, disinformation, and inaccuracies learned from one realm of science upon the controlling ideas of other realms, sinful self-interest, the weakening of mental energies, the internal disorganization and emotional disfunctions of sin-skewed life-harmonies, and most importantly, their autonomous detachment from the ποῦ στῶ (*pou stō*)[3] to be found only in the revealed knowledge of God, that alone justifies human knowledge and from which alone justified human predications may be launched – now, I say, men must face the fact that any and all of these noetic effects of sin can and do bring them in their search for knowledge a large part of the time to unrecognized and thus to unacknowledged ignorance.

I may say in passing that it is also evident from these passages of Scripture that the Reformers were far more sensitive to the teaching of Scripture when they taught the total corruption of all mankind than were the Roman Catholic apologists at the Council of Trent and their modern followers who assert that fallen men are not depraved but rather only deprived of the superadditional gift (*donum superadditum*) of original holiness and righteousness.[4]

---

[3]By ποῦ στῶ (*pou stō*) ("[a place] where I may stand") I intend the ultimate heart commitment of whatever kind from which a person launches all his argumentation and all his predications. For the unbeliever it is his own autonomy; for the Christian it should be the revealed transcendent knowledge of God.

[4]The *Catechism of the Catholic Church* (1994) declares: "[Original sin] is a sin...transmitted by propagation to all mankind, that is, by the transmission of human nature *deprived of original holiness and justice* [righteousness]" (paragraph 404, emphasis supplied), and that "original sin does not have the character of a personal fault in any of Adam's descendants. It is a *deprivation of original holiness and justice* [righteousness], but human nature *has not been totally corrupted*: it is wounded in the natural powers proper to it; subject to ignorance, suffering, and the dominion of death; and inclined to sin – an inclination to evil that is called 'concupiscence'" (paragraph 405, emphasis supplied). Thus, according to Roman Catholic theology, man's fallen state is a *relapse* back to the state of pure nature (*status naturae purae*) that is *not* a state of sin, but only a state of the *tendency* to sin. The *Catechism* also states that Rome's teaching "was articulated in the sixteenth century [at

Total Inability

Because mankind is totally or pervasively corrupt, people are incapable of changing their character for the good or of acting in a way that is distinct from their corruption. They are unable to discern, to love, or to choose the things that are pleasing to God out of proper motives. As Jeremiah says: "Can the Ethiopian change his skin or the leopard his spots? Then [that is, if they can do these things] you also can do good who are accustomed to do evil" (Jer 13:23). The New Testament affirms several very significant moral/spiritual "cannots" (οὐ δύναται, *ou dunatai*) about unregenerate man:

Matthew 7:18: "...a bad tree *cannot bear* good fruit."

John 3:3, 5: "...unless a man is born from above, he *cannot see* the kingdom of God...unless a man is born of water and the Spirit, he *cannot enter* the kingdom of God."

John 6:44, 65: "*No one can come* to me unless the Father who sent me draws him...*no one can come* to me unless the Father has enabled him."

John 8:43: To some Jews interrogating him Jesus said: "...you are *unable to hear* what I say."

John 15:4-5: "*No [branch] can bear fruit* by itself; it must remain in the vine. *Neither can you bear fruit* unless you remain in me. I am the vine...apart from me *you can do nothing* [good]."

John 14:17: "The world *cannot accept* [the Spirit of truth], because it neither sees him nor knows him."

Romans 8:7-8: "...the sinful mind...does not submit to God's law, *nor can it* do so. Those controlled by the sinful nature *cannot please* God."

1 Corinthians 2:14: "The man without the Spirit does not accept the things that come from the Spirit of God, for they are foolishness to him, and he *cannot understand* them, because they are spiritually discerned."

---

the Council of Trent] in opposition to the Protestant Reformation," whose first leaders "taught that original sin has radically perverted man and destroyed his freedom" (paragraph 406). Here we see Rome protecting the libertarian freedom of the human will over against the biblical teaching that the human will (which is simply the mind choosing) is corrupt and incapable of choosing the good for the proper motives.

1 Corinthians 12:3: "...*no one can say*, 'Jesus is Lord,' except by the Holy Spirit."

James 3:8: "...*no man can tame* the tongue."

This second point means that people in their natural state are not only morally and spiritually corrupt but are also incapable of the understanding, the affections, and the will to act that, taken together, enable them to be subject to the law of God, to respond to the gospel of grace, to appreciate the things of the Spirit, to do those things that are well-pleasing in God's sight and to love God. Paul calls this universal ability a form of death, the fallen heart being "dead in transgressions and sins" (Eph. 2:1; Col. 2:13).

It is important that we note that total depravity and total inability are of one piece. That is to say, they do not exist apart from each other. Because man is by nature corrupt and wicked (total depravity), he cannot incline himself toward spiritual good (total inability). Paul writes in Romans 8:7: "The sinful mind...*does not submit* to God's law [that is depravity], *nor can it do so* [that is inability]." Both are true and both are condemnatory.

Of course, these doctrinal conclusions have not gone unchallenged. Romanists and Arminians have always raised two objections in particular against these twin doctrines of total depravity and total inability. The first objection declares: "The teaching that mankind is totally corrupt and unable to please God is a counsel of despair to the lost and only encourages people to delay their response to the gospel." Of course, the opposite is true. It is only when a person, by the Spirit's enabling, knows that he is sinful and incapable of helping himself that he will seek help out of himself and cast himself upon the mercies of God in Christ Jesus. Nothing is more soul-destroying than the sinner's belief that he still has freedom of the will and that he is capable of remedying his situation anytime he wishes. And the teaching that man is natively able to do what is good in God's sight fosters this attitude. To encourage such a conviction is truly to plunge men into self-deception, and that is indeed a counsel of despair.

The second objection asks: "How can the teaching of total depravity and total inability be reconciled with God's commands? Do not the very commands of God presuppose mankind's ability to obey them? Can a person justly be required to do that for which he has not the necessary ability?" But God deals with man according to his obligation, not according to the measure of his ability. Before the Fall, man had both the obligation and the ability to obey God. As a result of the Fall, he retained the former but lost the latter. Man's inability to obey, arising from the moral corruption of his nature, does not remove his obligation to God to love him with all his heart, soul, mind, and strength and his neighbor as himself. His obligation to obey God remains intact. If God dealt with man today according to his ability to obey, he would have to reduce his moral demands to the vanishing point. Conversely, if we determined the measure of a man's ability from the sweeping obligations implicit in the divine commands, we would need to predicate total ability for fallen man, that is to say, we would have to adopt the Pelagian position, for the commands of God run the entire gamut of spiritual obligation and moral and ethical behavior.

Real Guilt Before God

The third condition of man's present state is this: Because of man's corruption and inability to please God, he is deserving of and liable to punishment, for his sin is not only real evil, morally wrong, the violation of God's law, and therefore undesirable, odious, ugly, disgusting, filthy, of infinite disvalue, with no right to be; it is also the contradiction of God's perfection, cannot but meet with his disapproval and wrath, and is damnable in the strongest sense of the word because it so dreadfully dishonors God. God must react with holy indignation against human sin. He cannot do otherwise. In sum, *mankind has incurred real guilt before God and thus faces the prospect of the miseries of this life and the pains of hell forever.*

Of the over fifty passages in the New Testament alone that speak of the final judgment, the bifurcation of destinies of the saved and the lost, and the conscious eternal torment of impenitent sinners, I will cite only four:

Matthew 25:34, 41, 46: "Then the King will say to those on his right, 'Come, you are blessed of my Father; take your inheritance, the kingdom prepared for you since the creation of the world'...Then he will say to those on his left, 'Depart from me, you who are cursed, into the eternal fire prepared for the devil and his angels;...Then they will go away to eternal punishment, but the righteous to eternal life."

John 3:18, 36: "Whoever believes in [God's Son] is not condemned, but whoever does not believe *stands condemned already* .... Whoever believes in the Son has eternal life, but whoever rejects the Son will not see life, for God wrath remains upon him."

Romans 2:5-10: "Because of your stubbornness and your unrepentant heart, you are storing up wrath against yourself for the day of God's wrath, when his righteous judgment will be revealed. God 'will give to each person according to what he has done.' To those who by persistence in doing good seek glory, honor and immortality [descriptive only of Christians], he will give eternal life. But for those who are self-seeking and who reject the truth and follow evil [non-Christians], there will be wrath and anger. There will be trouble and distress for every human being who does evil: first, for the Jew, then for the Gentile; but glory, honor and peace for everyone who does good: first, for the Jew, then for the Gentile."

Revelation 14:9-11: "If anyone worships the beast and his image and receives his mark on the forehead or on the hand, he, too, will drink of the wine of God's fury, which has been poured full strength into the cup of his wrath. He will be tormented with burning sulfur in the presence of the holy angels and of the Lamb. And the smoke of their torment rises forever and ever. There is no rest day or night for those who worship the beast and his image, or for anyone who receives the mark of his name."

And with the doctrine of hell as the just recompense for our guilt before God we come face to face, as John Murray observes:

> with a divine "cannot" that bespeaks not divine weakness but everlasting strength, not reproach but inestimable glory. He cannot deny himself. To be complacent towards that which is the contradiction of his holiness would be a denial of himself. So that wrath against sin is the correlate of his holiness. And this is just saying that the justice of God demands that sin receive its retribution. The question is not at all, How can God, being what he is, send men to hell? The question is, How can God being what he is, save them from hell? This is the import of [man's] *reatus* [state of guilt].[5]

But what does all this have to do with our original question: "Why the Godman?" Why did the eternal Son of God – the blessed Second

---

[5]John Murray, "The Nature of Sin," in *Collected Writings of John Murray* (Edinburgh, Banner of Truth, 1977), 2:81-2.

Person of the Holy Trinity – have to become flesh?" The answer to this question should now be plain: The terrible sin of man has offended the honor of the infinitely holy God, and the righteous requirements of his offended holiness demand satisfaction. But this satisfaction cannot be made for us by an angel but must be achieved by a human being inasmuch as it is the sins of human beings that must be removed from the sight of God. The author of Hebrews, under inspiration, states this fact this way:

> Since the children have flesh and blood, he too shared in their humanity.... For surely it is not angels he helps, but Abraham's descendants. For this reason he had to be made like his brothers in every way, in order that he might become a merciful and faithful high priest in service to God, and that he might make atonement for the sins of the people (Heb. 2:14-17).

But since every sin carries within its bosom *infinite disvalue* since it assaults the *infinitely* holy God and deserves God's infinite wrath and curse,[6] full satisfaction requires recompense that may be met only by a payment of *infinite worth*. This payment, however, cannot be made for any single human being by either another mere human being or by the entire human race but only a Being accredited with infinite worth before God, namely, by God himself! The One who makes such satisfaction must, therefore, be not only human but also divine. Hence the necessity of the God-man. And because his divine nature, in accord with God's eternal decree,[7] communes with, and

---

[6]Thomas Aquinas, *Summa Theologica*, Ia2ae. 87, 4, rightly states: "...the magnitude of the punishment matches the magnitude of the sin.... Now a sin against God is infinite, the higher the person against whom it is committed, the graver the sin – it is more criminal to strike a head of state than a private citizen – and God is of infinite greatness. Therefore and infinite punishment is deserved for a sin committed against him."

[7]John Calvin, *Institutes of the Christian Religion*, 2.17.1, writes: "In discussing Christ's merit, we do not consider the beginning of merit to be in him, but we go back to God's ordinance, the first cause. For God solely of his own good pleasure appointed him Mediator to obtain salvation for us. Hence it is absurd to set Christ's merit against God's mercy. For it is a common rule that a thing subordinate to another is not in conflict with it. For this reason nothing hinders us from asserting that Christ's merit, subordinate to God's mercy, also intervenes on our behalf. Both God's free favor and Christ's obedience, each in its degree, are fitly opposed to our works. Apart from

therefore concurs with, the suffering of the human nature in the one person of Christ in his work of redemption, the merit of Christ's suffering is of infinite and eternal worth.[8] Again, the author of Hebrews declares:

> Now there have been many [high] priests, since death prevented them from continuing in office, but because Jesus lives forever, he has a permanent priesthood. Therefore, he is able to save completely those who come to God through him, because he always lives to intercede for them. Such a high priest meets our needs – one who is holy, blameless, pure, set apart from sinners, exalted above the heavens. (Heb 7:23-26)

> How much more, then, will the blood of Christ, who through the eternal Spirit offered himself unblemished to God, cleanse our consciences from acts that lead to death, so that we may serve the living God.... In fact, the law requires that nearly everything be cleansed with blood, and without the shedding of blood there is no forgiveness. It was necessary, then, for the copies of the heavenly things to be purified with these [animal] sacrifices, but [it was necessary for] the heavenly things themselves [to be purified] with better sacrifices than these. For Christ did not enter a man-made sanctuary that was only a copy of the true one; he entered heaven itself, now to appear for us in the presence of God (Heb 9:14, 22-24).

As I said earlier, it is *this* state of affairs – man originally created good but now fallen and totally corrupt through willful disobedience and unable to save himself – that the Bible would have us believe lies behind and makes necessary the Incarnation and the cross work of Jesus Christ. This Creation/Fall backdrop is the Bible's context for Christ's incarnation and work of atonement. This is the biblical/ theological milieu in which these great redemptive events fulfill their purpose. And the Bible knows no other purpose for these central events of the Christian faith. There is no other background that will

---

God's good pleasure Christ could not have merited anything; but did so because he had been appointed to appease God's wrath with his sacrifice, and to blot out our transgressions with his obedience."

[8]It should be noted here that Christ's cross work, while of infinite worth and thus *sufficient* to save countless worlds such as our own, was particularistic in its design and thus is salvifically *efficient* only for God's elect.

do justice to Christ's Incarnation and his obedient life and atoning death.[9] To deny either man's original state of integrity or his self-willed fall from that estate into the estate of corruption and misery is to rob these events of the only context in which they have any meaning. Affirm the Bible's account of man's "golden age" of innocence and his subsequent rebellion against God and the cross fits man's need "hand in glove." For this reason, as unpopular as this teaching is today in many quarters, it is imperative that pastors and churches committed to the biblical faith continue to proclaim and to teach the doctrine of man's total sinfulness and inability. For if men are not corrupt, they have no need of the saving benefits of the cross! If men are not incapable of saving themselves, they have no need of the prevenient grace of God! If men are not guilty before God, they have no need of the saving mercies of God in Christ! It is only when men by God's enabling grace see themselves as they truly are – as pervasively sinful, as incapable of doing anything to save themselves, as guilty before God – that they will cry with Augustus M. Toplady:

Rock of Ages, cleft for me,
    let me hide myself in thee;
Let the water and the blood,
    from thy riven side which flowed,
be of sin the double cure,
    cleanse me from its guilt and power.

Not the labor of my hands
    can fulfill thy law's demands;
could my zeal no respite know,
    could my tears forever flow,
all for sin could not atone;
    thou must save, and thou alone.

---

[9]Jesus himself said: "...the Son of Man did not come to be served, but to serve, and to give his life a ransom for many" (Matt. 20:28; see also Mark 10:45); again, "...the Son of Man came to seek and to save what was lost" (Luke 19:10); and yet again: "...the Son of Man came not to destroy men's lives but to save them" (Luke 9:56, Received Text). And Paul writes: "Here is a trustworthy saying that deserves full acceptance: Christ Jesus came into the world to save sinners" (1 Tim. 1:15).

Nothing in my hands I bring,
    simply to thy cross I cling;
naked, come to the thee for dress,
    helpless, look to thee for grace;
foul, I to the fountain fly,
    wash me, Savior, or I die.

It should not be necessary to contend for these truths among Christians, but given the theological illiteracy and unbelief that everywhere abounds within Christendom today, it must be underscored that it is the biblical doctrines of man's total corruption, total inability, and real guilt before the high tribunal of heaven that made necessary the incarnation of the Second Person of the Godhead and the atonement he accomplished and applies. And it is just because professing Christians pretty generally across the board in our time have not been taught these fundamental biblical truths that they are willing to entertain the Romanist/Arminian synergistic soteriologies in which God and man both contribute something to man's salvation, with man even contributing the decisive part, or worse, even a Pelagian autosoterism in which man virtually saves himself. But wherever sinful men have come to understand that they are spiritually corrupt, that they can do nothing to rectify their lost condition, and that they have incurred real and infinite guilt before God, *there* they will revere the incarnation and glory in the atoning satisfaction that Christ's doing and dying alone provide.

Chapter Thirteen

The Sanders/Dunn "Fork in the Road" in the Current Controversy Over the Pauline Doctrine of Justification by Faith

The current controversy between the traditional Reformation position, on the one hand, and the "Shepherd" position, on the other, over the Pauline doctrine of justification by faith has a history. Evangelicals were confronted in the 1970s by several forks in the road where they chose the wrong road because their guides were highly respected theologians. The "Shepherd fork" that asks evangelicals to opt for justification both by a living faith in Christ and by the works this living faith produces came in the early to mid-1970s and has continued to plague the church to this day. The next significant fork on this wrong road where many evangelicals took a second wrong road was at the "Sanders/Dunn fork" in the late 1970s and early 1980s.[1] Now it is a truism that when one loses his way he should retrace his steps if he can, locate the fork (or forks) where he chose the wrong road, and take the other road. In order to assist evangelicals to retrace their steps, since O. Palmer Robertson has addressed the "Shepherd fork,"[2] I propose in this essay to address the second fork in the road, the "Sanders/Dunn fork."

The Most Debated Topic among Paul Scholars Today

The most debated topic among Paul scholars today is Paul's understanding of the law and more specifically the meaning of his key phrase, "works of law" (ἔργα νόμου, *erga nomou*).[3] By this phrase

---

[1]See E. P. Sanders, *Paul and Palestinian Judaism, A Comparison of Patterns of Religion* (Philadelphia: Fortress, 1977), and James D. G. Dunn, "The New Perspective on Paul" in *Bulletin of the John Rylands University Library of Manchester* 65 (1983), 95-122.

[2]See O. Palmer Robertson, *The Current Justification Controversy* (Unicoi, Tennessee: Trinity Foundation, 2003).

[3]Paul uses the phrase, "works of law," eight times in his writings: he affirms that no one can be justified by "works of law" (Gal. 2:16 [3 times];

he summarily characterized what he was so strongly setting off over against his own doctrine of justification by faith in Jesus Christ, namely, justification by "works of law." Obviously we will not be able fully to comprehend the precise nature of the doctrine Paul wants to put in its place if we do not grasp the precise nature of the teaching he so vigorously opposed. This debate is raging today between Protestant Pauline scholars, particularly German Lutheran scholars and historic Reformed theologians, on the one hand, and the "new perspective" views of E. P. Sanders, James D. G. Dunn and their followers, on the other. The former view – the "traditional Reformation view" – contends that Jews in general in Paul's day and the Pharisees in particular were obeying the law to accumulate merit before God for themselves and thereby to earn salvation, and that this is the reason Paul appears at times to inveigh against the law: his kinsmen according to the flesh or at least a large portion of first-century world Jewry (not all Jews, of course, since there was always "a remnant chosen by grace," Rom. 11:5) had come to view the law *legalistically* as the instrument for the acquisition of righteousness. C. E. B. Cranfield has argued that Paul's criticism of the law was a criticism of its then-current *perversion* into the legalism of works-righteousness; it is thus

---

Rom. 3:20, 28), that the Spirit is not received by "works of law" (Gal. 3:2, 5), and that all those whose religious efforts are characterized by "works of law" are under the law's curse (Gal. 3:10). Also the simple ἔργα, *erga*, in Romans 4:2, 6; 9:12, 32; 11:6; and Ephesians 2:9 almost certainly has the same meaning, thereby bringing the total number of texts in which Paul alludes to the concept to fourteen. I would argue that Paul intended by this phrase "things done in accordance with *whatever* the law commands – the moral law no less than the ritual, the ritual laws no less than the moral," with the intention of achieving right standing before God.

Although C. E. B. Cranfield argued in his essay, "St. Paul and the Law," in the *Scottish Journal of Theology* 17 (1964), 43-68, that Paul coined this Greek phrase because no designation was available in Greek to represent the idea of "legalism," close equivalents have been found in the Qumran material, for example, מעשי תורה, *m'sy thōrāh* ("works of law") in 4QFlor 1.1-7 (= 4Q174); מעשי בתורה, *m'sy bhthōrāh* ("works in the law") in 1QS 5:20-24; 6:18; and מקצת מעשי התורה, *mqtssh m'sy hthōrāh* ("some of the works of the law") in 4QMMT 3:29, all which seem to denote the works that the Qumran Community thought the law required of it in order to maintain its separate communal existence.

the "legalistic misunderstanding and perversion of the law," not the law itself, which kills.[4]

Sanders' "Covenantal Nomism"

The traditional Protestant view had not gone unchallenged, of course. For example, in 1894 C. G. Montefiore, a distinguished Jewish scholar, had argued that the rabbinic literature of the time speaks of a compassionate and forgiving God and of rabbis whose daily prayer was "Sovereign of all worlds! Not because of our righteous acts do we lay our supplications before you, but because of your abundant mercies" (*b. Yoma* 87b).[5] And in 1927 G. F. Moore had urged in his *Judaism in*

---

[4]C. E. B. Cranfield, "St. Paul and the Law," 43-68; see also his response to his critics, "'The Works of the Law' in the Epistle to the Romans" in *Journal for the Study of the New Testament* 43 (1991), 89-101. Of course, Paul's criticism of "covenantal legalism" was not an innovation: both the Old Testament prophets, by their denunciation of a preoccupation with the niceties of sacrificial ritual while obedience from the heart expressed in humility, compassion, and justice for the oppressed was non-existent (1 Sam. 15:22-23; Pss. 40:6-8; 51:16-17; Isa. 1:10-20; Amos 2:6-8; 4:4-5; 5:21-24; Mic. 6:6-8), and later Jesus himself, by his denunciation of the concern of the hypocritical scribes and Pharisees for their external, presumably merit-acquiring observance of the law while their hearts were far from the Lord (Matt. 5:21-6:18; 23:1-39; Mark 7:1-13; Luke 11:37-54), had spoken against such a perversion of the law's purpose.

So also Ridderbos ("Section 21: The Antithesis with Judaism" in *Paul: An Outline of His Theology*, 130-35), 132-4, who insists that for the Judaism of Paul's day

> the law is the unique means to acquire for oneself merit, reward, righteousness before God, and the instrument given by God to subjugate the evil impulse and to lead the good to victory...for the Jews the law was the pre-eminent means of salvation, indeed the real 'substance of life'...Judaism knew no other way of salvation than that of the law, and...it saw even the mercy and the forgiving love of God as lying precisely in the fact that they enable the sinner once more to built for his eternal future on the ground of the law...It is this redemptive significance that Judaism ascribed to the law against which the antithesis in Paul's doctrine of sin is directed.

[5]C. G. Montefiore, "First Impressions of Paul," *Jewish Quarterly Review* 6 (1894), 428-75; "Rabbinic Judaism and the Epistles of St. Paul," *Jewish Quarterly Review* 13 (1900-1901), 161-217.

the First Centuries of the Christian Era[6] that the earliest literature of rabbinic religion spoke constantly of grace, forgiveness and repentance. But New Testament theologians had largely ignored the implications of such studies. The publication of E. P. Sanders' programmatic *Paul and Palestinian Judaism*[7] in 1977, however, brought a "rude awakening" to what Dunn calls the "quiet cul-de-sac" that the field of New Testament study had become, making it necessary for anyone earnestly desiring to understand Christian beginnings in general or Pauline theology in particular to reconsider the traditional Protestant view.[8]

Sanders, in the name of what he terms "covenantal nomism," challenged the traditional view as being simply a myth. He argues, first, that traditional Protestantism, particularly Lutheranism, has been guilty of reading back into New Testament times *late* Jewish sources (such as those from the fifth century AD that picture the final judgment as a matter of weighing up merits and demerits) and thereby inappropriately construing the conflict between Paul and his Jewish opponents

---

[6]G. F. Moore, *Judaism in the First Centuries of the Christian Era: The Age of the Tannaim* (2 vols.; Cambridge, Mass.: Harvard University, 1927).

[7]E. P. Sanders, *Paul and Palestinian Judaism, A Comparison of Patterns of Religion* (Philadelphia: Fortress, 1977); see also his more important *Paul, the Law, and the Jewish People* (Philadelphia: Fortress, 1983), his *Paul* (Oxford: University Press, 1991), and his *Judaism: Practice and Belief, 63BCE-66CE* (London: SCM, 1992), all four works unified by their common conviction concerning the *non-legalistic* nature of first-century Palestinian Judaism and their corresponding rejection of the traditional Lutheran Reformation understanding of the law/gospel antithesis as the key to Paul's view of the law and the theology of his Jewish opposition. See also W. D. Davies, *Paul and Rabbinic Judaism: Some Rabbinic Elements in Pauline Theology* (1948; fourth edition; Philadelphia: Fortress, 1980), who argues that Paul's doctrine of justification by faith apart from "works of law" was only one metaphor among many of the time (221-23) and that Paul was simply a Pharisee for whom the messianic age had dawned (71-73).

[8]Dunn states that the reason Sanders' effort was heard while the previous efforts were largely ignored is traceable to the new historical situation and social climate which obtained at the time as the result of, first, the Nazi Holocaust in the aftermath of which the traditional denigration of Judaism as the negative side of the debate with the Protestant doctrine of justification could no longer be stomached, and second, Vatican II which absolved the Jewish people of deicide.

in terms of debates that occurred at the time of the magisterial Reformation between Luther and Rome, and second, that conversely first-century Palestinian Judaism had not been seduced by merit theology into becoming a religion of legalistic works-righteousness wherein right standing before God was earned by good works in a system of strict justice. He contends rather (1) that the covenant, the law, and the Jews' special status as the elect people of God were all gifts of God's grace to Israel; (2) that the Jews did not have to earn – and knowing this were not trying to earn – what they already had received by grace; (3) that Judaism did not teach that "works of law" were the condition for entry into the covenant but only for continuing in and maintaining covenant status (that is to say, that salvation comes not from meritorious works but through belonging to the covenant people of God),[9] which "pattern of religion," Sanders contends (I think wrongly), is also found in Paul; and (4) that the only real bone of contention between an (at times) incoherent and inconsistent Paul (who was not unwilling to distort his opponents' positions at times in order to safeguard his own) and his Jewish contemporaries was not soteriology (what one must do in order to be saved) but purely and simply *Christology* (what one should think about Christ). Which is just to say that Paul saw Christianity as superior to Judaism only because while the Jews thought they had in the covenant a *national* charter of privilege, Paul viewed covenantal privilege as *open to all* who have faith in Christ and who accordingly stand in continuity with Abraham. Or to put it more simply, Paul viewed Christianity as superior to Judaism only because Judaism was not Christianity.

It is indeed true, as Sanders demonstrates from his in-depth examination of the Qumran literature, the Apocryphal literature, the Pseudepigraphal literature, and the rabbinic literature of the first two hundred years after Christ that one can find many references in this material to God's election of Israel and to his grace and mercy toward the nation. And, of course, if Sanders is right about the non-legalistic nature of Palestinian Judaism in Paul's day, then Douglas J. Moo is correct when he asserts that the traditional Reformation view of Paul's polemic "is left hanging in mid-air, and it is necessary either to accuse Paul of misunderstanding (or misinterpreting) his opponents, or to find new opponents for him to be criticizing."[10] Regarding the

---

[9] Sanders, *Paul and Palestinian Judaism*, 422.

first of these possibilities, I can only say that the modern scholar, whether Christian or Jew, who supposes that he understands better or interprets more accurately first-century Palestinian Judaism than Paul did, is a rash person indeed! Moreover, Sanders makes too much of his, in my opinion, methodologically flawed findings on the "non-legalistic" character of first-century Palestinian Judaism, since first-century Palestinian Judaism, as he himself recognizes, also taught that the elect man was obligated, even though he would do so imperfectly (for which imperfections the law's sacrificial system provided the remedy), to obey the law in order to *maintain* his covenant status and to *remain* in the covenant. But this is to acknowledge, as Moo notes, that

> even in Sanders's proposal, works play such a prominent role that it is fair to speak of a "synergism" of faith and works that elevates works to a crucial salvific role. For, while works, according to Sanders, are not the means of "getting in," they are essential to "staying in." When, then, we consider the matter from the perspective of the final judgment – which we must in Jewish theology – it is clear that "works," even in Sanders's view, play a necessary and instrumental role in "salvation."[11]

Moo goes on to note in the same connection:

---

[10]Douglas J. Moo, "Paul and the Law in the Last Ten Years" in *Scottish Journal of Theology* 40 (1987), 293. See also Moo's "'Law,' 'Works of the Law,' and Legalism in Paul," *Westminster Theological Journal* 45 (1983), 73-100; and his *The Epistle to the Romans* (Grand Rapids: Eerdmans, 1996), particularly his comments on Romans 3:20 and the following "Excursus: Paul, 'Works of the Law,' and First-Century Judaism" (206-17), that take these developments into account, and Mark A. Seifrid, "Blind Alleys in the Controversy over the Paul of History" in *Tyndale Bulletin* 45.1 (1994), 73-95.

[11]Moo, *The Epistle to the Romans*, 215. In his somewhat dated but nonetheless very insightful *Biblical Theology* (Grand Rapids: Eerdmans, 1948), Geerhardus Vos also affirms that Judaism contained a large strain of legalism, stating that the Judaic "philosophy asserted that the law was intended, on the principle of meritoriousness, to enable Israel to earn the blessedness of the world to come" (142). He then explains why and how the Judaizers went wrong:

> It is true, certain of the statements of the Pentateuch and of the O. T. in general may on the surface seem to favor the Judaistic position. That the law cannot be kept is nowhere stated in so many words. And not only this, that the keeping of the law will be rewarded, is stated once and

...there is reason to conclude that Judaism was more "legalistic" than Sanders thinks. In passage after passage in his scrutiny of the Jewish literature, he dismisses a "legalistic" interpretation by arguing that the

---

again. Israel's retention of the privileges of the berith [covenant] is made dependent on obedience. It is promised that he who shall do the commandments shall find life through them. Consequently, writers have not been lacking, who declared, that, from a historical point of view, their sympathies went with the Judaizers, and not with Paul. Only a moment's reflection is necessary to prove that...precisely from a broad historical standpoint Paul had far more accurately grasped the purport of the law than his opponents. The law was given after the redemption from Egypt had been accomplished, and the people had already entered upon the enjoyment of many of the blessings of the berith. Particularly, their taking possession of the promised land could not have been made dependent on previous observance of the law, for during their journey in the wilderness many of its prescripts could not be observed. It is plain, then, that law-keeping did not figure at that juncture as the meritorious ground of life-inheritance. The latter is based on grace alone, no less emphatically than Paul himself places salvation on that ground. But, while this is so, it might still be objected, that law-observance, if not the ground of receiving, is yet made the ground for retention of the privileges inherited. Here it can not, of course, be denied that a real connection exists. But the Judaizers went wrong in inferring that the connection must be *meritorious*, that, if Israel keeps the cherished gifts of Jehovah through observance of His law, this must be so, because in strict justice they had *earned* them. The connection is of a totally different kind. It belongs not to the legal sphere of merit, but to the symbolico-typical sphere of *appropriateness of expression*. ...the abode of Israel in Canaan typified the heavenly, perfected state of God's people. Under these circumstances the ideal of absolute conformity to God's law of legal holiness had to be upheld. Even though they were not able to keep this law in the Pauline, spiritual sense, yea, even though they were unable to keep it externally and ritually, the requirement could not be lowered. When apostasy on a general scale took place, they could not remain in the promised land. When they disqualified themselves for typifying the state of holiness, they *ipso facto* disqualified themselves for typifying that of blessedness, and had to go into captivity.... And in Paul's teaching the strand that corresponds to this Old Testament doctrine of holiness as the indispensable (though not meritorious) condition of receiving the inheritance is still distinctly traceable. (142-4)

[12]Moo, *The Epistle to the Romans*, 216-7. While I disagree with Jacob

covenantal framework must be read into the text or that the passage is homiletical rather than theological in intent. But was the covenant as pervasive as Sanders thinks? Might not lack of reference in many Jewish works imply that it had been lost sight of in a more general reliance on Jewish identity? And does not theology come into expression in homiletics? Indeed, is it not in more practically oriented texts that we discover what people *really* believe? Sanders may be guilty of underplaying a drift toward a more legalistic posture in first-century Judaism. We must also reckon with the possibility that many "lay" Jews were more legalistic than the surviving literary remains of Judaism would suggest. Certainly the undeniable importance of the law in Judaism would naturally open the way to viewing doing the law in itself as salvific. The gap between the average believer's theological views and the informed views of religious leaders is often a wide one. If Christianity has been far from immune to legalism, is it likely to think that Judaism, at any state of its development, was?[12]

In support of Moo's contentions one could cite, as samplings of

---

Neusner's final conclusion, see his *Rabbinic Judaism: Structure and System* (Minneapolis: Fortress, 1995), 7-13, 20-3, which heaps scorn upon Sanders' literary efforts, not so much for his conclusions but because he tends by his method to join all Judaic religious systems into a single, harmonious "Judaism." While Neusner appreciates the methodology of Sanders' *Paul and Palestinian Judaism* much more than the methodology and conclusions reflected in his *Judaism: Practice and Belief 63 B.C.E.—66 C.E.*, he still faults Sanders' earlier handling of the Mishna and the other rabbinic sources because, says Neusner, the Pauline-Lutheran questions he brings to it are simply not these sources' central concerns: "Sanders's earlier work is profoundly flawed by the category formation that he imposes on his sources; that distorts and misrepresents the Judaic system of these sources" (22). He explains:

Sanders quotes all documents equally with no effort at differentiation among them. He seems to have culled sayings from the diverse sources he has chosen and written them down on cards, which he proceeded to organize around his critical categories. Then he has constructed his paragraphs and sections by flipping through these cards and commenting on this and that. So there is no context in which a given saying is important in its own setting, in its own document. This is Billerbeck scholarship.

The diverse rabbinic documents require study in and on their own terms... [But Sanders'] claim to have presented an account of "the Rabbis" and their opinions is not demonstrated and not even very well argued. We hardly need to dwell on the still more telling fact that Sanders has not

Judaic thought in this regard, Sirach (also known as Ecclesiasticus) 3:3, 14-15, 30-31, a second-century BC Jewish writing, that teaches quite clearly that human good deeds atone for sins:

> [3]Whoever honors his father atones for sins,...
> [14]For kindness to a father will not be forgotten,
> and against your sins it will be credited to you;
> [15]In the day of your affliction it will be remembered in your favor,
> as frost in fair weather, your sins will melt away....
> [30]Water extinguishes a blazing fire:
> so almsgiving atones for sin.
> [31]Whoever requites favors gives thought to the future;
> at the moment of his falling he will find support. (See also Sirach 29:11-13 and Tobit 4:7-11)

Sanders also ignores Flavius Josephus' frequent insistence that God's grace is meted out in response to merit,[13] and he simply discounts the argument of 2 Esdras[14] as an atypical exception here.[15]

---

shown how systemic comparison is possible when, in point of fact, the issues of one document, or of one system of which a document is a part, are simply not the same as the issues of some other document or system; he is oblivious to all documentary variations and differences of opinion. That is, while he has succeeded in finding rabbinic sayings on topics of central importance to Paul (or Pauline theology), he has ignored the context and authentic character of the setting in which he has found these sayings. He lacks all sense of proportion and coherence, because he has not even asked whether these sayings form the center and core of the rabbinic system or even of a given rabbinic document. To state matters simply, how do we know that "the Rabbis" and Paul are talking about the same thing, so that we can compare what they have to say? If it should turn out that "the Rabbis" and Paul are not talking about the same thing, then what is it that we have to compare. I think, nothing at all. (22-3)

[13]In his *Against Apion*, II, 217b-218, for example, Josephus writes: "For those...who live *in accordance with our laws* [νομίμως, *nomimos*] the prize is not silver or gold, no crown of wild olive or of parsley with any such public mark of distinction. No; each individual, relying on the witness of his own conscience and the lawgiver's prophecy, confirmed by the sure testimony of God, is firmly persuaded that *to those who observe the laws* [τοῖς τοὺς νόμους διαφυλάξασι, *tois tous nomous diaphulaxasi*] and, if they must needs die for them, willingly meet death, God has granted *a renewed existence* [γενέσθαι πάλιν, *genesthai palin*] and in the revolution of the ages the

And Qumran document 1QS 11:2, 3 states: "For I belong to the God of my vindication and the perfection of my way is in his hand with the virtue of my heart. And *with my righteous deeds* he will wipe away

---

gift of *a better life* [βίον ἀμείνω, *bion ameinō*]."

In his *Discourse to the Greeks on Hades* Josephus states that "to those that have done well [God will give] an everlasting fruition," and more specifically that "the just shall remember only their righteous actions, whereby they have attained the heavenly kingdom."

[14]2 Esdras is 4 Esdras in the appendix of the Roman Catholic Vulgate Bible, with chapters 3–14 being a late first-century AD work written by an unknown Palestinian Jew in response to the destruction of Jerusalem in AD 70.

[15]See, for example, the following statements in 2 Esdras:

7:77: "For you have a treasure of works laid up with the Most High."

7:78-94: "Now, concerning death, the teaching is: When the decisive decree has gone forth from the Most High that a man shall die...if [the spirits are] those...who have despised his law...such spirits shall not enter into habitations, but shall immediately wander about in torments, ever grieving and sad...because they scorned the law of the Most High.... Now this is the order of those who have kept the ways of the Most High, when they shall be separated from their mortal bodies. During the time that they lived in it, they...withstood danger every hour, that they might keep the law of the Lawgiver perfectly. Therefore...they shall see with great joy the glory of him who receives them...because...while they were alive they kept the law which was given them in trust."

7:105: "...no one shall ever pray for another on that day...for then every one shall bear his own righteousness or unrighteousness."

7:133: "[The Most High] is gracious to those who turn in repentance to his law."

8:33: "For the righteous, who have many works laid up with thee, shall receive their reward in consequence of their own deeds."

8:55-56: "Therefore do not ask any more questions about the multitude of those who perish. For they also received freedom, but they despised the Most High, and were contemptuous of his law."

9:7-12: "And it shall be that every one who will be saved and will be able to escape on account of his works...will see my salvation in my land...and as many as scorned my law while they still had freedom...these must in torment acknowledge it after death."

See also B. W. Longenecker, *2 Esdras* (Sheffield: Sheffield Academic, 1995).

[16]For the defense of "with my righteous deeds" and not "and in his righteousness" as the more likely original reading, see Mark A. Seifrid, "Blind Alleys," 81-2, fn. 28.

my transgressions."[16] 1QS 3:6-8; 8:6-10; 9:4 also attribute an atoning efficacy to the Qumran Community's deeds. Turning to the New Testament, one may also cite here the opinion of the "believers who belonged to the party of the Pharisees" (Acts 15:5) who declared: "Unless you [Gentiles] are circumcised, according to the custom taught by Moses, you cannot be saved" (Acts 15:1). I grant that the focus of these Acts verses is directed toward what the Pharisee party in the church thought Gentiles had to do in order to be saved, but it is surely appropriate to conclude, first, that they would have believed that they themselves had to do the same thing in order to be saved, and second, that they were apparently reflecting what at least the Pharisees – the strictest sect of Judaism – would also have believed.

Moreover, in Paul's "allegory" in Galatians 4:21-31, wherein he first declares that "Hagar stands for Mount Sinai in Arabia and corresponds to *the present city of Jerusalem* [lit. "the now Jerusalem," τῇ νῦν Ἰερουσαλήμ, *tē nun Ierousalēm*], because she is in slavery with her children," thereby placing "the now Jerusalem," which stands within his "Hagar-Sinai-law-bondage" matrix, in bondage to the law (4:25), and then contrasts "the now Jerusalem" with "the Jerusalem that is above [lit. "the above Jerusalem," ἡ ἄνω Ἰερουσαλήμ, *hē anō Ierousalēm*]" that is "free" and the Christian's "mother," it is apparent that Paul's expression, "the now Jerusalem," goes beyond the Judaizers who were troubling his churches and, in the words of Ronald Fung, "stands by metonymy for Judaism, with its trust in physical descent from Abraham and reliance on legal observance as the way of salvation."[17] In sum, Paul by this allegory is saying that the nation of Israel because of its unbelief and bondage to the law is actually a nation of spiritual Ishmaelites, sons of the bondwoman Hagar, and not true Israelites at all!

Finally, if the foregoing data are not sufficient to show Sanders'

---

[17]Ronald Y. K. Fung, *The Epistle to the Galatians* (NICNT; Grand Rapids: Eerdmans, 1988), 209; see also C. K. Barrett, "The Allegory of Abraham, Sarah, and Hagar in the Argument of Galatians" in *Rechtfertigung, Festschrift für Ernst Käsemann*, edited by Johannes Friedrich, Wolfgang Pöhlmann, and Peter Stuhlmacher (Göttingen: Vandenhoeck & Ruprecht, 1976); republished in *Essays on Paul*, 154-70.

[18]I construe δικαιοσύνης, *dikaiosunēs*, to be an ablative of means. Moo virtually says this when he concludes his discussion of the phrase νόμον δικαιοσύνης, *nomon dikaiosunēs*, here by saying: "'Law,' therefore, re-

error, and if one is willing as I am to give Paul his rightful due as an inspired apostle of Christ, then as the *coup de grace* to his "new perspective" on first-century Palestinian Judaism, Paul writes in Romans 9:30-32 and 10:2-4:

> When then shall we say? That the Gentiles, who did not pursue righteousness, have obtained it, a righteousness that is by faith; but Israel, *who pursued law [as a means to] righteousness*,[18] did not attain [the requirements of that] law. Why not? Because *they pursued it not by faith but as if it were by works* [of law[19]].... For I can testify about [the Israelites] that they are zealous for God, but their zeal is not based on knowledge. Since they did not know the righteousness that comes from God and *sought to establish their own*, they did not submit to God's righteousness. Christ is the end of "law-keeping" [lit. "law"] as a means to [εἰς[20]] righteousness to all who believe.[21] (emphasis supplied)

In sum, while both Judaism and Paul viewed obedience to the law as having an appropriate place in the covenant way of life, there was this difference: whereas Paul viewed the Christian's obedience as (at best) the *fruit* and *evidentiary sign* of the fact that one is a member

---

mains the topic of Paul's teaching throughout this verse and a half [Rom. 9:31-32a], but law conceived as a means to righteousness" (625-6).

[19]I have added this prepositional phrase only to bring out what I think is Paul's intended meaning and not because I think that it reflects the originality of the textual variant ἔργων νόμου, *ergōn nomou*, supported by ℵ² D K P Y 33 81 104 etc., a few church fathers, and a few versions.

[20]By construing the εἰς, *eis*, here as denoting "means," I have conformed Paul's statement here with his earlier phrase, "law [as a means to] righteousness," in 9:31.

[21]C. K. Barrett, in "Romans 9:30–10:21: Fall and Responsibility of Israel" in *Essays on Paul*, correctly explains Paul's intention in these verses this way: "...the only way to achieve righteousness (which is what the righteous law requires) is by faith. This way the Gentiles, who really had no choice in the matter, had adopted, when they were surprised by the gospel.... Israel had not done this. They had been given the law...and had sought to do what they understood it to mean; but *they had misunderstood their own law, thinking that it was to be obeyed on the principle of works*, whereas it demanded obedience rendered in, consisting of, faith" (141, emphasis supplied).

[22]For a detailed critical analysis of Sanders' thesis, see M. A. Seifrid, *Justification by Faith: The Origin and Development of a Central Pauline Theme* (NovTSup 68; Leiden: Brill, 1992); S. Westerholm, *Israel's Law and the*

of the covenant community, Judaism saw obedience to the law as the *instrumental basis* for continuing in salvation through the covenant. Thus the legalistic principle – even though it occurred within the context of the covenant as a kind of "covenantal legalism" – was still present and ultimately that principle came to govern the soteric status of the individual. This is just to say that Second Temple Judaism apparently over time became focused more and more on an "instrumental nomism" and less and less on a "gracious covenantalism of faith." Paul rightly saw that *any* obligation to accomplish a works-righteousness to *any* degree on the sinner's part would negate the principle of *sola gratia* altogether (Rom. 11:5-6), obligate him to obey the whole law (Gal. 3:10; 5:3), and make the cross-work of Christ of no value to him (Gal. 2:21; 5:2).[22] Finally, Paul does not represent Christianity as superior to Judaism only because of a kind of dispensational shift within salvation history from Judaism to Christianity. His differences with Judaism were far more radical and passionate than that.

Dunn's "New Perspective"

James D. G. Dunn, who accepts, not without some reservations, Sanders' understanding of first-century Palestinian Judaism, in his *Jesus, Paul and the Law*[23] urges that Paul's "works of law" phrase does not refer to works done to achieve righteousness, that is, to legalism, but to the Mosaic law particularly as that law came to focus for Israel in the observance of such Jewish "identity markers" as circumcision,

Church's Faith: Paul and His Recent Interpreters (Grand Rapids: Eerdmans, 1988); C. G. Kruse, *Paul, the Law and Justification* (Leicester: InterVarsity, 1996); and Karl T. Cooper, "Paul and Rabbinic Soteriology" in *Westminster Theological Journal* 44 (1982), 123-39.

[23]James D. G. Dunn, *Jesus, Paul and the Law: Studies in Mark and Galatians* (Louisville: Westminster/John Knox, 1990), 183-206, 215-36; see also his "The New Perspective on Paul" in *Bulletin of the John Rylands University Library of Manchester* 65 (1983), 95-122. Moo, *The Epistle to the Romans*, provides the "Dunn bibliography" on the issue (207, fn. 57), to which must be added his *The Theology of Paul the Apostle* (Grand Rapids: Eerdmans, 1998), 334-71.

[24]In his essay, "Echoes of Intra-Jewish Polemic in Paul's Letter to the Galatians" in *Journal of Biblical Literature* 112 (1993), Dunn states that the phrase refers to "acts of obedience required by the law of all faithful Jews, all

food laws and Sabbath-keeping. That is to say, Paul's "works of law" phrase refers to a subset of the law's commands that encapsulate *Jewish* existence in the nation's covenant relationship with God or, to quote Dunn himself, "the self-understanding and obligation accepted by practicing Jews that E. P. Sanders encapsulated quite effectively in the phrase 'covenantal nomism.'"[24] In sum, for Dunn the heart issue for Paul was the inclusion of Gentile Christians in the messianic community on an equal footing with Jewish Christians. In other words, for Paul his bone of contention with Judaism was not with an imagined attempt to acquire a merit-based righteousness before God as much as it was with Israel's *prideful* insistence on its covenantal racial exclusiveness: Israel shut Gentiles out of the people of God because they did not observe *their* ethno-social "identity markers." And apparently many Jewish Christians wanted Gentile Christians to observe these Jewish "identity markers" before they would or could share table fellowship with them (see Acts 10:28; Gal. 2:11-13). Paul by his "works of law" phrase was opposing then the Old Testament *ritual* laws that kept Israel in its national identity (see Num. 23:9) apart from Gentiles.

Whereas Sanders' conclusions, in my opinion, go too far, Dunn's interpretation of Paul's concern, in my opinion, is reductionistic and does not go far enough. Paul was indeed concerned with – and vigorously opposed – the spirit of racial exclusiveness within Messiah's community, but this does not appear to be his concern in his sermon in the synagogue at Pisidian Antioch when he declared that "through

---

members of the people with whom God had made the covenant at Sinai – the self-understanding and obligation accepted by practicing Jews that E. P. Sanders encapsulated quite effectively in the phrase 'covenantal nomism'" (466). In his more recent *The Theology of Paul the Apostle* Dunn declares quite forcefully: "I do not (and never did!) claim that 'works of the law' denote only circumcision, food laws, and Sabbath. A careful reading of my 'New Perspective' should have made it clear that, as in Galatians 2, these were particular focal or crisis points for (and demonstrations of) *a generally nomistic attitude*" (358, fn 97, emphasis supplied). If this is actually the case, then Dunn is saying that first-century Jewry held generally to a legalistic view of salvation and his "New Perspective" is not really new.

[25]Note too his universalistic phrases, "every mouth" (πᾶν στόμα, *pan stoma*) and "the whole world" (πᾶς ὁ κόσμος, *pas ho kosmos*) in Romans 3:19.

[26]Moo, *The Epistle to the Romans*, writes: "The 'works' mentioned [in

158

[Jesus] *everyone who believes* [πᾶς ὁ πιστεύων, *pas ho pisteuōn*] *is justified* [δικαιοῦται, *dikaioutai*] *from all things* [ἀπὸ πάντων, *apo pantōn*], from which you could not be justified by [keeping] the [whole] law of Moses" (Acts 13:39). Nor does he hesitate to relate his "works of law" terminology universally to "no flesh" (lit. "not...all flesh," οὐ...πᾶσα σάρξ, *ou...pasa sarx*] in Romans 3:20,[25] which surely includes both Gentiles (see Rom. 3:9) who obviously *were not obligated to observe Israel's circumcision or food laws* but who, according to Paul, were nonetheless regarded by God as transgressors of his law (see Rom. 1:18-32) and the people of Israel who *were obligated to observe and who were in fact observing their national identity markers* (see Rom. 2:25-29) but who also, according to Paul, were still regarded by God as transgressors of his law (see Rom. 2:21-24), both accordingly standing under the law's condemnation.[26] Which is just to say that Paul's "works of law" phrase in Romans 3:20 intended more than simply observance (or in the case of Gentiles, non-observance) of Israel's national identity markers. *The phrase included observance of God's moral law too.* But if the phrase in 3:20 includes observance of the moral law of God as well, it surely means the same in 3:28 where Paul declares: "For we maintain that a man [*any* man; see 3:29-30] is justified by faith apart from [legalistic] works of law." And immediately after he establishes mankind's guilt before God in terms of the inability of the "works of law" to justify anyone (3:20) Paul places those "works of law" as the false way to righteousness over against and in contrast to faith in Christ's saving work as the one true way to righteousness (see Romans 3:21-25: δικαιοσύνη θεοῦ διὰ πίστεως Ἰησοῦ Χριστοῦ, *dikaiosunē theou dia pisteōs Iēsou Christou*). Then when one takes into account Paul's reference to *human* "boasting" both in

---

Rom 3:20] must...be the 'works' Paul has spoken of in chap. 2. But it is not circumcision – let alone other 'identity markers' that are not even mentioned in Rom. 1-3 – that the Jew 'does' in Rom. 2; it is, generally, what is demanded by the law, the 'precepts' (v. 26; cf. vv. 22-23, 25, 27). Therefore, 3:20 must deny not the adequacy of Jewish *identity* to justify, but the adequacy of Jewish *works* to justify." (214).

[27]W. Gutbrod, νόμος, *nomos* (and the νομ-, *nom-*, word cluster), *Theological Dictionary of the New Testament*, translated by Geoffrey W. Bromiley (Grand Rapids: Eerdmans, 1967), IV:1072, also declares that Paul "works out his position" in regard to the law "primarily with ref. to the ethical command-

3:27 (καύχησις, *kauchēsis*) and 4:2 (καύχημα, *kauchēma*) and his insistence in Romans 4 that Abraham was not justified by his "works" (ἐξ ἔργων, *ex ergōn*, 4:2) or by his "working" (ἐργαζομένῳ, *ergazomenō*, 4:4-5) – which words, given their proximity to Romans 3:20 and 3:28, are almost certainly his theological shorthand for his earlier "works of law" expression – it should be again apparent that Paul's "works of law" phrase intends more than the observance (or in the case of Gentiles, non-observance) of certain Jewish identity markers *since Abraham lived before the giving of the ritual law of the Mosaic Law to Israel.*[27]

Then to Peter who, after enjoying table fellowship with Gentiles for a time at Antioch, succumbed to the pressures of the Judaizers Paul said:

> We [apostles] who are Jews by birth and not "Gentile sinners" know that a man is not justified *by observing the law* [ἐξ ἔργων νόμου, *ex ergōn nomou*], but by faith in Jesus Christ. So we, too, have put our faith in Christ Jesus that we may be justified by faith in Christ and not *by observing the law* [ἐξ ἔργων νόμου, *ex ergōn nomou*], because *by observing the law* [ἐξ ἔργων νόμου, *ex ergōn nomou*] no one [note again the universality in οὐ...πᾶσα σάρξ, *ou...pasa sarx*, "not...all flesh"] will be justified (Gal. 2:15-16).

Then, after asking the "Judaized" Gentile Christians of Galatia the twin questions: "Did you receive the Spirit *by observing the law* [ἐξ ἔργων νόμου, *ex ergōn nomou*], or *by believing what you heard* [ἐξ ἀκοῆς πίστεως, *ex akoēs pisteos*]" (Gal. 3:2), and "Does God give you his Spirit and work miracles among you because you *observe the law* [ἐξ ἔργων νόμου, *ex ergōn nomou*] or because you *believe what you heard* [ἐξ ἀκοῆς πίστεως, *ex akoēs pisteos*]" (Gal. 3:5), he declares:

> *All who* [ὅσοι, *hosoi*, "As many as"] *rely on observing the law* [ἐξ ἔργων νόμου εἰσίν, *ex ergōn nomou eisin*] are under a curse, for it is written: "Cursed is *everyone* [πᾶς, *pas*] who does not continue to do *everything*

---

ments, esp. those of the Decalogue which apply to all men."

[28]Observe his universalistic *everyone* [πᾶς, *pas*] and *no one* [οὐδείς, *oudeis*] in Galatians 2:16.

[29]S. Westerholm, *Israel's Law and the Church's Faith: Paul and his Recent Interpreters* (Grand Rapids: Eerdmans, 1988), 173.

[πᾶσιν, *pasin*] written in the Book of the Law." Clearly *no one* [οὐδεὶς, *oudeis*] is justified before God by the law, because, "The righteous will live by faith" (Gal. 3:10-11; see also Rom. 3:21-28; 4:1-5; Titus 3:5).

Who are these people who are "relying on observance of the law" for their salvation? Once again we are struck by Paul's universalistic language. It is true that in his letter to the Romans Paul describes the Jew as one who "*relies* [ἐπαναπαύῃ, *epanapaue*] on the law" (2:17). And it is also true that in the context of the Galatians letter his most immediate opponents are the Judaizers and his Gentile converts who had succumbed to the teaching of the Judaizers. But Paul's "no flesh" (οὐ...πᾶσα σὰρξ, *ou...pasa sarx*) expression in Galatians 2:16 appears once again to be applicable to anyone and everyone[28] – Jew or Gentile, *the latter of whom had no obligation to observe circumcision or Israel's food laws* – who trusts in his own law-keeping for salvation. And the same must be said for his "as many as" (ὅσοι, *hosoi*), his "everyone" (πᾶς, *pas*) and his "no one" (οὐδεὶς, *oudeis*) in Galatians 3:10-11. Finally, his descriptive "*everything* [πᾶσιν, *pasin*] written in the Book of the Law" in Galatians 3:10 suggests once again that he intended by his "works of law" expression not only Israel's identity markers of circumcision, food laws, and Sabbath-keeping but also the moral law.

Conclusion

It would appear then from these biblical references, first, that the "new perspective" theologians have not done adequate justice to Paul's teaching when they insist that first-century Palestinian Judaism was *not* a religion of legalistic works-righteousness for it clearly was (as were, of course, the myriad religions of the Gentiles), even though its legalism expressed itself within the context of God's gracious covenant with them in terms of a "maintaining" of covenantal status; second, that by his "works of law" expression Paul intended not just the ceremonial aspects of the law but the whole law in its entirety, and third, that "there is more of Paul in Luther"[29] and the other Reformers with respect to the critical salvific matters that concerned

---

[30]One would not be too surprised if Roman Catholic scholars, given their historical opposition to the Reformation interpretation of Romans, embraced Sanders' and Dunn's "new perspective," but Joseph A. Fitzmyer in his *Romans: A New Translation with Introduction and Commentary* (Anchor

them in the sixteenth century than some of the "new perspective" theologians are inclined to admit.[30]

In sum, these "new perspective" suggestions that would have Paul saying either more or other than he should have said (Sanders) or less than he actually and clearly intended (Dunn) are "blind alleys" which the church must reject if it hopes to understand Paul's doctrine of justification.[31] And I fervently hope that evangelicals who have been enamored with the influential "Sanders/Dunn fork in the road" will retrace their steps in the light of what I have pointed out in this essay and choose to come down once again on the side of the historic Reformation position on the doctrine of justification by faith alone in the preceptive and penal obedience of Christ alone for their justifying righteousness before God. For Paul insists

1. that there is only one gospel – justification by faith alone in Christ's righteous obedience and redeeming death alone (Rom. 1:17; 3:28; 4:5; 10:4; Gal. 2:16; 3:10-11, 26; Phil. 3:8-9);

2. that any addition to or alteration of the one gospel is another "gospel" that is not a gospel at all (Gal. 1:6-7);

Bible; New York: Doubleday, 1993), rejects the views of Sanders and Dunn, even arguing that Paul opposes merit theology. B. Byrne, also a Roman Catholic who holds a view of the law that is similar to Fitzmyer's view, like Fitzmyer dismisses the views of Sanders and Dunn in his *Romans* (Collegeville: Glazier, 1996).

[31] For readers who are interested in pursuing these topics for themselves, I recommend that they begin with E. Earle Ellis, "Pauline Studies in Recent Research" in *Paul and His Recent Interpreters* (Grand Rapids: Eerdmans, 1961), 11-34; Herman Ridderbos, *Paul: An Outline of His Theology*, translated by John R. De Witt (Grand Rapids: Eerdmans, 1975), 13-43; Scott J. Hafemann, "Paul and His Interpreters," and Thomas R. Schreiner, "Works of the Law," these last two articles appearing in *Dictionary of Paul and His Letters*, 666-79 and 975-9 respectively, and Thomas R. Schreiner, "'Works of Law' in Paul" in *Novum Testamentum* 33 (1991), 217-44.

[32] See Martin Luther's exposition of Psalm 130:4 in his *Werke* (Weimar: Bohlau, 1883 to present), 40.3.352:3.

[33] John Calvin, *Institutes of the Christian Religion*, 3.11.1.

[34] John Calvin, "Calvin's Reply to Sadoleto," *A Reformation Debate*, ed-

3. that those who teach any other "gospel" stand under the anathema of God (Gal. 1:8-9); and

4. that those who rely to any degree on their own works or anything in addition to Christ's doing and dying to merit their salvation nullify the grace of God (Rom. 11:5-6), make void the cross-work of Christ (Gal. 2:21; 5:2), become debtors to keep the entire law (Gal. 5:3), and in becoming such "fall from grace" (Gal. 5:4), that is, place themselves again under the curse of the law.

So what one thinks about justification, therefore, is serious business indeed. Quite correctly did Martin Luther declare Paul's doctrine of justification by faith alone to be the article of the standing or falling church.[32] And John Calvin, declaring it to be "the main hinge upon which religion turns"[33] and "the first and keenest subject of controversy" between Rome and the Reformers of the sixteenth century,[34] states:

> Wherever the knowledge of [justification by faith alone] is taken away, the glory of Christ is extinguished, religion abolished, the Church destroyed, and the hope of salvation utterly overthrown.[35]

---

ited by John C. Olin (Reprint: Grand Rapids: Baker, 1976), 66.

[35]John Calvin, "Calvin's Reply to Sadoleto," *A Reformation Debate*, 66.

Chapter Fourteen

Lord's Day Observance: Mankind's Proper Response to the Fourth Commandment

The observation that there is little respect for or observance of the Christian Lord's Day anymore will hardly come as a revelation to anyone. The Western world in general and the United States of America in particular, both having become increasingly secularistic, materialistic, and hedonistic in their orientation, have also become increasingly hostile to the so-called "blue-laws" on the books of civil government. Efforts abound to bring about a repeal of these laws that mandate societal observance of the sanctity of the first day of the week.

Such pervasive contemporary disdain for Lord's Day observance is not surprising when one considers the fact that only relatively few Christians themselves show any real concern for the sanctity of the day. Evidence would suggest that many Christians feel no obligation even to attend established Sunday worship services. And Sunday shopping and Sunday attendance at athletic events, theaters, and other entertainment attractions have become a common practice for Christians as well as for non-Christians.

This desacralizing of the day even among Christians is traceable, at least in part, to the widely-held opinion that the Fourth Commandment of the Decalogue is not, and has never been, normative for the New Testament church, much less for the world. If Christians are to regard any day differently from the other six days of the week (and even this is denied in some quarters), it is urged that they are to observe the "Lord's Day," *not* the Sabbbath, and that they are to do so because of such New Testament verses as Hebrews 10:25 and Revelation 1:10 and not because of the normativeness of the Fourth Commandment for mankind today.

Such teaching, however earnest and well-intentioned, in my opinion is dangerous in the extreme, for not only is proper Lord's Day

Note: This article first appeared in *Presbyterion: Covenant Seminary Review* (Spring 1987), Vol. XIII, Num. 1, 7-23.

observance undercut by such teaching, but also, by implication, the normativeness of God's entire moral law for Christ's church and society is rendered suspect inasmuch as the Fourth Commandment is a tenth part of God's "royal law," itself a unitary whole.[1] Accordingly, to the degree that the normativeness of any single part of God's moral law is denied for this age, just to the same degree the current trend toward the grounding of morality in humanistic rather than divine law is strengthened.

To counteract this harmful societal drift toward secularism I intend in this article to argue for the normativeness of the Fourth Commandment's *principial* teaching of one day in seven as a Sabbath for all mankind. I will also urge, once its principial normativeness is established, that mankind's proper response today to the Fourth Commandment should be first-day Lord's Day observance. I will begin by considering the expression, "the Lord's Day," itself.

The Meaning of the Expression, "the Lord's Day"

The expression, "the Lord's Day," occurs only in Revelation 1:10 as the English translation of the Greek τῇ κυριακῇ ἡμέρᾳ (*tē kurakē hēmera*). When one recalls that five or six decades had elapsed since the resurrection of Christ had occurred with no prior special designation for the day on which Christian gathered for worship having been given in the New Testament literature other than simply "the first day" (see Acts 20:7; 1 Cor. 16:2), such a sudden occurrence of this striking expression to designate the Christian day of worship is all the more intriguing. What is the explanation for this particular expression appearing in the New Testament literature at this time?

With the increasing ascription of super-human honors to the Roman emperors during this period, the cult of emperor worship had gradually emerged.[2] And in Asia Minor and Egypt the first day of the month, designated ἡ σεβάστη ἡμέρα ("the Emperor's Day"), had been set apart as a holiday.[3] It is a distinct possibility that the Apostle John,

---

[1]See Galatians 3:10; 5:3 and James 2:8-11, especially verses 10-11, for the scriptural enunciation of the principle of the Law's unitary wholeness.

[2]Emperor Domitian (AD 81-96), for example, the latter part of whose reign corresponded with the writing of the Apocalypse, attempted to compel his subjects to worship him.

[3]See G Adolf Deissmann, *Bible Studies* (Edinburgh: T. & T. Clark, 1901),

under divine inspiration, in order to distinguish the Christian day of worship from "the Emperor's Day," in opposition to the emperor cult was led to describe the Christian day of worship as "the Lord's [that is, Christ's] Day." But while such a historical exigency may explain the *need* for such a designation from a Christian perspective, it still remains to ask more pointedly the question: "What prompted the choice of the precise terminology of the phrase itself? There is no need to speculate here since Scripture itself suggests the direction in which one should look for the answer. I would submit that the words, "the Lord's Day," reflect the language of Isaiah 58:13 where the Sabbath is referred to as "*my* [that is, Yahweh's or the Lord's (LXX, κυρίου, *kuriou*) holy day," an Old Testament designation remarkably close to the Johannine "Lord's Day" expression. Both the Old Testament Sabbath and the Christian day of worship then are "the Lord's [holy] Day." By this striking description of the Christian day of worship as "the Lord's Day," the Apostle John not only highlighted the fact of Christ's ontological and resurrectional Lordship over the day but also by implication related the Christian day of worship to the Old Testament Sabbath principle of one day in seven to be set apart, that is, to be "kept holy," unto the Lord. More will be said about this later.

Scholars have not been unanimous in this opinion that "the Lord's Day" denoted the Christian day of worship, other suggestions as to its referent including (1) the Old Testament seventh-day Sabbath, (2) Christ's birthday, (3) Christ's crucifixion day, (4) the anniversary day of Christ's crucifixion, (5) the anniversary day of Christ's resurrection, and (6) the "day of the Lord" (see 2 Pet. 3:10). But if John had intended the Old Testament Sabbath, it is strange that he did not employ the customary term, "Sabbath." Also, neither the day of Christ's birth nor his crucifixion day held special honor, as far as is known, for the apostolic church. Indeed, the former day is not even known and the latter is still debated. Moreover, no early church father employs "the Lord's Day" to designate what today is referred to as Easter Sunday. Finally, the eschatological day of judgment is always referred

---

218-19; R. H. Charles, *The Revelation of St. John* (ICC; Edinburgh: T. & T. Clark, 1920), I, 23. See also Acts 25:21-26 where *ho Sebastos* ("His majesty") is employed with *Kaisar* ("Caesar") and with *ho kurios* ("the Lord"), both doubtless referring to Nero.

to as "the day of the Lord" (ἡ ἡμέρα τοῦ κυρίου, *hē hēmera tou kuriou*) in the Septuagint, never "the Lord's Day" (ἡ κυριακὴ ἡμέρα, *hē kuriakē hēmera*). It is quite safe to conclude, then, that the phrase, whatever it may mean, did not denote any of these. On the other hand, there are good reasons at hand to support the contention that it was, in fact, an early Christian designation of the church's day of worship. Beside (1) the reason already adduced (that is, the title was a protest against its counterpart in the cult of emperor worship), (2) since in the previous verse (verse 9) John tells his reader *where* he was when the vision recorded in the Apocalypse came to him, it is highly probable that he intended to tell him *when* it came by a designation recognizable to Christians everywhere (this reason would effectively eliminate "the day of the Lord"). Furthermore, (3) from church history Ignatius, bishop of Antioch (martyred *c.* AD 116), in his *Letter to the Magnesians*, IX.i, wrote of "no longer keeping the Sabbath [that is, the seventh day] but living according to the Lord's Day [*kuriakēn*], on which also our life has sprung up again by him." It is therefore extremely difficult, if not impossible, to escape the strong presumption (which the majority of scholars acknowledge to be present in these facts) that "the Lord's Day" is a term denoting the Christian day of worship. I will therefore proceed on the well-founded assumption that "the Lord's Day" refers to the Christian day of worship.

The Special Character of the First Day of the Week as "the Lord's Day"

That the Lord's Day, as the Christian day of worship, was also the *first* day of the week there can be no doubt. As the day on which Jesus rose from the dead and on which he first appeared to his disciples (Matt. 28:1; Mark 16:2; Luke 24:1, 13, 26; John 20:1, 19), the first day of the week became the day on which the early church regularly assembled under the sanction of the Apostles as spokesmen of Christ (John 20:26; Acts 20:7; 1 Cor. 16:2). This is not to deny that the early church often assembled itself locally on other days of the week as well, as noted in Acts 2:46. But Acts 2:46 should not be interpreted, as do some scholars like B. S. Easton, so as to conclude that first-day worship was never specifically sanctioned by the Lord or his apostles but arose rather as a matter of expediency and practicality because "waning of the first enthusiasm, necessity for pursuing

ordinary avocations, and increasing numbers of converts...made general daily gatherings impracticable."[4] The fact that the first disciples
gathered together on the second "first day" after Jesus' resurrection
(John 20:26) suggests that after Jesus' resurrection and his several
appearances on his resurrection day, the disciples immediately regarded that day of the week as a special day, its observance becoming then for them a sanctioned practice and an assumed obligation.

Easton, furthermore, ignores the apostolic sanction placed upon
the first day of the week as the Christian day for corporate worship in
1 Corinthians 16:2 ("on the first day of the week") when he writes:
"Worship is here not explicitly mentioned (the Greek of 'by him' is the
usual phrase for 'at home')."[5] To the contrary, the words *para
heautō* ("by himself"), according to Charles Hodge, "do not mean *to
lay by at home*, but *to lay by himself.* The direction is nothing more
definite than, *let him place by himself,* i.e. let him take to himself
[that is, set apart] what he means to give."[6] It is also needful to point
out that if every man had "treasured up" his money "at home," as
Easton contends is the intent of Paul's instruction, the end that Paul
desired to accomplish by his instruction would not have been attained
since a collection would still have been required when he arrived in
Corinth – the very thing he wished to avoid (16:2). The only conclusion one may fairly draw from the entire context is the assumption on
Paul's part that the Corinthian Christians, as were Christians elsewhere (see 16:1: "as I ordered the churches of Galatia"), were assembling themselves together on the Lord's Day already, and that
such assembling most advantageously provided the facility for doing
what he here enjoins concerning the collection. For any Christian to
have set aside his gift but "at home" would have been to ignore the
apostle's declared desire that "there be no collection when I come."
The obvious should not be overlooked here either: the phrase " on the
first day of the week," while not, true enough, the main point of the

---

[4]B. S. Easton (1939), "Lord's Day," in *International Standard Bible Encyclopedia*, Zondervan, III:1919.

[5]Easton, "Lord's Day," III:1919.

[6]Charles Hodge, *A Commentary on the First Epistle to the Corinthians*
(Reprint; Grand Rapids: Eerdmans, 1974), *in loc.*; see also J. Oliver Buswell,
Jr., *A Systematic Theology of the Christian Religion* (Grand Rapids:
Zondervan, 1962), I:370, who translates: "by himself without compulsion."

apostolic imperative, is still as much a required condition of the entire imperative as is the phrase "by himself," which simply means that the absence of this condition would entail that the demands of the Pauline imperative would not have been fully met. So even though special regard for the first day of the week by the church may be assumed by Paul to have been already in place, a certain categorical sanction is indirectly placed by him on that practice, thereby underscoring its obligatory character. Only by hazardous exegesis can one avoid the conclusion that the Apostle here mandates by implication first-day worship observance by the Christian community as a memorial to the Lord's resurrection on that day.

Some scholars reject this conclusion, insisting that "the observance of a given day as a matter of Divine obligation is denounced by Paul as a forsaking of Christ (Gal 4:10), and [that] Sabbath keeping is condemned explicitly in Colossians 2:16."[7] Such a statement, however, simply displays a failure to distinguish on the one hand between Paul's *condemnation* of the "observing of days" as a requirement of *soteric legalism* and on the other hand his *sanction* of the "observing of days" in 1 Corinthians 16:2 as a requirement for *proper Christian worship*; that is to say, what Paul condemns in Galatians 4:10 and Colossians 2:16 is an "observing of days" in order to be saved, *not* the "observing of days" in order to testify to the world and to other Christians concerning the resurrection of Christ and the Christian's own *de facto* position in the "community of Easter faith."

But what about Romans 14:5? Does not Paul, when he wrote: "One man regards one day above another, another regards every day alike. Let each man be fully convinced in his own mind," teach that the Christian man "might do as he pleased respecting the Lord's day?"[8] If those scholars are correct who so interpret Paul here, and if no day accordingly is to be regarded by the Christian as necessarily having any special day above any other day, then John's statement in Revelation 1:10, singling out as it does one day of the week as "the Lord's Day" is misleading at best, in conflict with Paul at worst, and casts John in the role of the "weak" brother spoken of in the Romans 14 context. The correct understanding of Paul must be sought in another

---

[7]Easton, "Lord's Day," III:1919.

[8]Easton, "Lord's Day," III:1919; see also C. C. Ryrie (1960), "Sunday," in *Baker's Dictionary of Theology*, ed. Everett F. Harrison, Baker, 506.

direction. Doubtless, Paul had in mind only the ceremonial holy days of the Levitical institution that some Jewish Christians were observing out of religious scrupulosity. John Murray quite rightly observes:

> Paul was not insistent upon the discontinuance of ritual observance of the Levitical ordinances as long as the observance was one of religious custom and not compromising the gospel (*cf.* Acts 18:18, 21; 21:20-27).... Many Jews would not yet have understood all the implications of the gospel and had still a scrupulous regard for their Mosaic ordinances. Of such scruples we know Paul to have been thoroughly tolerant, and they fit the precise terms of the text in question [Rom. 14:5]. There is no need to posit anything that goes beyond such observances. To place the Lord's day and the weekly Sabbath in the same category is not only to go beyond the warrant of exegetical requirements but brings us into conflict with principles that are embedded in the total witness of Scripture. An interpretation that involves such contradiction cannot be adopted. Thus the abiding sanctity of each recurring seventh day as the memorial of God's rest in creation and of Christ's exaltation in his resurrection is not to be regarded as in any way impaired by Romans 14:5.[9]

Finally, when it is urged that "the fact…that Christian worship was held on Sunday did not sanctify Sunday anymore than (say) a regular Wednesday service among us sanctifies Wednesday,"[10] it is sufficient in response simply to point out that those who observe first-day worship do not believe that it is their worship *per se* that sanctifies the day. Rather, it is the sanction of Christ and his apostles, evident in both their word and example (John 20:1, 19; Acts 20:7; 1 Cor. 16:2; Rev. 1:10 *et al.*), that they placed on the first day that sanctified it; and the first Christians, "devoting themselves to the apostle's teaching" (Acts 2:42) and example (Phil. 3:17; 4:9), submitted themselves to the apostles in this matter just as they felt obliged to do in other matters enjoined by the apostles.

---

[9]John Murray, "Romans 14:5 and the Weekly Sabbath," Appendix D in *The Epistle to the Romans* (Grand Rapids: Eerdmans, 1965), II:259.

[10]Easton, "Lord's Day," III:1919.

The Relationship Between the Lord's Day and the Old Testament Sabbath Institution

Among Christian scholars there is disagreement over the relationship between Christian first-day worship observance and the Old Testament seventh-day Sabbath observance. On the one hand, some sharply distinguish between them, either urging no relationship whatever or insisting that the Sabbath was only a shadow of things to come and that it passed away in the light of the New Covenant's "better promises."[11] On the other hand, there are those who insist that the Lord's Day is the Christian Sabbath that by divine arrangement took up into itself all of the essential and permanent features of the Old Testament Sabbath institution.[12] What are we to conclude? Two areas of consideration will provide the answer.

Man's Universal and Perpetual Obligation to Observe the Sabbath Principle
To assess this issue properly, the first undeniable fact that needs to be squarely faced at the outset is that Old Testament Sabbath observance was not first instituted by God simply as part of Israelite legislation that was only to be observed when and where that national legislation was in force. Rather, there are five incontrovertible reasons for insisting that, when instituted, Sabbath observance was intended to be universally and perpetually binding upon all men. Consider them in turn:

First, a day of Sabbath was instituted at the very beginning of the world, being at that time "blessed and sanctified [set apart]" by God for man, as the climax of the creation week (Gen. 2:3). Its institution had nothing to do with the conditions that were introduced later in to the human situation by Adam's fall and consequent need for redemption (though later it does pick up redemptive significance; see Exod. 20:2 and Deut. 5:15). As Murray states:

---

[11]James M. Boice (1976), *The Gospel of John*, Zondervan, 2:343-37; Ryrie, "Lord's Day," in *Baker Dictionary of Theology*, 330; Easton, "Lord's Day," in *International Standard Bible Encyclopedia*, III:1920; D. A. Carson (1982, ed.), *From Sabbath to Lord's Day*, Zondervan, special note on 23.

[12]*Westminster Confession of Faith*, XXI.vii; *Larger Catechism*, Question 116; Charles Hodge, *Systematic Theology*, III:321-48; Geerhardus Vos, *Biblical Theology*, 158-9; John Murray, "The Sabbath Institution," and "The Pattern of the Lord's Day," pamphlets published and distributed by The Lord's Day Observance Society.

…it is like the institutions of labor (Gen 2:15), of marriage (Gen 2:24), and of fruitfulness (Gen 1:28). The Sabbath institution was given to man as man, for the good of man as man, and extended to man the assurance and promise that his labour would issue in a Sabbath rest similar to the rest of God himself.[13]

And it must also be said that it appears in this context as being as continually binding upon man as are these other institutions.

Second, between the institution of the Sabbath in Genesis 2:1-3 and its formal inclusion within the Decalogue in Exodus 20:8-10, biblical evidence exists that would suggest that the seven-day cycle as a basic division of time was known and observed (Gen. 4:3,[14] 8:10, 12; 19:27-8; Exod. 16:5, 22-30, especially verse 26). From Exodus 16 the evidence, I would urge, is indisputable that there was a Sabbath obligation before the Mosaic Law was given.

Third, the first word of the Fourth Commandment, *"Remember the Sabbath day to keep it holy,"* implies that the Sabbath day was not a new institution being then and there established for the first time by the Decalogue, but rather it was already a part of biblical legislation requiring man's continued attentive observance.

Fourth, another fact that has only rarely received the consideration that it deserves is that the Sabbath commandment – appearing as it does within the summary statement of God's moral law for his redeemed people, which moral law purports to be both unitary in nature and of binding force by the fact that it is specifically these ten commandments that are written by the finger of God upon *tablets of stone* which very material suggests permanency – enjoys a position within the Decalogue alongside of nine other laws that no Christian would suggest are abrogated as the universal and perpetual standard of righteousness by which all men are to measure their lives. There simply is no basis for the insistence of some scholars that the Sabbath commandment was an aspect of the ceremonial law of ancient Israel

---

[13]John Murray, "The Sabbath Institution," 4; see Mark 2:27-8; Heb 3:7-4:11.

[14]The NASB's "In the course of time" here is literally, "at the end of days" (see margin), which suggests an established cycle of days, most likely the seven-day cycle established in Genesis 1–2 in light of the fact that at this "end" (seventh day?) of days Cain and Abel ceased from their labors and brought offerings to the Lord, a distinctly *religious* activity.

and that it is therefore not applicable to the church today.

Fifth, our Lord taught the universal and perpetual relevance of the Sabbath when he declared: "The Sabbath was established for man, and not man for the Sabbath. Therefore, the Son of Man is Lord also of the Sabbath" (Mark 2:27-8). Our Lord's statement contains an unquestionable allusion to the original institution of the Sabbath in Genesis 2. It is noteworthy that our Lord does not say that the Sabbath was established for Israel; rather, he says that it was established for man, its relevance being then as extensive as the extremities of mankind. Moreover, as he, as the Son of Man, is the Lord of the Sabbath, the obligation of Sabbath observance by mankind, for mankind's good, is as wide and as continuous as is the sphere of his sovereign lordship, which is just to say that it is both universal and perpetual (see John 17:2; Matt. 28:18).

Sabbath obligation appears in the Decalogue, in light of these incontrovertible data, not as a *de novo* requirement peculiar to and incumbent only upon the tiny nation of Israel within the family of nations and even there only for the period of time designated by Old Testament scholars as the period of Mosaism. Rather, it appears in the Decalogue quite naturally as fulfilling the dual role of a *reaffirmation* of an institution previously established and at an earlier time known (but doubtless forsaken) by men on a universal scale, and of a *reminder* to God's redeemed people particularly (see Exod. 20:2), *vis à vis* the "rest" of God as the divine sign to men (Exod. 20:8-11; see Gen. 2:1-3), of the future rest awaiting them that they will enter at the termination of their labors (Heb. 3:7-4:11 [note that this future rest is correlated with God's rest of creation in Hebrews 4:3-6, 9-11, and is expressly said to be a "Sabbath-resting" or "Sabbath-keeping" (σαββατισμος, *sabbatismos*) in Hebrews 4:9]; Rev. 14:13).

It should be apparent from these five points, then, that the principle of Sabbath obligation in the Decalogue (one day in seven to be the Lord's in a special sense) is as binding upon mankind in general as are the first or the second or the fifth or the seventh or the tenth commandments.

Sabbath Change from the Seventh to the First Day of the Week
What about the fact, however, that the Christian church celebrates its day of rest on the first rather than the last day of the week, as the Fourth Commandment seems to require? In the absence of a spe-

cific commandment in so many words, "You shall change the day of Sabbath from the last to the first day of the week," there is an understandable reticence in some quarters to accept the position that such a shift did in fact occur regarding a divine institution as significant as the Old Testament seventh-day Sabbath. But there are three factors, on the order of interpretive observations, that, once understood, should remove this hesitancy and that will at the same time be exegetically fair to the demands of Scripture.

First, it must always be remembered that some regulations prescribed in Scripture "are evidently intended to be understood with the qualification *ceteris paribus*, 'other things being equal.'"[15] The Old Testament Sabbath regulation *with respect to work restrictions* is a case in point. Concerning Sabbath observance, God expressly required in the Fourth Commandment that on the Sabbath "you shall not do any work" (Exod. 20:10). But in keeping with his principle that the Sabbath was instituted for man's benefit, Jesus Christ, who *is* the Lord and Institutor of the Sabbath, made it equally clear by his example and express statement that the Sabbath regulation was not against labor on the Sabbath so absolutely that it precluded works of necessity (Matt. 12:3-4), works of worship (Matt. 12:5), and works of mercy (Matt. 12:11-13; see Luke 13:10-16; 14:1-6).[16] These New Testament passages illustrate my point that there are divine regulations that are to be understood as binding, "other things being equal," but that there may well be the need, in the face of *sufficient reason* and *competent authority*, for qualifying the regulation, even changing the regulation in some details. I will urge in a moment that sufficient reason and competent authority mandated the alteration in detail of the specific day of the week on which the Sabbath is to be

---

[15]J. Oliver Buswell, Jr., *A Systematic Theology of the Christian Religion*, I:368.

[16]The "work" of the Sabbath violator described in Numbers 15:32-36, I would argue, could have been a "work of necessity" and therefore appropriate if the man involved had possessed a proper heart attitude toward the Sabbath regulation; but the placing of this incident in the ancient account immediately after the stated penalty for sins committed with a "high-handed" defiance of God's Word (verses 30-31) suggests that the incident is to be construed as an example of "sinning with a high hand"; the man, in other words, had deliberately conducted himself in conscious and spiteful disregard for God's Sabbath commandment.

observed.

Second, it must be remembered that some if not most biblical regulations had to await the full progressive revelatory unfolding of God's mind on the matter in order for the student of Scripture fully to comprehend which were their temporary and which were their abiding features. Again, the Old Testament Sabbath regulation, *with respect to its memorial significance*, is a case in point. Concerning what it was, specifically, that lay behind the reason for God's command regarding its observance and what it was to memorialize for its observers, we find that in Exodus 20:11 the reason for Sabbath observance is laid in God's original rest after creation that, as has been said, promised by example that a rest also awaited the child of God when his labors are completed. But in Deuteronomy 5:15 the reason for its observance, while not in disagreement with or abrogating the earlier reason (see the preface to the Decalogue in Exodus 20:2 where it is clearly stated that the *entire* Decalogue which followed is addressed to a redeemed people), highlights the *redemptive* note implicit in Exodus 20:1-17 by drawing Israel's attention to her deliverance from Egypt's bondage. The Sabbath day was now to symbolize and foreshadow redemptive deliverance from slavery and a future rest for men grounded not in their but in God's work of redemption. This redemptive work of God is placed still further in the foreground as the reason for Sabbath observance in Psalm 118:22-24: "The day that the LORD has made," in which the redeemed are to rejoice and to be glad, is prophetically related directly to the day on which "the Stone that the builders rejected" would become "the chief cornerstone," that is, to the day on which Jesus would rise from the dead (Acts 4:10-11; see also Psalm 2:7 and Acts 13:32-33). Here Old Testament prophetic material related the celebration of God's redemptive work directly to Jesus' resurrection day, urging the redeemed to rejoice on that day, and in doing so, prophetically anticipated by hundreds of years the shift of Sabbath observance from the seventh to the first day of the week.

Third, *with respect to detail*, it is a significant though often overlooked fact that the Fourth Commandment does not specifically state: "Remember the *seventh* day." I readily acknowledge that in the Old Testament context the seventh day was the designated day of Sabbath because it reflected the order of the Lord's activity during the creation week, which in turn foreshadowed the rest that awaits the child of God after his labors. But given a different contextual setting, the commandment could just as readily urge another day to be observed as the Sabbath without the alteration of single syllable in the commandment itself. It is the detail of a "different contextual setting" for the Fourth Commandment that the resurrection of Christ gives to the commandment that, as we shall now see, *required* the "detail" change in days from the seventh to the first day of the week.

To come now directly to the issue of the shift in days for Sabbath observance from the seventh to the first day of the week, in keeping with the three foregoing observations, it must be asserted, to paraphrase Charles Hodge, that there were only two *essential* elements in the Old Testament Sabbath regulation: first, that it should be a day in which one rests from his labors, and second, that it should be devoted to the worship of God and the service of religion (what these mean will be explained later). All else was circumstantial and variable. Even the particular day of the week was variable and might be changed, if changed (1) for sufficient reason, and (2) by competent authority. Indeed, where these two factors would be present, the change would be obligatory.[17] Were these two factors present in the first century, thereby legitimatizing the changing of the day of Sabbath observance from the seventh to the first day of the week? Indeed they were! A *sufficient reason* was patently present – the momentous event of Jesus' resurrection from the dead on the first day of the week! And *competent authority* was also patently present – the example and words of Christ himself, the Lord of the Sabbath, and his apostles (John 20:1, 19, 26; Acts 20:7; 1 Cor. 16:2; Heb. 10:25; Rev. 1:10). The inevitable conclusion that the Christian church reached was that the change of days was not only appropriate but also had Christ's and his apostles' sanction. For the church to continue to observe the seventh-day Sabbath, first, would have by implication either asserted that the *typical* redemptive event of the Exodus *vis à vis* the antitypical redemptive work of Christ was the more important redemptive event whereas in fact the Exodus was only the foreshadowing of the redemptive work of Christ, or denied the fact of the resurrection of Christ altogether; and second, would have meant the rejection of the authority of Christ and his apostles (not to mention the Old Testament prophetic scriptures as well) over the church. Which

---

[17]Charles Hodge, *Systematic Theology*, III:329-30.

is just to say that for the church to continue to observe the seventh-day Sabbath would have been to ignore the progressive nature of revelation that was here governing the situation. Geerhardus Vos elucidates:

> Inasmuch as the Old Covenant was still looking forward to the performance of the Messianic work, naturally the days of labor to it come first, the day of rest falls at the end of the week. We, under the New Covenant, look back upon the accomplished work of Christ. We, therefore, first celebrate the rest in principle procured by Christ, although the Sabbath also still remains a sign looking forward to the final eschatological rest. The O.T. people of God had to typify in their life the future development of redemption. Consequently, the precedence of labor and the consequence of rest had to find expression in their calendar. The N.T. Church has no such typical function to perform, for the types have been fulfilled. But it has a great historic event to commemorate, the performance of the work by Christ and the entrance of Him and His people through Him upon the state of never-ending rest. We do not sufficiently realize the profound sense the early Church had of the epoch-making significance of the appearance, and especially the resurrection, of the Messiah. The latter was to them nothing less than the bringing in of a new, the second, creation. And they felt that this ought to find expression in the placing of the Sabbath with reference to the other days of the week. Believers knew themselves [to be] in a measure partakers of the Sabbath fulfillment. *If the one creation required one sequence, then the other required another.*[18]

We must conclude then from the incontrovertible facts of (1) man's universal and perpetual obligation respecting Sabbath observance, and (2) the divinely instituted and authorized change of the day of Sabbath from the seventh to the first day of the week, that it is incontrovertibly certain that the Lord's Day, being the first day of the week, and the Sabbath observance mandated by the Fourth Commandment are for the Christian church to be regarded as essentially one and the same institution, the differences between them arising from the fact that the church after the resurrection of Christ entered into the age of

---

[18]Geerhardus Vos, *Biblical Theology*, 158, emphasis supplied. I demur from Vos's one turn of expression, "And they felt that this ought to find expression...," as though to suggest that the *church* decided to change the day on its own authority. Clearly, the change of days was mandated by Christ and his apostles and did not arise in the church as a merely human

fulfillment as over against the Old Testament age of anticipation (Col. 4:17). The church must affirm this representation of the matter, for only when this is fully understood can the proper observance of the Lord's Day be reestablished.

Three Objections

As might be expected, certain objections have been raised against the notion of a universal and perpetual first-day Sabbath obligation binding upon all men, Christians and non-Christians alike. It is often noted that "no observance of a particular 'day of rest' is contained among the 'necessary things' of Acts 15:28-29, nor is any such precept found among all the varied moral directions given in the whole epistolary literature."[19]

With respect to the first objection, it is enough to say that the same could be said about other precepts, the perpetual observance of which no Christian questions, such as the precept concerning the child's respect for his parent, the telling of truth, and the property rights of others.

As for the second, it would be enough simply to remind the reader of what has already been said with respect to 1 Corinthians 16:2. But it may also be noted that no such perpetuating precept is actually needed in the epistolary literature. Once the Decalogue was given, it would take an explicit directive from God to repeal it or any part of it. No such repeal has ever been issued. Even the change of the day is not a repeal but an adaptation of the Fourth Commandment to the New Testament situation. One should assume, therefore, that the Fourth Commandment, *mutatis mutandis*, is still in force.

Finally, it is frequently said that Sabbath obligation is out of keeping with the spirit of the gospel age that requires the consecration of *every* day of the week to the Lord. This objection, to begin with, is based on the false notion that the gospel age requires greater consecration to God on the part of his people that did the Mosaic administration. But the religion of Mosaism was no less a religion of the heart than that of the present age, requiring of men then as now to love God with all their being and their neighbor as themselves all the time. The devotion of the people of God in the Psalms exemplifies a religion of

---

convention.

the heart as well. But in neither age is the biblical religion exclusively a religion of the heart, for in both are found ordinances and institutions: divinely appointed services, stated ministries, and external helps (for example, the Bible and the sacraments). It certainly is not necessarily a denigration of the evangelical spirit of this gospel age then to insist that men are obligated to observe every recurring first day as a day set apart for the exercise of corporate and private worship. Furthermore, to assert that "every day is the Lord's day" may seem pious, but "we must not forget," as Murray writes:

> that there are different ways of serving God. We do not serve Him by doing the same thing all the time. If we do that we are either insane or notoriously perverse. There is a great variety in human vocation.... One of the ways by which this variety is enjoined is to set apart every recurring first day. This is the divine institution. The recurring seventh day is different and it is so by divine appointment. To obliterate this difference may appear pious. But it is piosity, not piety. It is not piety to be wiser than God; it is impiety of the darkest hue.[20]

Furthermore, I must point out again that John, writing the Apocalypse under the Spirit's superintendence, did not say that every day was "the Lord's Day." Rather, he implied that only *one* day of the week was, and he designated it as such.

Proper Observance of the Lord's Day

The apostolic church recognized as one of its obligations to God the assembling of itself together for corporate worship (see Heb. 10:25), and this on the first day of the week or "the Lord's Day" (1 Cor. 16:2; Acts 20:7). The service customarily included the singing of psalms, hymns and spiritual songs, the offering of prayers, the exercise of spiritual gifts, the reading of the Scripture, the preaching and teaching of God's Word, the giving of offerings for diaconal needs, the observance of the sacraments, and often the eating of the *agapē* feast together (Acts 20:7; 1 Cor. 11:20-22; 14:26; Col. 3:16; see also Justin Martyr, *First Apology*, chapters 45, 47). Apparently, much of the day, when circumstances permitted, was given over to the corporate expression of worship. In addition to works of worship, as has al-

---

[19]Easton, "Lord's Day," III:1920; see also Ryrie, "Lord's Day," 506.

ready been noted, works of necessity and works of mercy were also perfectly permissible and regularly practiced (Matt. 12:3-4, 11-13; Acts 20:9-11). But underlying the specific expressions of observance, and governing them all, was the recognition of the special character of the day as a day "set apart" by and for the Lord. This sanctity resides in the command to keep the day *holy*, that is, to recognize its "set apart-ness" and to adapt one's attitudes and actions to it (Exod. 20:8); and it comes to expression in (1) the recognition of the *distinction* of the day from the other six, and (2) the concentrated *adoration* of the triune God on that day.

In this connection it is important, where the Sabbath is said to be "a Sabbath of rest to the LORD" (Exod. 35:2), to note the meaning of the word "rest" and the following words "to the Lord." "Rest" cannot mean mere cessation of labor, much less recovery from fatigue. Neither idea is applicable to God's "rest" in Genesis 2:2-3. The former idea is denied by our Lord in John 5:17 where he affirms that "the Father is working [even] until now"; the latter is inappropriate to the very idea of God. "Rest" means then involvement in *new*, in the sense of *different*, activity. It means the cessation of the labor of the six days and the taking up of different labors appropriate to the Lord's Day. What these labors of the Sabbath-rest are is circumscribed by the accompanying phrase, "to the Lord." They certainly include both corporate and private worship and the contemplation of the glory of God as well as the other kinds of works already mentioned.

The Effects of Sabbath Neglect and Sabbath Observance

The Negative Effects of Sabbath Neglect
As might be expected, if men and nations neglect to remember the Lord's Day to keep it holy, dire consequences follow. The prophets speak with unmistakable clarity about the ruinous consequences that come jurisprudentially and providentially to the people who high-handedly disregard God's Sabbath:

> But if you do not obey me to keep the Sabbath day holy by not carrying any load as you come through the gates of Jerusalem on the Sabbath day, then I will kindle an unquenchable fire in the gates of Jerusalem that will consume her fortresses (Jer. 17:27).

> Yet the people of Israel rebelled against me in the desert. They did not

follow my decrees but rejected my laws – although the man who obeys them will live by them – and they utterly desecrated my Sabbaths. So I said I would pour out my wrath on them and destroy them in the desert (Ezek. 20:13).

Complaining that Israel's priests had backsliden, God declares:

[They] do violence to my law and profane my holy things; they do not distinguish between the holy and the common; they teach that there is no difference between the clean and the unclean, and *they shut their eyes to the keeping of my Sabbaths*, so that I am profaned among them (Ezek. 22:26).

In those days I saw men in Judah treading the winepresses on the Sabbath and bringing in grain and loading it on donkeys, together with wine, grapes, figs and all other kinds of loads. And they were bringing all this into Jerusalem on the Sabbath. Therefore I warned them against selling food on that day. Men from Tyre who lived in Jerusalem were bringing in fish and all kinds of merchandise and selling them in Jerusalem on the Sabbath to the people of Judah. I rebuked the nobles of Judah and said to them, "What is this wicked thing you are doing – desecrating the Sabbath day? Didn't your forefathers do the same things, so that our God brought all this calamity upon us and upon this city? Now you are stirring up more wrath against Israel by desecrating the Sabbath.' When evening shadows fell on the gates of Jerusalem before the Sabbath, I ordered the doors to be shut and not opened until the Sabbath was over. I stationed some of my own men at the gates so that no load could be brought in on the Sabbath day. Once or twice the merchants and sellers of all kinds of goods spent the night outside Jerusalem. But I warned them and said, "Why do you spend the night by the wall? If you do this again, I will lay hands on you." From that time on they no longer came on the Sabbath. Then I commanded the Levites to purify themselves and go and guard the gates in order to keep the Sabbath day holy. Remember me for this also, O my God, and show mercy to me according to your great love. (Neh. 13:15-22; see 2 Chron. 36:20-21)

One may apply the divine response to Sabbath-breaking to individuals, to families, or to nations; wherever the Lord's Day is presumptuously ignored or defiantly desecrated and people absent themselves from corporate worship of the living and true God, there true religious knowledge wanes and, without that, idolatry, immorality, and disrespect for law are spawned (see Rom. 1:18-32). In short, the result of Sabbath neglect on a wide scale is inevitably national and international paganism and moral perversity (recall here the outcome of the French "experiment" in 1793).

It must be said, of course, that the punitive regulations governing the profanation of the Sabbath that were operative under the Old Testament theocracy (see Exod. 31:14-15; Num. 15:32-36) are no longer within the province of the church's disciplinary measures under the New Testament economy (see *Westminster Confession of Faith*, XIX.4). But just because this is true, the conclusion should not be drawn that the Sabbath principle itself is no longer binding any more than it would be right to conclude, because adulterers and adulteresses are no longer put to death (Exod. 21:1; Lev. 20:10; Matt. 5:27-32), that the Seventh Commandment has been abrogated. The penalty for neglecting his Sabbaths God can and does exact in many other ways against his church and against mankind in general, not the least being the erosion of morality and respect for civil law that God allows to accrue in both the home and in the body politic. Such moral declension takes its toll in the rise of crime on a national scale, the ensuing increase in danger to life and property, and the ever-increasing imposition of taxes upon the citizenry to fund the necessary law-enforcement agencies to protect the citizenry from the ever-enlarging criminal element that preys on society. Then the ever-increasing curtailment of the rights and liberties of all follows as legislation has to be enacted to deal with the rising civil disobedience. Ultimately, of course, God will hold the Sabbath-breaker accountable in the Day of Judgment.

The Positive Effects of Sabbath Observance

The Scriptures promise specific blessings to those men and women and nations who observe and honor the Lord's Day. To demonstrate this, one can do no better than to quote the words of Scripture itself:

> Blessed is the man who does this, the man who holds it fast, who keeps the Sabbath without desecrating it, and keeps his hand from doing any evil. Let no foreigner who has joined himself to the LORD say, "The LORD will surely exclude me from his people." And let not any eunuch complain, "I am only a dry tree." For this is what the LORD says: "To the eunuchs who keep my Sabbaths, who choose what pleases me and hold fast to my covenant – to them I will give within my temple and its walls a memorial and a name better than sons and daughters; I will give them an

everlasting name that will not be cut off. And foreigners who bind themselves to the LORD to serve him, to love the name of the LORD, and to worship him, all who keep my Sabbath without desecrating it and who hold fast to my covenant – these I will bring to my holy mountain and give them joy in my house of prayer. Their burnt offerings and sacrifices will be accepted on my altar; for my house will be called a house of prayer for all nations." The Sovereign LORD declares – he who gathers the exiles of Israel: "I will gather still others beside those already gathered" (Isa. 56:2-8).

This passage, among other things, underscores the far reaches of the blessedness that Sabbath observance brings: to "foreigners" to Israel, indeed, to "all who keep my Sabbath…," God promises "joy in my house of prayer." Clearly Sabbath observance was to be taken seriously by men of other nations as well as by Israel, and blessings were promised to those honored God's Sabbath.

If you keep your feet from breaking the Sabbath and from doing as you please on my holy day, if you call the Sabbath a delight and the LORD's holy day honorable, and if you honor it by not going your own way and not doing as you please or speaking idle words, then you will find your joy in the LORD, and I will cause you to ride on the heights of the land and to feast on the inheritance of your father Jacob. The mouth of the LORD has spoken (Isa. 58:13-14).

But if you are careful to obey me, declares the LORD, and bring no load through the gates of this city on the Sabbath, but keep the Sabbath holy by not doing any work on it, then kings who sit on David's throne will come through the gates of this city with their officials. They and their officials will come riding in chariots and on horses, accompanied by the men of Judah and those living in Jerusalem, and this city will be inhabited forever (Jer. 17:24-25).

In lofty language full of promise and blessing, the prophets regale their readers with the divine blessing guaranteed the people who honor the Lord's Sabbath, the external religious institution perhaps above all others that sustains the people of God as a worshiping community. Of course, I certainly do not intend to suggest that men and nations can be made Christians merely by Sabbath-keeping, but observing the Lord's Day by the people of God (and by the nations) is certainly one of God's methods "for keeping the resurrection of Christ, on which salvation depends, in perpetual remembrance" (Charles Hodge) in all the earth, and this in turn does fall out to the salvation of men and, by an inevitable extension, to the moral improvement of people and nations. Charles Hodge well says: "If men wish the knowledge of [Jesus' resurrection] to die out, let them neglect to keep holy the first day of the week; if they desire that event to be everywhere known and remembered, let them consecrate that day to the worship of the risen Savior."[21] I would submit, as an application of Hodge's insight, that in the single fact that Christians have not maintained the sanctity of the Lord's Day we may well have pinpointed the major cause of the world's failure to take seriously the church's proclamation of Christ's resurrection and its implications! The non-Christian just does not perceive in the Christian church today any earnest recognition of the biblical significance of its first-day worship!

The Psalmist declares: "Blessed is the nation whose God is the LORD" (Ps. 33:12; see Ps. 144:15). There is no exegetical warrant to restrict this blessing solely to Israel (see verses 8, 12, 13-15, 18-19). Wherever a nation honors God and his holy precepts, God has pledged to bless that nation. And honoring his precepts certainly includes the passing and the maintaining of civil legislation to protect the sanctity of the Lord's Day and the right of the people of God to worship him on that day. It also means that a church faithful to her Lord will expect its office holders to affirm the binding character of the Lord's Day, to honor the Lord on this day, and to encourage by gentle instruction and example the people of God under their care to do the same.

Special Note

The 1982 symposium entitled *From Sabbath to Lord's Day*, edited by D. A. Carson, contends that the Lord's Day is not the Christian Sabbath. A key argument in the volume is its exposition of Hebrews 3:7-4:13 (see 197–220; 343–412). But Richard B. Gaffin, Jr. offers a Reformed biblical-theological response to this position in his article, "A Sabbath Rest Still Awaits the People of God," in *Pressing Toward the Mark: Essays Commemorating Fifty Years of the Orthodox Presbyterian Church*, edited by Charles G. Dennison and

---

[20]John Murray, "The Sabbath Institution," 7.
[21]Charles Hodge, *Systematic Theology*, III:330.

Richard C. Gamble (Philadelphia: Committee for the Historian of the Orthodox Presbyterian Church, 1986), 33–51.

Gaffin exegetically demonstrates that the *church*'s rest about which the author of Hebrews speaks in this context is not present, as the Carson volume argues, but is entirely future – as an eschatological *Sabbath*-rest (see 4:9). He trenchantly argues (1) that the (weekly) Sabbath is an eschatological sign or pointer to the eschatological rest. ("To deny this is to suppose that the writer…not only apparently coined the term 'Sabbath-resting' for eschatological rest himself but also connected that rest with Gen 2:2-3 (which elsewhere in Scripture is only used for instituting the weekly Sabbath), yet that he did so without any thought of the weekly ordinance – a rather unlikely supposition," 47) and (2) that the weekly Sabbath continues in force under the new covenant until the consummation ("To deny this is to suppose that for the writer the weekly sign has ceased to be, even though the reality to which it points is still future – again an unlikely supposition. What rationale could explain such a severing, by cessation, of sign and unfilled reality?" 47). Gaffin concludes that the author of Hebrews does not support the view that because of the "spiritual rest" already brought by Christ weekly Sabbath-keeping is no longer necessary or appropriate. I would urge my readers to read Gaffin's entire article. It addresses a "crucial and substantial" link in the central argument of the Carson symposium.

Chapter Fifteen

Children in the Covenant

Throughout history the people of God have always regarded their children as "a heritage from the LORD" (Ps. 127:2) and a blessing from him (Ps. 128:3-4). In a heightened sense is this true of the adherents to the Reformed faith as that faith is defined in the great Reformed creeds. According to the Reformed faith not only are the children of believing parents to be regarded as a heritage and blessings from the Lord but also they are regarded as *bona fide* members of both the covenant of grace and the church of Jesus Christ (see *Heidelberg Catechism*, Question 74; *Westminster Confession of Faith*, XXV.II). Furthermore, precisely because they view their children in this light, Reformed parents insist that certain rights and privileges accrue to their children that do not pertain to the offspring of unbelieving parents. Reformed parents believe as well that to withhold from their children these God-ordained rights is virtually to deny that they possess status in the Kingdom of God, a status that God himself guarantees to them, and is to commit "great sin" against God (*Westminster Confession of Faith*, XXVIII.5).

In this address[1] I will attempt to elucidate and to justify from Scripture the Reformed understanding of the status of children in the covenant of grace. By way of procedure I will first define what I mean by the term "covenant of grace" and give the biblical warrant for such a concept. I will then develop from key passages of Scripture the basis upon which Reformed parents believe that their children are members thereof and what is intended by regarding them as such. Finally, from this material I will set forth what I regard to be the more significant rights and responsibilities of these "children in the covenant."

Note: I delivered this address at a Congress sponsored by the National Presbyterian and Reformed Fellowship, held at Covenant College, Lookout Mountain, Tennessee, July 23-28, 1979. It appeared in *Presbyterion: Covenant Seminary Review* (Spring 1980), Vol. VI, Num. 1, 1-16. I have added one paragraph to this version of the address.

The Covenant of Grace

Its Relation to the "Covenant of Redemption"
The Holy Scriptures teach that before the creation of the world, in the eternal counsel of the triune God, the Father, the Son, and the Holy Spirit *covenanted together* to create the world and mankind, and to save an elect number out of mankind after Adam's sin plunged those descending from him by ordinary generation into the estate of sin and misery. On the Father's part, he would give those whom he foreloved and predestined to glory to his beloved Son, who promised in turn to make an atonement for their sin by taking into union with himself their human nature, then in the flesh by means of imputation taking their sin upon himself and paying the penalty for their sin by dying on the cross in their stead. The Father promised to prepare this body for him, preserving him in his time on earth from the natural corruption springing from Adam's sin, and empowering him with the spiritual gifts essential to the accomplishment of his Messianic work in the flesh. The triune Godhead also covenanted that the incarnate Son, after suffering and dying for the sins of the elect, would rise from the dead through his own power and that of the Father and of the Holy Spirit and would ascend to heaven to occupy the position of highest honor in the heaven as the Father's "firstborn Son" and as the redeemed community's Prophet, Priest, and King. He would then return to earth at the end of the age to destroy once and for all the kingdom of evil, destroy man's "last enemy," even death, by resurrecting all men from the dead, and after the judgment, would turn over his Messianic authority to the Father that God may be "all in all," who will then reign over the universe in a new heaven and a new earth. Also the Holy Spirit covenanted to apply the benefits and virtues of Christ's obedient life and substitutionary atoning death to the elect by regenerating them, working repentance and faith in them, sanctifying them through the means of grace, and forming them into one "new man" – even the Church. Finally, in conjunction with the incarnate Son's return to earth in final triumph over it, the Holy Spirit covenanted to raise from the death those who had died in faith and to bring them, together with transformed and glorified living Christians, into the final glorious Kingdom of Christ and of God. The rest of mankind would be judged and cast into the lake of fire.[1] All of this – indeed, everything that has occurred or will occur in earth history –

was included in the eternal purpose and decree of God that the triune Godhead determined before the creation of the world. This eternal covenant involving the salvation of men and the formation and glorification of the Church Reformed theologians designate for convenience as the "covenant of redemption."

God's providential execution of his eternal covenant of redemption in history Reformed theologians designate the "covenant of grace." That is to say, the "covenant of grace" refers to the tangible expression in creation history of God's prior covenant of redemption in eternity.

Its Relation to the Abrahamic Covenant

Immediately after Adam's tragically fatal transgression of the covenant that God his Creator had sovereignly imposed upon him (Hos. 6:7; Gen. 3:1-7), in the hearing of Adam God said to the serpent, the instrument of Satan in the temptation and by extension to Satan himself: "I will put enmity between you and the woman, and between your offspring and hers; he will crush your head, and you will strike his heel" (Gen. 3:15). Long have Christian theologians spoken of this divine declaration of war against the Kingdom of Evil as the inauguration of the covenant of grace and God's first gracious promise to fallen mankind of salvation from sin. Not without good reason have they designated this promise the *protevangelium*, the "first proclamation of the gospel." The promise, it is true, is in seed-form, indicating that out of the human race itself in the person of the "woman's seed" would come deliverance from sin, but it was sufficient to give our first parents hope (Gen. 3:20). In accordance with this promise, God extended grace to certain antediluvian descendants of Adam, for example, Abel (Gen. 4:4; Heb. 11:4), Enoch (Gen. 5:22-23; Heb. 11:5), and Noah (Gen. 6:8-9; Heb. 11:7) and his immediate family and daughters-in-law. It should be noted that the postlapsarian period prior to the great Genesis Flood saw only a minimal demonstration of divine

---

[1]These beliefs may be found in this general order in the following Scripture verses: Hebrews 13:20; Revelation 4:11; Ephesians 1:3-6; 2 Timothy 1:9; Romans 5:12-19; 8:29-30; 9:11; John 17; Hebrews 2:14; Acts 2:23; 4:27-28; Isaiah 53:4-6; Hebrews 10:5-7; Matthew 3:16; 4:1, 11; John 10:18; Ephesians 1:19-20; Romans 8:11; Acts 1:9; 3:22; Hebrews 4:14; 5:5-10; 1:3; Revelation 19-21; John 3:1-8; 1 Peter 1:2; Romans 4:5; 8:11; 1 Corinthians 15:51-52; Revelation 20:11-15.

grace, however, in order that the true nature of sin would be amply exhibited.[2] As a result mankind degenerated morally until "every thought and imagination of man's heart was only evil continually" (Gen. 6:5) and God determined to destroy mankind by the Flood. Nor was the situation much different during the postdiluvian period prior to the age of the Genesis patriarchs. There is only slight indication of the working of special or redemptive grace in this period of human history. In fact, the main feature of this period is the divine judgment that fell upon mankind in the form of the confusion of tongues at Babel (Gen. 11:1-11) and the resultant dispersion of the postdiluvian race over the face of the earth (Gen. 10) as punishment for man's manifest expression of pride at Babel (Gen. 11:4). I do not say "no indication" for there is the divine promise of grace set forth in Noah's prophetic statement that God would become in a unique sense the God of Shem and that the descendants of Japheth, as they "dwelt in the tents of Shem," would also receive redemptive benefit from Shem's God (Gen. 9:26-27).

With the call of Abraham, however, the covenant of grace underwent a remarkable advance, definitive for all time to come. The instrument of this advance is the covenant that God made with Abraham that guaranteed and secured salvific blessing for "all the families of the earth" (Gen. 12:3). So significant are the promises of grace in the Abrahamic Covenant, found in Genesis 12:1-3; 13:14-16; 15:7-21; 17:1-16; and 22:16-18, that it would not be an over-statement to hail these verses, from the perspective of the divine plan itself and covenantally speaking, as the most important verses in the whole Bible. In the covenantal sense, *everything that preceded the Abraham covenant in Genesis 1–11, may be viewed as introductory and preparatory to the revelation and making of the Abrahamic covenant, while all that God has savingly done and is savingly doing since its making may be viewed as the result and product of it.* In other words, God made a covenant with Abraham, and everything that he has done since to this present moment he has done in order to fulfill his covenant promise to Abraham. This is just to suggest that God's entire soteric program envisioned in the eternal covenant of redemption that came to expression in the covenant of grace as it came to expression in the Abrahamic covenant may be viewed in terms of the

---

[2]Geerhardus Vos (1954), *Biblical Theology*, Eerdmans, 56.

promise contained in the Abrahamic covenant – "I will be your God and you and your seed will be my people." God, of course, made temporal, earthly promises to Abraham, but these are neither primary nor central, and should be viewed, rather, as arising from the more primary and basic spiritual promise that envisioned the salvation of all God's elect.

If this representation of the significance of the Abrahamic covenant appears to be an overstatement, the following declarations of subsequent divine revelation should suffice to justify its propriety and to deliver it from the charge of injudicious indiscretion:

1. It is this covenant and none other that God later confirmed with Isaac (Gen. 17:19; 26:3-4) and with Jacob (Gen. 28:13-15).

2. The exodus deliverance of the people of God from Egypt (*the* Old Testament type of New Testament redemption in Christ) God specifically effected as his response to his "remembering" his covenant with Abraham, with Isaac, and with Jacob (Exod. 2:24; Deut. 7:8).

3. Again and again throughout Israel's history as a nation in Old Testament times the prophets trace God's extension of grace to the nation to his faithfulness to his covenant promise to Abraham (see Lev. 26:42, 45; Deut. 1:8; Josh. 24:3; 2 Kings 13:23).

4. Both Mary (Luke 1:54-55) and Zechariah (Luke 1:68-75) declared the advent of Jesus Christ to be a vital constituent part of the fulfillment of God's covenant promise to Abraham.

5. Jesus, who is himself *the* Seed of Abraham (Matt. 1:1; Gal. 3:15), declared that Abraham "rejoiced at the thought of seeing my day; he saw it and was glad" (John 8:56). Moreover, he strikingly describes the blessed state of those who enter into the future kingdom of glory as one in which the redeemed will take their places at the feast "with Abraham, Isaac, and Jacob in the kingdom of heaven" (Matt. 8:11).

6. Peter declared that God sent Jesus to bless the Jewish nation in keeping with his promise given to Abraham in Genesis 12:3, in turning them away from their iniquities (Acts 3:25-26).

7. Paul declared that Christ accomplished his redemption of sinners from the curse of the law on the basis of his substitutionary atone-

ment "in order that the blessing given to Abraham might come to the Gentiles" (Gal. 3:13-14).

8. Paul also taught that when God promised Abraham that "all peoples on earth will be blessed through you" (Gen. 12:3) he was announcing to Abraham in that promise the gospel of salvation. As a result, he declares, all believers "are blessed along with Abraham" (Gal. 3:8-9).

9. Paul also taught that Abraham is the "father of all who believe" among both Jews and Gentiles (Rom. 4:11-12) and are "Abraham's offspring and heirs according to the promise" (Gal. 3:29; see also 3:16-18).

Beyond dispute, these passages of Scripture make it clear that the promise of God, covenantally given to Abraham, that he would be the God of Abraham and his seed, and that they would be his people and would inherit the world (Rom. 4:13), extends temporally to the farthest reaches of the future and includes within its compass the entire community of the redeemed. Again, this is just to say that the Abrahamic covenant, in the specific prospects it holds forth of spiritual blessing in the salvation of the entire church of God, is identical with the soteric program of the covenant of grace, indeed, is identical with the covenant of grace itself. It also means specifically that the blessing of the covenant of grace that believers enjoy today under the sanctions of the New Testament economy are founded upon the covenant God made with Abraham. Said another way, the New Covenant itself is simply, in the words of John Murray, the current administrative "extension and unfolding of the Abrahamic covenant."[3] The organic unity and continuity of the one church of God composed of *all* the people of God of both the Old and New Testament dispensations, growing out of the one covenant of grace, is thus established and secured. If one desires further evidence of the unity of the covenant of grace and the oneness of the people of God in all ages he will find it in Paul's illustration of the olive trees in Romans 11:16-24 and his description of Christians as the "true circumcision" (Phil. 3:2-3) and the "Israel of God" (Gal. 6:16).

---

[3] John Murray (1962), *Christian Baptism*, Presbyterian and Reformed, 46.

Its Promises and Signs

Having determined the purpose and the locale of the covenant of grace, we are now in a position to discern the precise content of the divine promise contained therein, upon which the salvation of God's people in all ages is grounded. In the words of John Murray, it is

> undeniably and simply: 'I will be your God and you shall be my people' (cf. Gen. 17:7; Exod. 19:5, 6; Deut. 7:6; 14:2; Jer. 31:33). In a word, it is union and communion with Jehovah, the God of Israel.[4]

In light of biblical teaching generally, this union with God includes the constitutive declaration of pardon and righteousness handed down by God with regard to ungodly men (the doctrine of justification) that in turn is grounded upon the efficacy of Christ's accomplished atonement and is conditioned upon faith alone in Jesus Christ that is effected by the Holy Spirit's applicatory work. But this is precisely the reason that Abraham is the covenant father of all the faithful: just as "he believed the Lord, and he credited it to him as righteousness" (Gen. 15:6; Rom. 4:3, 18-24), so also they, and only they, who repudiate all self-effort and trust Christ alone are "Abraham's seed."

The sign and seal of the covenant of grace during its Old Testament administration, we learn from Genesis 17:1-16, was circumcision. Even in Old Testament times the rite was understood to convey symbolically the import of the removal of sin's defilement at the very source of life (the heart) (Exod. 6:13, 30; Lev. 19:23; 26:41; Deut. 10:16; 30:6; Jer. 4:4; 6:10; 9:25). In the New Testament Paul explained that it signified the imputation of righteousness through faith (Rom. 4:11). So closely connected is the sign and the spiritual reality it signifies that Stephen is willing to say that God "gave Abraham the covenant of circumcision" (Acts 6:7).

Under the New Testament administration of the covenant of grace circumcision as the Old Testament covenantal sign and seal was superseded by the sacrament of baptism. The import of baptism, however, is essentially the same as circumcision, namely, purification from sin's defilement through union with Christ in his death to the reign of sin and his resurrection to newness of life (Rom. 6:10; Tit. 3:5; see *Westminster Confession of Faith*, XXVII.5). Paul expressly relates

---

[5]Murray, *Christian Baptism*, 50; see also Charles Hodge (nd), *Systematic Theology*, Eerdmans, II:365.

the two ordinances with regard to their significance in Colossians 2:11-12: "in him you were also circumcised, in the putting off of the sinful nature, not with a circumcision done by the hands of men but with the circumcision done by Christ, having been buried with him in [the Spirit's] baptism and raised with him through…faith." Clearly for Paul, with respect to New Testament baptism – the outward sign and seal of the Spirit's baptismal work, its spiritual import is tantamount to that of Old Testament circumcision.[5] By the authority of Christ and his apostles, then, the church of the New Testament administers baptism in lieu of circumcision, with the spiritual significance of the former, however, being essentially the same as the latter.

In sum, the central promise of the covenant of grace guarantees mutual fellowship between God and the elect sinner. This fellowship is based upon Christ's accomplished atonement and the Holy Spirit's effectual application of its benefits to the elect sinner. The promise was signified and sealed in Old Testament times by circumcision; it is signified and sealed today by baptism.

The Relation of Children to the Covenant of Grace

While Scripture does not regard every child of minority age as having status within the covenant of grace, it does declare that the child of even one believing parent has such status. The biblical notices to this effect are many – indeed, more than one might imagine before actually researching the matter. Consider the following facts:

1. The Abrahamic covenant, when first made, included not only Abraham and other adults, but also those youths within his household of sufficient age and intelligence to exercise personal faith in

---

[5]Paul King Jewett, the noted Reformed Baptist theologian, acknowledges as much in his 1978 book, *Infant Baptism and the Covenant of Grace*, Eerdmans, 89, although he immediately thereafter aborts the significance of his acknowledgement, when he writes: "…the only conclusion we can reach is that the two signs [circumcision and baptism], as outward rites, symbolize the same inner reality in Paul's thinking. Thus circumcision may fairly be said to be the Old Testament counterpart of Christian baptism. So far the Reformed argument, in our judgment, is biblical. In this sense, baptism, to quote the Heidelberg Catechism, 'occupies the place of circumcision in the New Testament.'"

the God of Abraham as well as infant offspring. Even a cursory reading of Genesis 17:1-6 will put this beyond controversy. If there were any question as to whether children were to be regarded as properly within the compass of the promise of God to Abraham, Genesis 17:12 should remove any remaining doubt: "For the generations to come every male among you who is eight days old must be circumcised," that is, must have the sign of the covenant cut in his flesh. Any male not so marked was to be regarded as outside the embrace of the covenant promise (Gen. 17:14). Abraham clearly understood this as evidenced by the fact that he circumcised Ishmael who was thirteen years old at that time (Gen. 17:23-24) and later he circumcised eight-day-old Isaac (Gen. 25:3-4). Subsequent confirmations of the covenant with Isaac and Jacob (Gen. 26:3-4; 28:13-14) indicated that the children of the covenant within the patriarchal community were to be regarded as within the compass of the covenant promise.

2. The seriousness with which God takes both the covenant status of children of covenant parents and his insistence upon their receiving the sign of the covenant is strikingly portrayed when he "met Moses [on the latter's return trip to Egypt from the wilderness] and was about to kill him" for failing to circumcise his own son. "But Zipporah...cut off her son's foreskin and touched Moses' feet with it.... So the LORD let him alone" (Exod. 4:24-26).

3. Infants and young children were in the congregation of Israel on the Plains of Moab when Moses reconfirmed the covenant with the second generation after the exodus from Egypt. Here are Moses' words that indicate that children were included in the covenant confirmation at that time:

> Carefully follow the terms of this covenant [the Deuteronomic legislation], so that you may prosper in everything you do. All of you standing here today in the presence of the LORD your God – your leaders and chief men, your elders and officials, *together with your children* and your wives.... You are standing here in order to enter into a covenant with the LORD your God, a covenant the LORD is making with you today...*to confirm you this day as his people, that he may be your God as he promised you, and as he swore to your fathers, to Abraham, Isaac, and Jacob* (Deut 29:9-13).

4. When the covenant terms were later reviewed at Mount Ebal under Joshua's leadership, in keeping with Moses' requirements (Deut. 31:10-13), "there was not a word of all that Moses had commanded that Joshua did not read to the whole assembly of Israel, *including women and children...*" (Josh. 8:35).

5. When Jehoshaphat prayed for Judah's military victory over Moab and Ammon, "all the men of Judah, with their wives and children and little ones stood before the LORD" (2 Chr. 20:13).

6. When the prophets called Israel to repentance, children and nursing infants were expressly summoned to be present in Israel's solemn assemblies as a sign of national repentance (Joel 2:16). It is transparently clear from these Old Testament passages that children were looked upon as possessing covenant status in the community of Israel.

7. These Old Testament facts, furthermore, throw light on the reason for Christ's indignation over his disciples' attempt to send the parents away who were bringing their children (Luke 18:15 reads *ta brephē*, "the babes") to him that he might touch them and give them his blessing. Jesus Christ was and is the God of Abraham (John 8:56-58). Contrary to what the disciples assumed would be his attitude toward little children,[6] Jesus commanded them: "Let the little children come to me, and do not hinder them, for the kingdom of God belongs to such as these.... And he took the children in his arms, put his hands on them, and blessed them"[7] (Mark 10:13-16; see parallel passages in Matthew 19:13-15; Luke 18:15-17). From both his command and his remark that followed it to the effect that those who refuse to receive the kingdom of God like a little child will never enter therein, it is plain that Jesus regarded these Israelite children as members of the covenant community of

---

[6]Though the disciples should have known better, their attitude toward children may perhaps be explained from the fact that the status of children under then-current but totally unbiblical religious law consistently placed them in the company of the deaf and dumb, the weak-minded, the blind and crippled, the aged, Gentiles, women, and slaves. See Joachim Jeremias (1971), *New Testament Theology*, SCM, I:227, fn.

[7]Jesus' blessing, surely verbal and audible, was doubtless not comprehended by these infants, but this absence of comprehension (faith) on their part in no way nullified the fact of the blessing itself on his part.

Israel. It is worthy to note in passing that all three Synoptists thought Jesus' attitude toward these little children to be significant enough in their depictions of him that they mention this incident. Quite evident is it that Jesus loved these little children and recognized their covenant status, his attitude toward them serving to correct the unbiblical notion dominating his disciples' thinking.

8. On the day of Pentecost, when the Holy Spirit uniquely manifested himself in fulfillment of Joel's great prophecy pertaining to the last days (Acts 2:1-4; Joel 2:28-34), in his explanatory sermon concerning this epochal event, Peter affirmed that "the promise [of the Holy Spirit] is for you and your children and for all who are afar off – for all whom the Lord our God will call" (Acts 2:39). This Petrine declaration insures that the ancient divine promise that embraces children along with their parents continues unabated in this age. John Murray's comment on Peter's words is pertinent:

> Nothing could advertise more conspicuously and conclusively that this principle of God's gracious government, by which children along with their parents are the possessors of God's gracious covenant promise, is fully operative in the New Testament as well as in the Old than this simple fact that on the occasion of Pentecost Peter took up the refrain of the old covenant and said, "The promise is to you and to your children...."[8]

9. Paul too expressly declared that the children of even one Christian parent are *holy* (*hagioi*) (1 Cor. 7:14). Since he cannot mean by the word "holy" that these children are actually saved by virtue of the relation that they sustain to their parents, he doubtless intended by this exceptional word of description to ascribe covenant membership status to children of parents who are themselves members of the church – the New Testament form of the covenant community rooted spiritually in the Abrahamic covenant.

10. Paul also presupposes the covenant status of children when he includes them among the "saints" at Ephesus (Eph. 1:1; 6:1).

More examples of the same could be given, such as the New Testament's use of both the Genesis Flood and the Exodus as types of baptism (1 Pet. 3:20-21; 1 Cor. 10:1-2) in both of which "the covenantal action of God is not with individuals in isolation, but with fami-

---

[8]Murray, *Christian Baptism*, 71.

lies, or with individuals in families so that those belonging to the individuals are also separated as the people of God and in a very real sense come within the sphere of the divine covenant."[9] But I believe my point has been sufficiently demonstrated. It is this: In Scripture from the days of Abraham onward into the New Testament era itself children of covenant parents are expressly represented as possessing membership status in the covenant community. Reformed paedobaptist parents believe, therefore, that the baptism of their infants and young children today is a justifiable deduction from the following three *undeniable* biblical truths:

1. Infant males received the sign and seal of the covenant of grace under its Old Testament administration.

2. The covenant of grace has continuity and organic unity in which the people of God are essentially one in all ages, as was demonstrated earlier in our discussion of the salvific significance of the Abrahamic covenant throughout the Old and New Testaments to the farthest reaches of the future.

3. One can find no repeal in the New Testament of the Old Testament command to place the sign of the covenant of grace upon covenant children.

This fact having been established, we may now consider the question of precisely what is intended when children of believing parents are said to be in the covenant of grace and members of the church of Jesus Christ. How do we explicate the relation that this preposition "in" designates? What specifically does it connote?

It may be unequivocally stated at the outset that in neither the Old nor the New Testament is there any biblical warrant to justify the conclusion that these children are actually saved by the filial relation that they sustain to their parents. To the contrary, such a basis for salvation is expressly rejected (Matt. 3:9; John 1:13; Rom. 9:10-13), while personal faith in the atoning work of Christ is everywhere hailed as the necessary condition for individual salvation. In order that all fears due to misunderstanding for whatever reason may be allayed, I want to underscore the fact that the "in" in the phrase "children in the covenant" does not assert the personal salvation of these children

---

[9]Geoffrey W. Bromiley (1979), *Children of Promise*, Eerdmans, 16.

based upon natural descent. It does indicate, however, that the church as God's covenant community in this age regards these children as being as truly members in the visible church in this world as the elect of God are in the so-called invisible Church. Consider the representation of this matter by the Westminster Assembly: "The visible church...consists of all those throughout the world that profess the true religion, and of their children..." (*Westminster Confession of Faith*, XXV.II; see also *Larger Catechism*, Question 166). In other words, though they may not be saved and thus *of* spiritual Israel, they are still *in* the New Testament "Israel of God" and thus may be the recipients of its spiritual benefits, just as the Old Testament Jew as a Jew could receive the spiritual benefits God gave Israel (see Rom. 3:1-2; 9:4-5) by virtue of his connection to the Old Testament covenant community.

The Privileges, Rights, and Responsibilities of Children in the Covenant of Grace

Their privileges

Great privileges attend the child born in the covenant home. In addition to the fact that his most immediate authority (his covenant parents) recognizes the authority of God and attendant obligation to obey him, his is the most advantageous environment for the hearing of the gospel of Jesus Christ. He will also be assured normally of those influences conducive to moral and spiritual development, such influences including, first and foremost, parental Christian commitment and example, parental love for God and his Word, Christian training, the influence of the family's local church and of other Christians who are friends of the family, and so on.

Their rights

Beyond those common rights that all children normally have to loving parental provision of home, food, clothing, medical care, education, and so on, children in the covenant of grace possess the following additional rights that accrue to them by virtue of their position in the covenant.

The acknowledgement of covenant status itself

The first of these rights is the acknowledgement by their parents and the Christian church at large of their covenant status. It was this acknowledgement that underlay Paul's willingness to include children among those whom he addressed as "saints" at Ephesus.

It is a cause of deep sadness to paedobaptist Christians that multitudes of Christian parents are completely oblivious to the privileged status that their children possess by virtue of the fact that they – the parents – are Christians. I have personally heard parents aligned with Baptist churches insist with the best of intentions that their children are no different in God's sight from the children of the most spiritually darkened pagans until they have turned to Christ by faith. It is interesting, however, to observe these same parents instructing their children, even while the latter are able to speak only with childish lisps and before they are able to make a credible profession of faith, to think of God the Father as their heavenly Father and to pray the "Our Father" of the Lord's Prayer. The most immediate implication that an observer would draw from such instruction is that these parents believe, after all, that God does regard these little ones in some sense as his children. Their practice, though inconsistent, is better than their avowed theology. Apparently, in spite of their faulty theology, these Christian parents instinctively assume that their children are in some sense special to the Lord even though they do not possess the theological paradigm to justify their action. In my opinion, paedobaptist Christians, with their insights into the implications of the unity of the covenant of grace, should make a more concerted effort to educate evangelical Christian families with respect to the privileged status of their covenant children.

The sign and seal of the covenant of the grace
The second right is the right to the sign and seal of the covenant of grace that we have seen was circumcision in the Old Testament and baptism in the New, with the accompanying rights and responsibilities appertaining thereunto.

The baptism of infants and young children of believing parents under the New Testament administration of the covenant of grace, as we have already urged, is a justifiable deduction from (1) the undeniable fact that male infants and young children received the sign of the covenant of circumcision under its Old Testament administration, (2) the undeniable fact of the organic unity and continuity of the covenant of grace and oneness of the people of God in all ages, and (3) the undeniable fact of the absence of any repeal of the Old Testament command to place the sign of the covenant of grace upon covenant children in the New Testament. My point is this: just as the covenant sign was placed upon male infants and young children of covenant parents in Old Testament times, so also should the covenant sign be administered to all infants and young children of covenant parents under the New Testament administration of the same covenant of grace. Indeed, not to do so, the *Westminster Confession of Faith*, XXVIII.5, represents as "great sin."

This is not to suggest that Reformed paedobaptist Christians regard the infant so baptized as a saved individual by virtue of his baptism *per se* any more that they believe that the infant of Christian parents is saved by virtue of his relation to his parents. They in fact do not or, at least, should not believe so! Nor is it to suggest that these children are necessarily baptized on the *presumption* that they are elect and/or are *regenerate* children. Some highly placed Reformed theologians, it is true, have urged the baptism of infants on such grounds,[10] since there is some scriptural evidence that God can work and has worked faith in at least some infants in their infancy (Ps. 22:9-10; Luke 1:15, 41-44; see Isa. 49:1-6; Jer. 1:5; Gal. 1:15; see also Calvin, *Institutes*, 4.16.20 in this connection). Other Reformed theologians such as the late John Murray,[11] and I count myself among them, argue that the *divine command* that infants within the covenant community should receive the sign of the covenant is sufficient warrant for baptism to be administered to covenant children. On either ground, however, all of these theologians recognize that "the efficacy of baptism is not tied to that moment of time wherein it is administered" but that "the grace promised is…conferred, by the Holy Spirit, to such (whether of age or infants) as that grace belongeth unto…in [God's] appointed time" (*Westminster Confession of Faith*, XXVIII.6). Furthermore, they affirm that baptism, as the sign and seal of God's gracious covenant, is prescribed by God as a testimony to *his* saving work of grace in behalf of sinners and *not* to the Christian's confession of faith as such, and therefore, that it is not essential to its proper administration that the divine blessing that it signifies be either *consciously* appropriated or *consciously* appreci-

---

[10]See *First Helvetic Confession*, Article XXII, Abraham Kuyper, Charles Hodge, and Benjamin B. Warfield.

[11]Murray, *Christian Baptism*, 56-61.

ated by the recipient at the time of its administration.

The Baptist Christian, who denies the teaching of paedobaptism, argues that a command to baptize infants and young children prior to personal faith cannot be found in the New Testament. This the Reformed paedobaptist readily acknowledges, but he argues, in light of (1) the organic oneness of the covenant of grace in all ages, (2) the *parallelism of meaning* between circumcision and baptism, and (3) the New Testament inferences that infants of believing parents are covenant children, that it is not he who needs a command to *continue* the two-thousand-year-long practice of the Old Testament into this age, but it is rather the Baptist Christian who must produce a command to *discontinue* the age-long practice of placing the covenant sign on covenant children if he would justify his anti-paedobaptist stance. In the absence of such a command, or until such a command is forthcoming, the paedobaptist Christian contends that the practice of marking out the covenant child as such by the administration of the current sign of the covenant must be continued. He would further urge that every argument leveled against infant baptism as understood by the Reformed faith is ultimately an argument against Old Testament circumcision as well.

Training and instruction in our most holy faith
In light of their two preceding rights, the third right of covenant children is the right to be brought up "in the training and instruction of the Lord" (Eph. 4:6), a work that our Puritan forebears spoke of as "improving" their children's baptism. This imposes a solemn responsibility upon both parents and the local church.

In the home, covenant parents, particularly the father (Eph. 6:4), bear the responsibility to make available the means of grace necessary to bring their children to conscious repentance toward God and faith in Jesus Christ. They must take whatever steps are necessary to insure that the character of spiritual commitment lived out in the home environment conduces to their children's growth in grace. Discussions of biblical truths and themes should be a normal, natural part of family social interaction. This means that regular times of Bible reading and study, singing praises to God, and prayer should be observed (see Deut. 6:4-25). Scriptural discipline also should be administered in love and with a concern for the proper development of the whole child, mentally, psychologically, and spiritually. General demeanor in the home should comport with the Christian profession of the home. Early should the child begin to be taught to realize the spiritual benefits that accrue to him by virtue of his status as a covenant child in the Christian home.

Christian parents should also take their children regularly to a good Sunday school and worship service where as a family they can be further taught by lesson and sermon "what man is to believe concerning God and what duty God requires of man" (*Westminster Shorter Catechism*, Question 3), and where they can observe the administration of and participate in the sacraments. In this way the children will experience first-hand the blessings that flow from Christian fellowship and the mutual sharing of the benefits of the Holy Spirit's gifts to the church as the body of Christ. When, in God's gracious providence, the children come to conscious faith in Christ, they then have the right, upon public confession of faith before the ruling body of elders, to be received into the membership of the church as communicant members and thus participate in the sacrament of the Lord's Supper.

Finally, with primary and secondary state-provided education increasingly becoming philosophically humanistic, anti-Christian, academically inferior, and morally infirm and hedonistic, and in light of the fact that in Jesus Christ "are hidden all the treasures of wisdom and knowledge" (Col. 2:3), Christian parents should have serious reservations about the value of any educational program in which Christ is consciously and legislatively denied his rightful place. Where primary and secondary Christian educational alternatives are available, covenant parents should consider these preferable to state-provided programs, even if it means financial sacrifice. Where these are not available, local church leaders and the Christian community at large should be challenged to launch such educational programs for the benefit of their children, under the supervision of either a local church or a parent-controlled association. Information concerning the steps to starting Christian school programs is readily obtainable from many Christian educational organizations.

Another alternative preferred by increasing numbers of Christian parents is home-schooling in which through parental networks Christian parents share their several areas of educational expertise with the children in their network in order to give these children a God-honoring education.

In this context I want to call attention to the Presbyterian doctrines of covenant succession and covenant nurture. Robert S. Rayburn is doubtless correct when he claims "that far and away the largest part of the Christian church at any time or place – except that historical moment when the gospel first reaches a place and people – are those who were born and raised in Christian families."[12] Accordingly, when the church contemplates its growth, either quantitatively or qualitatively, it cannot afford to ignore its responsibility to its own children. The church must always remember that (1) "it is God's will and declared purpose that his saving grace run in the lines of generations" (Gen. 17:7-9; Exod. 20:6; Deut. 6:6-7; Ps. 103:17-18; Isa. 44:3; 54:13; 59:21; Ezek. 37:25; Acts 2:38-39; 16:14-15, 31; 1 Cor. 7:14), and (2) "the biblical paradigm is for covenant children to grow up in faith from infancy" (Pss. 22:9; 71:6; Eph. 6:4; 2 Tim. 3:15). Since their children are members of the covenant community Christian parents are charged to nurture their children in Christian faith and love, "which nurture when carried out faithfully becomes the divine instrumentality of their awakening to spiritual life." Rayburn is right again when he concludes his discussion by declaring:

> The [church's] appropriation by faith of this divine promise and summons of [covenant succession] is the means appointed to furnish the church with generation after generation of great multitudes of Christian servants and soldiers who reach manhood and womanhood well-taught, sturdy in faith, animated by love for God and man, sophisticated in the way of the world and the Devil, polished in the manners of genuine Christian brotherhood, overshadowed by the specter of the Last Day, nerved to deny themselves and to take up their cross so as to be counted worthy of greater exploits for Christ and Kingdom. Currently the church not only suffers a terrible shortage of such other-worldly and resolute Christians, superbly prepared for spiritual warfare, but, in fact, is hemorrhaging its children into the world. Christian evangelism will never make a decisive difference in our culture when it amounts merely to an effort to replace losses due to widespread desertion from our own camp. The gospel will always fail to command attention and carry conviction when large numbers of those who grow up under its influence are observed

---

[12]Robert S. Rayburn, "The Presbyterian Doctrines of Covenant Children, Covenant Nurture, and Covenant Succession," *Presbyterion: Covenant Seminary Review* (1996), Vol. XXII, Num. 2., 96, 98, 103, 109.

abandoning it for the world. Recovering our Presbyterian inheritance and inscribing the doctrine of covenant succession upon the hearts of family and church must have a wonderfully solemnizing and galvanizing effect. It will set Christian parents seriously to work on the spiritual nurture of their children, equipping them and requiring them to live the life of covenant faith and duty to which their God and Savior called them at the headwaters of life. And, ever conscious of the greater effect of parental example, they will forsake the easy way, shamelessly and joyously to live a life of devotion and obedience which adorns and ennobles the faith in the eyes of their children. This they will do, who embrace the Bible's doctrine [of covenant succession], lest the Lord on the Great Day should say to them: "You took your sons and daughters whom you bore to me and sacrificed them to idols."

Their responsibilities

"Every privilege is attended by responsibility." This adage is certainly true of covenant children. Weighty and solemn are the responsibilities that accrue to them by virtue of their covenant status.

Obedience to parents

Covenant children are responsible to acknowledge parental authority over them and to obey without murmuring every legitimate command their parents give them (Eph. 6:1-3; Col. 3:20). When they disobey, they should receive parental discipline respectfully, hopefully coming eventually to understand that such discipline "produces a harvest of righteousness and peace for those who have been trained by it" (Heb. 12:9-11).

Repentance and faith

When they mature sufficiently to comprehend the truth of their sinfulness and need of salvation, covenant children are personally responsible to live lives of repentance toward God and of faith in our Lord Jesus Christ, thereby actualizing in their lives that which their baptism signified. For them not to respond affirmatively to the privileges extended to them by their status in the covenant of grace is to apostatize from the covenant community of faith within which they lived since infancy (Heb. 10:29).

Communicant church membership

Finally, in God's providential timing, covenant children are responsible to profess Christ credibly and publicly before the elders of their local church. Then, as communicant members, they are to enter responsibly into the life of the visible church on the basis of their profession and vows to the eldership, and to submit themselves with piety and obedience to the teaching and discipline of their local church. As they become adults, marry, and begin to have children of their own, they are to rear their children, as they were reared, in their most holy faith.

* * * * *

In this address I have attempted to explain what the covenant of grace is, the place that children of believing parents occupy within it, and the privileges, rights, and responsibilities that accrue to them from their covenant status.

In conclusion I would like to make a personal reference. I wish to praise God for his covenant faithfulness to my wife and me and our children. In their infancy when my children were baptized, at each baptismal ceremony my wife and I responded affirmatively to the following two questions:

1. Do you acknowledge that, although your children are conceived and born in sin and therefore are subject to condemnation, they are holy in Christ and as members of his church ought to be baptized?

2. To you promise to instruct your child in the principles of our holy religion as revealed in the Scriptures of the Old and New Testament, and as summarized in the Confession of Faith and Catechisms, of this church; and do you promise to pray with and for your child, to set an example of piety and godliness before him, and to endeavor by all the means of God's appointment to bring him up in the nurture and admonition of the Lord?

While I confess with shame that I have not been as faithful to these vows as I should have been, through the years we have instructed our children in our most holy faith and have prayed hundreds of times with and for them. Together we regularly attended a Bible-believing Presbyterian church on the Lord's Day. Our children, at times with some sacrifice to the family, we enrolled in Christian primary and secondary schools. Today I can testify that God has kept his promise to my family – my children have made credible professions of faith in Jesus Christ as their Lord and Savior, love God, and speak comfortably and knowledgeably of spiritual things, and seek to live obediently before their God – by no means perfectly, of course.

Hundreds of thousands of other covenant parents could similarly testify to the faithfulness of the God to Abraham to his covenant promise to them. Christian couples contemplating parenthood or those who are already parents can be confident, if they will faithfully rear their children in the fear of the Lord as God has given instruction in his Word, that he will keep his promise to them and their family will realize innumerable blessings.

In a day when, perhaps as never before, the forces of evil seek the spiritual downfall of our children, when the very future of the family unit in American life is under attack and uncertain, Christian parents cannot afford to be unfaithful to their covenant responsibilities. We must renew our vows, taken when we presented our children for baptism, to rear them to know and to serve the God of Abraham. We must make the effort to take as seriously as God does the covenant status of our children. We parents must regard our children as our most precious possessions after our own personal relation to God and to one another as husband and wife, and be willing, therefore, to make whatever personal or monetary sacrifices are necessary for the sake of providing our children with the benefits that accrue to them as the "little people" in God's covenant of grace. We must have the vision to see that among the future leaders of our churches tomorrow are our own children and that the soundness of the future health of the Church of Jesus Christ depends much upon our parental faithfulness today to the rearing of our covenant children in our most holy faith.

Chapter Sixteen

Brunner's Dialectical Encounter

Emil Brunner (1889–1966) attended the Universities of Berlin and Zurich, taking a Th.D from the latter, researching in the writings of Kant and Husserl. He made a trip to America in 1919 and taught at Union Theological Seminary, New York City. In 1924 he was appointed to the Chair of Systematic and Practical Theology at the University of Zurich, which post he held until his retirement from active teaching in 1955, with brief visits in the meantime to America again in 1938 to fill a guest professorship at Princeton Theological Seminary and to Japan in 1953 as Lecturer at the new International Christian University at Tokyo. Prior to his death, in spite of failing health he worked on and completed his *magnum opus*, a three-volume neoorthodox *Dogmatics*. Brunner's major works include *Revelation and Reason*, *Divine-Human Encounter*, *Man in Revolt*, *The Divine Imperative*, *The Mediator*, and the previously mentioned twelve hundred page *Dogmatics*. Works about Brunner of interest to the American reader are Cornelius Van Til's *The New Modernism*, Paul King Jewett's *Emil Brunner's Concept of Revelation*, and *The Theology of Emil Brunner*, a collection of essays edited by Charles W. Kegley.

The emergence of Neo-orthodoxy in the 1920s was a protest against several widely-held theological viewpoints. Among these were the romantic idealism of Schleiermacher, the Neo-Kantianism of Ritschl, an immanentistic Hegelian pantheism, the "comparative religions school" of Troeltsch, and biblical orthodoxy. The two theologians who spearheaded this new theological expression were Karl Barth and Emil Brunner. And though Emil Brunner is regarded as the secondary figure, it was he, through his visits to America, and not Karl Barth who introduced neoorthodox thought to the American student. Furthermore, in comparison with Barth's still unfinished *Church Dogmatics*, Brunner's writings are a model of brevity and clarity. For these reasons, as John B. Cobb, Jr. observes "... when [the American]

Note: This article first appeared as a monograph published by Presbyterian and Reformed in 1967.

undertakes to state the position in questions, it is more likely to sound like that of Emil Brunner".[1] A knowledge of Brunner's basic theological thought is absolutely essential, therefore, to an intelligent understanding of the contemporary theological scene in America, for even though his ideas have lost much of the excitement they fostered sixty years ago simply because of the Church's familiarity with them, they have done much to determine the direction of American theology today.

The Historical Roots of Brunner's Thought

Every theological innovation is the offspring of a preceding epistemological situation, and Brunner's theological thought is no exception. The nineteenth century was an infamous period in the history of the Church insofar as biblical orthodoxy is concerned. An extremely destructive biblical criticism was exhibited in the work of Graf, Kuenen, Wellhausen, Cornhill, and others. Philosophers and theologians alike were prone to discredit any ability to know God. Kant, in denying to man any knowledge of *das Ding an sich* of the noumenal world, limited man to a knowledge of the phenomenal world (which man himself allegedly creates by his own reasoning process) and to "pious guesses" about the noumenal. Fichte even did away with the noumenal, saying it was the Ego. In biology and geology respectively, Darwin introduced his theory of organic evolution by means of natural selection, and Lyell, working from a theory of uniformity in nature, postulated long periods of time for the development of geological deposits, a view apparently compatible with the theories of organic evolution. Furthermore, a general antipathy toward the supernatural pervaded the academic centers of learning. There was an overlooking of the Biblical doctrine of the awfulness of sin. Ritschl, it is said, declared that he would walk into heaven erect! In general, no need was felt for the atoning work of Jesus Christ; "God will forgive; it is his profession" was the flippant response to the evangelical appeal of the earnest parish minister. And this was the legacy willed to the Church of the twentieth century.

Because of the attacks of this liberal brand of Christianity upon the theological orthodoxy of the Church, many scholars no longer regarded the theology of the Reformation to be tenable. The

---

[1]John B. Cobb Jr., *Living Options in Protestant Theology* (Philadelphia: Westminster, 1962), 143.

Reformers' doctrine of the depravity of man, for example, was manifestly untrue, was it not, in the light of all that man had been able to accomplish toward the betterment of himself and society? Indeed, the twentieth century, it was said, was to inaugurate a new and glorious era in the history of man. The preaching of the Social Gospel of Henry Churchill King, Gerald Birney Smith, and Walter Rauschenbusch here in America was to usher in the Kingdom of God. The twentieth century would be "the Christian century". But then the world was plunged into the chaos and destruction of the First World War, and a few years later came the American Stock Crash. No doubt for many in the Western Hemisphere it was almost as if some giant demon had turned off all the lights around the world, plunging even the universe into darkness.

What influence did such a turn of events have upon the liberal theological enterprise? Certainly for many young theologians trained in the great liberal theological centers of Europe it meant a re-examination of their liberal foundations. Liberal theology had not been equal to the task of ushering in the Kingdom of God! Thus it was within this context that new young voices appeared on the theological scene, Emil Brunner's among them, all crying out that the world was in the throes of *Krisis* and standing under the judgment of God. Out of this movement – now known as Neo-orthodoxy – developed several theological systems which have made lasting impressions upon theological thought, all having in common (at least overtly) hostility to philosophical reasoning and a stress upon the uniqueness of the religious experience as the foundation of the theological structure. We shall now show the historical and philosophical background of Brunner's acceptance of this position. Then, the discussion will turn directly to Brunner's thought pertaining to revelation and the dialetic of eternity and time.

The exponents of Neo-orthodoxy traced their position back as far as the New Testament. They pointed out that the New Testament writer felt no compulsion to justify his affirmations by appealing to analogies in Greek philosophy or to elucidate his faith systematically along the lines of philosophical categories. And certainly this is true.

Many of the Church's theological utterances after the Apostolic Age until the sixteenth-century Reformation, however, were consciously framed in philosophical categories of thought. There were theologians, of course, who resisted (sometimes with little success) the impulse to rely upon Greek philosophy to make Christian theology intelligible, such as Tertullian (c. 160–230) and the later Augustine (354–430). Then too, the mystics, such as Pseudo-Dionysius (fifth century), Bernard of Clairvaux (1090–1153), Meister Eckhart (1260–1327), and Nicholas of Cusa (1401–1464), may be regarded as standing historically in the line leading toward the contemporary autopistic systems of Neo-orthodoxy, in that they emphasized faith almost to the exclusion of reason as the ground of religious certainty. But even with these exceptions, by and large, the Reformation was a legitimate protest against the corruption of the pure faith of the early Church and the first five ecumenical councils by Scholastic philosophy.

The vital force of the Reformation lay in its return to the Scriptures of the Old and New Testaments as the final authority in matters of faith and practice and in its aversion to philosophical speculation in theology. Unfortunately, however, scholasticism entered both Lutheran and Calvinistic thought in the seventeenth and eighteenth centuries. Among Calvinistic scholars, for example, traces of scholasticism may be found in Petrus Ramus (1515–1572) and Theodore Beza (1519–1605), reaching a highwater mark in the writings of Gisbertus Voetius (1589–1676). However, the writings of several philosophers, especially David Hume, through their cogent argumentation against Christian doctrine grounded in philosophical conclusions, "reopened for theologians the possibility that faith must work out its form and content in independence of all speculative reason."[2]

Nineteenth-century European theology may be viewed as an effort to accomplish just such an end. But by this time, it should be noted, the thinkers of the Enlightenment, through their labors in Biblical criticism, philosophy, theology, and science, had raised a large question mark over the possibility of knowing anything absolutely about God. Consequently, those theologians who had never committed themselves to the Reformers' doctrine of Scripture as the inscripturated self-revelation of God were reluctant to affirm God's ontological reality on the basis of revelation as the sixteenth-century Reformers had unhesitatingly done. As a result the theological enterprise took a novel turn. Theologians began to frame theological affirmations in confessional terms as an account of the faith of the religious community (because this was an empirical fact that few philosophers

---

[2]John B. Cobb Jr., *Living Options*, 126.

could deny) rather than in revelational or dogmatic terms. Inasmuch as such a "faith" was really a description of experiential faith, both individually and collectively, and not the description of a faith that was necessarily the exclusive work of God, nineteenth-century theological expression became, for the most part, anthropocentric. And it is primarily against this anthropocentrism in theology that Brunner, as well as Barth and the other leading voices of Neo-orthodoxy, reacted.

Throughout his writings Brunner discerns what, in his opinion, are misconceptions of true Christianity by prejudiced theologians.[3] Religion in general, as to its essence, has been wrongly viewed by anthropology as the simple outgrowth of a basic human trait such as fear or as the result of sociological development. Also theological Liberalism had sought to ground religion in some basic structure of mankind such as the feeling of dependence (Schleiermacher) or valuational judgments (Ritschl). Brunner became convinced that Schleiermacher and Ritschl laid the groundwork for modern theological liberalism by the former stressing the view that religion is the feeling of absolute dependence with dogmatics being the expression of this feeling in speech, and the latter, building upon a Kantian idealism, stressing a moral Christianity centred in the historical Jesus. Against these systems Neo-orthodoxy reacted, both Barth and Brunner inveighing against them. Barth, for example, speaks of Schleiermacher's theology as *Bewusstsein-theologie* – a "consciousness theology" beginning with the fact of man's self-consciousness as something given and proceeding from this consciousness to inquire about the possibility of knowing anything about God. And as early as 1928 Brunner wrote a criticism of Schleiermacher entitled *Die Mystik and das Wort*.

Furthermore, Brunner lamented, theologians for too long have used the methodologies of philosophy and science, failing to work out and employ their own special methodology. The danger of alien methodology is the abstracting of God that such a procedure invariably produces.

Roman Catholicism also suffered from misconceptions. Its type of authoritarianism degenerates the conscience and produces religious serfs rather than free men in Jesus Christ. It reduced dogma to

---

[3]For the following brief analysis of the misconceptions of Christianity as Brunner sees them, I am indebted to Bernard Ramm, *Varieties of Christian Apologetics* (Grand Rapids: Baker, 1961), 67-70.

rationalization when it wed theology to Aristotelian Thomism, and it wrongly defined faith as intellectual assent to authority and a body of dogma.

The worst misconceptions of all, however, were those of orthodoxy: ignoring the "unimpeachable" results of biblical criticism, it conceived of revelation as the communication of doctrinal disclosure and imposed upon Scripture a doctrine of mechanical inspiration Applying a false hermeneutic of literalism, it forced Scripture into head-on collision with modern science with the result that orthodoxy lost the day in the areas of Copernican astronomy, Lyellian geology, and Darwinian evolution. To all of the foregoing misconceptions Brunner offered his theology as a corrective.

Søren Kierkegaard's Influence

Thus far we have noted only those men and movements against which Brunner reacted in the formulation of his theology. But if we are to grasp fully his peculiar contribution to contemporary theology, we must look briefly at a thinker who influenced Brunner in a positive manner.

Brunner has been influenced by many men, not the least of whom are Martin Luther, Immanuel Kant, Ferdinand Ebner, and Martin Buber, but probably it is Søren Kierkegaard, more than any other single man, who made the greatest lasting impression upon Brunner's theological development. Indeed, Brunner himself acknowledged this debt when he wrote: "Today I, in contrast to Karl Barth, still profess allegiance to this great thinker [Kierkegaard] to whom present-day theology, Catholic no less than Protestant, owes more to than anyone since Martin Luther."[4] For this reason, it is necessary that we now briefly consider the thought of the "Danish gadfly".

Søren Kierkegaard (1813–1855) was born, according to some authorities, a hunchback, to a father who believed he had been cursed by God and to a mother with whom his father had had premarital sex relations. He inherited a deeply melancholic nature from his father who burdened his young son with the knowledge of his own somber religious experiences and profligate tendencies. In 1840 Kierkegaard became engaged to Regina Olson, a virtuous young lady, but feeling great guilt because of his own youthful debaucheries, he soon broke

---

[4]Emil Brunner, "Intellectual Autobiography," *The Theology of Emil Brunner*, edited by Charles W. Kegley (New York: Macmillan, 1962), 11.

the engagement. Throughout the literary period of his life he was the target of a weekly newspaper in Copenhagen, while in turn he relentlessly attacked Danish Christendom until his death at the age of forty-two. Yet in the short span of his life he established in Denmark a literature so original and rich that it is absolutely without parallel in that country.

To understand Kierkegaard's theology, one must first understand his enemies.[5] First, having studied Hegelian philosophy with Schelling in Berlin, Kierkegaard waged relentless war against the Hegelian system that viewed the truth of Christianity as merely the necessary part of an absolute system whose content is determined by pure rationality. According to Cobb, Kierkegaard distinguished three errors that Hegelianism made.[6] The first is its attribution to pure, impersonal rationality a power of construction that in fact it does not have. Its second flaw is its inability to account for the concrete individual in his passionate concern. In other words, Hegelianism failed to take into account life's contingencies and problems; life just does not flow as unhesitatingly smooth as the Hegelian dialectic would assume. Against this error Kierkegaard heaps clever sarcasm, portraying, for example, the Hegelian philosopher being interrupted in the middle of a lecture on the glories of the "System" by an impulse to sneeze! Its third mistake is its profound misunderstanding of the nature of the Christian faith in identifying this faith with rational conviction that certain affirmations are true. If it is sarcasm that he heaped upon the second error of Hegelianism, it is a vehement hatred that Kierkegaard expressed toward any interpretation of faith which would involve rational belief.

Kierkegaard's second enemy was the pervasive Romanticism of his day. He felt that the Romanticist takes too easy a view of the problems of human existence. He represents a life of no disorder and no decision, no inwardness and no suffering. In his *Stages of Life's Way* Kierkegaard describes life as subsisting in three levels: the aesthetic, the ethical, and the religious, moving from lower to higher. And the Romanticist Kierkegaard describes as being on the lowest or aesthetic level, never passing beyond the mere desire for pleasure

---

[5] I am indebted to Ramm, *Varieties of Christian Apologetics*, 49-65, for the major ideas of this treatment of Kierkegaard's theology.

[6] Cobb, *Living Options*, 133

and the immediate gratification of want.

Finally, Kierkegaard deplored the apathy of Danish Christendom. In his day to be born a Dane was tantamount to being born a Christian. Baptism was equivalent to conversion. But such Christianity meant neither cross-bearing nor discipleship. For Kierkegaard, such "orthodoxy" was only playing the game of Christianity. His *Attack on Christendom*, containing his most severe diatribe, is one of his best known works.

For Kierkegaard, God is a hidden God (*Deus absconditus*) and existentially transcendent, that is, absolutely different from man. Man does not find God by searching for him; it is God who determines the condition of the "Moment" or the "Encounter". Also God is always *Subject*, never object. This means for Kierkegaard that, although there is an ontological objectivity about God, God is never the object of man's knowledge like a tree can be. God is always known as a person is known. Ramm comments on Kierkegaard's thought here: "If God were known as objects are known, one could know God and remain the same sinful, selfish creature. Unless knowing transforms, it is irreligious.... If God is Subject, he is Person, and therefore is known by 'subjectivity in inwardness', or in more prosaic language, existentially."[7]

Kierkegaard grants to man a freedom concerning "inwardness"; that is, man is capable of inward action. This places *man as individual* above *humanity as class*. Against Hegelian categories that classified particulars into general classes, thus losing the *individual* man in the *class* of humanity, Kierkegaard protests that inward human existence is higher than any philosophical category of humanity.[8] As an individual, however, man is infinitely different from God, according to Kierkegaard, and therefore is sinful.[9] In addition as an individual, man is an existent, involved in existence and in need of finding Truth and the true form of existence. Man is not a detached observer sitting on the "balcony" of some philosophical vantage point (as the Hegelian

---

[7]Ramm, *Varieties of Christian Apologetics*, 53.

[8]By taking this position, Kierkegaard anticipates the modern existentialist cliché: "Existence precedes essence."

[9]If there is a fall of man at all in Kierkegaard's theology, it is this infinite qualitative difference between God and man. In other words, man's sinfulness is psychologically understood in terms of his finiteness.

philosopher supposes) and observing the universe below as the rational outworking of Absolute Mind.

Kierkegaard's understanding of Truth is a radical departure from the philosopher's concept of Truth. For Kierkegaard real truth is existential truth; that is, it is personal and religious, not philosophical and scientific. Real truth is "truth for me". Furthermore, existential truth is paradoxical. Hegel had said that thought (principles of logic) and being (reality) are one. Kierkegaard, however, claims that thought is free from any metaphysical significance; therefore, a view of Being different from Hegel's is necessary. Now if the principles of thought are not the principles of reality (and Kierkegaard obviously thought so), then Reality or religious truth will appear to man the existent as a paradox. And this paradox, Kierkegaard believed, will never resolve itself by the Hegelian three-term dialectic into a synthesis. Religious truth will always remain di-polar in nature to the existent, and no amount of intellectual mediation will remove the contradiction. Only faith can relieve the illogical "logic" of religious or existential truth. Finally, Kierkegaard contends that real truth, if it is to exist at all for the individual, must be subjectively appropriated. "Truth is Subjectivity," is his famous byword, developed most fully in his *Concluding Unscientific Postscript*. Truth does not exist for the individual until he as a human existent existentially responds to it in existential confrontation. Although God is Truth, statements about God are not truths in and of themselves. They are only formulas for action or calls for decision. They become truths-in-subjectivity when the existent responds to them. Gordon Clark explains Kierkegaard's thought at this point in this way: "For Kierkegaard God is truth; but truth exists only for a believer who inwardly experiences the tension between himself and God. If an actually existing person is an unbeliever, then for him God does not exist. God exists only in subjectivity."[10]

The human response to paradox Kierkegaard regards as faith. Faith is not rational; it is not an act of the mind. It is a personal leap, a venture, a risk, a "not-knowing". The responding existent can be neither accompanied nor counselled in his leap; he must venture all upon objective uncertainty. Furthermore, he may expect no objective certainty after the faith-response. Faith is the decision to *live* in objective uncertainty and subjective certitude. Kierkegaard was well

---

[10]Gordon H. Clark, *Thales to Dewey* (Boston: Houghton Mifflin, 1957), 488.

aware that this position is reprehensible to the philosopher, but the man of faith, Kierkegaard was assured, knows subjectively that he has been *transformed* by the paradox and that is enough "proof" for him that he is *in truth*.

Of the paradoxes of faith, the most crucial is the Incarnation of God. Consequently, for Kierkegaard, faith, aroused by this particular paradox – the Absolute Paradox – will have for its object solely a Person – Jesus Christ – and not doctrines about Jesus Christ. Or, as Ramm succinctly states Kierkegaard's position on this point: "The object of faith is not a truth to be communicated but a Person to be chosen."[11]

Not only was Kierkegaard's understanding of the Christian life one of loneliness, subjectivity, and suffering, but it also was a personal life in contemporaneity with Christ. The Christian man is unconcerned with the span of time between the Absolute Paradox and himself. In fact, he is unconcerned with the historical as far as Jesus Christ is concerned. By faith he mediates the distance between them and recovers Christ for himself. In existential terms, by faith he mediates time and eternity.

When one understands only this much of Kierkegaard's thought, he does not need to read far in Brunner's writings to discover that in nearly every area of theological thought the Dane has been given his dues. His stress upon God as being radically beyond the grasp of reason and knowable only in faith seizes Brunner at every turn. Indeed, Brunner's very vocabulary is Kierkegaardian – he constantly speaks of existence, existential, incognito, encounter, contemporaneity, anxiety, and decision, to name just a few terms. This, of course, is not to say that Brunner is uncreative, that he merely parrots Kierkegaard's thought. To the contrary, Brunner brings to the theological task a massive accumulation of knowledge and a creativity rarely found in human kind. It is merely to point up the obvious, a fact which even Brunner himself recognized, namely, that Kierkegaard's was the most influential voice to address Brunner's intellectual needs.

With this background we now turn directly to the nerve center of Brunner's system – his concept of revelation and the dialectic between eternity and time.

---

[11]Ramm, *Varieties of Christian Apologetics*, 63.

Brunner's Concept of Revelation

The heart of Brunner's theology is his concept of revelation. An understanding of it, therefore, is absolutely essential for progress into his religious thought. He regards revelation as essentially *God's activity in salvation*: "... 'divine revelation' always [means] the whole of the divine activity for the salvation of the world, the whole story of God's saving acts, of the 'acts of God' which reveal God's nature and His will, above all, Him in whom the preceding revelation gains its meaning, and who therefore is its fulfillment: Jesus Christ. He Himself is the Revelation. Divine revelation is not a book or a doctrine; the Revelation is God Himself in His self-manifestation within history. Revelation is something that *happens*, the living history of God in His dealings with the human race: the history of revelation is the history of salvation, and the history of salvation is the history of revelation."[12] He continues: "The real content of revelation in the Bible is not 'something,' but *God* Himself. Revelation is the self-manifestation of God. The real revelation, that is, the revelation with which the whole Bible is concerned, is God's self-manifestation."[13] And still further: "... by 'revelation' [the Bible] does not mean a supernaturally revealed doctrine; nor does it equate 'revelation' either with a collection of books or with one particular Book; in the Bible 'revelation' means God's mighty acts for man's salvation."[14] Thus Brunner refuses to identify revelation with the words of the Bible as such, gaining thereby (so he says) a dynamic, moving "accomplishing" revelation, rather than the "static" revelation of Orthodoxy which is bound to the Bible.

But these mighty acts which comprise Brunner's concept of revelation are always personal acts, for revelation is the personal encounter of two subjects in the "I-Thou" relation. God meets man in a truth-encounter; thus revelation is never one-way communication, never a monologue, but always a dialogue: "... revelation actually consists," so Brunner writes, "in the meeting of two subjects, the divine and the human, the self-communication of God to man. Jesus Christ is not 'revelation' when He is not recognized by anyone as the Christ, just as He is not the Redeemer if He does not redeem anyone.

---

[12]Emil Brunner, *Revelation and Reason*, translated by Olive Wyon (Philadelphia: Westminster, 1946), 8.

[13]Brunner, *Revelation and Reason*, 25.

[14]Brunner, *Revelation and Reason*, 118.

The Biblical doctrine of revelation means this transition from the divine to the human subject."[15] The point should be simply noted at this juncture that, for Brunner, for the act of revelation to actually occur, man is as essential in his role of recipient to the "possibility" of revelation as is God in the role of revealer.

Since revelation is conceived as a personal divine-human encounter, it is unique (*Einmalige*), absolute, transcendent, non-repeatable, and unverifiable by logic or science. "Revelation has always and everywhere the character of a sudden event.... But in the Bible alone is this sudden happening understood in an absolute sense, as the unique, as that which can never be repeated."[16]

Is this revelation historical? Does it occur in history in the same sense in which Napoleon's defeat at Waterloo took place in history? Brunner is convinced that revelation must not be so understood, for should revelation be so related to history, it would imbibe of all the relativity of the historian's history. Rather, Brunner explains the relation of revelation to history tangentially, that is, revelation touches history but does not enter into it. He writes: "When we have discovered what history really is, we realize that we cannot seek for the decisive within history."[17] "It is impossible to introduce the eternal into the chain of historical events as though it were a specially precious and magnificent pearl. The eternal as an event, the revelation, as such, *possesses no historical exension.*"[18] "The eternal in history, the revelation as the absolutely unique, *cannot be perceived in terms of historical extension.* Revelation is not the actual fact which is made known through history: the life of Jesus and the historical personality of Jesus – but the invisible secret of the Person of Jesus, hidden behind the veils of history and of human life, not the Christ after the flesh but the Christ after the Spirit, the 'Word made flesh'."[19] "The revelation of Christ is therefore absolutely decisive, for in it the non-historical, the eternal, breaks through into time at one point, and in so doing makes it a place of decision."[20] Now lest from this last quotation

---

[15]Brunner, *Revelation and Reason*, 33.

[16]Brunner, *Revelation and Reason*, 30-31.

[17]Brunner, *The Mediator*, translated by Olive Wyon (Philadelphia: Westminster 1947), 304.

[18]Brunner, *The Mediator*, 305 (italics mine).

[19]Brunner, *The Mediator*, 305.

[20]Brunner, *The Mediator*, 308

one conclude that he does indeed allow revelation to "enter into" time and thereby become historical, Brunner explains what he means by this "breaking through": "The 'breaking through' would be in reality ...'Supranaturalism' if we were here concerned with the insertion of a new supernatural 'section'. But in so far as the 'breaking through' does not in any way result in any visible historical phenomenon, but only in the mystery of the Person of Christ on the one hand and in faith in this mystery on the other, it does not lead to the isolation of a 'section' of eternity in the midst of time, which indeed would be supranaturalism in the bad sense. Hence it is so important to distinguish between the Christ *in* the flesh and the Christ *after* the flesh."[21]

If revelation is not the actual fact which is made known through history, but still it does "break through" and touch time, where does revelation actually occur and what is the precise relation of revelation to history? Brunner's answer is "primal history" (*Urgeschichte*) that he regards as actual occurrence that is related to our space-time world but yet does not lie within it. "The general character of our history as a whole is to be recognized only from the perspective of 'primal history'. The kernel of all history is this 'primal history', the time-space manifestation of which is that which the historian narrates for us as 'history'."[22] He further declares that the historian never sees real history, that is, primal history, but only the "after-history" (*Nachgeschichte*) that has primal history as its *prius*. It is as when "he sees the tree that is struck by lightning, never the stroke of lightning itself."[23] In the light of these remarks, it is clear that Brunner sees revelation as a personal encounter of God with man which lies not in history but rather behind and touching history and that determines history.

The foregoing may be regarded as Brunner's fundamental conception of revelation. This notion will now be placed in sharper relief by a discussion of the "Christ event". In his analysis of Brunner's Christ event Cobb writes: "Revelation is the all-inclusive category for God's saving work; this work always takes place in the self-disclosure

---

[21]Brunner, *The Mediator*, 308.

[22]Cited by Paul King Jewett, *Emil Brunner's Concept of Revelation* (London: James Clarke, 1954), 25.

[23]Brunner, *The Philosophy of Religion from the Standpoint of Protestant Theology*, translated by Farrer and Woolf (New York: Charles Scribner's and Sons, 1937), 121.

of personal encounter; and this encounter never occurs except through the person of Jesus Christ."[24] In other words, as Cobb has correctly perceived, Jesus Christ is for Brunner the point of contact in the divine-human encounter: God meets man in the act of revelation in Jesus Christ and, in a "saving" way, nowhere else. Since revelation is dynamic and not static, for Brunner the revelational encounter between God and man in Christ in a very real sense is an "event", hence the term "Christ event". Thus revelation, viewed most sharply, is "God's action in Jesus Christ".[25]

But what is the relationship of this Christ in Brunner's Christ event with Jesus of Nazareth? When Brunner talks of God's revealing himself to man in Jesus Christ, does he mean by that what Orthodoxy has traditionally meant by that statement? In light of what has been said earlier regarding the relationship (as Brunner sees it) of revelation to history, it should be obvious that he does *not* equate the Christ event with Jesus of Nazareth or with the Jesus Christ of Orthodoxy. In fact, Brunner declares: "The question whether Jesus ever existed will always hover upon the margin of history as a possibility, in spite of the protests of the theologians.... Even the bare fact of the existence of Christ as an historical person is not assured. It would be a good thing once for all to admit this consequence of (necessary) historical relativism."[26] And in a footnote to this remark, he continues: "That [the existence of Jesus of Nazareth] is less certain historically, than that of Caesar, for instance, is in no wise accidental. It is only attested by those whom it actually concerns, and this means: the believers."[27]

With regard to the Virgin Birth narratives, Brunner devotes two long sections in *The Mediator* (322-27) and his *Dogmatics* (II, 352-56) to a denial of this "theory", contending that the New Testament's affirmation of it "has ... helped to 'mingle unwisely with one another' the historical and pneumatical elements".[28] Besides, "if the idea of a Virgin Birth had really meant anything to the Apostle Paul he would hardly have laid so much stress on the fact that Christ was 'born of a woman' as an element which He shared with all other human beings, and on His origin from the 'seed of David'."[29]

---

[24]Cobb, *Living Options*, 161.
[25]Brunner, *Revelation and Reason*, 10.
[26]Brunner, *The Mediator*, 187.
[27]Brunner, *The Mediator*, 187.
[28]Brunner, *The Mediator*, 187.

Then perhaps the revelation in the Christ event should be identified with Jesus' teaching? No, says Brunner: "What Jesus said if it be taken by itself, is just as far from being the revelation, the Gospel, as His historical personality, the picture of His life and of His inner life taken by itself is the revelation."[30]

Perhaps then the revelatory act is the atonement? Not so, says Brunner: "The atonement is not history [*Historie*]. The Atonement, the expiation of human guilt, the covering of sin through His sacrifice, is not anything which can be conceived from the point of view of history. This does not belong on the historical plane. It is super-history; it lies in the dimension which no historian knows in so far as he is merely an historian. It is an 'event' which is only an 'event' for faith. That it actually happened faith alone knows. It is not a fact which has its place in world history. It would be absurd to say: in the year 30 the Atonement of the world took place. But we can say: This event, which those who know history tell us probably took place about the year 30, is the same as that which we know through faith as the Divine Act of Atonement."[31]

Then perhaps the resurrection? To this query, Brunner rejoins: "... we cannot imagine what the Resurrection of Jesus means. It is as invisible, as unthinkable, as the Incarnation."[32] Assuming this attitude because of what he imagines as inconsistencies in the New Testament reporting of this event, he contends: "Whoever asserts that the New Testament gives us a definite consistent account of the Resurrection is either ignorant or unconscientious."[33] And on and on Brunner goes, denying the historicity of the post-resurrection ministry of Jesus Christ[34] and his bodily ascension into heaven.[35] Thus with no specific event in the life of Jesus of Nazareth will Brunner equate the revelatory act of God. This seems very strange and yet it is no misrepresentation of Brunner. He simply refuses to identify the Christ event, or the divine-human encounter between God and the individual, with the historical as such. Rather he insists that the actual event itself be consistently

---

[29]Brunner, *The Mediator*, 361.

[30]Brunner, *The Mediator*, 429.

[31]Brunner, *The Mediator*, 504-05.

[32]Brunner, *The Mediator*, 573.

[33]Brunner, *The Mediator*, 577.

[34]Emil Brunner, *Dogmatics* (Philadelphia: Westminster, 1956), II, 373.

[35]Brunner, *Dogmatics*, 373-76, 377.

kept outside the range of history [*Historie*] in primal history [*Urgeschichte*], a relationship which Brunner expresses by the phrase "Christ *in* the flesh" but not "Christ *after* the flesh."

As primal history Christ touches time but does not enter into time: "... He can be known only 'in the flesh' but not 'after the flesh'. This distinction is only another way of expressing this unique fact, which, while it is really and truly historical, yet transcends all historical barriers. Historical actuality is the way in which the Eternal Divine Word, as the Eternal Son, touches the historical world. This actuality means a real entrance into the historical mode of existence, but so far as its significance is concerned this entrance merely touches the fringe of existence."[36]

With such a construction of the relation of the Christ event to Jesus of Nazareth, Brunner actually sees a sharp disjunction between, and rigidly applies an unbending dichotomous attitude toward, eternity and time and God and man. *Urgeschichte* is absolute; *Historie* is relative.

Since this is so, Brunner contends, the Christ must be viewed as *incognito* in Jesus. And this, it may now be seen, is the real relationship, as Brunner conceives it, existing between the Christ event and Jesus of Nazareth. The Christ event is there all right; there is no denying it. But Christ is there *incognito*. With nothing in the life of Jesus may he be identified. He is there but not in history; rather he is there *behind* the historical Jesus in primal history. Only by this manner of viewing things is Brunner convinced that room is made for faith; only by this manner of viewing things is Brunner convinced that the absoluteness of the revelation can be retained and spared the relativity of our earthly existence. He writes: "The personality of God is 'most hidden yet most manifest,' that is, it is revealed to faith alone in the disguise [*Inkognito*] of an historical personality, which as such, as a phenomenon which can be recognized within the sphere of history, is precisely not the true personality, namely, the personality divine."[37] He continues: "The Person is ... the Word, the Revelation, the personal Presence.... But this Person is not the historical personality who can be perceived as such. The historical personality who can be perceived is the incognito under which the Person is concealed."[38] And again:

---

[36]Brunner, *The Mediator*, 156-57.
[37]Brunner, *The Mediator*, 270.

"Jesus Christ has not imparted Himself directly, in order that the decision to which He calls us may be really the decision of faith. The category of this life – in contrast with every other life – is mystery, in the essential fundamental meaning of the word, the 'incognito'. Only because the deity of Christ appears in the incognito of His humanity is it possible to have a relation of faith toward Him, a real decision."[39] Thus the Christ event is, for Brunner, a Paradox: it is at one and the same instant a complete revelation and a complete veiling. "As a revelation it is complete because a real personal approach can only take place through a real person whom we meet personally. As a veiling, however, it is complete, because to us there is nothing more ordinary, less striking, more familiar, than a human person like ourselves, thus the very opposite of something which must first of all be given unto us."[40]

At this point the reader perhaps is baffled by what appears to be contradictory: a Christ *in* the flesh but not *after* the flesh, a Christ event that wholly reveals God yet wholly conceals him, a Christ who touches time yet does not actually enter time. And all this in the interest of real decision? It is difficult, when one remembers that Brunner has drunk deeply at the metaphysical spring of Kantian thought, not to simply see here a Kantian interpretation of Christianity. Has he not simply followed Kant and even for some of the same reasons made a distinction between reality (the noumenal world) and appearance (the phenomenal world), positing all of the so-called events of redemption in the former? One may seriously question whether this is the *biblical* representation of the matter! But before any real criticism is made of Brunner's thought, the analysis must continue with Brunner's view of the relationship in which the Bible stands to this Christ event. Does he think he is being biblical? What is his view of the Bible?

Brunner's View of the Bible

Throughout his writings Brunner heaps disdain upon orthodoxy for its verbal plenary view of inspiration. The equation of the words of the Bible with the words of God is "actually a breach of the Second Commandment: it is the deification of a creature, bibliolatry."[41]

---

[38]Brunner, *The Mediator*, 271.
[39]Brunner, *The Mediator*, 337.
[40]Brunner, *The Mediator*, 333-34.

Because orthodoxy will not admit the validity of the "assured results" of biblical criticism, it fails to see what is so clear to Brunner, namely (among other things) that Genesis 1–11 is a late Priestly production; the creation story, the fall of man, the flood, and the Babel incident being myths or representations of religious truths under the inadequate form of historical events; that Wellhausen's view – first the Prophets and then the Law – as a whole is true; that Isaiah is not a unity but the work of several writers; that the Virgin Birth stories are legendary; that the resurrection narratives are hopelessly in conflict; that the Gospel of John is not an historical source; and that the Pauline Pastorals are late. Such results in the fields of higher and lower criticism constitute the main reason, contends Brunner, that, regardless of where they may go in the future, theologians can never return to orthodoxy.

On biblical doctrine Brunner writes the following: "[Revelation] is not a doctrine which is the object of faith, but Jesus Christ Himself. The doctrine is only a means which serves to lead us to Him, and therefore it is never infallible."[42] "Doctrine is only a pointer, though it may be a clear and useful pointer. Therefore faith is not directed to it, but its skims past, as it were, like a ball from the barrel of a gun, toward a goal."[43] "God's Word is not a doctrine, but it is the self-manifestation of Christ which is accomplished through the instrument of the doctrinal message."[44] And finally, "The revelation of God must be told, not taught; the doctrine only has validity as a means of serving the 'telling' of the Good News. Where narrative is replaced by doctrine, Greek thought triumphs over the thought of the Bible."[45]

Brunner discerns not just one system of doctrine but several within the covers of the Bible, which serve to correct each other. "There is a Synoptic, a Pauline, and a Johaninne type of doctrine; each differs considerably from the other, and no theological art reduces them to the same common denominator. What they all have in common is this: He Himself, Jesus Christ, is the Word of God; He is the center of their testimony; but their witness to Him, their particular doctrines, whether according to Matthew, or Paul, or John, are like radii which point toward this center from different angles, while none of them

---

[41]Brunner, *Revelation and Reason*, 120.
[42]Brunner, *Revelation and Reason*, 156.
[43]Brunner, *Revelation and Reason*, 156.
[44]Brunner, *Revelation and Reason*, 150.
[45]Brunner, *Revelation and Reason*, 201.

actually reaches the goal."[46] "Between the Synoptic Gospels and the Fourth Gospel, as well as between the teaching of Jesus and that of the Apostles, there is a great, and indeed, a radical difference. In my opinion, this is the most important result of the whole work of Biblical criticism."[47] He continues: "...the Epistle of James contributes something to our knowledge of Christ that we should not gain from Paul alone, and which, so far as Paul is concerned, is not only complementary, but also acts as a corrective. Every Apostle needs to be complemented and corrected by the others."[48] He sees, similarly, many "theologies" in the Old Testament as well.[49]

If all this is so, and Brunner thinks it is, then one may well wonder just what value Brunner places on the Bible. Just what is the relationship between this badly confused body of writing and the Christ event. Biblical orthodoxy in the past believed, and still so believes, that all that one knows authoritatively about Christ must be gathered from Scripture. But if the Scriptures are hopelessly uncertain about what did actually happen during a specific period of thirty or so years approximately two millennia ago, can one then be certain about the truth-content of the Christ event? Brunner replies in the affirmative, averring that the resolution of the imagined problem lies in an understanding of the real value of the Bible and of faith itself.

Brunner never tires of quoting Luther's remark to the effect that the Scriptures are the crib in which Christ is laid. The Scriptures are, in a remote or secondary form, revelation.[50] Though it is not, itself, the primary revelation, the Bible is a trustworthy "pointer" to the primary revelation or Christ event. "The Bible is the word of God because in it, so far as He chooses, God makes known the mystery of His will, of His saving purpose in Jesus Christ."[51] The Bible is the Word of God in those places where it bears witness to the Word, that is, where it is a Word-bearer, but "we cannot maintain that everything that is Biblical – not even everything in the New Testament – is in the same way, or to the same extent, the 'bearer' of the Word of God."[52] But in spite of

---

[46]Brunner, *Revelation and Reason*, 129.
[47]Brunner, *Revelation and Reason*, 288.
[48]Brunner, *Revelation and Reason*, 290.
[49]Brunner, *Revelation and Reason*, 291.
[50]Brunner, *Revelation and Reason*, 132.
[51]Brunner, *Revelation and Reason*, 135.

all the Bible's inadequacies, Brunner is still prepared to affirm (and it must be in the light of such remarks as these just quoted that one must understand his affirmation): "Just as no one can come to the Father save through the Son, so also it is true that no one can come to the Son save through the Holy Scriptures."[53] This is so because the Scriptures, and only the Scriptures, are the crib wherein the Christ is laid.

If his mere affirmation that the Bible is a trustworthy witness to the Christ event is not convincing to his reader, Brunner is quite sure that with a proper understanding of faith, any lingering doubts which his reader might still entertain will be dispelled.

Brunner's Concept of Faith

The divine side of the divine-human encounter Brunner certainly sees as the Word of God to man in the Person of Jesus Christ. But what is its correlate on the human side? If the human side is essential to the encounter (and Brunner thinks it is), how is the encounter effected or appropriated by the human element? With these questions we are brought to Brunner's discussion of faith. *In nuce*, the human response to the revelatory Word on the divine side is faith.

How faith arises Brunner admits is an impossible proposition to answer fully. "How the heart of man opens to receive the Word of God, and *how* the reason receives and understands the Word, is as mysterious as the incarnation of the Son of God."[54] However, this realization should not, Brunner feels, exempt the theologian from the necessity of making an effort to understand as much of it as he can. Therefore, he feels some analysis is in order.[55]

When the eternal in the form of the divine Word in the Person of Jesus Christ confronts man, that historical moment is thereby raised, Brunner declares, to the moment of decision. The man who has been confronted knows in that moment nothing of a "still-having-time, of not yet." He knows he must decide in that moment. (This *necessity* on the part of the human element to decide is the basis of Brunner's

---

[52]Brunner, *Revelation and Reason*, 129.

[53]Brunner, *Revelation and Reason*, 136.

[54]Brunner, *Revelation and Reason*, 415.

[55]Brunner, *Revelation and Reason*, 415.

ethics.) And the instant in which he, confronted with the divine Word, decides, is the *moment [Augenblick]*, or as Jewett writes, the place where an "atom of eternity" has pierced time.[56]

But this is only descriptive; what is faith's (or decision's) explanation? Brunner is sure that in that moment of decision, man has not simply made an affirmative choice; rather he hears of *Krisis*, that is, he learns that his whole existence stands under the judgment of God. The subjective side of *Krisis* is *Angst* (dread), or the feeling of not being at home in the universe. *Angst* leads him to the moment in which man must make a decision *[Entscheidung]*. Of course, men may accept or reject the voice of God (Brunner unequivocally rejects any doctrine of predestination that denies to man the final authority and responsibility for how he reacts to God's offer), but by *faith* some men become willing to cast aside all assurance of sense perception, mathematical proof, and logical consistency, and to *decide* for the Word to them in free venture, risking all on the personal revelation which has come to them, of course, individually.

Brunner is perfectly aware, as are all of the "encounter theologians," that such a construction of things offers no objective certitude, but he cannot see how it can be otherwise, if true faith is actually to occur. "Where personal truth is concerned, proof is neither possible nor fitting. For this truth is both trust and decision: we must decide either for proof or for trust, either for rational evidence or for the evidence of personal encounter."[57] But just to the degree that there is no objective certitude, to the same degree the divine-human encounter gives subjective certitude. The experience itself is its own best and only proof. It is credible in itself (autopistic), suprarationalistic (not capable of rational analysis), and unique, not to be confused with any other human action. In short, the only proof for this Word-faith encounter is the encounter itself: "Truth is encounter; encounter is truth." "... when a believer is asked: Why do you believe that Jesus is the Christ?, he can only answer: Why should I not believe, since Jesus confronts me as the Christ, when He meets me...."[58]

Faith, then, can have only one proper object – a Person who ever remains Subject, Jesus Christ. "... faith is not a relation to 'something',

---

[56]Jewett, *Brunner's Concept of Revelation*, 50.

[57]Brunner, *Revelation and Reason,* 179.

[58]Brunner, *Dogmatics*, II, 255.

to an idea, a truth, or a doctrine – not even a 'divinely revealed' doctrine – but it is wholly a personal relationship....'[59] "The sole object of faith is Jesus Christ, God in His personal revelation. The 'object of faith is not a general truth, not a timeless and nonhistorical metaphysic, but the Person of Christ;...' Faith, therefore, 'has one sole aim, not a variety of doctrines, but one only, which faith, in its universal application, apprehends with increasing clarity'. Faith is 'solely our relation to Jesus'."[60]

What are the "results" of the Word-faith encounter? First, the individual is transformed, which faith as intellectual assent fails to do. Second, he acknowledges the paradox of both the guilt and the forgiveness of sin.[61] "Man is far too profoundly a sinner to be able to admit his sin. That is the dialectic [paradox] of repentance: that man admits his true and vital need, the need which lies in himself, and which he could know himself only when he is no longer in this distress."[62] Third, he becomes a "contemporary" of Christ. "The revelation in Jesus Christ produces the illumination in my heart and mind, so that I can now see what I could not see before, and what so many are unable to see: that this man is the Christ. Suddenly, all the barriers of time and space have faded away; I have become 'contemporary' with Christ, as much His 'contemporary' as Peter was, though Caiaphas, who cross-examined Him, was never His contemporary (in this sense)."[63] And fourth, for him the scandal and offense of the Cross is removed. For an understanding of the Cross "the historical imagination is no help at all; for the better it functions, the more clearly do we perceive the 'scandal and folly'. Sympathetic 'feeling' and deep human understanding do not help us here, for I cannot understand the message of the Cross, as the Bible means it, from my point of view.... For the Cross and its meaning ... is unique, never to be repeated, and therefore far above all human analogies; it can never be understood along the lines of intellectual argument."[64] But when faith has occurred, "at that moment when man's sense of

---

[59]Brunner, *Revelation and Reason*, 36.

[60]Brunner, *Revelation and Reason*, 36-37.

[61]Brunner, *Dogmatics*, III, 292-93.

[62]Brunner, *Revelation and Reason*, 425.

[63]Brunner, *Revelation and Reason*, 170.

[64]Brunner, *Revelation and Reason*, 166.

autonomous independence vanishes there dawns upon him the meaning of God's self-revelation and self-giving in Jesus Christ; at the moment when the pride of self breaks down, the message of Christ ceases to be 'folly' and 'scandal'."[65]

Brunner's entire thought is grounded in this divine-human encounter. God acts in a redemptive way by revealing himself to man in the Person of Jesus Christ. Man responds in faith to this voice from God, thereby "completing the circuit". Though he cannot (and would not if he could) offer any objective evidence for the truth-content of the encounter, the involved individual is nonetheless certain of the encounter, for "encounter is truth". Faith works transformation, the confession of guilt and the reception of forgiveness, contemporaneity with Christ, and the removal of the "scandal" of Christianity in the believer. All else that Brunner has to say is grounded in this dialectical relationship between God and man.

Criticism

In his construction of the revelational problem, Brunner obviously sees the theologian's main task as that of successfully grappling with the relation of eternity to time.[66] "Brunner's basic assumptions ... are the following. History, as such, is the sphere of the relative. Revelation on the other hand is the communication of absolute truth. The problem is, how to preserve the Christian concept of an historic revelation against a mystical or idealistic negation of history, without involving oneself in historical relativism."[67] The answer, as Brunner conceives it, is the Kierkegaardian dialectic of eternity and time in which no direct identity between revelation and history, that is, no predication of absolute significance to any event in time and space, is permitted. Like a tangent to a circle, revelation *touches* time but does not *enter* it in an extension.

Jewett makes several telling criticisms of Brunner at this juncture, for after an impeccably sound discussion in which he demonstrates

---

[65]Brunner, *Revelation and Reason*, 173.

[66]For the following criticism of Brunner's concepts of the paradox of time and eternity and the truth-content in the divine-human encounter, I am indebted to Jewett's monograph on Brunner's concept of revelation and heartily commend it to the reader.

[67]Jewett, *Brunner's Concept of Revelation*, 140.

that Brunner is unable to carry this approach out in practice,[68] he then demonstrates that Brunner is unable to carry it out even in thesis.[69] To this demonstration we now turn.

When Paul Althaus complained that Brunner "had defined the Jesus event too narrowly for the minimal interests of faith", Brunner conceded that "the picture of the story of Jesus is of fundamental importance for our faith. The line of absolute withdrawal which Kierkegaard tries to set up as one that cannot be touched lies too far behind the lines of the actual encounter with Christ to do justice to faith. [There is a definite] necessity of the stories of Jesus for leading people to the Christian faith ..."[70] To this concession Jewett rejoins: "If it be true that it belongs to the *essence* of the Christian concept of faith 'that the *divine* revelational presence be set in antithesis to the world ...' then, as Brunner himself repeatedly asserted in *Der Mittler*, all discussion about the empirical extent of the Jesus event is immaterial to faith. When he subsequently concedes that Kierkegaard defined the ground of faith too narrowly and proceeds to extend the historical basis of faith, this does not constitute a *corrective* to his Kierkegaardian dialectical approach, but a repudiation of it. This much ought to be made emphatically clear, that one cannot expand the point at which a 'perpendicular from above' bifurcates the horizontal plane of history, nor the vortex of a parabola. Points are *per definitionem* without extension. An extended point is no longer a point. In trying to do the impossible, Brunner has altered the face of the whole problem."[71] Jewett concludes, therefore, that "this leaves the issue right where it was when the dialectical theologians appeared on the scene; that is to say, either Jesus was the kind of person described in the Gospel tradition or else Christianity is a mistake ... the dialectical approach has not proven a successful instrument in getting above the Orthodox-Liberal antithesis. 'If history is given its right, then the dialectic must disappear. If the dialectic triumphs, however, then one can no longer talk about a historical revelation.'"[72]

But Brunner's troubles are not over simply with his inability to

---

[68] Jewett, *Brunner's Concept of Revelation*, 140.

[69] Jewett, *Brunner's Concept of Revelation*, 142.

[70] Brunner, *Revelation and Reason*, 284, footnote 21.

[71] Jewett, *Brunner's Concept of Revelation*, 144.

[72] Jewett, *Brunner's Concept of Revelation*, 145-46.

retain his Christianity as long as he persists in a dialectical construction of it. He cannot consistently show that even the divine-human encounter, wherein the apprehension of truth is alleged to be subjectively certain, yields truth for sure. Though he claims that "something which, to the historian is only a point of relative certainty in the historical continuum, is absolutely certain to faith in an entirely different way,"[73] he cannot explain how this can be. For example, Brunner argues that "the Gospel writers did not intend to give us a scientific biography, but rather to tell us who Jesus was as seen by the eye of resurrection faith. He calls the Christ whom the historian sees 'the Christ after the flesh'."[74] A critical problem, however, arises for Brunner when, while having to admit that if any ever did behold the Christ by faith, it was the apostolic witness, he has to likewise admit, because of the "assured results" of Biblical criticism, that their witness was a witness with only "more or less historical fidelity". In fact, as we saw earlier, he feels he must describe the respective witnesses of Matthew, Paul, John, and the other New Testament writers as "radii which point toward this center from different angles; while none of them actually reaches the goal." In short, as Jewett strikingly states: " ... not only is the picture of the critical historian defective, because lacking the dimension of the transcendental, but so also is the picture of faith."[75] It may be legitimately asked, where is the certainty in the Word-faith event?

Certain other attitudes of Brunner are equally problematical to the orthodox theologian. At least in the area of communication, God, according to Brunner's construction, needs man as much as man needs God in salvation. God cannot reveal himself unless man apprehends the revelation, and the decision to apprehend the revelation remains ultimately man's decision. Man has it in his power, then, to render God a deaf mute, a God who can act but who cannot reveal his act. This does away with a God-in-himself and substitutes a God-for-man. No longer is there an ontological Trinity; rather, only a functional or economical Trinity remains.

Nor can the truly Reformed Christian have anything at all to do with any theology which grants to man the final authority and

---

[73]Cited by Jewett, *Brunner's Concept of Revelation*, 151.
[74]Jewett, *Brunner's Concept of Revelation*, 153-54.
[75]Jewett, *Brunner's Concept of Revelation*, 154.

responsibility for how he responds to the divine offer of salvation. He knows that the unbeliever is made a partaker of the redemption purchased by Christ by the effectual application of it to him by the Holy Spirit of God (*Westminster Shorter Catechism*, Q. 29), that the Spirit of God works faith in the unbeliever, thereby uniting him to Christ in his effectual calling (*Catechism*, Q. 30), and that effectual calling is solely the work of God's Spirit, whereby the unbeliever is persuaded and enabled to embrace Jesus Christ as he is freely offered to him in the gospel (*Catechism*, Q. 31). Moreover, the truly Reformed Christian knows that it could not be otherwise, for he is well aware that the unbeliever is spiritually dead in trespasses and sins (Eph. 2:1), that is, he is incapable, in himself, of correctly comprehending anything spiritual (Rom. 1:21-22; 3:11; 1 Cor. 1:20-21; 2:14; Eph. 4:17-19).

Of course, he knows, on the other hand, that Paul does not deny that all men, as men, have an innate knowledge of God's existence. Indeed, Paul affirms that all men do know God, though not in a saving way (*gnontes ton theon*, Rom. 1:21), that all men know experientially God's ordinance that the sinner is worthy of death (*dikaiōma tou theou epignontes*, Rom. 1:32), and that all men "show the work of the law written in their hearts, their conscience bearing witness" (Rom. 2:15). Does Paul mean by these words that men may in themselves respond to God's call? The Reformed Christian is certain that Paul should not be so understood, for Paul is equally insistent that the unbeliever, although he knows all these things in the deepest recesses of his heart, cannot face this knowledge squarely, because to become genuinely *God*-conscious would require his becoming at the same moment epistemologically *self*-conscious. And since genuine self-consciousness is identical with *covenant*-consciousness, attendant upon such self-consciousness is the realization of his own creaturehood, his apostasy from the Creator, his guilt before God, and the justice of divine retribution upon his sin. Consequently, though revelation streams into man's consciousness from nature continually (Rom. 1:20; cf. Ps. 19:1) and though man, made in the image of God, is himself revelational of the Deity to himself, *since it is no longer his nature to own this revelation, the natural man suppresses* (*katechontōn*) *this truth through his own unrighteousness* (Rom. 1:18). Why then would man respond any differently when encountered by the Christ of Brunner's Christ event unless he be *compelled* to respond, an affirmation which Brunner is not prepared to make? Would he not just as assuredly suppress this revelation as well? Beyond controversy, any revelation which comes to the unregenerate man apart from the irresistible grace of God will be immediately suppressed. Thus at this point too, Brunner's theology, when compared with the teaching of Scripture, is found deficient and sub-Christian.

Finally, Brunner's refusal to identify the saving acts of God with any particular fact or event of the Incarnation should be regarded as dangerous in the extreme to the gospel of the grace of God and must be rejected by a genuinely Christian theism. A gospel whose Christ did not actually take to himself a true body and a reasonable soul, that is, did not actually become incarnate; whose Christ did not live obediently under the law, thereby obtaining a righteousness which is peculiarly fitted to man's need and which could be imputed to man through faith; whose Christ did not actually die a vicarious death for the sins of his own on a specific calendar day on a particular hill outside of Jerusalem some two thousand years ago; whose Christ did not literally and bodily leave the tomb on the third day after death; whose Christ did not literally and bodily ascend into heaven after his resurrection, there to intercede in behalf of those for whom he died – such a gospel is no gospel at all! A gospel whose Christ is a phantom, whose cross is merely a symbol, and whose resurrection occurs only in primal history but not in our history simply has no salvation in it! As J. Gresham Machen said many years ago, even the simple biblical statement, "Christ died for our sins," includes both history and theology. "Christ died" – that is history; "for our sins" – that is theology. And both must be retained in the fullest sense of their respective meanings if the gospel as the life-giving channel of the grace of God is to be maintained.

Brunner's problems all stem from his refusal to admit the existence of objective truth in the inscriptured revelation of God and his correlative definition of truth in terms of subjectivity or inwardness. As we have seen, Brunner believes that the religious encounter is credible in itself, that it is so self-validating to the one involved that it is its own basis for credibility. The writers of Scripture, however, never define truth in such a manner or by such a criterion. Truth is, for them, primarily objective, coming to man *ab extra*, found ultimately in the ontological Trinity and the incarnate Son of God and derivatively in the written Word of God, the Holy Scriptures. God is, to them, no deaf mute who acts but cannot, or at least does not, speak. Quite to the contrary, the biblical God is light in himself and his Word gives light to all. Furthermore, their conception of the nature of revelation, though not exhausted by it, clearly allows for the existence of revealed propositional truths. Revelation may take the form of declarative, imperative, interrogative, and interjectional sentences. The Bible is replete with the notion that behind the words of Scripture is the God who revealed himself to man and then superintended the recording of that revelation so closely that the written product was rendered inerrant (not liable to be false or mistaken) and infallible (not liable to the teaching of error). The alleged indisputable results of Biblical criticism, when closely examined, are not as problematical as they might seem (though admittedly problems will always remain), and the proffered lists of alleged Scriptural discrepancies are embarrassingly archaic. Most have been grappled with with a high degree of successful harmonization (in the minds of many scholars) and are consequently regarded as inconsequential. Certainly none seems so compelling that the Scripture's claim for itself must *necessarily* be relinquished. This, of course, Brunner is unable to accept. Consequently, Brunner who would seek, above all else, to have a "theology of the Word" has, in reality, no Word from heaven at all since he rejects the objective written revelation of God, the Sacred Scriptures. Though a man of massive breadth of learning, a man of unquestionably great intellectual and literary achievement, Brunner is unable to overcome a very poorly defined and colorless Christ event, about which, as soon as he says anything at all, he must speak in biblical terms, terms the truthfulness of which he is not at all sure. Biblical orthodoxy is convinced that it has something far more trustworthy, pistically speaking, and satisfying, epistemologically speaking, than this in its Word become flesh, set forth in an inspired, inerrant Scripture.

Chapter Seventeen

Barth's Doctrines of Election and Reconciliation

Karl Barth (1886–1968), born in Basel, Switzerland, was educated at the Universities of Berne (under his father, a New Testament theologian), Berlin (under Adolf von Harnack, the Ritschlian church historian), and Marburg (under Wilhelm Herrmann). During the second decade of the twentieth century he pastored a church in Safenwil, Switzerland, becoming there increasingly disenchanted with his liberal theological training because of the backing that his mentors had given to the military policy of Kaiser Wilhelm II and because of the fact of World War I itself. Between 1915 and 1919 Barth and Eduard Thurneysen, an intimate friend and also a pastor, re-evaluated their theology, the result of Barth's research being his *Römerbrief.* Therein, besides the Bible, was the influence of Kierkegaard, Overbeck, and Dostoievski. During the 1920s, that may be regarded as the decade of his existentialist approach to theology, Barth taught at the Universities of Göttingen and Münster. The year 1927 saw the publication of the first (and only) volume of his *Christian Dogmatics*, an effort which he later began anew and replaced with his monumental *Church Dogmatics*. From 1930 to 1934 he taught at the University of Bonn, at the end of which time he returned to his home town of Basel and taught there in the University until his retirement in 1961. The last years of his life witnessed an amazing literary creativity, his unfinished *Church Dogmatics* eventually filling thirteen large volumes in English translation. In 1962 he visited the United States for the first time under the auspices of Chicago Divinity School and Princeton Theological Seminary.

In addition to his *Dogmatics*, he authored some forty or fifty books and several hundred articles covering a wide range of topics, many of a non-theological nature.

Books about Barth of interest to the American reader are Gerrit

---

Note: This article first appeared as a monograph published by Presbyterian and Reformed in 1967.

C. Berkouwer's *The Triumph of Grace in the Theology of Karl Barth*, Cornelius Van Til's *The New Modernism* and *Christianity and Barthianism*, Gordon H. Clark's *Karl Barth's Theological Method*, Fred Klooster's *The Significance of Barth's Theology*, and A.D.R. Polman's *Barth*. Neoorthodox treatments of Barth which are also valuable are those by Torrance, Weber, and Come.

Barth is regarded by many theologians today as the foremost twentieth-century voice on the theological scene. Certainly in creativity and originality his peers are few indeed. Though their opinion could be seriously debated, some qualified thinkers even see him as continuing the line of orthodoxy extending from Paul and running through Augustine and Anselm, Luther and Calvin.

This prominence is no doubt due primarily to the fact that Barth spearheaded the theological revolt in the 1920s against classical Liberalism and to the fact that he refused to be silent throughout his long career but continued to speak to the world's leading theologians through his *Church Dogmatics*, the publication of which spanned some thirty-five years since the appearance of the first instalment in 1932. This time factor has led Cobb and many others to insist that Barth "needs to be understood in terms of the development of his thought",[1] though Cobb admits that throughout Barth's literary activity lies a profound consistency. T. F. Torrance distinguishes between a critical liberal period prior to the third decade of the twentieth century, an existential period in the 1920s, and then a post-existential period in which (so he says) Barth has repudiated any and all reliance upon philosophy.[2] Of course, it is true that Barth's *Römerbrief* (1919) had refused to ground Christian faith in objective history and objective knowledge, this refusal rendering his dialectic theology wholly compatible with existential emphases and in broad early agreement with Bultmann's redirecting the dialectical approach until the latter insisted that the Christian faith demands no historical foundation other than the mere "thatness" of Jesus' existence and that the New Testament is to be understood only existentially. It is also true, of course, that to forestall any existential takeover of his position, Barth

---

[1] John B. Cobb, Jr., *Living Options in Protestant Theology* (Philadelpia: Westminster, 1962), 171.

[2] T. F. Torrance, "Karl Barth," *Ten Makers of Modern Protestant Thought*, edited by George Hunt, New York: Association Press, 1958), 59-63.

broke with Bultmann in the late 1920s and rejected existentialism in the 1932 *Church Dogmatics*, steadily adding since then "objectifying" elements to his theological structure.[3] But there are sound reasons for thinking that this much-discussed "development" has been greatly exaggerated and that Barth is still controlled today in his methodology by the presuppositions which bound his thinking in the second edition (1921) of his *Römerbrief*. In the Preface to the second quarter-volume of Volume IV of his *Dogmatics* (English translation published in 1956), Barth himself bears this conclusion when he writes: "... at the decisive points [evangelical groups] cannot fail to hear something of the rolling thunder of the 1921 *Romans*.... Perspicuous readers will surely notice that there is no break with the basic view which I have adopted since my parting from Liberalism."[4] Klooster views this development in Barth as one of *emphasis* mainly: Barth's resounding divine *No* upon man in his earlier writings only prepared the way for his even more resounding and final divine *Yes* in man's behalf in his later work.[5] It would appear that Klooster's analysis is correct. Consequently, direct regard for this development will not play a prominent role in the present discussion.

According to Barth, the two doctrines which are central to all the ways and works of God are election and reconciliation, the former because it is the sum and substance of the gospel and of all words that can be said it is the best, the latter because it is the center of all Christian knowledge.

Barth's Doctrine of Election

Barth's doctrine of election is found in the second half-volume of Volume II of the *Dogmatics*, which volume the *Union Seminary Quarterly* suggests "may turn out to be the most important volume in Karl Barth's massive *Church Dogmatics*".[6] Klooster reports: "After Barth spoke to a ministers' conference in Germany in 1949, the

---

[3]Carl F. H. Henry, "Cross-currents in Contemporary Theology," *Jesus of Nazareth: Saviour and Lord*, edited by Carl F. H. Henry (Grand Rapids: Eerdmans, 1966), 5-6.

[4]Karl Barth, *Church Dogmatics*, (edited and translated by G. T. Thomson, G. W. Bromiley, T. F. Torrance (Edinburgh: T. & T. Clark, 1956), IV/2, x.

[5]Fred Klooster, *The Significance of Barth's Theology* (Grand Rapids: Baker, 1961), 20.

[6]*Union Seminary Quarterly* (May, 1959), 55; cited by Klooster, 39.

response of some was that this doctrine of election gave them new joy in preaching."[7] How does Barth himself feel about his construction of this doctrine? He writes: "The work has this peculiarity, that in it I have had to leave the framework of theological tradition to a far greater extent than in the first part on the doctrine of God. I would have preferred to follow Calvin's doctrine of predestination much more closely, instead of departing from it so radically.... But I could not and cannot do so. As I let the Bible itself speak to me on these matters, as I meditated upon what I seemed to hear, I was driven irresistibly to reconstruction."[8] What importance does Barth place upon the doctrine of election in his "system"? He declares: "The doctrine of election is the sum of the Gospel because of all words that can be said or heard it is the best."[9] And still more to the point he affirms: "The election of grace is the sum of the Gospel – we must put it as pointedly as that. But more, the election of grace is the whole of the Gospel, the Gospel *in nuce*."[10]

The foundation of election

Barth begins his construction of election by rejecting tradition, experience, and any preconceived notion of God as proper bases for a truly Scriptural notion of election.[11] Rather, he declares: "... we must begin as we seek to be taught by the self-revelation of God attested by Holy Scripture."[12] Of course, he recognizes that the Reformers had sought to do the same thing: "We must not overlook the fact that these older theologians did read their Bible carefully, and that in the teaching they did intend to comment as we do on Romans 9–11 and other passages in the scriptural witness."[13] Why then does Barth feel that he must depart from their earlier teaching? In brief, Barth disagrees with the way that the Reformers read their Bibles. On this reading of the Bible Barth writes:

---

[7]Klooster, *The Significance of Barth's Theology*, 41, fn.

[8]Barth, *Church Domatics*, II/2, x.

[9]Barth, *Church Dogmatics*, 3.

[10]Barth, *Church Dogmatics*, 13-14.

[11]Barth, *Church Dogmatics*, 35, 38, 44.

[12]Barth, *Church Dogmatics*, 52.

[13]Barth, *Church Dogmatics*, 148.

The decisive point is the reading of the Bible itself. It is the question where and how we find in the Bible itself the electing God and the elected man, and therefore that reality of the divine election as a whole which must shape our thinking about the election and form the object of all our individual reflection and speech concerning it.[14]

How then does Barth read his Bible at this point? The Reformers read the Bible as a body of divinely revealed information about God's decrees, but this avenue of approach Barth is not willing to follow. Rather, Barth speaks of the "christological basis and starting point for the doctrine".[15] We will let Barth explain himself at this point:

... in the name and person of Jesus Christ we are called upon to recognize the Word of God, the decree of God and the election of God at the beginning of all things, at the beginning of our own being and thinking, at the basis of our faith in the ways and works of God.[16]

And he adds:

When it is a question of the understanding and exposition of what the Bible calls predestination or election, why and on what authority are we suddenly to formulate a statement which leaves out all mention of Jesus Christ? How is it that at this point there suddenly arises the possibility of looking elsewhere?[17]

Barth believes that there must be "a continuity between the christological centre and *telos* of the temporal work of God ... and the eternal presupposing of that work in the divine election."[18] What is the significance for Barth of this christological starting point for election? Klooster quite correctly answers: "Barth means to say that from the work of Jesus Christ one must be able to conclude backwards to a knowledge of the whole will of God."[19] He continues: "Since Jesus Christ came to save men, Barth concludes that God's will is the election and not the rejection of man."[20] Barth wonders "how could

---

[14]Barth, *Church Dogmatics*, 148.

[15]Barth, *Church Dogmatics*, 145.

[16]Barth, *Church Dogmatics*, 99.

[17]Barth, *Church Dogmatics*, 153.

[18]Barth, *Church Dogmatics*, 149.

[19]Klooster, 45.

[20]Klooster, 45.

one ever deduce a doctrine of reprobation from an analysis of the crucifixion and death of Jesus Christ? Obviously this was the work of grace..."[21] And so Barth strikes his hermeneutical note of Christomonism, which asserts that at every point the theologian who would be biblical must begin with Christ and Christ alone in the formulation of doctrine. Would the theologian wish to pronounce in the area of election? Then to be biblical, he must view election from Jesus Christ as God's expression of all his will, ways, and works. And it is this note that Barth consciously seeks to hear in all of his theological pronouncements. What are the results for his construction of election of Barth's rigid following of this hermeneutical procedure? To answer this question, we must turn to Barth's construction itself.

The election of Jesus Christ

Barth understands election to be primarily the election of Jesus Christ,[22] the genitive "of Jesus Christ" being taken here both subjectively and objectively. Barth rejects both the "covenant of redemption" and the "covenant of works" of traditional Reformed thought. Of the former he writes:

> Can we really think of the first and second persons of the triune Godhead as two divine subjects and therefore as two legal subjects who can have dealings and enter into obligations one with another? This is mythology, for which there is no place in a right understanding of the doctrine of the Trinity as the doctrine of the three modes of being of the one God.[23]

Of the latter he writes:

> There never was a golden age. There is no point in looking back to one. The first man was immediately the first sinner.[24]

Barth is left then with only *one covenant* (and this is what he was after all along) – the covenant of grace – and *one decree* – the decree of election of Jesus Christ. "In its simplest and most comprehensive form the dogma of predestination consists ... in the

---

[21]Klooster, 46.
[22]See Barth, *Church Dogmatics*, II/2, 94-194.
[23]Barth, *Church Dogmatics*, IV/1, 65.
[24]Barth, *Church Dogmatics*, 508.

assertion that the divine predestination is the election of Jesus Christ."[25] Claiming simply to follow John 1:1-2, Barth asserts:

> Jesus Christ was in the beginning with God. He was so not merely in the sense that in view of God's eternal knowing and willing all things may be said to have been in the beginning with God, in His plan and decree.... He was also in the beginning with God as ... Himself the plan and decree of God, Himself the divine decision with respect to all creation and its history whose content is already determined."[26]

This means, according to Barth, that *Jesus Christ is both the Electing God and the Elected Man:* "... of Jesus Christ we know nothing more surely and definitely than this – that in free obedience to His Father He elected to be man, and as man, to do the will of God."[27] As the Elected Man, "Jesus Christ is not merely one object of the divine good-pleasure side by side with others. On the contrary, He is the sole object of this good-pleasure."[28] Jesus Christ, then, is *the* God who does the electing, he is *the* man who is elected.

But such a construction has removed the double election of traditional Reformed theology, has it not? For where is the decree of reprobation pertaining to the non-elect? Barth agrees that the Reformers' construction of a double election is removed by this viewing of things, but he feels quite confident that a double object of election still remains, and this time the construction is a truly Biblical one. "In so far as [Jesus Christ] is the electing God, we must obviously ... ascribe to Him the active determination of electing," that is, the electing which is "the divine determination of the existence of Jesus Christ ..."[29] "In so far as He is man, the passive determination of election is also and necessarily proper to Him," that is, the election (the being elected) which is "the human [determination of the existence of Jesus Christ]."[30] Thus a double election – and Barth thinks this is the only double election which Scripture will tolerate – remains, namely, that God has "elected fellowship with man for Himself," and "fellowship

---

[25]Barth, *Church Dogmatics*, II/2, 103.
[26]Barth, *Church Dogmatics*, 104.
[27]Barth, *Church Dogmatics*, 105.
[28]Barth, *Church Dogmatics*, 104.
[29]Barth, *Church Dogmatics*, 103.
[30]Barth, *Church Dogmatics*, 103.

with Himself for man."[31] Furthermore, election has a new double content now. God has willed that he himself shall lose, that Christ will be reprobated, that the No of election concerns only himself, that for himself alone there is reprobation, perdition, and death. On the other hand, God has willed that man shall only gain, that man shall be elected, that the Yes of election concerns man, that for man there is only election, salvation and life. In short, "When we look into the innermost recesses of the divine good-pleasure," Barth writes, "predestination is the non-rejection of man. It is so because it is the rejection of the Son of God."[32]

A summary of Barth's doctrine up to this point may perhaps clarify Barth's thoughts concerning election. In his own words, "the simplest form of the dogma may be divided at once into the two assertions that Jesus Christ is the electing God, and that he is also elected man."[33] "Starting from John 1:1f., we have laid down and developed two statements concerning the election of Jesus Christ. The first is that Jesus Christ is the electing God. This statement answers the question of the subject of the eternal election of grace. And the second is that Jesus Christ is elected man. This statement answers the question of the object of the eternal election of grace. Strictly speaking, the whole dogma of predestination is contained in these two statements."[34]

Barth sees two chief values in his construction of election over that of the Reformers. *First*, the theologian is no longer dealing with unknown quantities, with abstractions; he is now dealing with the living electing God and with the living elected man. In the older interpretation of the doctrine, "ultimately and fundamentally the electing God is an unknown quantity," and "ultimately and fundamentally elected man is also an unknown quantity."[35] But now, says Barth, "our thesis that the eternal will of God is the election of Jesus Christ means that we deny the existence of any such twofold mystery."[36] He continues: "The thesis does avoid this twofold obscurity. It does give a single and known form to the unknown God and unknown man. The two together acquire one name and the name of one person...."[37]

---

[31]Barth, *Church Dogmatics*, 162.

[32]Barth, *Church Dogmatics*, 167.

[33]Barth, *Church Dogmatics*, 103.

[34]Barth, *Church Dogmatics*, 145.

[35]Barth, *Church Dogmatics*, 146.

[36]Barth, *Church Dogmatics*, 146.

Second, the theologian is done with the Reformers' *decretum absolutum* which involves, so Barth feels, a static view of God's relation to the universe, so that God himself becomes a prisoner of his own decree. Declares Barth: "The substitution of the election of Jesus Christ for the *decretum absolutum* is ... the decisive point in the amendment of the doctrine of predestination,"[38] and, continues Barth, "It is one of the great puzzles of history that the step which we are now taking towards a true form of the electing God and elected man was not taken long ago."[39] But with no hesitation Barth takes this step: "There is no such thing as a *decretum absolutum*. There is no such thing as a will of God apart from the will of Jesus Christ."[40] Calvinism was "pagan rather than Christian" because "it thought of predestination as an isolated and given enactment which God had decreed from all eternity and which to some extent pledged and committed even God Himself in time."[41] Barth elaborates further: "The point that we have to make against the older doctrine is this, that while in other respects it laid too great stress upon God's freedom, in this context it came very near to thinking of this freedom in such a way that in predestination God became His own prisoner."[42] And so Barth concludes: "At root, can there be anything more unchristian or anti-christian than the horror or the peace which is given by the thought of the *decretum absolutum* as the first and last truth from which everything else proceeds?"[43]

Having disposed of the Reformers" *decretum absolutum* by replacing it with the election of Jesus Christ, Barth is now prepared to draw out the full implications of his doctrine. "It is now possible and necessary for us to make the controversial assertion that predestination is the divine act of will itself and not an abstraction from or fixed and static result of it."[44] That is, Barth means to say that what we actually see Jesus Christ working out and doing in history is that which is predestinated, and not something else. "The order proclaimed in the

---

[37]Barth, *Church Dogmatics*, 147.
[38]Barth, *Church Dogmatics*, 161.
[39]Barth, *Church Dogmatics*, 147.
[40]Barth, *Church Dogmatics*, 115.
[41]Barth, *Church Dogmatics*, 181.
[42]Barth, *Church Dogmatics*, 184.
[43]Barth, *Church Dogmatics*, 158.
[44]Barth, *Church Dogmatics*, 181.

work of revelation and atonement must be regarded and respected as also the order of the divine predestination."[45] In short, predestination is itself history, encounter, and decision,[46] which is simply another way of saying in Barthian terminology that predestination is Jesus Christ. And this in turn makes Jesus Christ an "event" or an "act". States Barth:

> The fundamental significance of the character of predestination as act ought to be clear without further discussion. If it is unchanged and unchangeably the history, encounter and decision between God and man, there is in time an electing by God and an election of man, as there is also a rejecting by God and a rejection of man, but not in the sense that God Himself is bound and imprisoned by it, not as though God's decree, the first step which He took, committed Him to take a corresponding second step, and the second a third. If it is true that the predestinating God not only is free but remains free, that He does not cease to make use of His freedom but continues to decide, then in the course of God's eternal deciding we have constantly to reckon with new decisions in time. As the Bible itself presents the matter, there is no election which cannot be followed by rejection, no rejection which cannot be followed by election. God continues always the Lord of all His works and ways.[47]

And he concludes: "Ultimately there is only one reason that we can give for deciding in favor of an activist understanding, and that is that the predestination which we know in the person and work of Jesus Christ is undoubtedly event, the history, encounter and decision between God and man."[48]

What does this all mean? What precisely has Barth done by such a construction?

First, Barth has disposed of a decreeing God who is ontologically detached from this world. Or at least we can know nothing of such a God. The only decreeing God we can know is the God who continues to decree in time and who works in time as history, encounter, and decision. As far as our knowledge of a divine decree is concerned, it must be a knowledge related far more to time than to eternity.

Second, Barth has "activated" the Incarnation, that is, he conceives

---

[45] Barth, *Church Dogmatics*, 174.
[46] Barth, *Church Dogmatics*, 184.
[47] Barth, *Church Dogmatics*, 186.
[48] Barth, *Church Dogmatics*, 187.

of the Incarnation as an ongoing process by interpreting the person of Christ as his work. Christ, then, becomes an event. Or Jesus Christ, it can be said, is predestination, and nothing is predestined outside the work which Jesus Christ accomplishes. And what is this work? It is his electing to be man, and his election of himself to be both the Elect and the Reject. Of course, Barth is aware that Christ's Incarnation has been understood traditionally in an historical sense, namely, as referring to that time in human history when the Son of God took to himself a true body and reasonable soul in the person of Jesus of Nazareth. But with this understanding, Barth contends, the grace of God is bound to certain happenings in Palestine a good many years ago and cannot be the original relation of every man to God. But if Jesus Christ be regarded, not primarily as *Historie* (the kind of history that historians write), but primarily as *Geschichte* (revelational history which includes everything that exists and which makes human nature what it is because of its participation in *Geschichte*), then Christ's human nature will not be understood statically but as event. "In Jesus Christ it comes about that God takes time to Himself, that He Himself, the eternal One, becomes temporal, that He is present for us in the form of our existence and our own world, not simply embracing our time and ruling it, but submitting Himself to it, and permitting created time to be the form of His eternity."[49] *Geschichte* takes *Historie* up into itself, and Christ as the presence of God in *Geschichte* becomes event. Christ is *Geschichte*, and man is man because he participates in this *Geschichte*. The original relation of every man to God becomes thereby one of grace, for all men are related to Christ who is in his Incarnation *Geschichte*.

Third, in the interest of preserving God's freedom, Barth refuses to interpret the divine decreeing in any sense as inviolably fixed or unalterable. God continues to decree, new decisions actually making their appearances in time. We shall resist the temptation to comment upon Barth's construction at this juncture. Rather, we shall follow Barth's thought to discover what this election of Jesus Christ means for mankind.

---

[49]Barth, *Church Dogmatics*, II/1, 616.

The election of the community

Barth sees election as secondarily the election of the community.[50] "The election of grace, as the election of Jesus Christ, is simultaneously the eternal election of the one community of God."[51] Barth feels that the Reformers were too quick to deal with the election of the individual:

... if we keep to Holy Scripture, we find that unlike the classical doctrine of predestination it is in no hurry to busy itself with the 'many' men elected in Jesus Christ, either in the singular or plural. It does do this, of course, and we shall have to do so. But starting from the election of Jesus Christ it does not immediately envisage the election of the individual believer (and in this too we shall have to follow it), but in the first place a mediate and mediating election. The Subject of this is indeed God in Jesus Christ, and its particular object is indeed men. But it is these men as a fellowship elected by God in Jesus Christ and determined from all eternity for a peculiar service.[52]

The task of this elected community, as Barth understands it, is to attest to Jesus Christ before the whole world and to summon the world to faith in Jesus Christ.[53] It carries out this twofold task by its very *nature* and by its *message*.

What is the nature of this elected community? To answer this question, Barth turns to Romans 9–11 and, interpreting Paul existentially rather than historically as Paul intended to be understood, applies Israel and the Church to this elected community as two aspects or phases of the one community of God.

Commenting on Romans 9, Barth concludes that as Israel the community serves the representation of the divine judgment; as the Church it serves the representation of the divine mercy.[54] "The specific service for which Israel is determined within the whole of the elected community is to reflect the judgment from which God has rescued man and which He wills to endure Himself in the person of Jesus of Nazareth."[55] "The service for which the Church as the perfect form of the one elected community is determined ... consists always in the

---

[50]See Barth, *Church Dogmatics*, II/2, 195-305.
[51]Barth, *Church Dogmatics*, 195.
[52]Barth, *Church Dogmatics*, 195-96.
[53]Barth, *Church Dogmatics*, 195.
[54]Barth, *Church Dogmatics*, 195.
[55]Barth, *Church Dogmatics*, 206.

fact that it is the reflection of the mercy in which God turns His glory to man. The community in the form of the Church is the community of the risen Lord Jesus Christ."[56] Commenting on Romans 10, Barth concludes that as Israel the community is determined (destined) to hear the promise sent to man; as the Church it is determined (destined) to believe the promise sent to man.[57] "The special service of Israel within the totality of the elected community consists ... in the hearing, the reception and the acceptance of the divine promise."[58] "In the perfect form of the one elected community of God the service of the Church consists ... in the fact that it secures attention for the promise heard by putting faith in it."[59] Finally, commenting on Romans 11, Barth concludes that Israel is the passing form of the community, the Church the coming form of the community.[60] "The specific service which within the whole of the elected community is Israel's determination is the praise of the mercy of God in the passing, the death, the setting aside of the old man, of the man who resists his election and therefore God."[61] "... the service of the Church as the perfect form of the one community of God consists in attesting, by faith in the Word heard, by laying hold of the divine mercy, the coming kingdom of God as the end of all human need, the coming of the new man and his eternal life."[62]

One thing is apparent from Barth's analysis of Israel and the Church as aspects of the one elected community. The two terms do not refer to a past and a present of the elected community in the sense that the community is not now what it once was, and was at one time in the past something that it now is not; rather, there was and never will be a time when the elected community is not both Israel and the Church, the former merely speaking of that impossible possibility that God in his grace passed by, the latter speaking of what all men are, though they perhaps do not realize it not.

This new understanding of Israel and the Church is brought out even more clearly in the message which, according to Barth, the

[56]Barth, *Church Dogmatics*, 210.

[57]Barth, *Church Dogmatics*, 195.

[58]Barth, *Church Dogmatics*, 233.

[59]Barth, *Church Dogmatics*, 237.

[60]Barth, *Church Dogmatics*, 195.

[61]Barth, *Church Dogmatics*, 260.

[62]Barth, *Church Dogmatics*, 264.

elected community is to proclaim. The community in Jesus Christ is not really two but one: in Christ the elect triumph in the "gracious end" which Israel manifests and in the "new gracious beginning" which the Church reflects.[63] In this dual role the one community approaches every man with the promise that "he, too, is an elect man,"[64] for although it is fully aware of man's perverted choice, fully aware of man's godlessness, it remembers that "it consists itself of godless men who were enabled to hear and believe this promise, and who still need to hear and believe it. It must and does reckon continually with the original godlessness of its members. It is fully aware, too, of the eternal condemnation of the man who is isolated over against God, which is unfailingly exhibited by the godlessness of every such man.... It knows the wrath and judgement and punishment of God in which the rejection of the man isolated over against God takes its course. And it also knows of the shadow into which every man does actually move because he desires and undertakes at all costs to be a man isolated, and therefore rejected, in relation to God; because he behaves and conducts himself at all costs *as though he were this rejected man*. But it knows, *above all*, about Jesus Christ.... It knows that God ... has taken upon Himself the rejection merited by the man isolated in relation to Him; that on the basis of this decree of His *the only truly rejected man is His own Son*.... And *this is the very goal which the godless cannot reach, because it has already been taken away by the eternally decreed offering of the Son of God.... It testifies to them that the way in which they find themselves was ... nullified before the world began*. They may choose as they do. They may proceed as far as they are able. But *the situation and reward of the rejected for which they stretch out their hands in their folly when they reject God, will assuredly not be secured by them*.... It knows supremely that Jesus Christ died and rose for [the rejected] also. And because of this it must address him without reserve.... *It is to say to each of them that he is the actual object of the divine election of grace*."[65]

From this rather lengthy quotation it is obvious that the message of the elected community, as both Israel and the Church, is actually and

---

[63]Barth, *Church Dogmatics*, 259.

[64]Barth, *Church Dogmatics*, 318.

[65]Barth, *Church Dogmatics*, 318-20 (italics mine).

purely a message of grace. Though it understands, because of its own nature as Israel, the godlessness of all men, yet it understands even better, because of its nature as the Church, that all men are the actual objects of divine grace in election, that no man is actually outside of Jesus Christ, that try as he might the godless man is unable to undo what God in Jesus Christ has graciously decreed in his behalf. In short, God's wrath is always and only penultimate; his grace is always and finally ultimate. Klooster observes that, beyond question, Barth teaches a universal election.[66] As to whether this affirmation by Barth teaches a universal salvation will be considered shortly. At this point the discussion will simply continue to follow Barth as he proceeds to the election of the individual.

The election of the individual

Barth arrives, only after treating the election of Jesus Christ and the election of the community in him, at the election of the individual,[67] an approach which he thinks is the only biblical one. He writes: "Included in His [Jesus Christ] election there is ... this 'other' election, the election of the many (from whom none is excluded)."[68] Indeed, "the election of the individual [is] the *telos* of the election of the community."[69] Barth is critical of the traditional Reformed doctrine of election for its "over-anxious" approach to the election of the individual. As a result, its construction was more in the interest of a non-Biblical humanism than in the interest of true Biblical exposition: "... the doctrine [of election as the Reformers understood it] is not merely one of those factors which have paved the way for Pietism and Rationalism within the Church itself, but is also one of the presuppositions without which the further development of secular individualism would have been inconceivable (the development from J. J. Rousseau and the younger Schleiermacher through Max Stirner and Kierkegaard to Ibsen and Nietzsche)."[70] This is so because the older doctrine involved the "conviction that the beginning and end of all the ways of God, and even the essence of all divine truth, are to be recognized and honoured in individual human beings."[71]

---

[66]Klooster, *The Significance of Barth's Theology*, 59.
[67]See Barth, *Dogmatics*, II/2, 306-506.
[68]Barth, *Dogmatics*, 195.
[69]Barth, *Dogmatics*, 311.
[70]Barth, *Dogmatics*, 308.

One cannot but feel that Barth is very reluctant to deal with the non-elect in his construction of election, for still Barth refuses to deal with them separately apart from the elect. Rather, he first treats the elect and the non-elect together, avoiding the very terms "non-elect" or "reject," preferring the neutral and colorless term, the "others" (but see Eph. 2:3). What is the difference for Barth between the elect and these others? Answers Barth:

> This, then is how the elect and others differ from one another: the former by witnessing in their lives to the truth, the latter by lying against the same truth. *It ought to be clear that to this extent they belong together.* The elect are obviously to be found in the sphere of the divine election of grace, in the hand of the one God, under the reign whose beginning and principle are called Jesus Christ. *But the others are also to be found there.* The former are there in obedience, the latter in disobedience.... If the former testify by their truthful witness to what God wills, the latter no less expressively testify by their lying witness to what God does not will. Thus both serve the revelation of the divine will and decree which by nature are wholly light, but which cannot be revealed or recognized except as light and shade. Believers "are" the elect in this service so far as they bear witness to the truth, that is, to the elect man, Jesus Christ, and manifest and reproduce and reflect the life of this one Elect. The godless "are" the rejected in the same service so far as by their false witness to man's rejection they manifest and reproduce and reflect the death of the one Rejected, Jesus Christ. Because this One is the Elect and the Rejected, He is – attested by both – the Lord and Head both of the elect and also of the rejected. Thus not only the former, but no less indispensably, in their own place and after their own totally different fashion, the latter, are His representatives, just as originally and properly as He is theirs.[72]

It is beyond debate that Barth still does not take seriously a group which could actually be designated the "non-elect". Rather, both the elect and the non-elect find themselves within the sphere of the grace of God, serving correlative purposes. Neither is dispensable; each needs the other to testify to opposing principles with which they have to do. Barth continues: "It is from this solidarity of the elect and the rejected in the One Jesus Christ that there arises a very definite recollection for the elect and equally definite expectation for others."[73]

---

[71]Barth, *Dogmatics*, 308.

[72]Barth, *Dogmatics*, 346-47 (italics mine).

[73]Barth, *Dogmatics*, 347.

What is the recollection for the elect and the expectation for the "others" to which Barth refers?

> The recollection for the elect is this ... As they work out their election, in faith in Jesus Christ, they can never think of the basis of their election without thinking simultaneously of the rejection which has been diverted from them in their election ...[74]

> The expectation for others is this. The original and proper distinction of Jesus Christ, which alone makes possible and actual the distinction of the elect, is the truth which also transcends, comprehends and illumines their existence, but which does not appear to be theirs because they are obviously involved in the evil, perilous and futile manifestation, repetition and reproduction of the life of men rejected by God. In this respect we must not forget that the distinction of the elect, which originally and properly is that of Jesus Christ alone, is also valid for these others; that they do not possess it only in so far as they do not recognize and accept it as their own distinction.... They can, of course, dishonour the divine election of grace: but they cannot overthrow or overturn it. They cannot prevent God from regarding them as from all eternity He has willed to regard and has actually regarded sinful men in His own Son.... A limit is fixed by the fact that the rejected man, who alone and truly takes and bears and bears away the wrath of God, is called Jesus Christ. They can be only potentially rejected. They may indeed conduct themselves as rejected, but even if they deserved it a thousand times they have no power to bring down on themselves a second time the sword of God's wrath now that it has fallen.[75]

It would seem, then, that still for Barth there are no truly and ultimately non-elect men, but let us not be hasty in our judgement. Let us continue to let Barth speak:

> Both the necessary recollection for the elect and the necessary expectation for others means, then, that we have every reason to consider the elect and others together for all their opposition. We cannot, at any rate, regard their opposition as absolute. For all its distinctive sharpness, the opposition between them can only be relative, because both are in the one absolute hand of God.[76]

---

[74]Barth, *Dogmatics*, 347-48.
[75]Barth, *Dogmatics*, 349.
[76]Barth, *Dogmatics*, 350.

Barth readily affirms that according to Scripture these two lines are followed out in human history which is "the history of the continually renewed consolidation, separation and encounter of these two peoples,"[77] but this contrast is clearest, declares Barth, where these two are not two but one – namely, Jesus Christ who is the Elect and the Rejected. "He is *the* Rejected, as and because He is *the* Elect. In view of His election, there is no other rejected but Himself."[78] And so Barth concludes that both groups are necessary: "We can no more consider and understand the elect apart from the rejected than we can consider and understand the rejected apart from the elect."[79]

Only now, after he has treated the elect and the "others" together in such a way that the two groups are equally within the sphere of the divine election of grace, does Barth consider the elect separately and the non-elect separately. But still it is the elect which come in for treatment first.[80] This treatment, however, is largely repetitious of all the expressions of grace which Barth has previously written concerning the elect: no new decisions or conclusions are reached. Consequently, we are here primarily concerned with what Barth does with the "others."[81] But the suspicious reader can hardly be blamed for thinking that the decisions concerning them have already been made in preceding sections of Barth's discussion or for being less than surprised when he is confronted with Barth's actual handling of the matter. For, as we shall show, Barth does not regard the non-elect as being essentially different from the elect. In fact, he actually denies the independent existence of the unbeliever. He writes: "Because Jesus Christ takes [the rejected man's place], He takes from him the right and possibility of his own independent being and gives him His own being. With Jesus Christ the rejected can only *have been* rejected. He cannot *be* rejected anymore."[82] Thus a rejected man is not independently really actual or actually real. Barth sees man only in Jesus Christ, which means that only Jesus Christ is a person; we achieve participation in personhood only in him. Apart from believing participation in Jesus Christ there are no real persons at all. Of course,

---

[77]Barth, *Dogmatics*, 351.

[78]Barth, *Dogmatics*, 353.

[79]Barth, *Dogmatics*, 353.

[80]See Barth, *Dogmatics*, 410-49.

[81]See Barth, *Dogmatics*, 449-506.

[82]Barth, *Dogmatics*, 453.

Barth does not mean by all this that the rejected man is an imaginary entity or that he would not meet empirical tests of existing. But, as Cobb has rightly observed, Barth is using "real" in a very special sense.

> [Barth's sense of "real"] can be grasped, if at all, only by imaginatively sharing in his own vision of the sole agency of God and the unlimited graciousness of that agency. From this point of view we must see by faith, and in spite of all appearances, that what resists God's grace is *really* nothing – is already negated, wholly negative. Hence those men who attempt to stand in that rejection have in fact nothing to stand upon and no being or power to oppose to God's grace. Barth does, it is true, allot a certain limited and negative reality to the rejected, but this he insists is derived from the elect. One exists as rejected by virtue of being known as such by the elect. He represents man in this need for election and in that negative condition which is the only alternative to faith. As such he too exists by the will of God as the shadow of his gracious election.[83]

But what about Judas? Surely if ever there were one, here is one whom the Scriptures regard as actually and independently real and as rejected by God. Barth is not so convinced, for he devotes forty-eight pages to a demonstration that Judas may be regarded as an elect individual. He does this by arguing that the Greek word *paradidomi* does not mean "betray" with reference to Judas' actions concerning the Christ. Rather, it means "a handing over". And Judas' "handing over" was only one of three "handings-over". First, there was the "handing over" of the Son by the Father.[84] Second, the apostolic mission "handed over" the Christ in the preaching and teaching of the gospel.[85] And third, there was Judas' "handing over" of Jesus to the religious leaders and the Roman soldiers. Now the Christian should not be too harsh with Judas, so thinks Barth, for if redemption may for the moment be compared to a huge stone, it is this stone which Judas starts rolling – but only starts rolling.

> ... this almost incidental denunciation by Judas is the first link in the chain: the smallest, but one which involves and controls all that follow....

---

[83]Cobb, *Living Options in Protestant Theology*, 187-88.
[84]Barth, *Dogmatics*, II/2, 488; see Rom. 4:25; 8:32; Gal. 2:20; Eph. 5:2, 25.
[85]Barth, *Dogmatics*, 484; see 2 Thess. 2:15; 1 Cor. 11:2, 23: 15:3.

At this point it is a disciple and apostle of Jesus who makes the decisive movement. It is quite a small movement, trifling as compared with everything that follows once it has taken place. It is carried out by the kiss, which, in point of fact, attests and seals the fellowship of the perpetrator with Jesus. Judas delivers Jesus, and in so doing he initiates the decisive moment which Jesus had to perform for the accomplishment of His work – His suffering and death.[86]

... the treacherous kiss by which Judas distinguishes Jesus from the surrounding disciples is ... the sign of the gratitude of lost men for the existence of Him who now wills to intervene for him.[87]

And Barth concludes:

In one sense Judas is the most important figure in the New Testament apart from Jesus. For he, and he alone of the apostles, was actively at work in this decisive situation.[88]

In this manner Barth vindicates the actions of Judas and denies to him the status of the rejected. But even though it undoubtedly is true that Judas' betrayal of Jesus did initiate the first movement which eventuated in Christ's death on Calvary's tree (although Barth's viewing of the kiss of betrayal as an attestation and seal of the fellowship which Judas enjoyed with Jesus stretches legitimate biblical exegesis beyond the breaking point), is not the testimony of Scripture clear to the effect that Judas died and "went to his own place"? Is it not the clear intent of Scripture to portray Judas as a lost man? Barth answers this objection by declaring that we need not accept as true the Scripture concerning Judas' final destiny. For one thing, does not the Scripture disagree with itself regarding the manner of Judas' death, the Gospel account ascribing his death to suicide by hanging but Peter in Acts speaking of his death in far more violent terms – as a falling down followed by a bursting open in the middle and the gushing forth of his bowels? To Barth this disagreement speaks of an uncertainty within the early Church itself over what did actually happen to Judas. Consequently, he argues, from this factor, that all the disparagement of Judas found within the pages of Scripture simply reflects the early

---

[86]Barth, *Dogmatics*, 460.

[87]Barth, *Dogmatics*, 502.

[88]Barth, *Dogmatics*, 502.

Church's effort to cover up the faithlessness of the other disciples by portraying Judas in deep shades of greed, selfishness, disloyalty, and dishonor. In this manner Barth feels he has succeeded in opening to Judas the doors of grace.

In the light of all that we have seen Barth affirming concerning the blessed position of both the elect and the "others" as objects of the divine election of grace, it cannot be denied that a universal salvation should be the logical outcome of Barth's construction of election. But Barth will neither affirm nor deny the theory of universal salvation. He writes:

> If we are to respect the freedom of divine grace, we cannot venture the statement that it must and will finally be coincident with the world of man as such (as in the doctrine of the so-called *apokatastasis*). No such right or necessity can legitimately be deduced. Just as the gracious God does not need to elect or call any single man, so He does not need to elect or call all mankind. His election and calling do not give rise to any historical metaphysics, but only to the necessity of attesting them on the ground that they have taken place in Jesus Christ and His community. But, again, in grateful recognition of the grace of the divine freedom we cannot venture the opposite statement that there cannot and will not be this final opening up and enlargement of the circle of election and calling ... We would be developing an opposing historical metaphysics if we were to try to attribute any limits ... to the loving-kindness of God.[89]

In his book *The Humanity of God*, after describing his construction of election, Barth writes:

> Does this mean universalism? I wish here to make only three short observations, in which one is to detect no position for or against that which passes among us under this term. 1. One should not surrender himself in any case to the panic which this word seems to spread abroad, before informing himself exactly concerning its possible sense or non-sense. 2. One should at least be stimulated by the passage, Colossians 1:20, which admittedly states that God has determined through His Son as His image and as the first-born of the whole Creation to "reconcile all things (*ta panta*) to himself," to consider whether the concept could not perhaps have a good meaning. The same can be said of parallel passages. 3. One question should for a moment be asked, in view of the "danger" with which one may see this concept gradually surrounded. What of the

---

[89]Barth, *Dogmatics*, 417-18.

"danger" of the eternally sceptical-critical theologian who is ever and again suspiciously questioning, because fundamentally always legalistic and therefore in the main morosely gloomy? Is not his presence among us currently more threatening than that of the unbecoming cheerful indifferentism or even antinomianism, to which one with a certain understanding of universalism could in fact deliver himself? This much is certain, that we have no theological right to set any sort of limits to the loving-kindness of God which has appeared in Jesus Christ. Our theological duty is to see and understand it as being still greater that we had seen before."[90]

Thus Barth concludes his treatment of election that at every turn pointed on the surface at least toward a clear unequivocal universalism by declaring himself an agnostic with reference to the final outcome of the divine election of grace. Only this attitude, he feels, preserves the divine freedom.

Criticism

The Reformed Christian will have already discerned that Barth's construction of election does, as Barth readily admits, differ at almost every point from the view which he has been taught. But just why this is so is due to several reasons. The following discussion of these reasons will form in the main our criticisms of Barth's doctrine of election.

First, Barth begins his construction of election with a very low view of the inspiration and infallibility of Scripture. The surprising thing is that he refers to Scripture as much as he does and employs its terminology as much as he does in the light of the fact that he does not believe that the Bible is the Word of God. For Barth the Bible only *becomes* God's Word from time to time. Writes Barth: "The Bible is God's Word so far as God lets it be His Word, so far as God speaks through it."[91] Barth assumes this position because, raised as he was in the liberal tradition, he accepts the "unimpeachable results" of the destructive Biblical criticism which arose on the European Continent during the nineteenth and early twentieth centuries. He does not hesitate to speak of errors and contradictions within the pages of Holy Scripture. The Bible simply is not the Word of God for Barth. It

---

[90]Karl Barth, *The Humanity of God* (Richmond: John Knox, 1960), 61-62.
[91]Barth, *Dogmatics*, I/1, 123.

is a book through which God may choose from time to time to reveal himself through certain of its statements, but no man has the guarantee that he will be confronted by the Word of God when he turns to its pages, and no two men have the guarantee that the same statement will be the Word of God alike to both. Gordon H. Clark has correctly perceived the end result of this position when he writes: "... rationality requires that each Scriptural statement be true permanently or untrue permanently. Ambiguous sentences, such as the favorite Stoic example 'It is daytime now,' can change from true to false as the meaning of 'now' is changed. But if unambiguous sentences can become true and then become false, if they are true only from time to time, there is no defense against scepticism."[92] Yet Barth continues to claim that "we do the Bible a poor honour, and one unwelcome to itself, when we directly identify it with ... revelation itself."[93] Thus in spite of all his claims to the effect that he seeks above all else to let the Bible speak to him in all matters, Barth in actuality sits in judgment, as the autonomous man, on what the Bible can and cannot say. This must be true from the very nature of the case. By denying to the words of Scripture any inherent infallibility and viewing God's Word as "God's Word to me" in the moment of revelation, Barth has removed all objectivity from God's Word and has subjectivized all religious truth. The Biblical writers, however, never subjectivized truth in such a manner. For them truth is primarily objective, coming to man *ab extra*, found ultimately in the ontological Trinity and the incarnate Son of God and derivatively in the written Word of God, the Holy Scriptures. Nevertheless, in "proof-text" fashion, Barth quotes those Scriptures that "speak" to him (that is, aid him) in his construction of his doctrine whereas those Scripture statements which contradict his construction he rejects. A clear case in point is his treatment of the passages relating to Judas. He does not hesitate to affirm that Scripture contradicts itself in the matter of Judas' death, for this "fact" allows him to interpret Judas' actions in the manner he deems will best aid his reconstruction of election. And this reading into Scripture that which he wishes to see there Barth extends throughout his writing. Thus there can be no controversy that over the question of whether or not the Bible is the inspired, infallible Word of the living God Barth remains ever an

---

[92]Gordon H. Clark, *Karl Barth's Theological Method* (Philadelphia: Presbyterian and Reformed, 1963), 164.

[93]Barth, I/1, 126.

unbeliever. And it is this unbelief that gives rise to and shapes all of the other errors in his doctrine.

Second, his christomonistic principle of interpretation, that is, his effort to view all of the decreed ways and works of God only from the work of Jesus Christ is simply unbiblical. Barth rejects the orthodox understanding of the Trinity, that is, that there are three Persons in the Godhead, the Father, the Son and the Holy Spirit, and that these three are one God, the same in substance, equal in power and glory. Rather, though he rejects likewise the formulation of historic Modalism, Barth describes the three Persons as simply "three modes of being of the one God." He is adamant in his insistence that the only God man can know is the God who reveals himself in Jesus Christ; therefore, he will not speak of the God "behind" Jesus Christ, for then, he declares, he would be no better off than the Reformers who spoke about a decreeing God other than Jesus Christ and his *decretum absolutum*. For Barth, then, though he will refer to the election of the Father and the Holy Spirit, God for all practical purposes is simply and solely Jesus Christ.

Because of his practical Unitarianism of the Second Person Barth must twist the clear meaning of many passages of Scripture in order to speak of Jesus Christ as being the pre existent God-man who decreed to become both the Elect and the Reject. In fallacious proof-text fashion Barth affirms on the basis of John 1:1ff. "two statements concerning the election of Jesus Christ. The first is that Jesus Christ is the electing God.... And the second is that Jesus Christ is the elected man."[94] Now it just simply is not biblical to speak of Jesus Christ alone as the electing God. For while Scripture certainly speaks of the eternal pre existence, prior to his Incarnation, of the Second Person of the Holy Trinity as the Logos of God who did participate in the decisions of the covenant of redemption, who later in our time and in our history took to himself a true body and a reasonable soul in a genuine Incarnation, who bore his humanity through the tomb and to heaven at his ascension, and who will continue to bear his assumed humanity forever in behalf of his elect, Scripture nowhere ascribes election solely to Jesus Christ. Eternal pre existence applies only to Christ's deity, and to speak of the eternal pre existence of Jesus rather than the eternal pre existence of the Logos of God is simply fallacious exegesis. The very compound name, Jesus Christ, refers to his human and divine natures in his Incarnation.

Furthermore, it is simply is not biblical to conclude backward from the earthly work of Jesus Christ to a knowledge of the whole decretive will of God. The work of Jesus Christ pertains in its redemptive aspect only to his elect; this means that with reference to the non-elect the triune God has decreed to regard them as outside of Jesus Christ and to leave them to their ordained perdition. But, of course, it is this very teaching of Scripture which Barth refuses to hear, preferring his own construction which, if carried to its logical end, leads to an unqualified universalism.

Third, it is actually Barth's view of election that involves an unknown God.[95] For in Barth's opinion, although all men are elect in Jesus Christ, so that what Jesus Christ has done has been done for all men, in the interest of preserving God's freedom in his sovereignty, Barth leaves open the question of a possible universalism, affirming that "the gracious God does not need to elect or call any single man,"[96] and that "there is no election which cannot be followed by rejection, no rejection which cannot be followed by election."[97] In short, Barth is prepared to affirm that "if it is true that the predestinating God not only is free but remains free, that He does not cease to make use of His freedom but continues to decide, then in the course of God's eternal deciding we have constantly to reckon with new decisions in time."[98] But if a man can never be sure at any moment what God is going to decide about his election or rejection, does this not mean that God is unpredictable? And an unpredictable God can never become a God who can be irrevocably known. He remains forever an unknown God.

But does God's eternal decree which must necessarily "bind" him to his word deny to him his freedom? Who forced this binding upon him? No one. Whose will is being done? His own. The Christian is grateful that God eternally wills to bind himself even by oath to an eternal covenant of grace with those whom he fore loved before the world was made. In the eyes of the Christian such a God is not less than free; indeed, it is through his eternal willing that as the Sovereign

---

[94]Barth, II/2, 145.

[95]I am indebted to Klooster for this criticism of Barth. Indeed, I must acknowledge the profound debt I owe to his *The Significance of Barth's Theology*.

[96]Barth, *Dogmatics*, II/2, 417.

[97]Barth, *Dogmatics*, 186.

[98]Barth, *Dogmatics*, 186.

of the Universe, he has, according to the counsel of his own will and for his own glory, foreordained what ever comes to pass. It is by his eternal willing that, as far as man is concerned, his sovereignty is established. And this is simply to say that it is *his* freedom of choice which is working itself out in our history. Indeed, as Klooster declares, "Scripture indicates that the unchangeable God never desires to change his decree. It is because he eternally wills that he is never the prisoner of the decree laid before the foundation of the world."[99]

Fourth, though Barth admittedly does not affirm in so many words universal salvation, it would appear that he does not do so simply because he does not choose to do so. His voiced fear that such an affirmation would deny to God his freedom is groundless if it is universal salvation that the Scriptures teach. It would seem that this is just another example of the irrationalism which pervades his whole theological construction – the unwillingness to assume a position which is the only logical result of his methodology. Everything in his methodology and treatment points as straight as the arrow's flight to a universalism, but then, having advanced to the very threshold of this affirmation, he is unwilling to step across the threshold, but haltingly affirms that he is not sure what God will do. "The frontier from election to rejection and vice versa can be repeatedly crossed and crisscrossed."[100] The Christian, of course, rejoices that Barth does not affirm a universalism; in this Barth is right. But the Christian must always have strong objections to a construction which leads beyond doubt to a universalism.

Finally, it is clear from his description of the message of the elect community that for Barth it is not one primarily of warning and crying out against sin; it is not one of beseeching men in Christ's stead to be reconciled to God. Rather, it is an informing them that all men are already elected in Jesus Christ, that even the "others," choose as they may, "can be only potentially rejected. They may conduct themselves as rejected, but even if they deserved it a thousand times they have no power to bring down on themselves a second time the sword of God's wrath now that it has fallen"[101] on *the* rejected Man, Jesus Christ. With such a message, the Scriptural warning against

---

[99]Klooster, *The Significance of Barth's Theology*, 68.
[100]Klooster, *The Significance of Barth's Theology*, 70.
[101]Barth, *Dogmatics*, II/2, 349.

apostasy as well as the Church's call to conversion is minimized if not completely aborted. Barth's construction of election cuts the very heart out of all true evangelism.

Barth's Doctrine of Reconciliation

Barth's doctrine of reconciliation, found in Volume IV of his *Church Dogmatics*, includes what theologians have usually distinguished as Christology, hamartiology, soteriology, and ecclesiology. Barth himself describes this area as the "centre of all Christian knowledge", and attaches such importance to it that he exclaims: "... to fail here is to fail everywhere. To be on the right track here makes it impossible to be completely mistaken in the whole."[102]

The schema of Barth's construction

Traditionally, the biblical message has been schematised under the three terms of creation, fall, and redemption. Barth is quite familiar with this fact, of course: "Between the doctrine of creation and that of atonement it was and is customary (and logically it is very instructive and didactically most illuminating) to interpose a special section *De peccato*: a doctrine of the fall, of original sin and its consequences, of the state and constitution of sinful man, of individual or actual sins."[103] But Barth feels compelled to substitute for the traditional schema the "dialectic of covenant, sin and reconciliation."[104] Barth does not speak first of creation but of covenant. This is due, first, to Barth's contention that one must begin with John 1 rather than Genesis 1 if a genuinely christological starting point is to be made. (For this reason Barth is regarded as a supralapsarian by many of his readers, the decree to create being subordinated to the covenant.) Second, the fact that he rejects the historical authenticity of the first chapters of Genesis, viewing them as *Saga*, that is, as description of events having to do with Adam as representative man, and as such, events that happen again and again, contributes to his aversion to begin with the creation of man.

Barth regards the covenant of grace as the first presupposition of reconciliation. As we saw earlier, Barth rejects orthodoxy's traditional handling of the covenant program, failing to see either its "covenant

---

[102]Barth, *Dogmatics*, IV/1, ix.

[103]Barth, *Dogmatics*, 139.

[104]Barth, *Dogmatics*, 80.

of redemption" or its "covenant of works". Consequently, he posits the one covenant of grace, after assuming an original gulf between God and man which may be bridged only by God's reconciling action. It is true that Barth speaks of an "original fellowship" between God and man, but it should be carefully noted that this original fellowship between God and man is described as the fellowship of the *covenant of grace*: "The fellowship which originally existed between God and man, which was then disturbed and jeopardised, the purpose of which is now fulfilled in Jesus Christ and in the work of reconciliation, we describe as the covenant."[105] Consequently, Barth regards the first man as "immediately the first sinner"[106] standing in need of the grace of the covenant. It may be legitimately asked, where is the golden age of Eden, where is the fall of man from his created position of holiness in all of this? Of course, Barth removes both, insisting that only in this way may one actually be able to begin from a genuinely christological starting point. It may be said in passing that one can hardly be blamed for seriously questioning the validity of Barth's christological starting point that necessitates the setting aside of the teaching of entire blocks of Scripture.

Barth looks upon the doctrine of sin as the second presupposition of reconciliation. But what is sin in Barth's system? It is essentially a breaking of the covenant of grace which asks that man be thankful for God's grace! "... man is called to hold to the grace of His Creator, to be thankful for it, to bow to it and adapt himself to it, to honour it as the truth. And the essence of sin is that he does not do this."[107] This definition is certainly a far cry from the definition of sin in the *Westminster Shorter Catechism*: "Sin is any want of conformity unto, or transgression of, the law of God." What is the relation of sin, as Barth sees it, to grace? Traditionally, God's grace has been viewed against the backdrop of sin since the Bible always represents grace as God's response to man's sin; consider, for example, "Where sin abounded, grace did much more abound (Rom. 5:20), and "God commendeth his love toward us, in that, while we were yet sinners, Christ died for us" (Rom. 5:8). But Barth reverses this order and maintains that sin can only be seen in the light of grace, otherwise sin is an abstraction. "... we cannot with a good conscience," writes

[105]Barth, *Dogmatics*, 22.
[106]Barth, *Dogmatics*, 508.
[107]Barth, Dogmatics, 140.

Barth, "follow the procedure which would give [sin] a treatment which is independent, self-originating and self-contained."[108] "... there can be no place in dogmatics for an autonomous section *De peccato* constructed in a vacuum between the doctrine of creation and that of reconciliation."[109] "If it takes place as a breach of one covenant [of grace], and not in any other way [and this is the burden of Barth's entire discussion to this point], it can be known only in the light of the covenant. But since man has broken the covenant, that can mean only in the light of the covenant fulfilled and restored in Jesus Christ and therefore in the light of the atonement made in Him."[110] And this is simply saying that sin must be seen as already regarded by God in the light of the covenant of grace and hence negated. "In all its forms it exists and is only as that which negates and therefore as that which is itself negated, on the left hand of God, where God in saying Yes has already said No, where in electing He has rejected, where in willing He has not willed. But the divine Yes which sin negates and by which it is negated is the Yes of God's covenant with man...."[111] Barth continues:

> ... we have no option but to consider and answer the question of sin in the light of the Gospel and therefore within the doctrine of reconciliation, to take it up into that doctrine instead of giving it precedence over it as though it were an autonomous question. In this context we shall find a natural place for it immediately after the Christology. It is in the knowledge of Jesus Christ as the revelation of the grace of God that we shall necessarily perceive step by step both the fact that man is a transgressor, and the nature of the transgression in which he contradicts the grace of God and for the sake of which he is decisively contradicted by that grace.[112]

The result of this christological approach to sin is really the viewing of sin as an "impossible possibility." Barth has terrible pictures of sin to paint and he does so, but he can afford to do so in his thought because he sees this sin, no matter how black and hideous, as already taken up into and dealt with in reconciliation.

---

[108]Barth, *Dogmatics*, 139.

[109]Barth, *Dogmatics*, 141.

[110]Barth, *Dogmatics*, 140-41.

[111]Barth, *Dogmatics*, 140.

[112]Barth, *Dogmatics*, 142.

The "christological aspects" of reconciliation

With this background we come now to the "christological aspects" of Barth's construction of reconciliation. The sections on Christology in IV/1, IV/2, and IV/3 of the *Church Dogmatics* will provide one with an adequate amount of material in order to understand Barth's christomonistic construction of the doctrine of reconciliation. He himself avers that the christological sections stand "at the head and contain the whole *in nuce*."[113] In these sections "the decisions are made".[114] Barth writes further: "We have to develop the whole doctrine of reconciliation in accordance with our Christology and the three basic christological aspects.... The Christology is the key to the whole. From each of the three aspects suggested it will be our starting point and will necessarily control all the detailed developments."[115]

As at so many other points Barth replaces with his own view the traditional view of Christology.

Traditionally, theologians have distinguished between Christ's person and Christ's work. This was done not out of deference to scholastic mentality but because it was regarded as scriptural and for facility of handling all of the material. In connection with Christ's person, his natures are distinguished. As an example, the *Westminster Shorter Catechism* declares: "The only Redeemer of God's elect is the Lord Jesus Christ, who, being the eternal Son of God, became man, and so was, and continueth to be, God and man, in two distinct natures, and one person, forever." In regard to his work, theologians treated both the threefold office of prophet, priest and king, and the two states of humiliation and exaltation within which he exercised his threefold office. Barth, of course, is aware of these facts.

> It was and is customary in dogmatics to have a single complete and self-contained chapter on Jesus Christ, the so-called "Christology," (as the climax in the whole presentation.) This includes (1) a special doctrine of the "person" of Christ, i.e., the incarnation of the Word of God, and also His Godhead and manhood in their relationship the one to the other, (2) a special doctrine of His work (following the *munus triplex* arrangement of the Reformation period), and usually (3) a special doctrine of the two "states" of Christ, His humiliation and exaltation.[116]

---

[113]Barth, *Dogmatics*, IV/2, x.

[114]Barth, *Dogmatics*, IV/2, x.

[115]Barth, *Dogmatics*, IV/1, 138.

[116]Barth, *Dogmatics*, 123.

Feeling that such a treatment tends only to abstractionism, Barth, however, brings together into intimate relationship the doctrines of the two natures and the two states, together with the three offices:

> An abstract doctrine of the person of Christ may have its own apparent importance, but it is always an empty form, in which what we have to say concerning Jesus Christ can never be said. Again, it is almost inevitable that a doctrine of the work of Christ separated from that of His person will sooner or later give rise to the question, and perhaps even impose it, whether this work cannot be understood as that of someone other than that divine-human person.[117]

Barth then wants to view Christ's work as his person and his person as his work.

> It is in the particular fact and the particular way that Jesus Christ is very God, very man, and very God-man that He works, and He works in the fact and only in the fact that He is this One and not another. His being as this One is His history [*Geschichte*], and His history [*Geschichte*] is His being. This is the truth which must light up the doctrine of reconciliation as Christology."[118]

From this it is apparent that for Barth *reconciliation is Christology and Christology is reconciliation.*

We see then that Barth has substituted for the traditional view his own Christology. But of what details does his Christology consist? We shall look at this Christology (that the reader should keep constantly in mind is for Barth equivalent to reconciliation) in greater detail, but a summary of Barth's Christology at this point will stand the reader in good stead in his effort to comprehend the intricate thought of Barth on this matter.

First, Jesus Christ as very God corresponds to the humiliation of God and to the priestly office.[119] Second, Jesus Christ as very man corresponds to the exaltation of man and to the kingly office.[120] Third, Jesus Christ as the God-man corresponds to no specific state but

---

[117]Barth, *Dogmatics*, 127.

[118]Barth, *Dogmatics*, 128.

[119]See Barth, *Dogmatics*, 128-30 and IV/1 – "Jesus Christ, the Lord as Servant."

[120]See Barth, *Dogmatics*, 130-35 and IV/2 – "Jesus Christ, the Servant as Lord."

does speak of the prophetic office.[121] These then are Barth's three "christological aspects", and a careful study of them will reveal that Barth does seek to relate the person of Christ to his work and his work to his person. Each of these aspects will now be discussed in greater detail.

What is involved for Barth in his affirmation that Jesus Christ is very God? Barth responds: "The content of the doctrine of reconciliation is the knowledge of Jesus Christ who is ... very God, that is, the God who humbles Himself, and therefore the reconciling God."[122] Barth further elucidates:

> God became man. That is what is, i.e., what has taken place, in Jesus Christ. He is very God acting for us men, God Himself become man. He is the authentic Revealer of God as Himself God. Again, He is the effective proof of the power of God as Himself God. Yet again, He is the fulfiller of the covenant as Himself God. He is nothing less or other than God Himself, but God as man. When we say God we say honour and glory and eternity and power, in short, a regnant freedom as it is proper to Him who is distinct from and superior to everything else that is. When we say God we say the Creator and Lord of all things. And we can say all that without reservation or diminution of Jesus Christ.[123]

At first blush the unwary reader might conclude that Barth has certainly listened to Scripture in his description of Jesus Christ as very God. But there is sound reason to believe that Barth, in spite of all that is good and proper in what he says about Christ, is not talking about the Scriptural Christ at all. For, to Barth, the deity of Jesus Christ is not a self-contained, ontological deity, but rather *it is the nature of this God to humble himself and to turn himself into his opposite, namely, the creature.* Scripture speaks of God as a Spirit, infinite, eternal, and unchangeable, in his being, wisdom, power, holiness, justice, goodness, and truth. There are three persons in this Godhead, and this Trinity is ontologically independent, self-contained, and self-subsisting. Any turning on the part of the triune God to this creation is done, not out of necessity, but out of loving interest and concern. In truth, God does not need anything (Acts 17:24-25). But Barth does not have an ontological Trinity in his theology at all. For Barth the

---

[121]See Barth, *Dogmatics*, 135-38 and IV/3 – "Jesus Christ, the Guarantor."

[122]Barth, *Dogmatics*, 79.

[123]Barth, *Dogmatics*, 128-29.

Trinity is a modal revelational representation and essentially functional in nature. Barth himself describes Jesus Christ as "the One whose eternity ... commands Him to be in time and Himself to be temporal".[124] He continues: "He, the true God, is the one whose Godhead ... plainly consists in essence in the fact that ... He ... wills this condescension."[125] And finally, "He is God in that He takes [the fallen] creature to Himself.... He is God in the fact that He can give Himself up and does give Himself up not merely to the creaturely limitations but to the suffering of the human creature, becoming one of these men, Himself bearing the judgment under which they stand, willing to die, and, in fact, dying the death they have deserved. *That is the nature and essence of the true God as He has intervened actively and manifestly in Jesus Christ.*"[126] This simply means, as Van Til has seen, that Jesus Christ is God *because* he turns himself completely into the creature. This means in turn for Christianity that it no longer has a God-in-himself. It has only a God-for-man, with all the correlativity between Creator and creature which this implies. God needs the creature in order to be God just as much as the creature needs God in order to be saved. Only a functional Trinity remains for the needy creature. All of this must be clearly kept in mind if one is to comprehend what Barth means when he speaks of Jesus Christ as very God.

Corresponding to Jesus Christ as very God, in Barth's Christology, is what traditionally has been termed the state of humiliation. Traditionally, it has been said that "Christ's humiliation consisted in his being born, and that in a low condition, made under the law, undergoing the miseries of this life, the wrath of God, and the cursed death of the cross, in being buried and continuing under the power of death for a time" (*Westminster Shorter Catechism*, Q.27). That is, Christ's state of humiliation pertains to the time of his Incarnation, extending up to and including his burial in the tomb. Christ's humiliation, then, necessarily included and refers to the atoning deeds of both his active and passive obedience, that is, his *atoning work*. But in the interest of relating Christ's work to his person, Barth refuses to speak of Christ's humiliation as that specific time of his earthly career extending from his birth to his enclosure in Joseph's tomb. Rather, he relates the

---

[124]Barth, *Dogmatics*, 129.

[125]Barth, *Dogmatics*, 130.

[126]Barth, *Dogmatics*, (italics mine).

state of humiliation to Jesus Christ's *divine* nature. "... what is the humiliation of Jesus Christ? To say that He is lowly as a man is tautology which does not help us in the least to explain His humiliation."[127] "The humiliation, therefore, is the humiliation of God."[128] Christ's divine nature, then, corresponds to the work included in his state of humiliation. And it is to this aspect that Barth relates Christ's priestly office.

Barth's second "christological aspect" refers to Jesus Christ as very man. "The content of the doctrine of reconciliation is the knowledge of Jesus Christ who is ... very man, that is, man exalted and therefore reconciled by God."[129] He elaborates:

> The second christological aspect is that in Jesus Christ we have to do with a true man. The reconciliation of the world with God takes place in the person of a man in whom, because He is also true God, the conversion of all men to God is an actual event. It is the person of a true man, like all other men in every respect, subjected without exception to all the limitations of the human situation. The conditions in which other men exist and their suffering are also His conditions and His suffering. He is altogether man just as He is altogether God.... To say man is to say creature and sin, and this means limitation and suffering. Both these have to be said of Jesus Christ.[130]

Corresponding to Jesus Christ as very man, in Barth's Christology, is what traditionally has been termed his state of exaltation. Traditionally, Christ's exaltation has referred to "his rising again from the dead on the third day, in ascending up into heaven, in sitting at the right hand of God the Father, and in coming to judge the world at the last day" (*Westminster Shorter Catechism*, Q. 28). In other words, his exaltation has been regarded as having followed temporally his humiliation, and this certainly is the Scriptural representation (see Phil. 2:6-11). But again in the interest of relating Christ's work to his person, Barth speaks of exaltation in reference to Christ's *human* nature. "... what is the exaltation of Jesus Christ? To say that as God He is transcendent, free, sovereign, above the world, and therefore above the limitation and suffering of the human situation is again tautology

---

[127]Barth, *Dogmatics*, 134.
[128]Barth, *Dogmatics*, 134.
[129]Barth, *Dogmatics*, 79.
[130]Barth, *Dogmatics*, 130-31.

which does not help us to understand His exaltation."[131] Christ's exaltation is the exaltation of man,[132] because it is of the nature of this man to exalt mankind. "What has happened in Him as the one true man is the conversion of all of us to God, the realisation of true humanity. It is anticipated in Him, but it is in fact accomplished and revealed. As in Him God became like man, so too in Him man has become like God.... That is the atonement made in Jesus Christ in this second aspect. *In Him humanity is exalted humanity, just as Godhead is humiliated Godhead.*"[133] Christ's humanity, then, corresponds to the work included in the state of exaltation. And it is to this aspect that Barth relates Christ's kingly office.

Barth's third "christological aspect" pertains to Jesus Christ as the God-man. "The content of the doctrine of reconciliation is the knowledge of Jesus Christ who is ... in the unity of the two [natures] the guarantor and witness of our atonement."[134] This aspect, however, does not add materially to our understanding of reconciliation in Jesus Christ. "There can be no question," writes Barth, "of our trying to see a third thing in what we have called the third christological aspect. Everything that can be said materially concerning Jesus Christ and the atonement made in Him has been said exhaustively in the twofold fact ... that He is very God and very man, i.e., the Lord who became a servant and the servant who became Lord, the reconciling God and the reconciled man. [Only the bringing together of these two things historically] is the new thing in the third christological aspect. Jesus Christ is the actuality of the atonement."[135]

While there is no specific corresponding state to this union of natures, it is to this aspect that Barth relates Christ's prophetic office.

The results of this construction

What are the results of Barth's relating Christ's person to his work? In a word, Barth has again "actualised" the Incarnation and resultingly has interpreted Christology as the work of reconciliation. For Barth, as we have seen, Christ's two states (which he regards as equivalent to his work) cannot be separated from his two natures. Jesus Christ,

---

[131]Barth, *Dogmatics*, 134.

[132]Barth, *Dogmatics*, 134.

[133]Barth, *Dogmatics*, 131 (italics mine).

[134]Barth, *Dogmatics*, 79.

[135]Barth, *Dogmatics*, 136.

then, as the God-man was never humiliated apart from being exalted or exalted apart from being humiliated. "Where and when is He not both humiliated and exalted, already exalted in His humiliation, and humiliated in His exaltation?"[136] "Both aspects force themselves upon us. We have to do with the being of the one and entire Jesus Christ whose humiliation detracts nothing and whose exaltation adds nothing. And in this His *being* we have to do with His action, the work and event of atonement."[137]

By seeing in the work of Christ also the person of Christ, Barth declares that the Incarnation is "actualised", that is, made into an ongoing process. This is done in the interest of interpreting Jesus Christ as "event". By this event which contains both the person and work of Christ,

the being of Jesus Christ, the unity of being of the living God and this living man, takes place in the event of the concrete existence of this man. It is a being, but a being in history. The gracious God is in this history, so is reconciled man, so both are in their unity. And what takes place in this history [*Geschichte*], and therefore in the being of Jesus Christ as such, is atonement. *Jesus Christ is not what He is – very God, very man, very God-man – in order as such to mean and do and accomplish something else which is atonement. But His being as God and man and God-man consists in the completed act of the reconciliation of man with God.*"[138]

For Barth the Incarnation itself is unquestionably the reconciling act!

We conclude this survey of Barth's christological construction of reconciliation with his summary of the atonement:

The atonement as it took place in Jesus Christ is the one inclusive event of this going out of the Son of God and coming in of the Son of Man. In its literal and original sense the word *apokatallassein* ("to reconcile") means "to exchange." The reconstitution and renewal of the covenant between God and man consists in this interchange – the *exinanitio*, the abasement, of God, and the *exaltatio*, the exaltation, of man. It was God who went into the far country, and it is man who returns home. Both took place in the one Jesus Christ. It is not, therefore, a matter of two different and successive actions, but of a single action in which each of the two elements is related to the other and can be known and understood only in

---

[136]Barth, *Dogmatics*, 133.

[137]Barth, *Dogmatics*, 133.

[138]Barth, *Dogmatics*, 126-27 (italics mine).

this relationship: the going out of God only as it aims at the coming in of man; the coming in of man only as the reach and outworking of the going out of God; and the whole in its original and proper form only as the being and history of the one Jesus Christ.[139]

Criticism

There can be no doubt that Barth's doctrine of reconciliation, taking up into itself Christology, hamartiology, soteriology, and ecclesiology as it does, is a new doctrine in which older traditions and themes have been thoroughly recast. Yet it is from the older traditional (and we believe biblical) position that we make the following criticisms.

First, because of his low view of the historicity of Genesis, Barth fails to adopt the biblical view of the origin of man, his original state, and the origin and nature of sin. This is the seed-bed of all of Barth's erroneous thinking; because unless one takes seriously a genuine creation of man in a state of original knowledge, righteousness, and holiness, he will never understand the biblical references to the fall of man. And unless one takes seriously the biblical teaching of the fall of man, he will never understand the nature of sin as "any want of conformity unto, or transgression of, the law of God" or understand the present desperate estate of man as one of sin and misery. And unless one takes seriously the biblical teaching of man's present estate of sin and misery, he will never understand the Bible's unique doctrine of redemption. In any construction of the atonement, it will invariably be deficient and sub-Christian unless a genuine creation and a genuine fall are affirmed. For this reason, the traditional schema of the biblical message was summarized under the three terms of creation, fall, and redemption. Regardless of what he may feel about this traditional schema, the honest interpreter must admit that Barth's construction, whatever else it may be, certainly is not biblically oriented in this regard.

In the interest of an acceptable affirmation of the universality of sin, it might be objected, why not accept Barth's view of Adam as representative man? For Barth's view of Adam as representative man standing in the need of the grace of God universalises sin, does it not? To this objection it must be pointed out that such an interpretation of the Adam of Genesis, though on the surface appearing to make sin universal, actually denies other important doctrines, not the least of

---

[139]Barth, *Dogmatics*, IV/2, 20-21.

which, as we have already seen, is the Genesis account of the fall of man from a state of created holiness, not to mention the exceedingly important doctrine of the imputation of Adam's guilt to all those who have descended from him by ordinary generation as set forth by Paul in Romans 5:12 ff. Now there is a legitimate sense in which Adam represented every man, that sense being as the covenant head of his race and his obedience or disobedience under the covenant of works being imputed to his natural progeny. As the *Westminster Shorter Catechism* (Q. 16) states: "The covenant being made with Adam, not only for himself, but for his posterity, all mankind descending from him by ordinary generation, sinned in him, and fell with him, in his first transgression." And it is through a similar principle of imputation of Christ's righteousness that the redeemed are made acceptable in God's sight. But Barth wants nothing to do with such a view of Adam. For him Adam depicts the essential state and attitude of every man. Every man sins like Adam. Of course, this view denies the biblical doctrine of original sin, for it just is not true that all men sin like Adam. Adam had a choice; there was nothing within him that inclined him toward evil. Indeed, his created state inclined him toward good. But that is not the condition in which men, according to Scripture, now enter this world. Adam's descendants now begin life with a propensity toward evil. They are born in sin. They are dead in trespasses and sins by nature. Hence, Barth's understanding of Adam can hardly be regarded as biblical, and for this reason it is unacceptable to a Christian.

Second, Barth's failure to distinguish between the person and work of Christ is unbiblical. Scripture makes this distinction: the Second Person of the Trinity existed prior to his Incarnation and birth by the Virgin. Furthermore, his mediatorial work of redemption was performed, according to the Scriptures, once and for all (*ephapex*) in history and is now a complete work, a redemption accomplished and remaining only to be applied historically to God's elect.[140]

Third, in spite of all his talk about their unity, Barth destroys the unity of Christ's two natures when he ascribes the humiliation of Jesus Christ only to his divine nature and the exaltation of Jesus Christ only to his human nature. Chalcedon's description of the union included the terms, "indivisibly" and "inseparably": "... one and the same Christ, Son, Lord, Only-begotten, to be acknowledged in two natures

---

[140] See Klooster, *The Significance of Barth's Theology*, 94.

inconfusedly, unchangeably, indivisibly, inseparably ..."[141] An unscriptural division of Christ's natures also results from Barth's ascription of Christ's priestly office to his divine nature and his kingly office to his human nature.

Fourth, in Barth's view the Incarnation is the really crucial event in man's reconciliation to God. Jesus' suffering and death on the cross are little more than revelatory of the depth of the humiliation resulting from God turning into his opposite, namely, the creature. The resurrection is essentially only revelatory of the exaltation of man that occurs in the Incarnation.[142] But this understanding of reconciliation by no means does justice to the biblical doctrine of reconciliation. Again and again at various stages in his earthly ministry, Christ declared: "Mine hour has not yet come." But standing in the shadow of the cross, he exclaimed: "For this hour came I into the world." Paul nowhere speaks of our being reconciled by the mere event of the Incarnation, but rather proclaims our reconciliation to God through the death of his Son (Rom. 5:10; Col. 1:22) and Christ's having made peace through the blood of his cross (Col. 1:20; Eph. 2:16). Barth is completely incapable of harmonizing the teaching of these Scripture passages with his construction.[143]

Finally, and this criticism applies equally both to his construction of election and to his construction of reconciliation, Barth has, as Berkouwer has so aptly declared, no transition for the sinner from wrath to grace in history. The sinner has always stood under both the wrath and the grace of God. But the wrath of God is always and only penultimate; the grace of God is always and finally ultimate. Though man has always been rejected in Jesus Christ as *the* one rejected Man, he has also and ultimately always been elected and therefore exalted in Jesus Christ as *the* one elected Man. Barth cannot avert an ultimate universalism.

Because of the shattered liberal dogmas of man's inherent goodness, the breakdown of confidence in humanistic man, the discredited assumptions of the optimism of the Enlightenment, modern culture

---

[141]Klooster, *The Significance of Barth's Theology*, 94-95.

[142]See Barth, *Dogmatics in Outline* (New York: Harper & Row, 1959), 101-02.

[143]Klooster, *The Significance of Barth's Theology*, 95-96.

has drifted toward despair. Because of his inability to explain his own history logically, modern man has sought his salvation in mysticism and irrationalism.

Instead of challenging this nihilistic culture to face its despair squarely and pressing upon it the rationality to be found in the Christian gospel, Barth, in dependence upon a Kantian metaphysics and a destructive biblical criticism, has followed his culture into the same mood of irrationalism by substituting his own plan of salvation and a reconstructed gospel for the biblical plan of salvation and the only gospel (Gal. 1:6-9) which can meet the real need of "modern" man. For Barth, the words of the Bible may ever remain fallible and human as long as the Word of God in *Geschichte* is believed; creation may be affirmed as long as it has no relation to the Genesis account of a *creatio ex nihilo* of the Universe or to man in an original state of righteousness and holiness; the fall of man may be believed as long as Adam's personal existence as the first man is denied; the figure of Jesus of Nazareth may remain shrouded in mystery as long as the Christ of faith is proclaimed; the Cross may be proclaimed as long as the sacrificial blood of Christ is neglected; and the resurrection of Christ may be spoken of as long as it is understood that this "event" is for believers only. But, of course, such a gospel is no gospel at all, certainly not the biblical gospel.

The only answer to man's need is to be found in the gospel of historic Christianity, which rejects all of the ambiguity and theological doubletalk of modern Neo-orthodoxy and projects a message that is rationally and historically true. Only a Christian theism that is grounded in the authority of the infallible Bible, in a genuine creation and real historical fall, and in the atonement wrought out by the God of the Incarnation – only this will supply the cures for the spiritual ills of mankind.

Chapter Eighteen

Bultmann's Demythologized Kerygma

Rudolf Bultmann (1884–1976), born in Oldenburg, Germany, received his theological education under Karl Müller at Tübingen, Hermann Gunkel and Adolf von Harnack at Berlin, and Adolf Jülicher, Johannes Weiss, and Wilhelm Herrmann at Marburg. He served as Professor of New Testament at Marburg from the autumn of 1921 until his retirement from active teaching in 1951. During the time of Nazi domination he took active part in the opposition to Nazism that the "confessing church" built up. Bultmann's prominence in Continental theology is usually dated from his programmatic essay of 1941 entitled *New Testament and Mythology* in which he outlined a felt need to "demythologize" the New Testament in order to discover the pure New Testament *kerygma*. Since that time his thought has even gained ascendancy over Barth's thought, though recent years have seen a "revolt" among his students toward more "objectivity" in the construction of a New Testament theology. After his retirement he lectured in Sweden, Holland, Denmark, Scotland, and the United States. Some of the choicest theological chairs in Europe have been filled by his pupils or disciples, for example, Günther Bornkamm at Heidelberg, Hans Conzelmann at Göttingen, and Ernst Käsemann at Tübingen.

Important works by Bultmann are *Jesus and the Word, Jesus Christ and Mythology, The Presence of Eternity*, and his two-volume *Theology of the New Testament*.

Works about Bultmann or Bultmannism are *Kerygma and Myth*, edited by H. W. Bartsch, *Christ Without Myth* by Shubert Ogden, *Myth in the New Testament* by Ian Henderson, *The New Testament in Current Study* by Reginald Fuller, *A New Quest of the Historical Jesus* by James M. Robinson, *The Theology of Rudolf Bultmann*, edited by Charles W. Kegley, *Bultmann* by H. Ridderbos, and *Jesus of Nazareth: Saviour and Lord*, edited by Carl F. H. Henry.

In the early years of Neo orthodoxy's revolt against classic

Note: This article first appeared as a monograph published by Presbyterian and Reformed in 1967.

Liberalism, Karl Barth and Rudolf Bultmann were the chief exponents of an existential Christianity. Gradually, the former became disenchanted with any and all efforts to construct a theology in conjunction with any philosophy and since around 1930 endeavoured to purge theology of alien elements. Bultmann, however, remained unwaveringly convinced that Christianity must be interpreted existentially and devoted his entire academic career to the development of a program and a methodology of a truly existential Christianity. His program is popularly described by the phrase, "demythologization of the New Testament," and his methodology, aiming at a "positive" (existential) construction of the Christian faith, has been "borrowed" from the school of form criticism and the existential philosophy of Martin Heidegger.

Bultmann claims that his entire program is simply a consistent following through of the Reformation principle of *sola fide*. As Bornkamm correctly discerns: "Bultmann cannot accept any 'objective' revelatory realm of being that can be recognized, established, and understood in and by itself prior to its relation to faith."[1]

Bultmann's Modern Scientific World-View

Bultmann begins by taking very seriously the modern scientific world-view. Cobb views Bultmann's attitude here as a major key to his thought:

> ... one must begin with [Bultmann's] understanding of the relation between God and the world. He understands the world as the totality of spatio-temporal phenomena, the whole object of human knowledge. It may be approached both externally, in an objectifying way that is appropriate to the physical sciences, and internally, in the way that is appropriate to the study of man and human history. In either case, we find a closed system of cause and effect – objective causal relations in the former instance, subjective motivations and human decisions in the latter. In so far as our knowledge is concerned, any failure to find a cause simply means that we do not yet have adequate tools at our command. We always properly presuppose that the causes of this-worldly phenomena are this-worldly. This means that God can never be introduced as a factor into the explanation of this-worldly phenomena.[2]

---

[1] Günther Bornkamm, "The Theology of Rudoph Bultmann," an essay in the book by that title, edited by Charles W. Kegley (New York: Harper & Row, 1966), 16.

And to this axiom there are no exceptions. Bultmann himself declares:

> ... modern man acknowledges as reality only such phenomena or events as are comprehensible within the framework of the rational order of the universe ... When a strange or marvellous accident occurs, he does not rest until he has found a rational cause.[3]

Furthermore,

> ... there are still many superstitions among modern men, but they are exceptions or even anomalies. Modern men take it for granted that the course of nature and of history, like their own inner life and their practical life, is nowhere interrupted by the intervention of supernatural powers.[4]

And finally:

> Although modern physical theories take account of chance in the chain of cause and effect in subatomic phenomena, our daily living, purposes and actions are not affected. In any case, modern science does not believe that the course of nature can be interrupted or, so to speak, perforated, by supernatural powers.[5]

Bultmann frankly admits that his program "takes the modern world-view as a criterion".[6]

What are the results for one's understanding of the New Testament of this acceptance of the world-view of modern science? Simply this: the New Testament becomes to a large degree "mythological". Bultmann declares: "... the world-view of Scripture is mythological and is therefore unacceptable to modern man whose thinking has been shaped by science and is therefore no longer mythological."[7] By "myth" Bultmann, of course, does not mean fiction or fairytale. He has reference to the use of imagery to express the other-worldly in terms of this world, the divine in terms of human life, and the "other

---

[2]John B. Cobb, Jr., *Living Options in Protestant Theology* (Philadelphia: Westminster, 1962), 227-228.

[3]Rudolf Bultmann, *Jesus Christ and Mythology* (New York: Charles Scribner's Sons, 1958), 37-38.

[4]Bultmann, *Jesus Christ and Mythology*, 16.

[5]Bultmann, *Jesus Christ and Mythology*, 15.

[6]Bultmann, *Jesus Christ and Mythology*, 35.

[7]Bultmann, *Jesus Christ and Mythology*, 36.

side" in terms of "this side".[8] But it must be noted here that such description or imagery is anthropological and not specifically cosmological. In other words, Bultmann means that though in a myth man appears to be describing the world, he is actually describing his own existence. (This demythologization of the New Testament, as we shall see, does not consist merely in eliminating what one concludes is mythology. Rather, it involves interpreting the New Testament anthropologically, or, as Bultmann prefers to say, existentially.) Understood in this way, mythology constitutes, in Bultmann's opinion, a great amount of New Testament teaching.

To illustrate this understanding of the so-called mythological teaching of the New Testament, one could do no better than to turn to his 1941 essay, *New Testament and Mythology*, wherein he specifies what he feels are distinct mythological elements surrounding the New Testament kerygma:

> The cosmology of the New Testament is essentially mythical in character. The world is viewed as a three-storied structure, with the earth in the centre, the heaven above, and the underworld beneath. Heaven is the abode of God and of celestial beings – the angels. The underworld is hell, the place of torment. Even the earth is more than the scene of natural, everyday events, of the trivial round and common task. It is the scene of the supernatural activity of God and his angels on the one hand, and of Satan and his deamons on the other. These supernatural forces intervene in the course of nature and in all that men think and will and do. Miracles are by no means rare.... *This then is the mythical view of the world which the New Testament presupposes when it presents the event of redemption which is the subject of its preaching.* It proclaims in the language of mythology that the last time has now come. "In the fullness of time" God sent forth His Son, a pre-existent divine Being, who appears on earth as a man. He dies the death of a sinner on the cross and makes atonement for the sins of men. His resurrection marks the beginning of the cosmic catastrophe.... The risen Christ is exalted to the right hand of God in heaven and made "Lord" and "King." He will come again on the clouds of heaven to complete the work of redemption, and the resurrection and judgment of men will follow.... All this is the language of mythology, and the origin of the various themes can be easily traced in the contemporary mythology of Jewish Apocalyptic and in the redemption myths of

---

[8]Rudolf Bultmann, "New Testament and Mythology," *Kerygma and Myth*, edited by Hans Bartsch (New York: Harper and Brothers, 1961), 10.

Gnosticism. To this extent *the kerygma is incredible to modern man, for he is convinced that the mythical view of the world is obsolete*. We are therefore bound to ask whether, when we preach the Gospel today, we expect our converts to accept not only the Gospel message, but also the mythical view of the world in which it is set. If not, does the New Testament embody a truth which is quite independent of its mythical setting? If it does, theology must undertake the task of stripping the Kerygma from its mythical framework, of "demythologizing" it. Can Christian preaching expect modern man *to accept the mythical view of the world as true?....*
Man's knowledge and mastery of the world have advanced to such an extent through science and technology that it is no longer possible for anyone to hold the New Testament view of the world.... Now that the forces and the laws of nature have been discovered, we can no longer believe in *spirits, whether good or evil.... The miracles of the New Testament* have ceased to be miraculous.... *The mythical eschatology* is untenable for the simple reason that the parousia of Christ never took place as the New Testament expected. History did not come to an end, and, as every schoolboy knows, it will continue to run its course. [Whether modern man regards himself as pure nature or as pure spirit], he finds *what the New Testament has to say about the "Spirit" (pneuma) and the sacraments utterly strange and incomprehensible....* Again, the biblical doctrine that *death is the punishment of sin* is equally abhorrent to naturalism and idealism.... The same objections apply to *the doctrine of the atonement.* How can the guilt of one man be expiated by the death of another who is sinless – if indeed one may speak of a sinless man at all? What primitive notions of guilt and righteousness does this imply? And what primitive idea of God?... What a primitive mythology it is, that a divine Being should become incarnate, and atone for the sins of men through his own blood!... The *resurrection of Jesus* is just as difficult for modern man.... It is only with effort that modern man can think himself back into such an intellectual atmosphere.[9]

So it is beyond debate that, though Bultmann (as we shall see more fully later) recognizes the existence of a genuine New Testament proclamation which is relevant to today's "modern man," this New Testament kerygma is couched in and covered over with a great amount of first-century mythology. The New Testament writers were definitely attempting to tell us something of a meaningful nature but they related this message in existential terminology. That is, steeped as they were in a pre-scientific understanding of the world and spirits, they could

---

[9]Bultmann, "New Testament and Mythology," 1-8, emphasis supplied.

not avoid relating their message in mythological terms. But the modern man, instructed as he is in the scientific world-view of the twentieth century, must now face the realization that he lives in a closed cause-and-effect cosmic system. He is not afforded the 'luxury' of falling back upon explanations of a supernatural nature to account for mysterious enigmas. God can never be introduced as a factor into the explanation of any this-worldly phenomenon! This acceptance of the modern scientific world-view is basic to Bultmann's theology.

Bultmann's Understanding of Faith and Its Task

In light of the foregoing summary of Bultmann's scientific world-view, one might easily conclude that the theological task was ruled out at the outset prior to any statement about God. But for Bultmann the way has only now been cleared for a truly biblical faith relationship between man and God. For Bultmann faith is a "nevertheless" perception. In other words, although an event may be fully and correctly understood in terms of this-worldly causes, "nevertheless" by faith it may be seen as having an essentially different meaning. To support his view Bultmann refers to such passages as Psalm 73:22-23: "So foolish was I, and ignorant; I was like a beast before thee. Nevertheless, I am continually with thee! Thou hast held me by my right hand," and 1 Corinthians 7:29-31: "But this I say, brethren, The time is short; it remaineth that both they that have wives be as though they had none; And they that weep, as though they wept not; and they that rejoice, as though they rejoiced not; and they that buy, as though they possessed not; And they that use this world, as not abusing it, for the fashion of this world passeth away." Illustrations of his use of these rather uncommon verses to support his construction of faith as a *nevertheless* concept are the following:

> In faith I deny the closed connection of the worldly events, the chain of cause and effect as it presents itself to the neutral observer.... This is the paradox of faith, that faith "nevertheless" understands as God's action here and now an event which is completely intelligible in the natural or historical connection of events. This "nevertheless" (the German *dennoch* of Psalm 73:23; and Paul Tillich's *in spite of*) is inseparable from faith. Only this is real faith ...,"[10]

and

---

[10]Bultmann, *Jesus Christ and Mythology*, 64-5.

... our relation to the world as believers is paradoxical. As Paul puts it in 1 Corinthians 7:29-31, "Let those who have wives live as though they had none, and those who mourn as though they were not mourning, and those who rejoice as though they were not rejoicing, and those who buy as though they had no goods, and those who deal with the world as though they had no dealings with it." In terms of this book [*Jesus Christ and Mythology*], we may say, "Let those who have the modern world-view live as though they had none."[11]

Ridderbos correctly interprets Bultmann at this point:

> In Bultmann's theology, the world and human personality retain their own independence and are completely shut off from God. At the very most, only something which occurs within this closed order can be *understood* by faith as an act of God.[12]

In short, then, for Bultmann a given event or phenomenon, though no doubt having a this-worldly explanation, can be for the believer, but *only* for the believer, an act of God. By faith, God is made real and effective in relation to human existence.

It might be well if at this point a word is said concerning Bultmann's understanding of God. Just who is this one who is made real and effective by faith. Bultmann declares that God is the "absolutely transcendent One", "the Wholly Other"; therefore, we cannot say what God is like. We can only say what God does for us. Hence to speak of God means to speak of man. Theology, then, for Bultmann is the explanation of the self-understanding which man achieves when God speaks to him through the *kerygma*. In other words, God and all talk about him, if genuine, can never be understood as mere abstractions. If God is genuinely apprehended by faith's "nevertheless" perception, it transforms the way in which the individual understands his own existence: "faith is a new understanding of personal existence. In other words, God's action bestows upon us a new understanding of ourselves."[13] And further,

---

[11]Bultmann, *Jesus Christ and Mythology,* 85.

[12]Herman Ridderbos, *Bultmann* (Philadelphia: Presbyterian and Reformed, 1960), 31.

[13]Bultmann, *Jesus Christ and Mythology*, 73.

the most important thing is that basic insight that the theological thoughts of the New Testament are the unfolding of faith itself growing out of that new understanding of God, the world, and man which is conferred in and by faith – or, as it can also be phrased: *out of one's new self-understanding.* For by the believer's new understanding of himself we, of course, do not mean "understanding" as in a scientific anthropology which objectifies man into a phenomenon of the world, but we do mean an existential understanding of myself which is at one with and inseparable from my understanding of God and the world.[14]

In other words, an apprehension of God's action for me by faith is actually at the same time an acquisition of a new existential understanding of myself. Furthermore, not only do I have a new *self*-understanding, but also by faith all of nature and existence is viewed in its boundedness by and radical dependence upon that which altogether transcends it, that is, God.

Bultmann's Demythologizing Program

Thus far we have determined that, for Bultmann, we live in a closed world system, free from all supernatural intrusion, but by faith we may nevertheless perceive that God acts in our behalf, this perception resulting in a new understanding of ourselves, which is the *telos* of the faith perception. Immediately, it may justly be asked, is this the Bible's understanding of God, the world, faith, and faith's *telos* or task? If one understands the Bible as a trustworthy document respecting its cosmology, eschatology, and historicity, then, of course, Bultmann's understanding of these items is incorrect. But Bultmann is convinced that the Bible, specifically the New Testament as it is this which concerns him as a New Testament scholar, is on the face of it, for the most part, outdated mythology. Yet underlying this mythology is something else with deep meaning – namely, the New Testament proclamation of the act of God, or, in short, the *kerygma*. For instance, Jesus' disciples, say Matthew, for example, were convinced that through their association with Jesus of Nazareth they had by faith perceived God acting in Jesus Christ for them, giving them a new understanding of themselves and the world in which they lived. Being "children of their age", they naturally and unconsciously

---

[14]Bultmann, *Theology of the New Testament*, translated by Kendrick Grovel (New York: Charles Scribner's Sons, 1955), II, 239.

expressed this new self-understanding derived from their apprehension of God's action for them in pre-scientific mythological terms. Bultmann is convinced that the New Testament kerygma is absolutely essential to modern man's own self-understanding, but it can only be made relevant to him if the New Testament is stripped of the mythological shell which surrounds the true New Testament kerygma. "This method of interpretation of the New Testament which tries to recover the deeper meaning behind the mythological conceptions," affirms Bultmann, "I call *de-mythologizing*."[15] By demythologising the New Testament, Bultmann declares that the true proclamation of the act of God may be seen and understood for what it is and not taken as itself a bit of outdated mythology. How does he propose to carry out this program?

Before his actual methodology is considered, it must be made clear that Bultmann views demythologisation as neither an attempt to discover certain New Testament passages which are not mythological and to regard these as the gospel for our day, nor is it an effort to go behind the form of the New Testament to the teaching of Jesus, for this too is mythological, made more so by the interpretation which the faith of the early Church placed upon his words and deeds. Rather it is a program to *identify* the existential intention of myth and to *reaffirm* this intention in non-mythological categories, that is, in categories devoid of the cosmological and eschatological categories of the New Testament.[16] The result of such a program is our hearing "in the Bible authoritative words about our existence".[17]

To arrive at a proper comprehension of the true kerygma, Bultmann follows a basic twofold methodology: first, the "form-historical" (*Form-Geschichtliche*) method, expressed in a highly detailed, voluminous work entitled *Die Geschichte der synoptischen Tradition* (1921), and second, what may be termed for lack of a more precise designation, the "presuppositional-existentialist" method, developed in his *Glauben und Verstehen* (I, 1933; II, 1952) and *Theologie des Neuen Testaments* (1953).

---

[15]Bultmann, *Jesus Christ and Mythology*, 18.
[16]Cobb, 232.
[17]Bultmann, *Jesus Christ and Mythology*, 53.

Bultmann's form-historical method

"Form history," more popularly known as "form criticism," endeavors "to get behind the written Gospels and their literary sources to the oral stage of the Gospel tradition, and so to classify and examine the various "forms" or types of story, utterance, etc., represented in that oral tradition."[18] "These [oral] forms are supposed to have provided material for the Gospels and are also thought to have been so thoroughly shaped by the needs of the early Church as to preclude a full historical basis for all the events recorded in the Gospels."[19] Hence, though for him Jesus is nothing other than a man whom the later faith of the Church made a deity, Bultmann is well aware that, contrary to Liberalism's efforts to free the "life of Jesus" of all supernaturalism, the history of Jesus as recorded in the Gospels is very definitely a supernatural history which at the same time is freighted with the character of preaching. But according to Bultmann, "this preaching does not give us a trustworthy account of what occurred; it represents only the faith of the later church."[20] Moreover, "this faith of the later church (and its accompanying "theology") has taken such a thorough hold of what was originally said by Jesus that it is extremely difficult to derive, from this proclamation of faith, a clear picture of what Jesus actually said and did."[21] (It is for this reason that one rarely hears the Bultmann scholar declare, "Jesus said"; rather, he prefers to say, "Jesus is purported to have said," or "It has been put into the mouth of Jesus that 'such and such' is the case.") Bultmann is willing to concede that the words and sayings ascribed to Jesus actually have historical kernels, but these sayings are no longer to be taken with any certainty. For example, whether Jesus ever regarded himself as the Messiah cannot be determined by any information presently available to us. Actually, the Gospels, so declares Bultmann, are not concerned with Jesus but with the faith and preaching of the Church with respect to Jesus. By going behind the Gospels as simple expressions of the faith of the early Church to the original forms of

---

[18] F. F. Bruce, "Form Criticism," *Baker's Dictionary of Theology,* edited by Harrison, Bromiley, and Henry (Grand Rapids: Baker, 1960), 227.

[19] *The New Scofield Reference Bible* (New York: Oxford University Press, 1967), 989.

[20] Ridderbos, 11.

[21] Ridderbos, 11.

the Gospel tradition (insofar as they are capable of determination) before they were brought together into the unity exhibited in the present Gospel records, Bultmann is convinced that the *Sitz im Leben* (the life-setting) of these oral traditions may be in many instances readily grasped, thus enabling the New Testament interpreter to more easily determine the precise influences – whether Jewish apocalyptic, whether Gnostic – which bore upon the original saying. Such a determination in turn will aid the interpreter in his demythologization of a given narrative or saying. Herein resides the value of a form-critical method for Bultmann's *Entmythologisierungsprogam.*

Bultmann's presuppositonal-existentialist method
Bultmann maintains that if one would demythologize the New Testament writer's expression of his self-understanding in order to understand his theology, he must come to the New Testament with some kind of question or previous understanding (*Vorverständnis*). Herein lies Bultmann's presuppositionalism. He declares:

> It is important to remember that every interpretation is actuated by the framing of specific questions, and without this there could be no interpretation at all. Of course these questions need not be framed explicitly or consciously, but unless they are framed the texts have nothing to say to us.[22]

When the objection is raised that the presuppositional approach to the text inevitably colors one's findings, Bultmann's argument, while readily admitting this to be the case, presses for the recognition that there is no interpretation of any document without preconceived concepts:

> It would be a fallacy to suppose that exegisis can ever be pursued independently of profane terminology. Every exegete is dependent upon a terminology which has come down to him by tradition.[23]

Thus having cleared the way for the framing of a certain question to be directed to the New Testament text in his approach to it, Bultmann declares what this question should be:

---

[22]Bultmann, *Kerygma and Myth*, 191.
[23]Bultmann, *Kerygma and Myth*, 193.

I think I may take for granted that the right question to frame with regard to the Bible – at any rate within the Church – is the question of human existence. I am driven to that by the urge to inquire existentially about my own experience. But that is a question which at bottom determines our approach to and interpretation of all historical documents. For the ultimate purpose in the study of history is to realize consciously the possibilities it affords for the understanding of human existence.[24]

In another place Bultmann affirms:

Our task ... is to discover the hermeneutical principle by which we can understand what is said in the Bible.... In other words, the question of the "right" philosophy arises.... Our question is simply which philosophy today offers the most adequate perspective and conceptions for understanding human existence. Here it seems to me that we should learn from existentialist philosophy, because in this philosophical school human existence is directly the object of attention.[25]

In particular, Bultmann feels that Martin Heidegger's existentialist construction of human existence, as a philosophical anthropology, provides a sound basis for asking sensitive questions. Writes Bultmann:

Heidegger's existentialist analysis of the ontological structure of being would seem to be no more than a secularised, philosophical version of the New Testament view of human life. For him the chief characteristic of man's Being in history is anxiety. Man exists in a permanent tension between the past and the future. At every moment he is confronted with an alternative. Either he must immerse himself in the concrete world of nature, and thus inevitably lose his individuality, or he must abandon all security and commit himself unreservedly to the future, and thus alone achieve his authentic Being. Is not that exactly the New Testament understanding of human life? Some critics have objected that I am borrowing Heidegger's categories and forcing them upon the New Testament. I am afraid this only shows that they are blinding their eyes to the real problem. I mean, one should rather be startled that philosophy is saying the same thing as the New Testament and saying it quite independently.[26]

---

[24]Bultmann, *Kerygma and Myth*, 191.
[25]Bultmann, *Jesus Christ and Mythology*, 54-55.
[26]Bultmann, *Kerygma and Myth*, 24-25.

Bultmann is confident that this existentialist methodology as *phenomenology* seeks to be objective and as *ontology* limits itself to the sphere of what is universal to human existence as such and omits the variety of actual forms which human existence can take.

The Results of Bultmann's Demythologizing Program

The form-critical, existentialist analysis of the New Testament, declares Bultmann, demythologizes the texts and results in the New Testament's untrammelled proclamation of the Christian message that God, the wholly transcendent, has acted decisively for man's salvation in Jesus Christ. As proclamation of God's past act in Jesus Christ, the kerygma is likewise promise of God's act in the here-and-now as it functions as a call to the radical decision of faith (total surrender of self to God). Faith, as the authentic response to the *kerygma*, is at the same time God's act in the present in the believer's "death" to self and "resurrection" to the life of freedom. All this sounds, of course, on the surface something like the traditional message of the Church, but Bultmann's program actually alters the traditional message in nearly every feature. Specifically, how has Bultmann's construction altered the Church's traditional understanding of man, his world, and God?

In his interpretation of man, Bultmann treats Paul's antithesis of flesh and spirit. Here, for Bultmann, Paul is speaking of two modes of human existence; however, in Bultmann's opinion, Paul's terminology leads to confusion. But informed by Heidegger's analysis of *Dasein*, Paul's two modes are seen to be respectively unauthentic and authentic existence, the former alluding to the way of understanding one's self from the world of things and which leads to a care for that world that prevents man from being truly himself, the latter describing life lived in terms of the real potentialities of the existent personality, free from past ancestry, achievement, and failure, and open to the future and responsible decision.[27] The transition from the former to the latter mode of existence occurs when the existent responds in faith to the *kerygma*.

Bultmann's reinterpretation of the New Testament message replaces New Testament cosmology and eschatology with a new understanding of nature and history. In the sphere of nature, the New Testament confronts us with a three-tiered cosmology, the *supra-*

---

[27]Cobb, 234.

worldly (God's world) being treated, for example, as an objectively real world alongside of the spatio-temporal world. But interpreting this aspect of the New Testament cosmology existentially, Bultmann asserts that the conception of heaven as the abode of God is simply the conception by means of the category of space of the transcendence of God. In the sphere of history, the New Testament sets forth an eschatology in which a new kind of world will in the chronological future replace this one. But again, his methodology leads Bultmann to view this "mythology" similarly as simply the conception by means of the category of time of the transcendence of God, but in the special sense of God's transcendence in judgment over finite man.[28] In short, Bultmann completely disposes with the traditional understanding of New Testament cosmology and eschatology.

Bultmann's understanding of God was seen earlier to involve a conception of him as the absolutely transcendent, wholly other One who is hidden to every eye except the eye of faith. It is through faith alone that God becomes relevant to our existence, for apart from faith we live in a closed world-system of cause and effect. Yet it is this God, Bultmann insists, who reveals himself in Jesus Christ for man's salvation, this affirmation being in a unique sense *the* New Testament proclamation. With this we are brought to Bultmann's Christology.

At the outset it must be understood that Bultmann's view of the *relationship* between God's act in Christ and Jesus of Nazareth is paradoxical. Because of his form-critical approach to the Gospels, Bultmann is sure that we possess today exceedingly little real information about Jesus of Nazareth: "I do indeed think that we can know almost nothing concerning the life and personality of Jesus."[29] Furthermore, because of his modern scientific world-view with its corollary – the rejection of the New Testament world-view, Bultmann is equally insistent that knowledge about Jesus is of little or no interest to him. For him, the Christian faith is essentially indifferent to what Jesus said or did or how he understood himself. He writes:

---

[28]Bultmann, *Jesus Christ and Mythology*, 22, 25-26.

[29]Bultmann, *Jesus and the Word* (New York: Charles Scribner & Sons, 1934), 8.

The facts which historical criticism can verify cannot exhaust, indeed they cannot adequately indicate, all that Jesus means to me. How he actually originated matters little, indeed we can appreciate his significance only when we cease to worry about such questions. Our interest in the events of his life, and above all in the cross, is more than an academic concern with the history of the past. We can see meaning in them only when we ask what God is trying to say to each one of us through them.[30]

In another context he states:

If I desire an encounter with the Jesus of history, it is true that I must rely on certain historical documents. Yet the study of these documents can bring us to an encounter with the historical phenomenon "Jesus" only on the basis of one phenomenon of past history. Yet we can hope, by means of this study, to recognize the historical phenomenon "Jesus" only on the basis of one's own historic [*geschichtlich*] encounter. That was the aim and method of my *Jesus and the Word*. The Jesus of history is not *kerygma*, any more than my book was. For in the *kerygma* Jesus encounters us as the Christ – that is, as the eschatological phenomenon *par excellence*. Neither St Paul nor St John mediate an historic encounter with the historic Jesus. Even if the synoptic gospels appear to do so, that is only when they are read in the light of the historical problems which have arisen since their day, not when they are read in their original sense.... So far, then, from running away from *Historie* and taking refuge in *Geschichte*, I am deliberately renouncing any form of encounter with a phenomenon of past history, including an encounter with the Christ after the flesh, in order to encounter the Christ proclaimed in the *kerygma*, which confronts me in my historic situation.[31]

From these remarks it is evident that Bultmann is unconcerned, apart from the mere "thatness" of Jesus, with Jesus of Nazareth, simply because Jesus of Nazareth is not *the* subject of the *kerygma*. Right here appears the paradox to rationality. Bultmann believes that God acts only with human existence here and now (which act is revelation) and this act can never become an event of the past.[32] Yet the *kerygma* is the proclamation that God acted in the historical Jesus of Nazareth, although we can know little about and should be interested

---

[30]Bultmann, *Kerygma and Myth*, 35.

[31]Bultmann, *Kerygma and Myth*, 117.

[32]George E. Ladd, "What Does Bultmann Understand by the Acts of God?" *Bulletin of the Evangelical Theological Society*, 5, 3: 91-97.

even less in this Jesus "after the flesh". (The mere "thatness" but not the "whatness" of Jesus is all that is essential to the *kerygma*.) Certainly, knowledge about this one in whom God acted for man's salvation would seem on this construction to be reduced too much for even the barest interests of faith; certainly, any *proof* of this act is rendered impossible. Nevertheless, Bultmann is positive that God did "speak" in the historical Jesus and that this "Word" demands decision. In fact, this is the only way, in Bultmann's opinion, to preserve the *skandalon* of Christianity, for it is only in this manner that all objectivity, upon which the interests of faith might rest (which would in turn rend the true nature of faith), is removed.

Bultmann's attitude toward faith as decision apart from all objectivity may at this juncture be related to his view of this world. As we saw earlier, Bultmann views the objective world as closed to divine causality. We will miss a fine nuance in his thought if we assume here that his view of the world as a closed system is due *solely* to his scientific *Weltanschauung*. This is one but not the main factor.[33] For behind his view of the objective world is an even more basic commitment, namely, his view of faith. In his opinion it is only the scientific world-view with its view of the world as a closed system which does justice to or allows for a proper understanding of faith. Cobb explains Bultmann's point in this way:

> Faith knows that what is seen apart from faith is always explicable in categories that make no reference to the act of God and that no kind of historical event points more clearly to God than any other. But faith sees that *nevertheless* precisely these events are the act of God for the believer. Hence, *for faith*, the events that for the historian are the historical Jesus are the act of God. Faith connects the act of God to the historical event, not on the basis of historical evidence that such a connection is warranted, but precisely *by faith* in spite of the lack of objective reason of any kind.[34]

Thus Bultmann does not demythologise the New Testament primarily in order to harmonize with his world-view; his most basic motivation is to do justice to faith itself.[35] For Bultmann, faith understands itself as a leap, as pure risk; it does not understand itself as based upon any

---

[33]Bultmann moved away from this emphasis in later years.
[34]Cobb, 241.
[35]Bultmann, *Jesus Christ and Mythology*, 72-73.

objective evidence. Moreover, Bultmann claims that only this view of faith is consonant with Paul's principle of justification by faith alone. In order to do full justice to faith, then, the principle of justification *sola fide* applied by Paul against seeking security in good works must be applied also against seeking security in objective facts of history. For to fail to do so, that is, to base faith on certain objective events in history, is a salvation by works! True faith is believing *in spite of* the absence of all objective evidence. Herein and only here is the *skandalon* of Christianity.

Regarding the *person* of Jesus of Nazareth, Bultmann does not hesitate to affirm that he was born like every other member of the race: and he denies that Jesus possessed any nature other than that common to all men. In fact, he sees a discrepancy between the doctrine of Christ's pre existence as given by Paul and John and the "legend" of the Virgin Birth in Matthew and Luke.[36] Bultmann finds it extremely difficult to harmonize in Jesus a concept of eternal pre existence on the one hand and a beginning in time through human birth on the other. This is due, of course, to his denial of Christ's two natures. He explains the doctrine of Christ's pre existence and the accounts of the Virgin Birth as merely attempts of the early Church to explain the meaning of the person of Christ for faith.[37]

As for the redemptive acts of God in Jesus Christ, that is, Christ's *work*, Bultmann demythologizes both the cross and the resurrection of Jesus and interprets them existentially.[38] He declares that the idea of an incarnate God-man who vicariously atones for man's sin by enduring man's punishment and death is a mythological interpretation of the crucifixion of Jesus consisting of "a mixture of sacrificial and juridical analogies, which have ceased to be tenable for us today".[39] And as for the resurrection of Jesus, it is a mythical event pure and simple, not an objective event of past history at all.[40] What then are these "events" intended to convey if they do not indicate a vicarious atonement and an objective event of past history? When one recalls that for Bultmann mythology is essentially anthropological and not

---

[36]Bultmann, *Kerygma and Myth*, 34.

[37]Bultmann, *Kerygma and Myth*, 35.

[38]Bultmann, *Kerygma and Myth*, 35-43.

[39]Bultmann, *Kerygma and Myth*, 35.

[40]Bultmann, *Kerygma and Myth*, 38.

cosmological, that is, that in myth, though he appears to be describing the world and certain events in the world, man is really describing his own existence, one is not surprised when Bultmann interprets the redemptive acts of God as set forth in the New Testament anthropologically, or perhaps better, existentially. The cross becomes then a symbol of human self-mastery over the passions, and the resurrection becomes an attempt to explain the significance of the cross to faith.

Concerning the cross, Bultmann writes: "To believe in the cross of Christ does not mean to concern ourselves with a mythical process wrought outside of us and our world, with an objective event turned by God to our advantage, but rather to make the cross of Christ our own, to undergo crucifixion with him."[41] By thus entering by the leap and risk of faith into Christ's sufferings, the "flesh with passions and lusts thereof" (Gal. 5:24) is crucified, which means existentially "the overcoming of our natural dread of suffering and the perfection of our detachment from the world."[42] In so far as man is judged and delivered from his passions and concern for the world by his understanding of the cross, so far is Christ crucified "for us", but not in the sense of any theory of sacrifice or satisfaction.[43] And the proclamation of the cross as the event of redemption from these things challenges all who hear it to appropriate this significance for themselves. Existentially, this all means simply a challenge to modern man to abandon unauthentic living, to surrender himself to the invisible and to freedom to face the future with individual responsibility.

Concerning the resurrection, Bultmann insists that it must be viewed with the cross in an inseparable unity as a faith affirmation that the cross is actually the salvation of the world. "... the cross and the resurrection form a single, indivisible cosmic event which bring judgment to the world and opens up for men the possibility of authentic life."[44] This means that the resurrection itself is not an event of past history. Rather, it means that the affirmation of faith in the resurrection is simply the affirmation of faith that the salvation of God works itself out in the cross.[45] Bultmann avers:

---

[41] Bultmann, *Kerygma and Myth*, 36.
[42] Bultmann, *Kerygma and Myth*, 37.
[43] Bultmann, *Kerygma and Myth*, 37.
[44] Bultmann, *Kerygma and Myth*, 38-39.
[45] Bultmann, *Kerygma and Myth*, 41.

The resurrection itself is not an event of past history. All that historical criticism can establish is the fact that the first disciples came to believe in the resurrection. The historian can perhaps to some extent account for that faith from the personal intimacy which the disciples had enjoyed with Jesus during his earthly life, and so reduce the resurrection appearances to a series of subjective visions. But the historical problem is not of interest to Christian belief in the resurrection. For the historical event of the rise of the Easter faith means for us what it meant for the first disciples – namely, ... that act of God in which the redemptive event of the cross is completed.[46]

Existentially, this means the affirmation, by faith, that the cross has "saving" efficacy. And these events – the cross and resurrection – when proclaimed constitute the New Testament *kerygma* – a message of deliverance from unauthentic living and translation into authentic living.

A summary at this point of the *kerygma* which Bultmann feels needs to be proclaimed to modern man may aid in solidifying what has just been said. Bultmann is asking the modern preacher to proclaim that God acted in Jesus Christ in his death and resurrection. Of course, he is to make it clear to his hearers that this death and this resurrection are expressed in the New Testament in mythological, that is, in existential language – in language of a pre-scientific age intended to express and to explain the New Testament writers' own existence, how their lives were shaped by this man Jesus. As intimate followers of Jesus, by the crucifixion of their friend, the disciples entered into his suffering, no longer fearing the same, and thus became open to what God had for them. In faith (which was God's act in them) they believed that somehow God had acted in this one for the forgiveness of their sins. They expressed this faith in this act of God for them in Christ by picturing him as on the third day rising from the dead. Finally, by believing the same *in spite of* the evidence of modern science to support the view of this world as a closed system of cause and effect, modern man too may know God's act for him, no longer fearing the past and opening up to the future. In short, he may know the meaning of authentic existence as freedom in love and as freedom toward responsible decision.

As for Bultmann's understanding of the Holy Spirit, his

---

[46]Bultmann, *Kerygma and Myth*, 42.

demythologized concept of that divine person consists in his being the "factual possibility of the new life" which the modern man can acquire through faith.[47]

Christian Theology or Heideggerian Philosophy?

For many interpreters of Bultmann, his understanding of New Testament theology is, as Cobb puts it, simply "baptizing" Heidegger's philosophy as Christian theology. Bultmann emphatically denies that he has done such, since Heidegger's existentialism tells us only *that* we should live authentically and not *what* constitutes authentic existence, *since* Heidegger's existentialism, though insisting on the attainment of authentic existence, cannot prescribe how it is to be attained, and *since* Heidegger's existentialism assigns a decisive place to "being-toward-death," whereas Christian thought assigns the decisive place to the encounter with a "Thou".[48] The Christian faith provides in the *kerygma* the call to decision and the content of authentic existence. The Christian faith places before the religious existent an encounter with God in Jesus Christ and opens up the possibility of authentic *freedom* from one's past and the *experience* of faith, love, hope, and joy which characterizes Christian existence.

Viewing the relationship between Heidegger's philosophy and Christian theology in this manner, Bultmann, as we have seen, simply allows existentialism to frame the sensitive questions of and for modern man, but the New Testament "act of God in Christ," he insists, must give the answers. In short, Bultmann begins with and builds his theology upon existentialist philosophy.

Has Bultmann's *Entmythologisierungsprogram* removed the scandal of Christianity for modern man? Bultmann vehemently denies this, insisting that there is still a scandal – indeed, a scandal of even greater moment than the scandal of traditional Christianity since he has removed the latter's objective basis of faith, namely, Christianity's continuing insistence that it is only faith in the decisive act of God in the Jesus Christ of history that transforms man and delivers him up to true authenticity.

---

[47]Cited by Ridderbos, Bultmann, 28.
[48]Cobb, 234-35.

Criticism

George E. Ladd is certainly correct when he writes that "the most superficial reading of [Bultmann's] writings would show that he is not and does not desire to be an orthodox theologian."[49] When Bultmann rejects all of the cardinal articles of the orthodox Christian faith, he certainly places himself beyond the confines of Orthodoxy. Indeed, it would seem that only in the sense that Bultmann continues to insist that God acts in *Jesus Christ* for man's salvation and not, say, in Buddha that he may be considered a *Christian* theologian at all. He rejects the infallibility and inerrancy of the Old and New Testaments; he denies the orthodox understanding of God as subsisting eternally in three persons, the Father, the Son, and the Holy Spirit, all three possessing the same essential deity and equality in power and glory; he repudiates the eternal pre existence of the divine nature of Jesus Christ, averring that Jesus was only a man, born like all other men. Though willing to speak of Jesus' cross as an event of past history, Bultmann rejects all ideas of his death as in any sense a vicarious atonement for the sins of the world. Jesus' resurrection is pure mythology as is his ascension into heaven. At best, from the point of view of orthodoxy, the most that can be said for Bultmann's view of God is that it is absolutely deistic, with God and the world as two independent, mutually exclusive, non-intervening entities.

When Bultmann's analysis of Paul's antithesis in man between "flesh" and "spirit" concludes that these terms only describe what Heidegger has better distinguished as unauthentic and authentic existence – the former describing that existence wherein one's understanding of himself leads to concern for the world and wherein one finds security in externalities and history, the latter describing that existence wherein life is lived in terms of the real potentialities of the personality, free from the past and open to the future – such an analysis gravely fails to penetrate into the Biblical meaning of sin and grace. Sin defined as human self-assertion in the world of relativity and perishability seems hardly to scratch the surface of the Bible's portrayal of sin as any want of conformity to, or transgression of, the law of God (1 John 3:4). Human misery viewed as mere involvement in this world of relativity hardly does justice to the much fuller description of human misery found in the Bible and depicted as *loss* of communion

---

[49]Ladd, 91.

with God and *subjection* to God's wrath and curse, to all the miseries of this life, to death itself, and to the pains of hell forever (Gen. 3:8, 24; Eph. 2:3; Rom. 5:12, 14; 6:23; Matt. 25:41). Grace defined as that which is necessary to bring man into a state of freedom and the enablement of man to attain authentic existence fails to do justice to the Biblical depiction of grace as the unmerited love of God in action in the very presence of sin (Rom. 5:20), and manifested in a saving way in his acts of justification and adoption, in his work of sanctification, and in the benefits to the believer which accompany these, namely, assurance of God's love, peace of conscience, joy in the Holy Spirit, increase of grace, and continuing perseverance in the faith to the end (Eph. 1:7; 1 John 3:1; 2 Thess. 2:13; Rom. 5:1-5; Col. 1:10-11; Prov. 4:18; 2 Pet. 3:18).[50]

Certainly the salvation that is consonant with Bultmann's view of God and man fails to meet adequately the spiritual needs of man and is radically unbiblical. The Bible declares man's basic need to be the deliverance out of his state of sin and misery and a new birth into a state of salvation, this need being met only in the life, death, and resurrection of a personal Redeemer, the Lord Jesus Christ, as the benefits of his redemption are applied to the believer by the Holy Spirit.

These facts alone sufficiently indicate that Bultmann is not able to propagate the biblical faith or to instruct the saint. And from the point of view of orthodoxy this criticism could stop here. However, since Bultmann's demythologized kerygmatic theology raises several pertinent issues and contains definite inconsistencies and discrepancies, no criticism would be complete without some word concerning them.

Irrationalism

First, a basic irrationalism pervades Bultmann's theology. Bultmann is guided throughout his theological work by the very practical concern of removing all unnecessary obstacles to the faith of modern man. We should not, so he says, insist that modern man accept the pre-scientific view of the world, the New Testament teaching on miracles, spirits, etc., and the mythical idea of a Savior God-man dying on a cross for sinners. Yet it seems extremely arbitrary on Bultmann's part to stop with the *kerygma* as he formulates it, namely, that God

---

[50]For Bultmann's definitions of sin and grace, see Ridderbos, *Bultmann*, 44.

acts for man's salvation in the death and resurrection of Jesus Christ, and not to demythologize it too. Thielicke is justified in remarking: "We are left wondering why the event of Christ is not myth like everything else. Surely '*logos sarx egeneto*' implies an intervention in the closed system of reality."[51] Is not such an insistence, particularly when Bultmann is unwilling to provide any objective basis for accepting the same, an unnecessary obstacle to modern man, if, as it would appear to be, the removal of unnecessary obstacles is Bultmann's desire. If obstacle there must be, why not simply retain the New Testament picture of things? Now it will not do to reply that this criticism misunderstands the nature of myth and the purpose of demythologization, and that while it is true that the New Testament is to be demythologized completely, yet only that which is myth can be mythologized, and since the *kerygma* is not myth, it must be retained. For there is absolutely no *defensible* criterion which Bultmann can produce which can demonstrate why his *kerygma* is not as equally mythical as the mythology which he regards as unnecessary. His *kerygma* definitely proclaims divine intrusion into man's affairs in order to provide the *only* remedy for man's lack of authenticity.

Bultmann, of course, attempts to skirt this difficulty by reminding his critic that God does not *actually* intervene. Only *by faith* is God made relevant to the human situation. Though the human existent knows that he lives in a world into which God *never* intrudes, *nevertheless* by faith God becomes real in the human situation. But herein as well is Bultmann's irrationalism evident. Either an event is or is not an act of God. It cannot both be and not be an act of God at the same time, all of Bultmann's protestations to the contrary notwithstanding. If it is not, no amount of "faith" on my part makes it an act of God; if it is, it is so, regardless of whether I believe it to be so or not. Now, of course, in the Reformed view, everything that happens is decreed by God and either mediately or immediately governed by God (Eph. 1:11; Acts 4: 27-28; Ps. 145:17; 104:24; Heb. 1:3). Bultmann's assertion that God does not intervene in human affairs is really a deistic view at best, which allows no room for divine providence, either general or special. Actually, there is considerable reason to wonder whether Bultmann even has a God at all. And is not

---

[51]Helmut Thielicke, "The Restatement of New Testament Mythology," *Kerygma and Myth*, 154.

the "crucifixion of our passions" which is purported by Bultmann as being accomplished when we believe in the cross of Christ (even though we know that Jesus did not really die for us), as Schniewind suggests, nothing more than a "striking euphemism for self-mastery, which is the quest of all the higher religions and philosophies"?[52] It definitely seems to be so!

The irrationalism which pervades Bultmann's theological pronouncements is representative of a much more extensive mood – never seriously considered as viable prior to Kierkegaard and biblical criticism – to be found throughout modern theology, and expressed by a divided field of knowledge. The "upper story" contains concepts to be accepted without any kind of empirical verification but only on the ground of a leap of faith since the "lower story" – the world of rationality and testable science – offers no key to the meaning and significance of man. In such a dichotomy man must leap to a faith commitment – which one being of little consequence – in which he can feel at home. Of course, in this leap the fact of faith seems to be the important thing, the object of faith inconsequential. This shift toward a divided field of knowledge, Pinnock analyses as an attempt to escape the tangle of logic and history by creating one's own meaning of human existence by an act of the will.[53] Through this expression of will as "ultimate concern", man experiences "salvation". It is little wonder that such a mood is considered by the uninitiated laymen as theological doubletalk, "full of sound and fury, signifying nothing."

A misunderstanding of Biblical faith
Second, Bultmann's concept of faith is unbiblical is its assertion that faith, to be faith, must be devoid of all genuine objective knowledge content. He sees this to be simply a consistent application in the area of cognition of the Reformers' principle of justification by faith alone in the area of good conduct. As the Reformers demolished all human security in meritorious works, so he desires to remove a false confidence in human knowledge. But, as Pinnock rejoins, "The analogy is tragically fallacious. There is a world of difference between leaving one's moral bankruptcy and finding refuge in the objective and finished

---

[52] Julius Schniewind, "A Reply to Bultmann," *Kerygma and Myth*, 65.

[53] Clark H. Pinnock, "The 'Upper' and the 'Lower' Story in Modern Theology," Classroom notes, New Orleans Baptist Theological Seminary.

work of Christ, and turning from intellectual doubt about the veracity of Scripture only to leap into the abyss of blind faith."[54]

Though a theologian's view of the nature of faith will always depend on the views he holds of Scripture, of God and man, and of their relationship, one with the other, yet if he is willing to heed the teaching of Scripture, the theologian will learn that the Bible does not repudiate an objective knowledge basis for faith. Rather, he will discover that the Bible regards faith as including rational assent grounded in certain specific objective facts and events. To illustrate this point, one could cite Hebrews 11:6: "he that cometh to God must believe that he is [*estin*], and that he is a rewarder of them that diligently seek him." From this text alone one learns that biblical faith involves intellectual assent to at least two affirmations of such a nature that they could become articles of creeds, namely, that God *exists* and that he is the *rewarder* of them who diligently seek him. But the assumption of the writer of this epistle in making this assertion (which he makes abundantly clear throughout his discourse) is precisely these things, namely, that God is and that he rewards the one seeking him, not that God does *not* exist or that he does not reward the one seeking him. He would never be so foolish as to demand that the one coming to God must believe that God exists if he knew that God did not exist. He would never be so irrational as to require the one coming to God to believe that God will reward his searching if he knew that God would not reward him. Yet Bultmann seems to be just this irrational when he asks the modern man to *believe* that a given act is the act of God when he *knows* that that act is not and cannot be an act of God.

Another verse (among many) is Romans 10:14: "How then shall they call on him in whom they have not believed? And how shall they believe in him of whom they have not heard?" This verse makes it as clear as it can be made that at least some knowledge of Christ is absolutely essential as a *precondition* to trust. Our Lord taught the value of objective evidence as the proper basis for faith when he instructed Thomas to thrust his finger into his wounds and to believe (John 20:27). Paul in the Damascus road incident, asked, "Who are you, Lord?" (Acts 9:5; 26:15). The knowledge gained in each case cited led on to faith.

---

[54]Pinnock, *A Defense of Biblical Infallibility* (Philadelphia: Presbyterian and Reformed, 1967), 6.

Of course, knowledge of objective fact as here described does not and from the nature of the case cannot refer to knowledge based on facts that can always be scientifically and empirically verified. Whether Jesus rose from the grave on the third day cannot be scientifically proven in the sense that the word "scientifically" conveys for modern scientism. But knowledge can be knowledge nonetheless if it is based on *trustworthy testimony*. As Packer correctly declares, "Whether particular beliefs should be treated as known certainties or doubtful opinions will depend on the worth of the testimony on which they are based."[55] And the objective events and facts in which the Bible urges that we place our faith rest on the testimony of a God who cannot lie (Titus 1:2) and which is, therefore, *absolutely* trustworthy. Now, of course, this last affirmation rests on a particular view of the Bible, but it is a view claimed by the Bible for itself and recognized by the Church (a *motivum credibilitatis*) as the only true view for eighteen and a half centuries. In the Bible God requires him who would be saved to recognize his need of salvation and to believe in certain objective historical events (the meanings of which are divinely interpreted), namely, that Jesus died (actually and literally on a particular calendar day on a particular hill in the land of Palestine) for our sins (which is the divine interpretation) according to the Scriptures (which is the testimony to be believed), that he was buried, and that he rose again (actually and literally) the third day (after the particular day on which he died) according to the Scriptures (which is the testimony to be believed but which is abundantly supported by the eye-witness testimony of Peter [see 1 Cor. 15:5 and 2 Pet 1:16-18], the twelve, five hundred disciples at one gathering, and finally James, the apostles, and Paul [1 Cor. 15:5-8]). Now none of this testimony, of course, can be scientifically verified – none of these witnesses are present in person for interrogation; however, *no* reason has yet been advanced which must *necessarily* demand the denial of the veracity of any one of them. To the contrary, much evidence may be cited to show that they all gave trustworthy testimony. Certainly God did and must. Therefore, since the testimony of God is manifestly true, it is to be believed, and only rejected at the peril of one's own soul.

To rebut the testimony of Scripture to the resurrection of Jesus, the claim is often made that since only the disciples saw Jesus after

---

[55] James I. Packer, "Faith," *Baker's Dictionary of Theology*, 209.

his resurrection, therefore the event of the resurrection is of interest only to believers. Bultmann, in particular, insists that the early disciples' Easter faith gave rise to the story of the resurrection rather than the resurrection serving as the ground of that faith in the disciples. But such a claim is simply not true to the very witness on which the claim is based. First, many disciples found it extremely difficult to believe in Christ's resurrection even after the Lord "showed himself alive after his passion by many infallible proofs" (Acts 1:3; Matt. 28:17; John 20:25-28). Second, and perhaps even more important for the point presently being made, at least one *unbeliever* saw the resurrected and glorified Lord and as a result of that revelation believed, namely, Saul of Tarsus on the Damascus road. Ridderbos demonstrates the weakness in Bultmann's view when he writes:

> If Christ did not rise from the dead and this story is a myth, the question confronting us is how this myth originated. It is undeniable that this "myth" originated several days after the death of Jesus. A very abrupt change had to take place in the thoughts and deliberations of the disciples with respect to their dead Master. To think of this as the mythical formation of the significance...which the disciples abruptly ascribed to Jesus' crucifixion without any new fact as its basis, a fact which originated outside of themselves, is a postulate that is dictated by Bultmann's concept of reality, but which is at the same time absolutely unintelligible from an historical point of view. It is especially incomprehensible if one remembers that this resurrection witness, in the primary sense of an eye witness..., was the starting point and center of the Christian proclamation and formed the foundation of Christian certainty.[56]

There can be no doubt whatever, then, in light of this discussion that the Bible does set forth definite objective facts and events based upon trustworthy testimony as the knowledge basis of faith. The Bible knows nothing of a leap into the dark for no rational reason. One cannot ignore the Bible on this point with impunity. To follow Bultmann in his concept of faith is to be misled completely; it is to be led away from the biblical faith which is rationally defensible and pistically satisfying to a faith whose object is extremely difficult to define, whose authority is solely Bultmann himself, and whose verification is wholly subjective and non-verifiable.[57]

---

[56]Ridderbos, *Bultmann*, 34.

[57]It is for this very reason, namely, the absence of objectivity in Bultmann's

A false evaluation of modern science

Finally, Bultmann's claim that faith in God's acts must be based solely in the non-verifiable, non-rational, paradoxical revelation event itself and on nothing else because, besides the "fact" that this alone makes true faith possible, modern science has amply demonstrated that this is a closed world system operating on a cause and effect basis and into which the supernatural cannot and does not intrude – this claim, I say, is erroneous in that it ascribes powers to modern science which in fact it cannot and will never have. No scientific fact, in and of itself, can prove that this world is a closed system of cause and effect. It is invariably the interpretation which the scientist places on the fact which determines the meaning of the fact. Consequently, it is not with the specific facts of science that we take issue; rather, it is with the philosophy of science that controls modern science that we must be concerned. Obviously, Bultmann assumes the validity of the principles (the philosophy) that control the modern scientific enterprise and which guide it in all of its affirmations. But he fails to distinguish between an unbelieving philosophy of science and a Christian philosophy of science. The former, we readily admit, is unable (and unwilling) to allow a place for supernaturalism within its boundaries; the latter, however, is unable (and unwilling) not to allow a place for supernaturalism within its boundaries. Non-Christian scientism, in all of its efforts, *assumes* as pre-scientific givens the non-createdness and autonomy of man, the ultimacy of man's rational processes, and the non-createdness of every fact with which it has to do. Of course, all of its efforts will "prove" the non-existence of God or, at least, his non-intervention into this world's affairs. And this is so, even though the unbelieving scientist loudly claims that he makes, as a scientist, no religious value-judgements or moral decisions.

A Christian philosophy of science, to the contrary, delights in affirming the existence of the Creator, the createdness of all facts, human rationality as a divine gift, and a divinely-imposed cultural mandate to receptively "reconstruct" the universe as it thinks God's thoughts after him. Nor is there any incompatibility between this

---

theology, that the Bultmannian "school" has come upon "hard times" and has fragmented and until now his followers are known, for lack of a more precise name, as simply "post-Bultmannians". Many of Bultmann's pupils today are insisting upon more objectivity in theology.

approach to science and science *per se*, as is evidenced by the fact that here in America several hundred highly trained, indisputably qualified scientists are members of the Creation Research Society, an organization dedicated to the highest expression of true science within the framework of biblical revelation. Here are many scientific minds who insist that this world is not a closed system controlled solely by cause and effect. In fact, they insist that such a position as Bultmann maintains, as a universal negation, cannot be proven, while much evidence to the contrary may be cited which points by implication at least to the view that God has intruded himself, indeed, is constantly doing so, into man's affairs. Bultmann, as so many others in this day, has erroneously granted to modern science an infallibility and a finality which the modern scientist himself will admit it just does not have. Consequently, modern science need not be a hindrance to faith.

Bultmann speaks much of and shows great concern for "modern man". He means by the "modern man" that man who has "come of age", who can no longer tolerate the mythical elements of a pre-scientific age, who no longer believes in miracles, such as the resurrection, or a "three-storied universe" – heaven above, earth between, hell beneath. He seems to forget that unbelief in some forms of Biblical supernaturalism was as prevalent in the days of the events of the New Testament as it is today. Unbelief in miracle is not "modern"; unbelief in the resurrection is not the result of a sophistication newly learned in our day and unknown to the days of the Apostles. Ancient gnosticism, for example, was unable to relate Christianity's insistence on the Incarnation to its philosophy of matter as evil, so gnosticism refused to believe in the Incarnation. It is the same today. Unbelief is in so many instances, particularly on the academic level, simply the result of the inability to cope with the truth of revelation in the light of a previously assumed position. If the previously assumed position were given up, and upon examination it can so often be shown that there is no valid reason for not giving it up, the truth of revelation is easily assimilated. All of this simply means that the idea of the so-called "modern man" has been greatly exaggerated. Man's nature has not changed since the fall of his first parents; his needs are the same. Always some, as in Paul's day, at the preaching of the gospel will mock, others will say, "We will hear you again concerning this matter," but some will believe (Acts 17:32-34). And those who believe, after instruction concerning the nature of the resurrection body as to its material nature, when confronted with the "three-storied universe" of Scripture, will quickly see the need for and the reality of a "place" (John 14:2) called heaven for the elect and a "place" called hell (Matt. 25:41; Rev. 20:12-14) for the reprobated wicked, though the need to observe carefully the possible use of phenomenal language in the descriptions also must be stressed. Certainly there will always be the need to interpret the statements of Scripture as a body of divinely-revealed truths, but one only casts himself upon a subjective sea of conjecture with no guiding light when he denies that the Bible is the Word of God and declares, therefore, that man must fend for himself. The confusion with which modern theology is rife is abundant proof that every theological edifice so constructed is doomed at the outset to the ravages of time because its foundational planks are rotten. Feeling unable to accept the Scripture's claim concerning itself, Bultmann began with existentialist philosophy and constructed a New Testament theology in which the entire divine element exists only in the believer's mind. It would appear that Bultmann is only listening to a "recording" of his own inner voice.

Chapter Nineteen

Dr. John H. Gerstner on
Thomas Aquinas as a Protestant

In his article, "Aquinas Was a Protestant," that appeared in the May 1994 issue of *Tabletalk*, the popular monthly devotional publication of Ligonier Ministries, Inc., edited by R. C. Sproul, Jr., Dr. John H. Gerstner[1] declares that Thomas Aquinas (1225-74) "was a medieval Protestant teaching the Reformation doctrine of justification by faith alone" (13) – indeed, that he "taught the biblical doctrine of justification" (14)[2] – and that he was "one of Protestantism's greatest theologians" (14). While he acknowledges that Augustine did not adequately develop the forensic element in justification, he asserts that Aquinas "was not led astray" but "with Augustine taught the biblical doctrine of justification so that if the Roman church had followed Aquinas the Reformation would not have been absolutely necessary" (14).[3] He also calls the supposition, drawn by both Roman Catholic and Protes-

---

Note: This article was originally published in the *Westminster Theological Journal* 59 (1997) 113-21.

[1]I sent Dr. Gerstner this response to his article and requested that he carefully peruse it and indicate to me any place where he thought I may have misrepresented his view. However, Dr. Gerstner died in March 1996 before he had the opportunity to respond to my article. I regret that the reader will not have the benefit of his reaction.

[2]The Reformation (and biblical) doctrine of justification by faith alone is beautifully captured by the *Westminster Shorter Catechism* answer to Question 33, "What is justification?": "Justification is an act of God's free grace, wherein He pardoneth all our sins, and accepteth us as righteous in His sight, only for the righteousness of Christ imputed to us, and received by faith alone."

[3]Apparently Dr. Gerstner would disagree with Carl F. H. Henry's recent assessment of these two Fathers: "Augustine (354-430) conflated the immediate act of justification with the process of sanctification and consequently misrepresented justification as a 'making righteous.' Thomas Aquinas (1224-1274) also viewed justifying grace as a supernatural quality infused into the sinner. Justification he depicted in terms of operative divine grace transmitted in the sacraments. The Roman Church's elevation of Thomism as its

tant theologians alike, that Aquinas was a "modern tridentine Romanist" a "pernicious error" (14). He draws these conclusions because, he says, "Aquinas taught a doctrine of *iustificatio impii*, a justification of the impious" (14).[4] What is surprising – indeed, quite startling – about Dr. Gerstner's assessment of Aquinas is that in this same article he admits that Aquinas (1) "unfortunately attributed...undue power to the sacraments" (13-14); (2) understood *iustificatio impii* in terms of "remission and infusion of sanctifying grace" (14)[5]; and (3) "does not state the 'imputation' of Christ's righteousness" (14). But in spite of these doctrinal deficiencies, Dr. Gerstner believes that Aquinas' teaching on justification is still "essentially the biblical (and Reformation) doctrine" (14).

---

official theology proliferated the view that justification is an inner state dependent upon sacramental observance." ("Justification: A Doctrine in Crisis," *JETS* 38/1 [March 1995] 58)

[4]Aquinas's use of the phrase *iustificatio impii* means nothing in itself; it is the language of the Latin Vulgate at *Romans* 4:5: *qui iustificat impium*. It is what he says "justification of the impious" is that is all-important, and it is just in this area that his theology of justification is defective.

[5]Far from Aquinas's understanding of justification as the "making of the sinner righteous" by remission (through the sacrament of baptism) and the infusion of sanctifying grace (by the sacraments of the Mass and penance) being rejected "with horror, as Protestant" by the Council of Trent (Gerstner, 52), his understanding was precisely how Rome's counter-Reformation Council of Trent was later to construe justification.

If Aquinas's writings erred so "horribly" in the very area where the Reformers were attacking Romish theology by siding with the Reformers, it is difficult to understand why the Reformers never claimed him or why Rome raised him in 1567, four years after the close of the Council of Trent, to the dignity of "doctor of the church" and regards him to this day as the *doctor angelicus*. David S. Schaff's remarks, found in Philip Schaff's *History of the Christian Church* (Grand Rapids: Eerdmans, 1960 reproduction of the 1907 edition, V, 662, 675, 754, 756) are clearly more on the mark:

> In the teachings of Thomas Aquinas we have, with one or two exceptions, the doctrinal tenets of the Latin Church in their perfect exposition as we have them in the Decrees of the Council of Trent in their final statement...the theology of the Angelic Doctor and the theology of the Roman Catholic Church are identical in all particulars except the immaculate conception. He who understands Thomas understands the mediaeval theology at its best and will be in possession of the doctrinal system

Perhaps one reason behind Dr. Gerstner's *apologia* on Aquinas' behalf (he does not advance it himself in the article under review, but I must assume that it is an aspect of his final conclusion concerning Aquinas) is that the latter teaches that justification is "instantaneous" and not successive (*Summa Theologi*ca, ii, 1, question 113, article 7). But Aquinas's exposition of justification here as elsewhere in his *Summa* is anything but "Protestant" in its content, and there is reason to believe, on the basis of his explanation in this particular article of justification being "instantaneous," that he is speaking only of the initial point at which God's infusion of grace first disposes the sinful mind toward holiness.

---

of the Roman Church.... No distinction was made by the mediaeval theologians between the doctrine of *justification* and the doctrine of *sanctification*, such as is made by Protestant theologians. Justification was treated as a process of making the sinner righteous, and not as a judicial sentence by which he was declared to be righteous.... Although several of Paul's statements in the *Epistle to the Romans* are quoted by Thomas Aquinas, neither he nor the other Schoolmen rise to the idea that it is upon the [condition] of faith that a man is justified. Faith is a virtue, not a justifying principle, and is treated at the side of hope and love.

Alister E. McGrath, *Luther's Theology of the Cross* (Oxford: Blackwell, 1985), 82, also writes:

During the thirteenth century the concept of a created habit of grace [that is, a permanent disposition within the believer, as distinct from the external influence of grace]...had become inextricably linked with the discussion of the mode of man's justification before God. The concept appeared to provide a solution to a dilemma which the theological renaissance of the twelfth century had highlighted: in what manner can God be said to dwell in the souls of the justified?... St. Thomas...located the solution to the problem as lying in the concept of a created habit which, although essentially indistinguishable from God, nevertheless remains an entity created within the human soul by him.

Underlying the implication of a created habit of grace in justification is a particular concept of causality. For St. Thomas,...the nature of grace, sin and divine acceptation were such that a created habit of grace was necessary in justification by the very nature of things.

In sum, it is this supernatural and intermediary change in human nature, according to Aquinas, rather than Christ's alien righteousness (*iustitia Christi aliena*), that is the basis of justification.

Dr. Gerstner explains the absence of any mention in Aquinas of the imputation of Christ's righteousness to the elect sinner this way: "[The imputation of Christ's righteousness] is *implied* by the infusion of sanctifying grace which would never have been infused into an unjustified soul" (14, emphasis supplied).[6] And he traces the "pernicious error"[7] that everyone (except, apparently, Dr. Gerstner himself) commits about Aquinas being a "modern tridentine Romanist" to the fact that Aquinas "mention[s] infusion *in connection with* justification" (14). "But," Dr. Gerstner declared, "so do Protestants, though they do not commonly use that term *infusion*" (14). Here Dr. Gerstner

---

[6]Dr. Gerstner says here in so many words that Aquinas believed that the soul would first have to be justified (in the Protestant sense) before God would infuse it with sanctifying grace. I am unaware of any place in his writings where Aquinas states this. To the contrary, he regularly declares that the infusion of grace and the movement of free choice toward God and away from sin are "in the order of nature" first required for the justification of the ungodly (*Summa Theologica*, ii, 1, question 113, article 8). And Rome regularly denies as a matter of course what Dr. Gerstner says here of Aquinas.

[7]These "pernicious errorists" would of necessity have to include the two great Reformers Martin Luther and John Calvin, for neither of them claimed Aquinas for the Reformation cause. Indeed, Luther, with characteristic bombast, spoke of him as "the fountain [*Brunn*] and original soup [*Grundsuppe*] of all heresy, error, and Gospel havoc [*aller Ketzerei, Irrthumb und Vertilgung des Evangelium*], as his books bear witness" (Schaff, *History*, V, 676). It has been argued, as does H. Denifle (*Luther und Luthertum in der erste Entwicklung* [Mainz: 1906, 2nd edition], I.2.535-56), that Luther, being the late medieval Augustinian that he was and educated within the *via moderna*, that is, within Occamism's metaphysical nominalism, knew only the early medieval theology, including Aquinas, from the historical sections of Gabriel Biel's *Collectorium* that had distorted the theology of the earlier medieval period. Thus Luther, Denifle argues, was prejudiced against "catholic" theology in general and the *via antiqua*, that is, Thomism's and Scotism's metaphyical realism, of the thirteenth century in particular. But Luther could and did read Aquinas's *Summa Theologica* for himself, even as his cited statement suggests.

Calvin declared that the definition of justification that the Council of Trent proffered at length "contains nothing else than the trite dogma of the schools [of which Aquinas was the most mature representative—RLR]: that men are justified partly by the grace of God and partly by their own works" ("On the Sixth Session of the Council of Trent," *Acts of the Council of Trent with the Antidote* [Grand Rapids: Baker, 1983 reprint of Calvin's *Tracts*], 3, 108.

says in effect that "Protestants do and Protestants don't" – that is to say, that they mention infusion in connection with justification but they do not use the term when they mention it! I say again, all this is quite startling, coming as it does from a renowned Reformed church historian who knows and accepts the Protestant doctrine of justification.[8]

Dr. Gerstner goes on to fault in quick succession several Protestant theologians by name for what he represents as their sub-biblical view of justification. He takes to task Kenneth Foreman, who wrote in the 1955 "Extension" to *The New Schaff-Herzog Encyclopaedia of Religious Knowledge*, for stressing that justification "does not refer to the state of man, only to his status," and for saying that justification "is nothing done to the man, it is God's way of looking at him." Dr. Gerstner declares Foreman's first statement to be true enough ("True, [justification] does not 'refer to the state of man,'" 15), but then he aborts any real significance in his concession by saying: "...but it does not exclude it" either (15). He faults Foreman's second statement, saying: "If nothing were done to the man, God would not look at him as justified" (15). Now one could agree with Dr. Gerstner here if he had gone on to say that what God did to the sinner in justifying him was to constitute him righteous in his sight by the divine act of imputation, but this is not what he says. Rather, what God did to the sinner, Dr. Gerstner said, is to regenerate him ("He is a *regenerate* man though God 'looks at him' as still among the *impii*!"; 15, emphasis original) – an assertion that no Protestant theologian would deny but that is not part of the Biblical definition of justification and that, if left as is, injects the same confusion into the meaning of justification that the Reformers had to address in the sixteenth century.

Dr. Gerstner criticizes as illogical J. P. Simpson, who wrote the article on justification in *Hastings Encyclopaedia of Religion and Ethics*, for saying that the term *justification* "implies a personal status or relationship, and not a subjective experience," and rejoins by

---

[8]One can only guess at the reason that lies behind Dr. Gerstner's *apologia* for a "Protestant" Aquinas in the area of justification, but one who knows of Dr. Gerstner's admiration of Thomistic natural theology cannot help but wonder if it is not his appreciation of the contribution that Aquinas's dichotomistic nature/grace scheme makes to his own apologetic system that is also driving his effort to "save" Aquinas *in toto* for Protestantism.

saying: "But what is faith if not a 'subjective experience?'" (15). He then goes on to say that it is this "big little slip" on Simpson's part that "throws his whole subsequent historical survey somewhat out of kilter, including Aquinas's view" (15). But it is Dr. Gerstner who confuses here. While faith in Jesus Christ, as a (Spirit-wrought) psychic act, is surely a subjective experience, it is not justification *per se* and it is not what the Bible means by justification. Faith is the necessary *precondition* to justification while justification – a constituting and declarative act – is the inevitable divine response to the sinner's faith in Jesus Christ. And Dr. Gerstner cannot deny that Aquinas does write in his *Summa Theologica*, ii, 1, question 100, article 12, that

> ...justification [properly so called] may be taken in two ways. First, according as man is made just by becoming possessed of the habit of justice; secondly, according as he does works of justice, so that in this sense justification is nothing else than the execution of justice. Now justice, like the other virtues, may denote either the acquired or the infused virtue.... The acquired virtue is caused by works; but the infused virtue [of the execution of justice] is caused by God Himself through His grace. The latter is true justice, of which we are speaking now, and in respect of which a man is said to be just before God, according to Rom. 4.2.[9]

If nothing more were to be said in response to this citation, one must surely insist that Aquinas commits grave exegetical error here. For the one thing Paul did *not* mean in Romans 4:2ff. is that the respect in which a man is said to be just before God is that of an "infused righteousness." Rather, the respect in which Paul declares that a man is just before God is through Christ's *imputed* or "credited" righteousness, which fact is made clear throughout Romans 4 by Paul's sustained employment of the verb λογίζομαι, *logizomai* ("count, reckon, credit, look upon as"):

Romans 4:3: "What does the Scripture say? 'Abraham believed God, and *it was credited* [ἐλογίσθη, *elogisthē*] to him as righteousness.'"

Romans 4:4: "...when a man works, his wages *are not credited* [οὐ λογίζεται, *ou logizetai*] to him as a gift, but as an obligation."

---

[9]Cited from *Thomas Aquinas: II*, Vol. 20 in *Great Books of the Western World*, ed., Robert Maynard Hutchins (Chicago: *Encyclopaedia Britannica*, 1952), 265.

Romans 4:5: "…to the man who does not work but trusts God who justifies the ungodly,[10] his faith *is credited* [λογίζεται, *logizetai*] as righteousness."

Romans 4:6: "…the man to whom God *credits* [λογίζεται, *logizetai*] righteousness apart from works."

Romans 4:8: "Blessed is the man whose sin the Lord *will never count* [οὐ μὴ λογίσηται, *ou mē logisētai*] against him."

Romans 4:9: "We have been saying that Abraham's faith *was credited* [ἐλογίσθη, *elogisthē*] to him as righteousness."

Romans 4:10: "Under what circumstances *was it credited* [ἐλογίσθη, *elogisthē*]?"

Romans 4:11: "…[Abraham] is the father of all who believe but have not been circumcised, in order that righteousness *might be credited* [λογισθῆναι, *logisthēnai*] to them."

Romans 4:22: "This is why '*it was credited* [ἐλογίσθη, *elogisthē*] to him as righteousness.'"

Romans 4:23-24: "The words '*it was credited* [ἐλογίσθη, *elogisthē*] to him' were written not for him alone, but also for us, to whom God *will credit* [λογίζεσθαι, *logizesthai*] righteousness – for us who believe in him who raised Jesus our Lord from the dead."

But more can be said. It was directly from the Schoolmen, including Aquinas,[11] that Trent derived its teaching of the condign and con-

---

[10]On the basis of Paul's statement here to the effect that God "justifies the ungodly" – the same Greek phrase as is used in the LXX in Exodus 23:7 and Isaiah 5:23 of corrupt judgments that God will not tolerate – J. I. Packer declares that Paul's doctrine of justification is a "startling doctrine" ("Justification," *Evangelical Dictionary of Theology*, 595). For not only does Paul declare that God does it but also that he does so in a manner designed "to demonstrate His justice" (Rom 3:25-26). Of course, Paul relieves what otherwise would be a problem of theodicy by teaching that God justifies the ungodly on just grounds, namely, that the claims of God's law upon them have been fully satisfied by Jesus Christ acting and dying in their stead.

[11]Thomas Aquinas, *Summa Theologica*, ii, 1, question 114, article 3, writes: "If…we speak of a meritorious work according as it proceeds from the grace of the Holy Spirit moving us to life everlasting, it is meritorious of life everlasting condignly." It must also be observed that the very fact that *Summa Theologica*, ii, 1, question 113, in which Aquinas sets forth his doctrine of the justification of the ungodly, is followed immediately by question 114, "Of Merit, Which is the Effect of Co-operating Grace," is alone sufficient indica-

gruous merit of good works.[12] But whereas Rome, still following Trent today,[13] affirms that it is fitting for God to reward the saints' congruous merit with eternal salvation, Paul and the Reformers[14] urged that the Bible's doctrine of grace puts all talk of human works and merit in

---

tion that he was thinking about justification as a medieval Schoolman and not as a pre-Reformation "Protestant."

[12]The Council of Trent stated in its Sixth Session, Chapter XVI: "...to those who *work well unto the end* and trust in God, eternal life is offered, both as a grace mercifully promised to the sons of God through Christ Jesus, and *as a reward* promised by God Himself, *to be faithfully given to their good works and merits*...nothing further is wanting to those justified [in Rome's sense of the word] to prevent them from being considered to have, *by those very works* which have been done in God, *fully satisfied the divine law* according to the state of this life and *to have truly merited eternal life*" (emphasis supplied).

[13]The *Catechism of the Catholic Church* (1994) declares: "The merit of man before God in the Christian life arises from the fact that *God has freely chosen to associate man with the work of his grace.* The fatherly action of God is first on his own initiative, and then follows man's free acting through his collaboration, so that the merit of good works is to be attributed in the first place to the grace of God, then to the faithful.... Filial adoption, in making us partakers by grace in the divine nature, can bestow *true merit* on us as a result of God's gratuitous justice. This is our right by grace, the full right of love, making us 'co-heirs' with Christ and worthy of obtaining 'the promised inheritance of eternal life.' The merits of our good works are gifts of the divine goodness" (paragraphs 2008, 2009).

[14]Luther declared: "These arguments of the Scholastics about the merit of congruence and of worthiness (*de merito congrui et condigni*) are nothing but vain figments and dreamy speculations of idle folk about worthless stuff. Yet they form the foundation of the papacy, and on them it rests to this very day. For this is what every monk imagines: By observing the sacred duties of my order I can earn the grace of congruence, but by the works I do after I have received this grace I can accumulate a merit so great that it will not only be enough to bring me to eternal life but enough to sell and give it to others." He says further: "There is no such thing as merit; but all who are justified are justified for nothing (*gratis*), and this is credited to no one but to the grace of God." Again he states: "For Christ alone it is proper to help and save others with His merits and works. The works of others are of benefit to no one, not to themselves either; for the statement stands: 'The just shall live by faith' (Rom. 1:17)" *What Luther Says: An Anthology* (Saint Louis: Concordia, 1959), II, 921-2.

any sense of the word, save for Christ's, off limits as worthy of or as earning salvation.

Dr. Gerstner also approves the Roman Catholic scholar Michael Root's faulting of Alister McGrath for saying that Protestants understand justification as "'strictly' a legal declaration of righteousness which works no 'real change' in the believer" (52). When Root states that according to "every Reformation theologian I know, however, coming to faith in the justifying righteousness of Christ constitutes a momentous change in the believer," Dr. Gerstner declares that Root is only demonstrating that he understands "historic Protestant justification" better than some Protestant theologians do, including McGrath apparently (52). But again, this is to confuse coming to faith in the justifying righteousness of Christ, that surely and inevitably brings about a momentous change in the believer and that no Protestant theologian denies for an instant, with the act of justification itself that follows logically upon one's coming to faith and that, as McGrath states, is strictly a legal declaration of righteousness that in and of itself works no "real change" *in* the believer. It is not McGrath, therefore, who has failed to distinguish carefully the Protestant doctrine of justification from regeneration, faith and sanctification. Regrettably, it is Dr. Gerstner who confuses all these doctrines when he writes:

> ...when Jesus Christ unites Himself with an elect soul, that person is so united with Him that his regenerated soul trusts Christ for eternal salvation, his sins' guilt is remitted, and divine righteousness received. *In this act* [!] instantly and forever after, the soul believes and obeys Jesus Christ [14].

Dr. Gerstner here describes union with Christ, regeneration (that is the Spirit's work), faith in Christ (that while it is produced by the Spirit is nevertheless the sinner's act and is always accompanied by repentance), forgiveness (that is the Father's act), the "reception" of divine righteousness (that is hardly the Protestant definition of justification according to which the sinner does not subjectively "receive" divine righteousness; rather, God declares it about or reckons it to him), and forever-after-obedience on the saved soul's part, that are six aspects of the Reformed *ordo salutis*, as "this act" – a grave and confusing over-simplification!

Of course, what Dr. Gerstner is concerned to underscore throughout his article – and this is another reason why he is so enamored of

Aquinas whom he believes was saying the same thing – is the inseparability of justification and sanctification in the saved person's experience. Dr. Gerstner hopes thereby to combat Antinomianism. His concern is proper enough, but the way he goes about making his case (1) skews the biblical meaning of justification; (2) is a bad "read" of Aquinas;[15] and (3) confuses distinct soteriological concepts that, while they never can be separated in the experience of the believer, must always be distinguished in theological writing for the sake of accurate communication of the redemptive truth revealed in the Holy Scriptures.

While no sound Protestant theologian would deny that progressive sanctification is the inevitable and immediate concomitant to justification (effected, however, not by the Father's justifying act but by the Spirit's regenerating act) and that in this sense justification and sanctification "can never be separated," I know of no sound Protestant theologian either who would bring the notion, much less the term, of the infusion of sanctifying grace into his definition of justification. But Dr. Gerstner does this when he insists, with Aquinas, that justification includes the state of man, his regeneration, his coming to faith, and his "forever-after-obedience."[16] And to do this is to commit serious theological error, for such teaching, against Scripture, means that one can never know in this life whether he is justified, thereby dishonoring the Savior, and thus makes impossible the full assurance to which, according to Scripture, justification should lead through the ministry of the Holy Spirit.

Finally, when Dr. Gerstner concludes his article by urging his readers "forward to the Reformation, to Thomas Aquinas, to the New Testa-

---

[15]Dr. Gerstner is asking us to believe that for seven hundred years no one except the Council of Trent "read" Aquinas correctly (and that Council, he avers, was "horrified" at what it read and rejected him), and that it is now he, without benefit of the discovery of a lost manuscript by Aquinas that throws new light on his intentions in his *Summa*, who is again reading Aquinas aright. Stranger things have happened in church history, I suppose, but I cannot think of one offhand.

[16]Jonathan Edwards in his "Five Discourses on Important Subjects, Concerning the Soul's Eternal Salvation," the first of which treats "Justification by Faith Alone," writes: "...in truth, obedience has no concern in justification, any otherwise than as an expression of faith" (*The Works of Jonathan Edwards* [Edinburgh: Banner of Truth, 1974], I, 642).

ment, to JUSTIFICATION BY CHRIST ALONE BY A FAITH THAT IS NOT ALONE" (52), without also first saying that faith is the *alone* instrument of justification, he fosters the Romanist confusion that justification is by faith and works and fails to exhibit the special care the *Westminster Confession of Faith* exhibits when it declares: "Faith, thus receiving and resting on Christ and his righteousness, is the alone instrument of justification: yet is it not alone in the person justified, but is ever accompanied with all other saving graces, and is no dead faith, but worketh by love" (XI.2).

No, Aquinas was not a medieval Protestant teaching the biblical and Reformation doctrine of justification by faith alone. Rather, he taught that justification was the making of the sinner righteous by means of the sacraments of baptism and the Mass as well as by acts of penance. Nor was he "one of Protestantism's greatest theologians" – for the reasons already noted as well as for many others that could have been. Rather, he was the Schoolmen's purest and maturest representative of medieval Latin theology and of Rome's sacerdotal system. For while he stressed the primacy of grace in the movement from sinner to saint, his explanation of justification (*Summa Theologica*, ii, 1, question 113) continued to rely upon the standard four-part schema that went back to Peter of Poitiers' *Sentences* (III.2) in which justification is represented as a *processus iustificationis* entailing the infusion of grace, the movement of the soul, arising from grace and free will, from a state of guilt to a state of righteousness, contrition, and the forgiveness of sins.[17]

Dr. Gerstner asserts, as we have already noted, that "if the Roman church had followed Aquinas the Reformation would not have

---

[17]Karl Froehlich, "Justification Language in the Middle Ages," in *Justification by Faith: Lutherans and Catholics in Dialogue VII*, edited by H. George Anderson, T. Austin Murphy and Joseph A. Burgess (Minneapolis: Augsburg, 1985), 158-59. See also Otto W. Heick's comments in J. L. Neve, *A History of Christian Thought* (Philadelphia: Muhlenburg, 1946), I, 202-3: "Grace is viewed [by Aquinas] from the standpoint of Aristotelian form which is at first a disposition in God and then becomes active in its object. By its infusion into man, he is restored and his nature is repaired. Thus *justification is not a judicial act; it rather is a gradual process of human recovery*" (emphasis supplied); and H. A. Oberman, "'Justitia Christi' and 'Justitia Dei.' Luther and the Scholastic Doctrine of Justification," in *Harvard Theological Review* 59 (1966) 1-26.

been absolutely necessary" (14). I have argued in this review article that Rome endorsed Aquinas's teaching on justification and that the Reformation was indeed necessary just because it did. G. C. Berkouwer speaks of the "polite aloofness" that has existed between Pauline thought and Roman Catholicism. He goes on to say:

> The neglect of Paul in the middle ages was not the result of a direct denial of his significance. Paul's letters did not go untouched. *Thomas Aquinas has left us a commentary on Romans. But one need only lay this commentary alongside of that of Luther to become aware of the profound difference between them.* The words of Paul were exegeted by Roman Catholic scholars, but they were not allowed to function in their original, radically evangelical power. It was first in the Reformation that the old words of Paul came through again in unprecedented religious clarity. They unleashed a storm over Europe, and yet brought peace and comfort to a generation of restless souls. Thomas wrote of Romans 5:1: "It is not that faith precedes grace, but far more that faith originates in grace, since faith is the first operation of grace in us." *It would be too much to expect a revolution in the thought and confession of the Church to be ignited by such words as these.* Thomas says about Abraham whose faith was reckoned to him for righteousness "that the righteousness which God accounts to a man is not that ascribed to external works, but to the inward faith of the heart that God alone sees. *This type of interpretation and its antithesis between the "external" and "inward" aspects of justification does not begin to approach the depth of Reformation exegesis.*[18]

With sixteenth-century Rome's doctrine of justification following, along with other Schoolmen, the theological thought of Thomas Aquinas, the Reformation was very much a necessity, and every educated Christian thanks God for it. My fear is that Dr. Gerstner's article, with its defective representation of what justification is and how it is obtained, will confuse those among Christ's sheep who have not received clear instruction about the doctrine of justification and who are not equipped therefore to think about these issues discerningly.

---

[18]G. C. Berkouwer, *Faith and Justification* (Grand Rapids: Eerdmans, 1954), 64-5 (emphasis supplied).

Chapter Twenty

Dr. Robert H. Schuller's
Self-Esteem: The New Reformation

Author's Note: I reviewed Dr. Robert H. Schuller's book, *Self-Esteem: The New Reformation*, in Πρεσβυτέριον: *A Journal for the Eldership* (Spring-Fall 1983), IX, 1-2:93-96, but not before sending it to Dr. Schuller[1] for his perusal and reaction. He was not happy with what I had written about his book and requested that Πρεσβυτέριον give him the opportunity to write a response to my review. As editor of Πρεσβυτέριον at the time, I assured him, after consulting with the editorial committee, that Πρεσβυτέριον would be quite willing to publish his response but only with the understanding that if I felt a rejoinder to his response was in order I would have the right to reply to his response. His response to my review appeared in Πρεσβυτέριον (Spring-Fall 1984), X, 1-2:111-13, and my reply to his response appeared in the form of an open letter in the same issue.

* * * * *

A Review of Dr. Robert H. Schuller's
Self-Esteem: The New Reformation

Dr. Schuller, senior minister of the Crystal Cathedral in Garden Grove, California, is deeply concerned. He has written a book about his concern and has arranged to have it distributed *gratis* to thousands of ministers across the country. There is, he says, a "desperate need" for a "new Reformation." It seems that the "old one" – the sixteenth-century Protestant Reformation – was a "reactionary movement" (39). Luther and Calvin, "possessed more by the spirit [note the lower case "s"] of St. Paul than by the Spirit (note the upper case "s") of Jesus Christ," looked to the Book of Romans for their primary inspiration" (39). Destructive and divisive results ensued for the church. Men were told that they were unworthy sinners. And "once a person believes he is an 'unworthy sinner,' it is doubtful if he can really honestly

---

[1]Dr. Schuller is the founder and senior pastor of the Crystal Cathedral in Garden Grove, California.

319

accept the saving grace God offers in Jesus Christ" (98). What is needed, Dr. Schuller contends, is a new reformation, a reconciling movement, beginning on the "safer ground" (than Paul) of our Lord's words in the Lord's Prayer (39) that will refocus the church's attention on "the sacred right of every person to self-esteem" (38).

Dr. Schuller believes that the six petitions of the Lord's Prayer deal with "the classic negative emotions that destroy our self-dignity" (48). The first ("Hallowed be...") deals with our sense of inferiority. The second ("Thy kingdom come, Thy will be done") answers to our depression. The third ("Give us...") speaks to our anxiety. The fourth (Forgive us...") deals with our guilt. The fifth ("...as we forgive...") addresses resentment. The sixth and final petition ("...and lead us not...") immunizes us against fear (49). (Anyone who has studied these petitions will question some of Dr. Schuller's divisions of them.) The major portion of his book (52-141) is then taken up with the development of this schema.

Before I address specific concerns that Dr. Schuller's book raises for me, I must say something about his use of the Lord's Prayer in the interest of demonstrating the self-worth of the individual.

Aside from the unholy denigration of the Spirit-of-Christ-inspired Book of Romans (the greatest theological treatise in the possession of the church) that is inherent in his remark quoted above, apparently it is of little significance to Dr. Schuller that there is no indication in the Scriptures that Christ intended that his model prayer should become the agenda for the restoration of human self-esteem and the pathway to world-wide evangelization. Both the context of his prayer in the Sermon on the Mount and the prayer itself make it abundantly clear that it is a prayer that actually should be prayed in corporate, not primarily individual, worship (see Matt 5:1 – "his disciples"; also the plural "our" in the prayer's address and the consistent use of the first person *plural* pronouns throughout). Furthermore, the exclusive presence of the second person singular "your" in the first three petitions makes it evident that the first and primary emphasis in the Lord's Prayer is on the character ('holy"), the sovereignty ("kingdom"), and the "lordship" ("will") of God. In short, it is the unabridged glory of God in the life of the church that receives primary emphasis in the Lord's Prayer. To use the Lord's Prayer as Dr. Schuller does is, to say the least, to handle Scripture in a cavalier fashion. No proof is offered to demonstrate that his usage of the prayer is in accord with our Lord's intention for it. One has only to compare Dr. Schuller's handling of the Lord's Prayer with Dr. Martyn Lloyd-Jones' careful exegetical treatment of the same material in the latter's sermons on the Sermon on the Mount to be struck immediately with the superficiality of Dr. Schuller's "exposition" and his apparent disinterest in sound canons of heremeneutics.

When one turns to a consideration of the specific details of Dr. Schuller's theology of the "new reformation" (this book does enter deeply into theology), one becomes painfully aware that, for Dr. Schuller, the touchstone for determining the truthfulness of any Christian teaching is whether the dignity or self-esteem of the individual is served by it. Every theological definition, in order to be true, must make peace with human self-esteem as understood by Dr. Schuller (see "Introduction"). For example, sin becomes "any act or thought that robs myself or another human being of his or her self-esteem," or again, sin is "any human condition or act that robs God of glory by stripping one of his children of their right to divine dignity" (14). Or yet again, "the core of sin is a lack of self-esteem" and "*at the deepest level* the heart of sin is found in what it causes us to do *to ourselves*. The *most serious* sin is the one that causes me to say, 'I am unworthy'" (98, emphasis supplied). One can hardly imagine a more radical departure than this from the biblical understanding of sin that sees the nature of sin as "any want of conformity unto, or transgression of, the law of God" (*Shorter Catechism*, question 14). Of course, to define sin as the *Catechism* does, for Dr. Schuller, is "shallow and insulting to the human being" (65). And with his definition of sin controlling his thought, Dr. Schuller, one is hardly surprised to learn, subjects virtually every other key biblical concept to radical revision. Salvation is no longer represented in terms of propitiation, reconciliation, redemption, and vicarious sacrifice; rather, salvation "means to be permanently lifted from sin (psychological self-abuse…) and shame to self-esteem… (99). The result of this salvation, not at all unexpected by those who have followed Dr. Schuller's ministry, is that the "saved" become "possibility thinkers" (99). The instrumentalities by which men become possibility thinkers, to be sure, are the incarnation, crucifixion, and resurrection of Jesus Christ. But for Dr. Schuller, "the Incarnation was God's glorification of the human being" (100). (And while on earth Christ "never called any person 'a sinner'" [100, 126] [but see Luke 11:13!].) The crucifixion of Christ becomes both the means by which the individual is assured that he is infinitely valuable in God's sight (74, 110), and the certain sign that "if God can forgive those who executed his Son,...then God can forgive me too" (74). The death of Christ on the cross Dr. Schuller does not portray in his book as possessing intrinsic vicarious propitiatory benefit for sinners standing in the presence of a wrathful God. At least in his proclamation of the gospel to the non-Christian he does not represent the nature of the atonement in such terms. Rather, as a sign that God is forgiving, the cross of Christ provides the ground of assurance that God accepts the self-abused, a kind of illustration that God wants to forgive him of his self-abuse and to restore genuine self-esteem to him. The resurrection of Christ, for Dr. Schuller, is the means whereby Christ "steps aside" to allow us to take his place and carry on his ministry of sharing "self-esteem love" with others (102). And to experience "existential encounter" with such unconditional love and acceptance is to be literally "born again" (100) and to escape hell that, with frightening consistency, Dr. Schuller defines as the "loss of pride that...follows separation from God" (14), the "loss of self-esteem" (15), the learning from God someday that one had wasted bright ideas, beautiful relationships, and, of course, possibilities (93).

As one reads *Self-Esteem*, it is impossible not to sense the passion with which Dr. Schuller writes. He is totally dedicated to his vision, because he has seen what has come of his own ministry by following it. And no one, certainly not this reviewer, doubts that his ministry has done much good and positively affected millions of people. Furthermore, no Reformed Christian can or will fault him for the concern he has expressed in *Self-Esteem* that the church give man his rightful due as created in God's image. All this is appropriate enough. But Dr. Schuller's book will not pass, by any stretch of the imagination, biblical muster. Elevating his understanding of the significance of human self-esteem, as he has, to the status of norm or benchmark for establishing the proper meaning of other biblical terms, his theology as a whole takes on a resemblance to the ever-increasing number of contemporary efforts whose bottom-line advocacy is what Paul Vitz terms "the cult of self-worship" in his book, *Psychology as Religion. Self-Esteem* fails to capture the biblical balance reflected in the Bible's willingness to say both things to fallen men – that they are bearers of the divine image and are therefore of worth before God and also that they are, by virtue of their fallenness, wicked and rebellious and haters of God. It is the latter biblical theme that is virtually ignored by Dr. Schuller in this book. The Reformed Christian can only grieve at the thought of the countless numbers of spiritually hungry, needy people being indoctrinated in this sub-biblical theology by the ministry being conducted by the Crystal Cathedral. Serious doubts about the lasting results of Dr. Schuller's ministry are surely justified when one reflects on the myriad numbers of people who are being led to believe that to be a Christian is to be a possibility thinker in the tradition of Dr. Norman Vincent Peale's religion of positive thinking. There is only one gospel (Gal. 1:6-9) – grounded in the work of Christ as interpreted in the great Reformation creeds and uniquely fitted to meet the needs of those who, under the convicting power of the Spirit of God, will acknowledge that they are by nature in revolt against God, rebels against God's holy laws, and who in their repudiation of their sense of self-worth will acknowledge the all-worthiness of the alone-righteous Christ of God as their only hope for forgiveness and heaven. This is not the gospel found in Dr. Schuller's book. Dr. Schuller's book, in a word, is a dangerous book and is not recommended to the Πρεσβψτέριον readership. Faithful ministers will pray that God will neutralize the effects of this book on the church of God that he has purchased at the price of his own beloved Son and, if the theology set forth in this book is in fact the theology undergirding the ministry and vision of Dr. Schuller, will warn their people of the diluted message being proclaimed from the pulpit of the Crystal Cathedral.

* * * * *

A Response by Robert H. Schuller to Robert L. Reymond's Review of *Self-Esteem: The New Reformation*

First let me express my thanks to the editorial committee of the Covenant Seminary Review for inviting me to write a response to the review of my book *Self-Esteem: The New Reformation*, reviewed by Robert L. Reymond.

Regrettably, Dr. Reymond has reviewed the book without adequately bringing to the subject a knowledge of established psychological truth. He may, indeed, have the academic credentials that qualify him to serve as a professor of systematic theology in a theological seminary that is accredited by the Association of Theological Schools. What must be understood is that it does not qualify him to teach a course in physics, chemistry, or psychology. It is from the psychological perspective that I am writing this entire book, *Self-Esteem: The New Reformation.*

I believe that he also violates fundamental principles of hermeneutics, both in logic and in homiletics. We are taught that we are not to "argue from silence," or use eisegesis. Both of these are fundamental strategies of interpretation that govern Mr. Reymond's review. Because I do not say that I believe in the substitionary atonement – which I, in fact, do believe and which I made adequate room for in the manuscript – he assumes that I do not. Therefore, he accuses me of not holding to this propitiatory position. I point out that the whole doctrine of the human person is rooted in the incarnation, crucifixion, and the resurrection of Jesus Christ which Dr. Reymond simply sweeps aside as a cavalier and unimportant basis! Again and again Dr. Reymond is accusing me of holding to positions that would be contrary to solid Reformed Theology simply because he does not "hear me say" that I believe in some of these cardinal reformed theological positions. To sum it up in a word – he is accusing me of not believing in some positions simply because I have not forthrightly said I hold to some of these positions! It's surprising me he has not accused me of denying the virgin birth of Christ, or the physical resurrection of Jesus Christ, or the literal second coming of Jesus Christ! The truth is that I hold to all of these theological positions. Dr. Reymond has argued from silence. And throughout he reads his own theological prejudices into my review accusing me of holding to viewpoints that distort and cause me to come across as something less than I am.

I am also concerned that his arguments against my positions are without solid Scriptural basis. He finds it easier to refer to dogmatic theological confessions than to Scripture itself. To illustrate: In the review he writes, "One can hardly imagine a more radical departure than this from the *Biblical understanding of sin* (italics mine) which sees the nature of sin as 'any want of conformity unto, or transgression of, the Law of God' (Shorter Catechism question 14)."

When defining the Biblical Understanding of Sin he does not even quote the Bible! He simply quotes the Shorter Catechism! One suspects that he places the Shorter Catechism on an equal par to the Bible as being the ultimate truth of the Sacred Scriptures much as a cultist does when the writings of Mary Baker Eddy are placed on a par with the Holy Bible.

In his closing part of the review he writes, "The Reformed Christian can only grieve at the thought of countless numbers of spiritually hungry, needy people being indoctrinated in this sub-Biblical theology …by the ministry being carried on by the Crystal Cathedral."

For this careless, reckless insult to the congregation of the Crystal Cathedral of the Reformed Church in America, I submit he owes 10,000 members and the elders and deacons on [*sic*] the local church a public apology! How can he slander and insult with a theological arrogance a body of God's believing people? Was this not to be a book review? What gave him the license to attack the spiritual integrity of the entire ministry of the congregation of the Crystal Cathedral?! It is simply another illustration of the roughshod and reckless style of one who hasn't taken the time to visit our campus and study in depth the ministry that goes on here!

Dr. Reymond says he "grieve(s) at the thought of the countless numbers of spiritually hungry, needy people"…is Dr. Reymond not aware of the fact that he may be, himself, a failure in meeting the needs of the spiritually hungry people in our country and our world? Does he dare to examine the track record of effectiveness and authentic evangelism by those who hold to such a narrow, negative, and prejudicial theological interpretation?

I can report that multiplied tens of millions of people have turned the church off, have thrown their Bibles away, simply because they have been intellectually and psychologically insulted by the strategies and spirit and style and substance of the type of religious leader that is evidenced by Dr. Reymond in this review.

If Dr. Reymond had the faith of the New Testament people, he would take this position as found in the Book of Acts: "If this is of God it will prevail – and if it is not of God it will fail." This was the wise and wonderful judgment of Gamaliel.

My main concern is not the danger that can happen to me because of the inaccurate and distorted misinterpretation of what the words say in the book that I have written. My concern is the number of unchurched persons who are living around the churches pastored by people who probably will be tempted to go into their pulpits and preach a very destructive, non-redemptive, doctrine that will fail to contain the beauties of the Gospels [*sic*] of our Living Savior and Lord of love, Jesus Christ.

For the record, I hold to the Reformed doctrines. For the record I believe in the Nicene Creed, the Athanasian Creed, the Apostles Creed. For the record I subscribe to the Canons of Dort with one exception. I believe that man has total inability – not total depravity. If a person is totally depraved he ought to be shot, gassed in the chamber, or hanged by the neck 'till dead. Total inability means that he is totally incapable of earning his own salvation but is completely dependent upon the grace of God in Jesus Christ and the power of the Holy Spirit for regeneration and sanctification. Total depravity are words that taken literally are irresponsible, unintelligent, and destructive – not redemptive! Furthermore, they are contrived by human theologians and are not scriptural. Total inability contains compassion and fits into the gospel spirit producing persons who become humbly dependent upon the goodness of God and the Grace of our Lord and Savior Jesus Christ.

I would respectfully request that Covenant Theological Seminary extend an invitation to me to lecture in the seminary and answer any questions by the students or faculty.

I would welcome such an invitation and respond positively to it with the hope that the Gospel of our Lord might be better served. Will such an invitation be forthcoming?

* * * * *

A Reply in the Form of an Open Letter to
Dr. Robert H. Schuller

March 26, 1984

Dear Dr. Schuller:

Your response to my review of your book, *Self-Esteem: The New Reformation*, that appeared in Πρεσβψτέριον: *A Journal for the Eldership* (Spring-Fall 1983), IX, 1-2, 93-96, arrived the morning of March 20 in the mail. Thank you for taking time out of a busy schedule to meet the requested deadline. Needless to say, I read your response with great interest. Because my review was more critical of your book than commendatory, I naturally anticipated that you would be unhappy with my analysis of your perspective on the need of man.

Be assured that I understand why you are unhappy. You believe that I do not have sufficient knowledge of "established psychological truth" to criticize a book that is written from "the psychological perspective (111).

You believe that I have "again and again" falsely accused you "of holding to positions that would be contrary to solid Reformed Theology" (111), and "of not believing in some positions" (111) such as the "propitiatory position." You say that my distortion of your viewpoints is due to my violation of "fundamental principles of hermeneutics," specifically, that I argue from silence and eisegetically (111). You believe that I have "inaccurately and distortedly misinterpreted your words" (113).

Furthermore, you believe that my arguments against your position are not based on Scripture as much as they are on "dogmatic theological confessions" (112).

Still further, you believe that I have, with theological arrogance, carelessly, recklessly, roughshodly, and slanderously insulted and attacked "the entire ministry of the congregation of the Crystal Cathedral" (112).

Finally, you believe that my "narrow, negative, and prejudicial theological interpretation" (112) and the "strategies and spirit and style and substance" (112) of religious leaders of my type are the reasons that "multiplied tens of millions of people have turned the church off, have thrown their Bibles away" (112). These multiplied millions have, to use your words, "been intellectually and psychologically insulted" by the perspective that I represent.

You can only wish that I "had the faith of the New Testament people" and had taken the position reflected in the "wise and wonderful judgment of Gamaliel" (112).

I hope you see, Dr. Schuller, from this abbreviated recounting of the several points of your response that I do understand why you are upset. If I thought you had insulted me and my congregation this way, I would be unhappy too.

I suppose that I could take the position, in light of your response, that whether I am in fact guilty of these very serious sins with which I am charged (I acknowledge that the word "sins" is my choice of words; you do not use this word to describe what you believe I have done), in the final analysis, temporally speaking, the readers of Πρεσβψτέριον will simply have to judge for themselves whether I have been as unkind as you suggest that I have been (I invite them to read my review); and someday, God will finally have to judge between us. But the Scriptures insist that I must seek reconciliation if I have offended a brother wrongfully and attempt to redress any injury or wrong that I have done. Consequently, I returned to your book and to my review and have reflected again on whether I misrepresented what you have written. Permit me to share, in light of this more recent reevaluation, my reactions to your response. I will address your points in the order in which you made them.

My inadequate knowledge of psychology

You begin, Dr. Schuller, by asserting that I bring to my review of your book an inadequate knowledge of "established psychological truth," and that I am therefore not qualified to review a book that was written from a psychological perspective. You obviously have a deep interest in and appreciation for psychology.

But what is this "established psychological truth" to which you refer, Dr. Schuller? Who established it? The psychologists? In what book (or books) is it carefully, clearly, and unassailably spelled out? And will all psychologists agree with it and with *your* knowledge of "established psychological truth"? Surely you will not have me believe that the field of psychology has concurred on a body of infallible, unchangeable "established psychological truth" with which the Christian can agree? Surely if there is one field that is in a constant state of flux and in which there is widespread disagreement over any number of issues, it is the field of psychology! And even if a body of "established psychological truth" were to be agreed upon by the secular psychologists, is the field of psychology to be allowed to function in isolation from the teaching of the Creator of man as that teaching is recorded in Holy Scripture? Surely Holy Scripture must provide the needed corrective to all of fallen man's endeavors, including psychology. I would like to think that you agree with this last statement, but I wonder, inasmuch as you say in *Self-Esteem* that "theology has failed to accommodate and apply proven insights in human behavior *as revealed* by twentieth-century psychologists" (emphasis supplied) and that "both [theology and psychology] can and must learn from each other. Neither can claim to have 'the whole truth'" (27, fn 3). Taken at face value, your statements simply mean that Holy Scripture is not to be viewed any longer as the theologian's sole and sufficient norm for theology, that he must now also look to the norm of "proven insights...revealed by twentieth-century psychologists" for his understanding of man. The upshot of this dual norm for theology is that the Word of Christ in Scripture no longer functions in the life of his church as the sole and final norm of and corrective to all our thinking. Now the redeemed mind must seek to be informed by the "proven insights" of psychology. Indeed, you insist that theology must "*begin* with...satisfying every person's hunger for personal value" (35, emphasis supplied). You even maintain that theology must *not* start with Scripture or Scripture's God (36); rather, theology must make its "theological benchmark" psychology's "proven insight" of the "universal right...of every person to be treated with great respect simply because he or she is a human being" (37). This certainly implies that whatever the theologian would learn later from Scripture must fit or be adjusted to (what you call) this "undebatable standard." This is the reason that I say that I wonder, in your model of the theological enterprise, whether Scripture can provide the needed corrective to psychology.

Of course, if you reply to my questions by saying that you have derived your "established psychological truth" also from your study of the Holy Scriptures (that is the source from which I hope we would both derive our opinions about the origin of man, his nature, and his needs), then you would grant, I hope, that I would not need to have advanced degrees in general psychology or child psychology or adolescent psychology or clinical psychology or in any other of the specializations of the field. I would only need to know the Holy Scriptures with a certain degree of proficiency and expertise to be justified in evaluating your position from a biblical perspective. I sincerely believe, Dr. Schuller, that this is all that I have done in my review, and that I have not evaluated your book or your ministry with a narrow, negative, and prejudicial theological interpretation – that I have simply evaluated your position from a scriptural perspective, a perspective from which we both must be willing to be judged. This is the reason that I concluded that I must be critical of your book. I still believe that my criticisms are biblically sound as I will demonstrate shortly, and that you must, for the sake of your ministry (1 Cor. 3:10-15), take my criticisms seriously and, at the very least, ask yourself if there is any merit to them.

My accusations based on the argument from silence
Several times, Dr. Schuller, you say that I accuse you of this or that, these accusations all based on argument from silence. Specifically,

you say I accuse you of not holding to the substitutionary theory of the atonement or to the "propitiation position." This appears to be a major reason for your unhappiness with me – that I represent you as not believing in or holding to the substitutionary view of the atonement that, you say, you in fact do believe in and hold to. Because this criticism is central to my concern respecting your book, it is important that Πρεσβψτέριον readers be reminded of precisely what I did say earlier in my review about your book. I wrote: "Salvation is no longer represented in terms of propitiation, reconciliation, redemption, and vicarious sacrifice...," and "The death of Christ on the cross Dr. Schuller does not portray in his book as possessing intrinsic, vicarious propitiatory benefit for sinners standing in the presence of a wrathful God. At least in his proclamation of the gospel to the non-Christian he does not represent the nature of the atonement in such terms" (94, 95). I assume these are the statements, Dr. Schuller, on the basis of which you conclude that I misrepresent you.

It is gratifying to learn from your response for *Presbyterion* that you affirm the substitutionary view of the atonement. But you must remember that I had to evaluate your position originally on the basis of your book. The question is then: In light of what you wrote, did I misrepresent you? I think not, and I will try to show you why I still say this. You deal with salvation and the work of Christ primarily on pages 99-102 of your book. In these pages you set forth the way in which Christ atones for our sins in these words:

> How does Christ's death atone for our sins? How can we say that we are saved by the blood of Christ? In three ways. (1) The Cross of Christ brings vitality to my dignity. If *the deepest curse of sin* is what it does to my self-esteem, then the atoning power of the Cross is what it does to redeem our discarded self-worth.... (2) The Cross of Christ makes atonement from guilt possible because it adds integrity to the positive Gospel.... (3) The Cross of Christ adds morality to divine forgiveness" (101, emphasis supplied).

It is on the basis of such statements as these, I feel sure, that you write in your response to my review: "I, in fact, do believe and...I make adequate room for" [the substitionary theory of atonement] in the manuscript" (111). But, Dr. Schuller, do your statements "make adequate room for" the substitutionary and propiatory atonement? I am sure you sincerely think so. Taken by themselves and read with some charity, one might conclude that they do. But the reading of such statements will inevitably be affected by the context in which you place them. Therefore, when you define sin elsewhere as you do as "any act or thought that robs myself or another human being of his or her self-esteem" (14), and then say that "at the *deepest* level the *heart* of sin is found in what it causes us to do to *ourselves*. The *most serious sin* is the one that causes me to say, 'I am unworthy'" (96, emphasis supplied; see also your first point quoted above), it is very difficult (perhaps impossible) to demonstrate the significance of or even the need for a substitutionary atonement accomplished by the death of Christ. If sin is what you say it is, why does God need to send his Son to die for a man whose sin at its most basic level is essentially against *himself*? Why should God need to get involved at all except for sympathy's sake? And why should man's sin against himself make Christ's *death* necessary? What is the nature of his death and what does his death accomplish other than provide a demonstration, as you state and as I report in my review (95), that if God can forgive those who executed his Son, then he can forgive the self-abused of his self-abuse? But even this suggestion is not very helpful since it is still not at all clear whose *place* Christ is taking substitutionally and why, and why God needs to forgive a man of his sin that is at heart [not against God but] against himself. Surely you can see this, Dr. Schuller.

But from yet another perspective it is difficult to see how your theological construction leaves room for a real substitutionary atonement. When you say: "It is essential that we constantly remember that every human being is a person for whom Jesus died on the cross..." (171; see also 110), then I have to conclude, unless you believe in the final salvation of all men (that I assume you do not believe), that Christ's death, as you represent it, is not truly substitutionary since some men for whom you say he died finally perish (see Matt. 25:31-46). One cannot have a universal atonement for men some of whom ultimately perish that is at the same time really substitutionary. The Synod of Dort saw this clearly (see *Canons*, First and Second Heads of Doctrine). Reformation theology has unanimously concurred in this analysis as Benjamin B. Warfield so brilliantly demonstrated in his little book, *The Plan of Salvation*, many years ago. A universal atonement *at best* can "make room for" a governmental theory of the atonement but not a real substitutionary atonement.

As for your view of the "propitiatory position," this is what I say in my review (95) – that you do not portray the death of Christ *in your book* as possessing intrinsic propitiatory benefit for sinners standing in the presence of a wrathful God, that you do not represent the nature of the atonement in these biblical terms in your depiction of the gospel. I do *not* accuse you of *not holding* to the "propitiatory position", though I now must say frankly that if you do (and I believe that you sincerely believe that you do hold to it), I think your view is defective and I will tell you why. Tell me, Dr. Schuller, what does Christ's death, when represented in Scripture as a propitiatory sacrifice (Rom. 3:25; Heb. 2:17; 1 John 2:2; 4:10), presuppose about God's attitude toward the sinner? Does it not presuppose the wrath of God against the unbelieving, unrepentant sinner? (See John 3:36; Rom. 1:18; 2:5, 8; 3:5, 25; Eph. 2:3; 1 Thess. 1:10.) What other attitude toward sinners on God's part can support the characterization of Christ's death as a propitiation? But this is precisely the attitude in God that you portray as a "fabrication" on the part of the unsaved sinner! Because "we *fabricate* our own images of God," you say, it is "no wonder…that the unsaved human being *imagines God to be angry* rather than loving" (66, emphasis supplied). Due to *our* fears, you say, we "have *pictured* [God] as a *threatening* rather than a redeeming figure" (66, emphasis supplied; personally I have found the average person much more inclined to think of God as loving than as angry). But, Dr. Schuller, the very God that you say the unsaved human being in his fear has fabricated the Bible says is *actually* there. Every moment he is angry with unrepentant sinners, and it is the matchless propitiatory work of Christ alone that quiets forever God's wrath toward the repentant believing sinner. I hope you see that it is impossible, on the one hand, to deny that God is angry and to represent this portrayal of God as a human fabrication and then, on the other hand, at the same time consistently to hold to the doctrine of propitiation. I must seriously question whether you have an adequate perception of the doctrine.

I would hope, Dr. Schuller, when I actually quote your own words as I am now doing (and as I could have done in my original review), that it is clear that I am not arguing from silence. It was certainly never my intention to read my theological prejudices into my review. But it is difficult to understand how you are holding to "solid Reformed Theology" when you affirm that Christ died for every human being, and that the depiction of God as wrathful is a human fabrication traceable to our fears.

I hope I do not appear to be disrespectful. I simply and sincerely hope that my concerns will contribute to a greater conformity on your part to the written Word of God that must be the Christian's final norm for his theology and preaching.

My arguments not based on scripture

Thank you, Dr. Schuller, for reminding me that my opposition to your positions cannot be based merely on a quotation from the *Shorter Catechism*. I assure you that I do not place the *Shorter Catechism* on an equal par with the inspired, inerrant Word of God. I do, however, believe that the *Shorter Catechism* correctly reflects the teaching of the Scripture and is therefore authoritative, but with this difference from Scripture. The Scripture possesses an *inherent* authority because it is the Word of God; the *Catechism*, because it reflects the teaching of Scripture, possesses a *derived* authority. But it is the same authority. That is why I thought it sufficient to quote the *Catechism* in support of the biblical definition of sin. But if Scripture itself would be helpful, in support of my definition of sin let me refer you to such passages as Romans 4:15; 5:13; 7:7-11; and 1 John 3:4. Take the last reference, for instance: "Everyone who sins breaks the law; in fact, sin is lawlessness." Whose law is referred to here? Is it not plainly God's law and not some innate law in the nature of man forbidding low esteem? Is not sin then transgression of God's law, as the *Catechism* affirms? And is not sin then *at its heart* against God and his glory as David declares in Psalm 51:4 at the moment of his clearest perception of the nature of his sins of adultery and murder: "Against you, you only, have I sinned and done what is evil in your sight" (NIV). Why then do you say, Dr. Schuller, that the heart of sin is found in what it causes us to do to *ourselves* (98)? Is not sin at its heart the creature's attack on the sovereignty, holiness, and purity of God his Creator?

While I am giving you Scripture for your consideration, as you suggest I should, Jesus (whom you say in your book [39] is "safer ground" than Paul) said that it was the man who stood at a distance and who would not even look up to heaven and who beat his breast and who cried: "God, have mercy upon me, the sinner," who went down to his house justified (Luke 18:13-14). Why, then, do you write that "once a person believes he is an 'unworthy sinner' it is doubtful if he can really honestly accept the saving grace God offers in Jesus Christ" (98).

I am not quoting the *Confession of Faith* or the *Catechism* now, Dr. Schuller. I am quoting from Scripture as you request. Have I mishandled it? I think not. Have you ignored it? I think so.

An insult to your congregation

I never intended to insult your congregaton, Dr. Schuller, but if anything I said was insulting, I here and now with shame offer the public apology that you believe should be forthcoming.

The truth is, my dear brother, I never intended to insult you either. I did intend to be critical of your theological position. And I think I have already said enough to give one pause before he agrees with you that what I have said about your teaching ministry is careless or reckless or slanderous or insulting to you. Surely you are willing to bring your ministry under the searching, penetrating, healing judgments of the light of God's Word. I live there too. So please, I beg of you, do not think for a moment that I am your enemy or the enemy of your ministry. I am not. But I do believe that your ministry needs the correction of Scripture in such areas as these that I have highlighted.

Three miscellaneous comments

1. I do not know how you can possibly report that it is because of religious leaders with my theological perspective that tens of millions of people have turned the church off and have thrown their Bibles away. Have you taken a poll of such proportions to learn this? And since when have we been instructed to judge the effectiveness and authenticity of a person's evangelistic method by numbers or lack of the same? Judged by these standards, Jesus' ministry was ineffective (see John 6:66).

2. As for the "wise and wonderful judgment of Gamaliel" to which you refer, I fail to see what "the faith of the New Testament people" or my faith has to do with his counsel at all. Could it be that you have incorrectly assumed because Luke quotes Gamaliel that Gamaliel's advice is intended as a principle of divine guidance for Christians? Gamaliel, an unsaved but learned Jewish Pharisee, in the providence of God, said essentially what you report – but to the Sanhedrin, *not* to the church. As a result of this bit of "worldly wisdom," after the

religious leaders had beaten the Apostles and ordered them not to speak any more in Jesus' name, they released them. But what this has to do with the faith of the New Testament church or with my faith escapes me completely. Since when is the church or its Christian leaders under obligation to follow the "wise and wonderful judgment" of this Pharisee? If we followed his advice, we would never object to anything. I would not have reviewed your book (that, of course, was your point). But then you would not have responded to my review either. Please, Dr. Schuller, do not ask me to believe that Gamaliel's counsel to the Sanhedrin is a proper guide for Christian action.

3. Finally, you say that you subscribe to the Canons of Dort with one exception – you reject total depravity in deference to total inability. What you then say about the person you envision as totally depraved makes me wonder if you understand what the Reformed Faith means by the doctrine. Now it goes without saying that this is no minor departure on your part away from the Canons of Dort. In fact, it is, in my opinion, the root problem with your "self-esteem hermeneutic" and the reason that you cannot do justice to the substitutionary atonement. Of course, it is not entirely clear from your stated rejection of total depravity whether it is the adjective "total" or the noun "depravity" at which you take umbrage. If it is only the adjective to which you take exception, the result being that you are willing to affirm that man is *partially* depraved, then, of course, you have the problem of explaining *which* part or faculty of man is not depraved, and how it is that man is unaffected by sin in this area – no small task I can assure you. If it is depravity *per se* that you are disavowing, then the only conclusion that I can draw is that you believe that man is essentially good but just psychologically malnourished due to his low self-esteem, and that his total inability to "earn his own salvation" springs from a psychological disorder and not from a nature that is morally corrupt and hostile to God. But in either case you have the problem of squaring your view of man with such Scripture passages as the following (emphasis supplied) that affirm both the corruption and the all-pervasiveness of that corruption throughout the human heart (nature):

> "The LORD looked down from heaven on the sons of men to see if there are any who understand, any who seek God. All have turned aside, *they have together become corrupt, there is no one who does good, not even one*" (Ps. 14:2-3; see also Rom. 3:9-18).

"The heart is *deceitful above all things* and beyond cure. Who can understand it?" (Jer 17:9).

"As for you, *you were dead in your transgressions and sins*, in which you used to live when you followed the ways of this world and of the ruler of the kingdom of the air, the spirit who is now at work in those who are disobedient. All of us also lived among them at one time, gratifying the cravings of our sinful nature and following its desires and thoughts. Like the rest, we were by nature objects of wrath" (Eph. 2:1-3).

"So I tell you this, and insist on it in the Lord, that you must no longer live as the Gentiles do, in the futility of their thinking. They are *darkened in their understanding*, and *separated from the life of God* because of the ignorance that is in them *due to the hardening of their hearts. Having lost all sensitivity*, they have given themselves over to sensuality so as to indulge in *every kind of impurity* with *a continual lust* for more" (Eph. 4:17-19).

And just why it is that telling a man that, apart from the grace of God, he is *incapable*, because of a psychological disorder, of doing anything or willing anything with regard to his salvation is compassionate and redemptive, and telling him that, apart from the grace of God, he does not *want to believe* and *will not believe* because he is morally corrupt (John 6:36) is irresponsible, unintelligent, and destructive is beyond my comprehension. Are we to judge the truthfulness of a doctrine by whether we think it is compassionate or redemptive? Of course not. Furthermore, Paul portrays depravity and inability as of one piece. That is, because man is by nature corrupt and wicked (total depravity), he cannot (total inability) incline himself toward spiritual good. He writes in Romans 8:7: "…the sinful mind…does not submit to God's law, nor can it do so" (NIV). The first clause asserts what we mean by depravity, while the second refers to what we mean by inability. But *neither* is commendatory and *neither* is more compassionate or redemptive than the other; *both* are condemnatory and *both* are true. Here is just another example of your willingness to advocate your particular version of one biblical theme and to reject another because it fits your "self-esteem hermeneutic."

Conclusion

Permit me to say, Dr. Schuller, as respectfully as I know how, that the areas of concern that I have raised (and I could cite more) both in my review and now in my open letter are areas of concern for many other evangelical pastors and teachers as well because vitals of the Christian gospel are involved. We do not think that it is right or fair for you to insist that we have to visit your church and to study in depth the ministry carried on there before we have the right to form an opinion of your ministry. We believe that we have the right and obligation to form an opinion in light of what we see and hear on television and what we read in your books, particularly in *Self-Esteem: The New Reformation*, and to warn our flocks who might be misled by error.

For many years I have known of your ministry. Though I have had reservations about it, I have never attempted to write an analysis of it before. Perhaps I should have written earlier to you. But when you wrote *Self-Esteem* and then had it sent *gratis* to 250,000 ministers and priests in which you accuse on a broad nationwide scale not one congregation but entire Christian denominations and tens of thousand of local churches of holding to theological views that are "negative," "shallow," and "insulting to men" simply because they hold to and proclaim the great evangelical doctrines of the Reformation tradition, and in which you call upon all of us to join you in your "new reformation," based not on Paul's writings but on what you regard as the "safer grounds" (39) of Jesus' words that by your own admission and practice are interpreted by your perceived body of "established psychological truth," then we who believe that the *entire* Bible is the Word of Jesus Christ (1 Pet. 1:11; John 16:12-15; 1 Thess. 2:15) and the *final* authority over all men and all their enterprises, including psychology, have become alarmed at what your book implies about Paul's writings and the Bible's authority as a whole and about the nature of the atoning work of Christ. For myself, as an ordained teaching elder in the Presbyterian Church in America (PCA) charged to protect the sheep of God and the Faith once for all delivered to the saints, I felt constrained to alert the church to what I and many others perceive as serious error in your teaching.

Not one word of what I have written, however, should be interpreted to mean that I do not regard you as a brother in Christ for whom I bear the responsibility to uphold and to help as God permits. But the Scriptures set forth the highest of standards for the teachers of Christ's church (1 Tim. 3:1-7; 2 Tim. 2:2; Tit. 1:5-11; Jam. 3:1) among whom you profess to stand as a leader, for you regularly sponsor seminars for other pastors and church leaders and write books to them. All the more then are you responsible to listen to Holy Scripture and to heed our admonitions when they are biblically based.

As for your request that Covenant Theological Seminary invite you to its campus to lecture, since I am not the one who decides such things myself, I cannot assure you that an invitation will be forthcoming. But I wonder if I can assume that you will invite me to your campus to lecture to you, your staff, and your congregation.

Thank you again, Dr. Schuller, for taking time out of your busy schedule to write your response to my review. I sincerely hope that we both have been helped by our exchange of views.

With cordial Christian greetings and brotherly respect,

Robert L. Reymond

Professor of Systematic Theology.

Chapter Twenty-One

Dr. John Stott on Hell

In a recent book[1] Dr. John Stott, famed rector emeritus of All Souls Church in London and currently president of the London Institute for Contemporary Christianity, tentatively makes the case for the doctrine of ultimate annihilation of the impenitent over against the longstanding orthodox doctrine that his final destiny is eternal conscious torment in hell.

I acknowledge with Donald Guthrie who espouses the orthodox doctrine that "the doctrine of eternal punishment is not an attractive doctrine and the desire to substitute for it the view that, at the judgment, the souls of the wicked will cease to exist, is understandable."[2] I would insist, however, that the Bible, which is, after all, our only infallible rule of faith for the doctrine of hell, will not endorse such a substitution. Nor is such a substitution really more acceptable to the majority of modern men than the traditional view, for the moment would still come even with Stott's representation of things when God annihilates the sinner by casting him into hell – a notion equally repugnant to the modern Western mind who would have God, if it retains him at all, to be a God only of love. But when a "world Christian" of John Stott's stature seriously pleads for a "frank dialogue among evangelicals on

---

Note: This article appeared in Πρεσβυτέριον: *Covenant Seminary Review* (Spring 1990), Vol. XVI, No. 1, 41-59. I have inserted in this version of the article a half-dozen or so paragraphs that the original article did not have.
[1]David L. Edwards and John Stott (1988), *Evangelical Essentials: A Liberal-Evangelical Dialogue*, InterVarsity. In this volume Edwards and Stott dialogue about the authority of Scripture, the nature of Christ's atonement, Christ's miracles, Christian ethics, and the content of the gospel for this day. I heartily endorse most of Dr. Stott's responses to Edward's concerns. The reader should know that it was only because Edwards asked Stott to respond directly to the issue of whether he held the belief that the wicked are tormented in hell or ultimately annihilated (292) that Stott offered his tentative case for annihilation.
[2]Donald Guthrie (1981), *New Testament Theology*, InterVarsity, 892. I recommend Guthrie's entire discussion of hell, 887-92.

the basis of Scripture" concerning this issue,[3] we honor him most by responding to his plea. To ignore his plea publicly while criticizing his view privately[4] is to treat him undeservingly with disrespect if not with disdain. It is in reponse to his plea for dialogue that I offer the following remarks.

Before I say anything else I want to disabuse those readers who have not read Dr. Stott directly of any notion that he advances the doctrine of annihilation because he is trying to find an "easier road" for the ungodly, for such is simply not the case. The sinner's banishment from God, for Dr. Stott, is "real, terrible (so that 'it would be better for him if he had not been born,' Mark 14:21) and eternal."[5] And few Christians will read Dr. Stott's discussion of hell without becoming deeply convicted regarding their lethargic, tearless efforts to reach the lost. My own reading of Dr. Stott made me realize afresh how little troubled I often am in my spirit over the plight of the lost, and I was driven to confess to God the sin of those large times in my life when I am not as concerned as I should be for the salvation of perishing men.

Nor is Dr. Stott's tentative advocacy of annihilationism due to an unwitting lapse away from the supreme authority of Scripture toward an unscriptural surrender to mere emotionalism. For while he admits that "emotionally, I find the [traditional] concept intolerable and do not understand how people can live with it without either cauterizing their feelings or cracking under the strain,"[6] he earnestly believes that he is listening to Scripture and that a case for the impenitent's annihilation can be made exegetically from Scripture itself.

He advances four arguments – related in turn to Scriptural language, Scriptural imagery, Scriptural justice, and Scriptural universalism – to make his case.[7] His first argument makes the basic point – since

---

[3]Edwards and Stott, *Evangelical Essentials*, 320.

[4]In the interest of Christian goodwill I permitted Dr. Stott to see this article in manuscript form before it was published to allow him the opportunity to correct any misrepresentations of his views and to write a response if he deemed it appropriate and necessary. Regrettably, his very busy schedule would not permit him to write a response within the time constraints *Presbyterion* had to impose upon him.

[5] Edwards and Stott, *Evangelical Essentials*, 314.

[6]Edwards and Stott, *Evangelical Essentials*, 314.

[7]Edwards and Stott, *Evangelical Essentials*, 315-20.

eternal perdition is often described in Scripture in terms of the sinner's "destruction" – that "it would seem strange…if people who are said to suffer destruction are in fact not destroyed."[8] Second, he contends that the imagery of hell as "eternal fire" suggests – since, he writes, "the main function of fire is not to cause pain, but to secure destruction, as all the world's incinerators bear witness" – that the sinner in hell is to be consumed, not tormented.[9] Third is his contention that a serious disproportion incompatible with the biblical revelation of divine justice would seem to exist between "sins consciously committed in time and torment consciously experienced throughout eternity."[10] Finally, he suggests that "the eternal existence of the impenitent in hell would be hard to reconcile with the promises of God's final victory of evil, or with the apparently universalistic texts which speak of Christ's drawing all men to himself (John 12:32), and of God uniting all things under Christ's headship (Eph. 1:10), reconciling all things to himself through Christ (Col. 1:20), and bringing every knee to bow to Christ and every tongue to confess his lordship (Phil. 2:10, 11), so that in the end God will be 'all in all' or 'everything to everybody' (1 Cor. 15:28)."[11] I will address each of his arguments in turn.

The Scriptural Language

The most fruitful way to address the meaning of the scriptural language pertaining to the eternal condition of the lost is simply to cite the pertinent passages themselves and to comment upon those whose meaning is not immediately transparent. Consider first some Old Testament data. J. A. Motyer has observed in this connection that the Old Testament contains the "suggestion of diversity of destiny for the godly and the ungodly."[12] What are these Old Testament "suggestions of diversity for the godly and the ungodly" to which Motyer refers (which diversity of destiny Dr. Stott, by the way, does not deny)? I cannot offer an exhaustive response here, but I will mention five such intimations.

   To begin, one should recall the distinction God drew between the

---

[8]Edwards and Stott, *Evangelical Essentials*, 316.

[9]Edwards and Stott, *Evangelical Essentials*, 316.

[10]Edwards and Stott, *Evangelical Essentials*, 318.

[11]Edwards and Stott, *Evangelical Essentials*, 319.

[12]J. A. Motyer (1960), "Destruction," *Baker's Dictionary of Theology*, ed. Everett F. Harrison, Baker, 260.

antediluvian world as a whole and Noah and his family:

> The LORD saw how great man's wickedness on the earth had become, and that every inclination of the thoughts of his heart was only evil all the time.... So the LORD said, "I will wipe mankind, whom I have created, from the face of the earth...." But Noah found grace in the eyes of the LORD (Gen. 6:5-8; see 1 Pet. 3:19-20; 2 Pet. 2:5).

To say the least, such a division among men would seem to disallow the doctrine of universalism.

This Old Testament distinction between the divine deliverance of the godly on the one hand and the divine destruction of the ungodly on the other may be seen in the destruction of Sodom and Gomorrah. Showing Lot mercy (Gen. 19:16), God delivered Lot and his family from Sodom.

> Then the LORD rained down burning sulfur on Sodom and Gomorrah from the LORD out of the heavens.... Early in the morning Abraham ...looked down toward Sodom and Gomorrah...and he saw dense smoke rising from the land, like smoke from a furnace (Gen 19:24, 27, 28).

Sodom's destruction is often used later in Scripture as a warning of the divine judgment that will befall those who sin against God (Deut. 29:23; Isa. 1:9; Jer. 23:14; 49:18; Lam. 4:6; Amos 4:11; Zeph. 2:9; Matt. 10:15; Luke 17:29; Rom. 9:29; Rev. 11:8). Particularly instructive for our present purpose are the two references to the destruction of Sodom and Gomorrah found in 2 Peter 2:6-9 and Jude 7 respectively:

> ...if [God] condemned the cities of Sodom and Gomorrah by burning them to ashes, and made them an example of what is going to happen to the ungodly; and if he rescued Lot, a righteous man, who was distressed by the filthy lives of lawless men... – if this is so, then the Lord knows how to rescue godly men from trials and to hold the unrighteous for the day of judgment, *while continuing their punishment* [κολαζομένους, *kolazomenous*; the present middle participle denoting continuous action].

> ...Sodom and Gomorrah and the surrounding towns gave themselves up to sexual immorality and perversion. They serve as examples of those who suffer the punishment of eternal fire.

Then the implicate of eternal loss respecting the ungodly may be seen in the Old Testament חֵרֶם, *herem* ("devoted," and hence "banned"), principle. Recall, for example, that in conquering Sihon, according to Moses' account, Israel "took all his towns and completely destroyed them – men, women and children. We left no survivors" (Deut. 2:34), "destroying [הַחֲרֵם, *haha̔rēm*] every city – men, women, and children" (Deut. 3:6). Here we see Israel carrying out the חֵרֶם, *herem*, principle – the irrevocable giving over of persons and things to the Lord, often by killing them. Liberal theologians and free thinkers, of course, have found this principle exceedingly distasteful and repugnant, and accordingly have concluded that the God of the Old Testament is barbaric in the extreme, governed by a sub-Christian ethic, and in no way to be identified with the loving "God and Father of our Lord Jesus Christ." But Meredith Kline rightly declares:

> Actually, the offense taken is taken at the theology and religion of the Bible as a whole. The New Testament, too, warns men of the realm of the everlasting ban where the reprobate, devoted to wrath, must magnify the justice of God whom they have hated. *The judgments of hell are the* חֵרֶם, *herem, principle come to full and final manifestation.* Since the Old Testament theocracy in Canaan was a divinely appointed symbol of the consummate kingdom of God, there is found in connection with it *an intrusive anticipation of the ethical pattern that will obtain at the final judgment and beyond.*[13]

Supporting this perception, the Preacher of Ecclesiastes declares: "God will bring every deed into judgment, including every hidden thing, whether it is good or evil" (12:14).

Then there are the two explicit Old Testament statements supporting the "diversity of destiny for the godly and the ungodly" found in Isaiah 66:22-24 and Daniel 12:2. Let us consider first Isaiah 66:22-24:

> "As the new heavens and the new earth that I make will endure before me," declares the LORD, "so will your descendants and your name endure. From one new moon to another and from one Sabbath to another, all [redeemed] mankind will come and bow down before me," says the LORD. [Note the suggestion of eternal life and blessedness here for God's

---

[13]Meredith Kline (1963), *Treaty of the Great King*, Eerdmans, 68 (emphasis supplied).

people.] "And they will go out and look upon the dead bodies of those who rebelled against me, for their worm will not die, nor will their fire be quenched, and they will be *loathsome* [דֵרָאוֹן, *dērā'ôn*] to all [redeemed] mankind." (Isa. 66:22-24)

In his commentary on Isaiah Franz Delitzsch states that דֵרָאוֹן, *dērā'ôn* is the strongest word in Hebrew for "abomination," adding:

It is perfectly obvious that the [picture] itself, as here described, must appear monstrous and inconceivable, however we may suppose it to be realized.... [Isaiah] is speaking of the future state, but in figures drawn from the present world. The object of his prediction is no other than the new Jerusalem of the world to come, and the eternal torment of the damned.[14]

Jesus' later citation of Isaiah 66:24 in Mark 9:48 would seem to bear out Delitzsch's comment (see discussion below):

Now let us consider briefly Daniel 12:2:

Multitudes who sleep in the dust of the earth will awake: some to *everlasting life* [חַיֵּי עוֹלָם, *hᵉyê 'ôlām*], others to *shame* [חֲרָפוֹת, *hᵃraphôth*] and *everlasting loathing* [דֵרָאוֹן עוֹלָם, *dērā'ôn 'ôlām*].

Note Daniel's use here of דֵרָאוֹן, *dērā'ôn*, intensifying its horror by placing it in construct with עוֹלָם, *'ôlam* ("everlasting"). The point must be made that some after the resurrection of the dead in the last day will enjoy *"everlasting* life" while others endure "shame and *everlasting* loathing." If the former is *conscious* everlasting enjoyment, one could be pardoned were he to conclude that the latter is also *conscious* everlasting loathing.

With respect to the New Testament data concerning the eternal condition of the lost, Motyer states, quite insightfully, that no sooner does Christ "bring life and immortality to light" than he

also reveals eternal loss and death, so that even Hades, otherwise equivalent to Sheol, cannot refuse the further significance. This *simultaneous maturing* of truth concerning eternal gain and loss is ignored by every attempt to divest the NT of its grim doctrine of eternal punishment.[15]

---

[14]Franz Delitzsch, *Biblical Commentary on the Prophecies of Isaiah* (Reprint, Eerdmans, 1949), II, 517.

What now is the New Testament evidence supporting this "maturing of truth concerning eternal loss" for the impenitent?

John the Baptist

To the multitudes John declared: "...the Messiah *will consume* [κατακαύσει, *katakausei*] the chaff with *unquenchable fire* [πυρὶ ἀσβέστῳ, *puri asbestō*]" (Matt. 3:12).

Annihilationists argue, of course, that the action depicted here by the word "consume" is not one of "tormenting" the chaff but one of burning up the chaff. And, of course, this is the Forerunner's language. But this argument ignores the fuller teaching of Scripture, as we shall see, and leaves completely unexplained why the Baptist characterizes the fire as "unquenchable" if every impenitent sinner at the final judgment is instantly consumed by it. To maintain that the adjective "unquenchable" means that that which is instantly consumed by the fire is consumed forever[16] does not really explain why the *fire* is described as unquenchable. If the chaff is instantly consumed by the fire, as the annihilationist maintains, there would be no need for it to be unquenchable. Once it had "done its job," it could be extinguished. Doubtless at least some of the language of Scripture describing the unseen world must be understood figuratively. But figurative language, if it has any meaning at all, intends something literal, and it is my contention that the figure of "unquenchable fire," in light of other Scripture references, intends at least *unending conscious misery.*

Jesus

The strongest support for the doctrine of unending conscious punishment for the impenitent is found in the teaching of Jesus, the Redeemer of mankind. *The Christian church and Christian pastors are not the authors of the doctrine.* Rather, Jesus, that omniscient Person, is more responsible than any other for the doctrine of eternal perdition. Accordingly, it is he, more than any other, with whom the opponents of the doctrine are in conflict. Consider now his witness:

---

[15]J. A. Motyer, "Destruction," *Baker's Dictionary of Theology*, 260 (emphasis supplied).

[16]Edwards and Stott, *Evangelical Essentials*, 316.

It is better for you to enter life maimed than with two hands to go into *hell where the fire never goes out* [τὴν γέενναν εἰς τὸ πῦρ τὸ ἄσβεστον, *tēn geennan eis to pur to asbeston*] (Mark 9:43).

Jesus' word translated "hell" here ("Gehenna") is the Aramaic word for "Valley of Hinnom." It is derived from the site name mentioned in 2 Kings 23:10, an idolatrous worship center from the time of Ahaz to Manasseh south of Jerusalem at which site children were burned in fire as an offering to the god Molech (2 Chr. 28:3, 33). It was later destroyed by Josiah and made a refuse dump for the city's garbage. Since fire burned continuously in the valley, Gehenna became a symbol of the "unquenchable fire" of hell. Topheth, that was in the valley of Ben Hinnom (2 Kgs. 23:10), became a synonym for the site as a whole: "Topheth has long been prepared; it has been made ready.... Its fire pit has been made deep and wide, with an abundance of fire and wood; the breath of the LORD, like a stream of burning sulphur, sets it ablaze" (Isa. 30:33).

It is better for you to enter the kingdom of God with one eye than to have two eyes and be thrown into *hell, where their worm [that is, their "maggot"] does not die, and the fire is not quenched* [τὴν γέενναν, ὅπου ὁ σκώληξ αὐτῶν οὐ τελευτᾷ καὶ τὸ πῦρ οὐ σβέννυται, *tēn geennan, hopou ho skōlēx autōn ou teleuta kai to pur ou sbennutai*] (Mark 9:47-48; see Isa. 66:24).

Because maggots, the larvae of flies, normally feed upon a corpse's flesh and are finally done with it (Job 21:26; 24:20; Isa. 14:11) and whereas here the impenitent's "maggot" is said never to die and Gehenna's fire is said to be "unquenched," the implication here is that his punishment is unending. Guthrie states that Jesus' description here of the unrepentant sinner's final state is that of a "continuous punishment."[17]

...anyone who says, "You fool!" will be in danger of the fire of hell [τὴν γέενναν τοῦ πυρός, *tēn geennan tou puros*] (Matt. 5:22; see verses 29, 30).

...wide is the gate and broad is the road that leads to *destruction* [ἀπώλειαν, *apōleian*], and many enter through it. (Matt 7:13)

---

[17]Donald Guthrie, *New Testament Theology*, 888.

In this context "destruction" appears to intend "[eternal] death," the antithesis of the "life" mentioned in the following verse.

> ...the subjects of the kingdom will be thrown *outside, into the darkness, where there will be weeping and gnashing of teeth* [τὸ σκότος τὸ ἐξώτερον· ἐκεῖ ἔσται ὁ κλαυθμὸς καὶ ὁ βρυγμὸς τῶν ὀδόντων, *to skotos to exōteron. Ekei estai ho klauthmos kai ho brugmos tōn odontōn*]" (Matt. 8:12; 22:13; 25:30; see 24:51).

Because "weeping and gnashing of teeth," suggesting as it does conscious pain and woe, exists in hell's "outer darkness," this expression too seems to describe a state of conscious continuous punishment.

> I tell you the truth, it will be *more bearable* [ἀνεκτότερον, *anektoteron*] for Sodom and Gomorrah on the day of judgment than for that town (Matt. 10:15; see 11:22, 24; also Luke 10:12, 14).

The New Testament often teaches that there will be degrees of punishment meted out to the impenitent, depending on such matters as the amount of spiritual light they had and their opportunities to repent and believe. Matthew 10:15 is one such expression of this teaching. It is difficult, to say the very least, to comprehend how this teaching can be squared with the annihilationist's position if the final outcome of the day of judgment for all the impenitent is the same, namely, annihilation.

> Do not be afraid of those who can destroy the body but cannot kill the soul. Rather, be afraid of the One who can destroy both soul and body in hell (Matt. 10:28).

Annihilationists such as Dr. Stott argue here that Jesus' terms of destruction suggest that annihilation is the impenitent's end, but "destruction" does not have to connote annihilation, that is, the cessation of existence. It can also connote a state of *existence*, the precise nature of which is to be determined by all language qualifying that existence. Accordingly, the impenitent can be described as "destroyed" when he has been cast into hell. And it is interesting that the Lukan parallel suggests precisely this connotation for the Matthean notion of destruction: "Fear him who, after the killing of the body, has power to throw you into hell" (Luke 12:5).

They will throw them into the fiery furnace, where there will be weeping and gnashing of teeth (Matt. 13:42).

It is better for you to enter life maimed or crippled that to have two hands or two feet and be thrown into *eternal fire* [πῦρ αἰώνιον, *pur aiōnion*] (Matt. 18:8).

It is better for you to enter life with one eye than to have two eyes and be thrown into the fire of hell (Matt. 18:9).

You snakes! You brood of vipers! How will you escape the judgment of hell? (Matt. 23:33).

Then he will say to those on his left, "Depart from me, you who are cursed, into the eternal fire prepared for the devil and his angels." (Matt. 25:41; see Rev 20:10 for an elaboration of the nature of the devil's punishment in the lake of fire in terms of "torment day and night for ever and ever").

Then they will go away to *eternal punishment* [κόλασιν αἰώνιον, *kolasin aiōnion*] but the righteous to eternal life (Matt. 25:46).

I can find no occurrence of κόλασις *kolasis*, where it connotes annihilation; it seems in every instance to mean "punishment." Ralph E. Powell correctly comments on this verse that "the same word 'eternal' is applied to the duration of the punishment in hell as is used for the duration of the bliss in heaven."[18]

...woe to that man who betrays the Son of Man! It would be better for him if he had not been born." (Matt. 26:24; see here Matt. 18:6; Luke 17:2).

But if Judas' final end was to be his soul's annihilation and thus simply nonexistence, how is his final state worse than his original nonexistent state prior to his birth?

That servant who knows his master's will and does not get ready or does not do what his master wants will be beaten with many blows. But the one who does not know and does things deserving punishment will be beaten with few blows. From everyone who has been given much, much

---

[18]Ralph E. Powell (1988), "Hell," in *Baker Encyclopedia of the Bible*, ed. Walter A. Elwell, Baker, 1:954.

will be demanded; and from the one who has been entrusted with much, much will be asked (Luke 12:47-48).

Again, while the degrees of punishment suggested here can be adjusted to the traditional doctrine of eternal conscious torment, it is difficult to see how these degrees of punishment can be adjusted to the annihilationist's contention that annihilation is the punishment for all the impenitent.

> In hell, *where he was in torment* [ἐν τῷ ᾅδῃ... ὑπάρχων ἐν βασάνοις, *en tō hadē... huparchōn en basanoios*].... "I am *in agony in this flame* [ὀδυνῶμαι ἐν τῇ φλογι ταύτῃ, *odunōmai en tē phlogi tautē*]".... "this *place of torment* [τὸν τόπον τούτων τῆς βασάνου, *ton topon toutōn tēs basanou*]" (Luke 16:23, 24, 28; see also 12:5; 13:27).

While one should not press every detail in any of our Lord's parables for its meaning, it is hardly likely that Jesus would have been unaware that his listeners on this occasion would have understood him to teach that, following physical death, the unrepentant sinner endures conscious torment in the fire of hell. If their conclusion was erroneous, one must conclude that Jesus did nothing to correct it. J. Oliver Buswell, Jr. declares: "That literal and intense suffering is the meaning intended [by 'torment' and 'agony' here] cannot be denied by any reasonable method of exegesis."[19]

As annihilationists commonly have done before, Dr. Stott interprets this parable to mean that lost men *in the intermediate state* between their physical death and their resurrection "will come to unimaginably painful realization of their fate. But this is not incompatible...with their final annihilation."[20] I grant that the parable may be describing most immediately the intermediate state, but there is nothing in the parable that suggests that the intermediate state's "torment" will cease for the lost after their resurrection and judgment. To the contrary, Jesus' description of the "great gulf" between the blessed and the lost as "fixed" (ἐστήρικται, *estēriktai*, the perfect passive of στηρίζω, *sterizō*, that is, "has been fixed and continues so") implies the unchanging character of the lost person's estate in hell.

---

[19]J. Oliver Buswell, Jr. (1962), *A Systematic Theology of the Christian Religion*, Zondervan, 2:308.
[20]Edwards and Stott, *Evangelical Essentials*, 317-18.

Do not be amazed at this, for a time is coming when all who are in their graves will hear his voice and come out – those who have done good will rise to live, and those who have done evil will rise to be condemned. (John 5:28-29)

Demons

What have we to do with you, O Son of God? Have you come here before the time *to torment* [βασανίσαι, *basanisai*] us? (Matt 8:29)

It would appear that demons believe that conscious torment, not annihilation, awaits them someday.

Paul

Concerning Paul's teaching regarding the judgment of unbelievers, Herman Ridderbos writes:

Paul declares the certainty of [punitive judgment on unbelievers and the ungodly] in an unmistakable way, in many respects with words that have been derived from the Old Testament preaching of judgment. He speaks of it as ruin, death, payment with an eternal destruction…, wrath, indignation, tribulation, anguish. But nowhere is the how, the where, or the how long "treated" as a separate "subject" of Christian doctrine in the epistles of Paul that have been preserved for us.[21]

Here are Paul's statements that deal with our topic:

If anybody is preaching to you a gospel other than what you accepted, let him be *condemned* [ἀνάθεμα, *anathema*] (Gal 1:9).

Jesus rescued us from the coming wrath (1 Thess. 1:10).

…*destruction* [ὄλεθρος, *olethros*] will come upon them suddenly…and they will not escape (1 Thess. 5:3).

Annihilationists press the word "destruction" here to mean the cessation of existence, but as I have already argued, the word does not need to connote a final state of nonexistence. To interpret the word so is to interpret the Scripture's embellished statements

---

[21]Herman Ridderbos (1975), *Paul: An Outline of His Theology*, Eerdmans, 554.

elsewhere on the state of the lost in hell by the unembellished word here (see comments on next verse) when the converse method should be followed.

> They will be punished with *everlasting destruction* [[ὄλεθρον αἰώνιον, *olethron aiōnion*] and shut out from the [approving] presence of the Lord. (2 Thess. 1:9; see *Westminster Larger Catechism*, Question 89).

This is the only passage in Paul where αἰώνιος, *aiōnios* ("everlasting"), is explicitly attached to ὄλεθρος, *olethros*. Geerhardus Vos offers the following comments on Paul's statement:

> This is the statement most frequently depended upon to tone down the principle of two-sided eternal retribution traditionally ascribed to the Apostle. It not being feasible to modify the eschatologically-constant value of *aiōnios*, the attack has centered upon the noun or nouns to which the adjective is attached. "*Olethros*[] and []*apōleia*" have been given the sense of annihilation.... As concerns the statement in 2 Thess. no one can deny that it posits a strong contrast between the destiny of believers and the end of their persecutors. Only, the question arises, whether the thought of annihilation is fitted to serve as the evil opposite pole in a contrast so sharply stressed by Paul. It will have to be remembered at the outset that "annihilation" is an extremely abstract idea, too philosophical, in fact, to find a natural place within the limits of the realistic biblical eschatology, least of all, it would seem, in this outburst of vehement indignation against the enemies of the Gospel. Closely looked at it is not a stronger but a weaker concept than that of protracted retribution to threaten with, so that, instead of contributing to the sharpness of the opposition intended, it would to a certain extent obliterate the latter....
>
> The problem of the relation of "*olethros*" and "*apōleia*" to existence or non-existence could be solved without much difficulty, were writers willing to test the Pauline statements by reference to the words of Jesus, because the latter on the one hand uses "*apōleia*" of the state and Gehenna of the place of eternal destruction and on the other hand combines with these the strongest predicates of unceasing retribution; cp. Matt. v. 29; vii. 13; Mk. v. 29, 30; ix. 43, 44, 46, 48; Lk. xii. 5.... Could Paul in a matter like this have shown less severity than Jesus?[22]

---

[22]Geerhardus Vos (1961), *The Pauline Eschatology* (Reprint, Eerdmans, 294-96.

Vos answers his own question in a footnote (296, fn. 12): "In none of [the passages where Paul employs ἀπώλεια, *apōleia*] is there noticeable a lack of pathos, rather the opposite."

Moreover, to describe the soul's annihilation in terms of being "shut out from the [approving] presence of the Lord" is very strange language, to say the least, to describe the state of nonexistence. Such an expression does not in itself imply annihilation in any sense that reasonable exegesis could justify.

> ...for those who...reject the truth and follow evil, there will be wrath, and anger; there will be trouble and distress for every human being who does evil (Rom. 2:8-9).

The last two descriptions of the evildoer's state does not comport easily with the notion of cessation of existence.

> ...all who sin...will perish (Rom. 2:12).

> [The things you are now ashamed of] result in death...the wages of sin is [spiritual] death (Rom. 6:21, 23).

> ...vessels of his wrath – prepared for destruction (Rom. 9:22).

> For we will all stand before God's judgment seat. It is written: "As surely as I live," says the Lord, "every knee will bow before me; every tongue will confess to God." So then, each of us will give an account of himself to God (Rom. 14:10-12).

> ...the message of the cross is foolishness to those who are perishing (1 Cor 1:18).

The verb for "perishing" here (the present middle of ἀπόλλυμι, *apollumi*) describes the *existing* people who are presently perishing. The verb does not suggest that their future state will be non-existence. The same verb in Luke 15:4, 6 describes the lost but *existing* sheep, in 15:8, 9 the lost but *existing* coin, and in 15:17 the lost but *existing* son. The same is true of the Hebrew word for "perish" (אבד, *'bd*). Kish's asses are described by this verb when they are simply lost but still exist (1 Sam. 9:3, 20). And Isaiah can speak of the righteous as perishing while they still exist (57:1). In none of these instances does the verb imply that the future state of these entities will be nonexistence.

Since the antithesis of perishing in the spiritual sense is "having eternal life," the "perishing" soul may be devoid of "eternal life" and thus be "dead" as far as the possession of eternal life is concerned but still exist, as in the case of those to whom Paul refers here.

> If anyone destroys God's temple, God will destroy him (1 Cor. 3:17).
> If anyone does not love the Lord – a curse be upon him (1 Cor. 16:22).

> For we must all stand before the judgment seat of Christ, that each one may receive what is due him for the things done while in the body, whether good or bad (2 Cor. 5:10).

The stress here on the individuality of these being judged ("each one") in the final judgment implies that there will be greatly varying results in this judgment. But if all the impenitent are annihilated, there is no room for any degrees of punishments.

> ...their [the enemies of the cross of Christ] destiny is destruction (Phil. 3:19).

The Author of Hebrews

This author includes among the "elementary teachings" and "foundation doctrines" of the Christian faith, the doctrine of "eternal judgment [κρίματος αἰωνίου, *krimatos aiōniou*]" (Heb. 6:2). About this judgment he writes: "...man is destined to die once, and *after that* to face judgment" (9:27). Note that this verse clearly states that men do survive the event of physical death and that *after* death they will stand before God in judgment. Then he writes:

> If we deliberately keep on sinning after we have received the knowledge of the truth, no sacrifice for sins is left, but only a fearful expectation of judgment and of *raging fire that will consume* [πυρὸς ζῆλος ἐσθίειν μέλλοντος, *puros zēlos esthiein mellontos*] the enemies of God (Heb 10:26-27; see verses 28-31 and also 12:29: "Our God is a *consuming fire* [πῦρ καταναλίσκον, *pur katanaliskon*]").

Annihilationists, of course, place a construction on these words not in keeping with the totality of Scripture teaching. Finally, he states: "But we are not of those who shrink back and are destroyed [εἰς ἀπώλειαν, *eis apōleian*]" (Heb 10:30).

Peter

...if God did not spare angels when they sinned, but *sent them to hell, putting them into gloomy dungeons* [σειραις ζόφου ταρταρώσας, *seirais zophou tartarōsas*; Tartarus is a classical word for the place of eternal punishment] to be held for judgment; if he did not spare the ancient world when he brought the flood on its ungodly people...; if he condemned the cities of Sodom and Gomorrah by burning them to ashes, and made them an example of what is going to happen to the ungodly... – if this is so, then the Lord knows how...to hold the unrighteous for the day of judgment, while continuing their punishment [κολαζομένους, *kolazomenous*; the present middle participle denoting continuous action] (2 Pet. 2:4-9).

Jude

...the angels who did not keep their positions of authority but abandoned their own house – these [the Lord] has kept in darkness, bound in everlasting chains for judgment on the great Day. In a similar way, Sodom and Gomorrah and the surrounding towns...serve as *an example of those who suffer the justice of eternal fire* [δεῖγμα πυρὸς αἰωνίου δίκην ὑπέχουσαι, *deigma puros aiōniou dikēn hupechousai*] (Jude 6-7).

John

...perish [ἀπόληται, *apolētai*]...stands condemned already... God's wrath remains [μένει, *menei*] on him (John 3:16, 18, 36).

If anyone worships the beast and his image and receives his mark on the forehead or on the hand, he too will drink of the wine of God's fury, which has been poured full strength into the cup of his wrath. He *will be tormented in fire* [βασανισθήσεται ἐν πυρὶ, *basanisthēsetai en puri*] in the presence of the holy angels and of the Lamb. And the smoke of their torment rises for ever and ever. There is *no rest day or night* [οὐκ ἔχουσιν ἀνάπαυσιν ἡμέρας καὶ νυκτὸς, *ouk echousin anapausin hēmeras kai nuktos*] for those who worship the beast and his image (Rev. 14:9-11; see 19:3).

Here unending conscious torment is said to be the punishment of those who receive the mark of the beast. Dr. Stott's comment here that "It is the smoke (evidence that fire has done its work) which 'rises for ever and ever'"[23] is somewhat facile, for while it is true that it is the smoke that is said to rise, it is equally true that it is the smoke of their *torment* that rises. And the smoke of their torment is said to be forever and ever. It is also said of these people that they experience "no rest day or night" – an expression hardly descriptive of a state of nonexistence.

[The beast and the false prophet] were thrown alive into *the lake of fire that burns with brimstone* [τὴν λίμνην τοῦ πυρὸς τῆς καιομένης ἐν θείῳ, *tēn limnēn tou puros tēs kaiomenēs en theiō*]" (Rev 19:20).

The devil, who deceived [the nations], was thrown into the lake of burning sulphur, where the beast and the false prophet had been thrown. They will be tormented day and night for ever and ever [βασανισθήσονται ἡμέρας καὶ νυκτὸς εἰς τοὺς αἰῶνος τῶν αἰώνων, *basanisthēsontai hēmeras kai nuktos eis tous aiōnos tōn aiōnōn*] (Rev 20:10).

Dr. Stott's argument here that since the beast and the false prophet "are not individual people but symbols of the world in its varied hostility to God" (with which view I am in essential agreement) and hence as symbols "they cannot experience pain"[24] seems to me to be a desperate measure to explain away the plain import of the passage. Surely the devil is a person, and if the beast and the false prophet are symbols surely they symbolize in some sense people.

And I saw the dead, great and small, standing before the throne, and books were opened. Another book was opened, which is the book of life. The dead were judged according to what they had done as recorded in the books. The sea gave up the dead that were in it, and death and Hades gave up the dead that were in them, and each person was judged according to what he had done. Then death and Hades were thrown into the lake of fire. The lake of fire is the second death. If anyone's name was not found written in the book of life, he was thrown into the lake of fire (Rev 20:12-15).

The fact that at the final judgment each person will be judged according to what he has done implies that degrees of punishment will be meted out by the Judge of all the earth who will do right by all (Gen. 18:25). This passage also implies that the same destiny awaits

[23]Edwards and Stott, *Evangelical Essentials*, 316.
[24]Edwards and Stott, *Evangelical Essentials*, 318.

the impenitent that awaits the devil, the beast, and the false prophet, namely, torment day and night forever and ever (see Rev. 20:10).

From such Johannine notices as these in the Apocalypse Guthrie declares that the New Testament makes it clear that divine judgment on evildoers is certain, just, and eternal. It is because the Apocalypse takes the fact of an eternal hell seriously, I would submit, that it concludes with the Spirit and the church urging any and all who are thirsty to come and to take the free gift of the water of life (Rev. 22:17). We as students of the Word have not been touched by our study of the Apocalypse as we should be if we have not been moved to take more seriously the evangelization of the world that is on a collision course with God's wrath to be revealed on "the day of wrath when God's righteous judgment will be revealed" (Rom. 2:5) – "on that day when God judges the secrets of men by Christ Jesus" (Rom. 2:16).

I must conclude from this survey of biblical texts pertaining to the last judgment and hell, interpreted both individually and in light of the analogy of Scripture, that their only natural meaning is that the retributive infliction of which they speak will be unending, and that the doctrines of the final judgment after death and of eternal conscious torment for the impenitent are clearly affirmed. If these texts speak only of the soul's annihilation, none of them intending to teach that the impenitent sinner consciously suffers eternal torment after the final judgment, then we must conclude that a large majority of the church's finest scholars through the ages has failed to do proper exegesis.

The Scriptural Imagery of Hell

It is true that hell is characterized in Scripture primarily in terms of fire. But in my opinion it goes beyond the evidence cited above to conclude from this fact, as Dr. Stott does, that "our expectation [of the effect of this fire]" would be the consummation or destruction of the soul. Leon Morris's observation is on point here:

> …against the strong body of NT teaching that there is a continuing punishment of sin we cannot put one saying which speaks plainly of an end to the punishment of the finally impenitent. Those who look for a different teaching in the NT must point to possible inferences and alternative explanations.[25]

---

[25]Leon Morris (1984), "Eternal Punishment," *Evangelical Dictionary of Theology*, ed. Walter A. Elwell, Baker, 370-71.

If the Scriptural imagery is to be taken figuratively at all (and many details are doubtless to be so construed), then the realities they seek to represent should surely be understood by us to be *more* – not less – horrible than the word pictures they depict, a position that I am confident Dr. Stott himself would espouse!

The Scriptural Justice of Eternal Torment

Assuming quite properly that scriptural justice implies that the penalty inflicted must be commensurate with the evil done, Dr. Stott draws from this what in my opinion is a *non sequitur*, namely, that a serious disproportion incompatible with justice would exist between sins consciously committed in time and torment consciously experienced throughout eternity. On this ground God could not even annihilate the sinner for his sins "committed in time" since annihilation is certainly eternal in duration.

Moreover, if Stott's argument is sound, then the justice in God's retribution against a whole host of what most people would view as rather insignificant sins recorded in Scripture is also highly questionable. To illustrate what I mean here, consider God's turning Lot's wife into a pillar of salt because she glanced back at Sodom and Gomorrah (Gen. 19:26), God's killing Nadab and Abihu for an irregularity in their priestly duties (Lev. 10:1-2), God's commanding an unnamed man to be stoned to death because he picked up some sticks on the Sabbath (Num. 15:32-36), God's disqualification of Moses entering the promised land because he struck the rock twice rather than speaking to it (Num. 20:11), God's commanding Achan's entire family to be executed because Achan stole something that God said he wanted (Josh. 7:11, 25), God's killing of Uzzah because he steadied the Ark with his hand (2 Sam. 6:6-7), and his striking down Ananias and Sapphira for lying to Peter (Acts 5:1-10). But beyond debate, the greatest example of "injustice" from the world's perspective is God's inflicting the entire human race with physical death and condemnation because Adam ate a piece of fruit that had been forbidden him (Gen. 3:5-6; Rom. 5:12-19). The world's justice systems would conclude that in not one of these instances did the divine reaction fit the crime, that these are only "little sins," if sins at all, hardly deserving the severe retribution God meted out against their perpetrators.

But are these "little sins"? The fact that Stott wants to stress – that men commit such sins in time and not in eternity is irrelevant to the nature and extent of their punishment. The only relevant fact, as David saw so clearly, is that all sin is transgression of the law of God: "Against you, only you, have I sinned and done what is evil in your sight, so that you are proved right when you speak and justified when you judge" (Ps. 51:4). Because all sin is finally against God, there is infinite demerit about the "tiniest" sin. Its infinite demerit may be seen by simply asking, with Anselm, "How great a consideration offered up to God would it take to make it right for me to disobey God and corrupt the original holiness of His creation?" The answer, of course, is that no consideration offered up to God – neither this entire universe nor all possible created universes – would ever make a single transgression of his law right. Every sin then deserves God's wrath and curse, for the justice of God demands that every sin receive its just retribution. Thomas Aquinas observed:

> The magnitude of the punishment matches the magnitude of the sin.... Now a sin that is against God is infinite; the higher the person against whom it is committed, the graver the sin – it is more criminal to strike a head of state than a private citizen – and God is of infinite greatness. Therefore an infinite punishment is deserved for a sin committed against him.[26]

God has certainly given evidence throughout the Old Testament that he will inflict the sinner with conscious *temporal* miseries (think of the Genesis Flood, the destruction of Sodom and Gomorrah, the plagues of Egypt in Exodus 7–12; the horrible threats of Leviticus 26:14-39; Deuteronomy 28:15-68; Habakkuk 1:5-11; Malachi 4:1-6). Of this there can be no doubt. If he has made known by subsequent New Testament revelation that final justice is served only by the judicial infliction of conscious *eternal* torment upon the impenitent – whose impenitence, we must not forget, also continues throughout eternity (since true repentance, as a gift of God, will not be granted; see Revelation 16:11, 21) – then the creature must acquiesce in his wise and just judgment.

---

[26]Thomas Aquinas, *Summa theologica*, 1a2ae. 87.4.

Scriptural Universalism: Eternal Suffering of the Impenitent Not an Infringement upon God's Final Victory over Evil

Dr. Stott is not a universalist. He is persuaded that the doctrine of the final judgment that will involve "a separation [among men] into two opposite but equally eternal destinies" is too deeply embedded in Scripture to be controverted.[27] One example of this conviction on his part is his total rejection of Pope John Paul II's statement, "Man – every man without exception whatever – has been redeemed by Christ, and…with man – with each man without any exception whatever – Christ is in a way united, even when man is unaware of it." Dr. Stott's exact words are as follows: "That kind of unconditional universalism…must be firmly rejected by those who look to Scripture for authoritative guidance."[28] Nevertheless, he suggests that "the apparently universalistic texts" (Eph. 1:10; Col. 1:20; Phil. 2:10-11; 1 Cor. 15:28)[29] are easier to reconcile with the awful realities of hell if hell means the destruction of the impenitent and not their continuing rebellion against God and God's corresponding continuing infliction of punishment upon them.[30]

The universalist, of course, will not be convinced by Dr. Stott's reasoning. He will argue that a judgment that eventuates in the

---

[27]Edwards and Stott, *Evangelical Essentials*, 319. The New Testament alone teaches the ultimate bifurcation of human destiny in more than fifty passages (Matt. 7:22, 23; 12:41, 42; 13:40-43; 24:51; 25:41-46; Mark 12:9; Luke 13:25-30; 16:19-28; 21:36; John 5:22-30; 12:47, 48; 15:6, 22-25; 16:8-11; Acts 17:31; 24:25; Rom. 1:32; 2:2, 3, 5; 5:16, 18; 14:10; 1 Cor. 5:13; 2 Cor. 5:10; Gal 6:7; 1 Thess. 4:6; 5:1-10; 2 Thess. 1:5-10; 2:3-12; 2 Tim. 4:1; Heb. 4:12, 13; 6:4-8; 10:26-31; Jas. 2:13; 4:12; 1 Pet. 2:7, 8, 23; 3:12; 4:17, 18; 2 Pet. 2:3-10; 3:7; 1 John 3:7, 8; Jude 4-6, 13, 15; Rev. 14:7, 9-11, 17-20; 15:1; 16; 19:1-3; 11-21; 20:11-15; 22:15).

[28]Edwards and Stott, *Evangelical Essentials*, 325; for Pope John Paul II's statement, see his papal encyclical, *Redemptor Hominis* (1979), paragraph 14.

[29]Leon Morris, "Eternal Punishment," *Evangelical Dictionary of Theology*, 370-71, is correct when he writes: "…to interpret such passages as meaning that in the end all will be saved is to go beyond what the writers are saying and to ignore the fact that in the contexts there are usually references to God's condemnation of the wicked, or to the final separation between good and evil, or the like."

[30]Edwards and Stott, *Evangelical Essentials*, 319.

annihilation of even one man equally overthrows the import of these universalistic passages. J. A. T. Robinson's words illustrate the universalist's concern here quite well:

> Christ, in Origen's old words, remains on the Cross so long as one sinner remains in hell. That is not speculation: it is a statement grounded in the very necessity of God's nature. In a universe of love there can be no heaven which tolerates a chamber of horrors; no hell for any which does not at the same time make it hell for God.[31]

I am persuaded that the universalist is more consistent here, for once Dr. Stott brings the "apparently universalistic passages" to the discussion as part of his basis for the doctrine of annihilation, he can find no exegetical warrant in them for stopping short of the universalist's unwarranted deduction of the final salvation of all men.

I would urge that the doctrine of hell, as traditionally understood and propounded, is not an infringement upon the notion of God's final victory over evil, nor is it an infringement upon his final joy. Victory over an enemy may be manifested in more than one way. An enemy's total destruction might be one of those ways, to be sure. But his deserved and permanent incarceration at hard labor might equally be a manifestation of victory over evil and could equally fall out to the praise of the victor's justice. In the case of God and of Christ, faced as they will be at the judgment with impenitent men guilty of sins of infinite magnitude against them, the sinner's eternal incarceration in hell will not infringe upon the final divine victory over evil but will in stark lines exhibit the divine triumph over it. I concur with James I. Packer's judgment that "the holy God of the Bible is praised no less for establishing righteousness by retributively punishing wrongdoers (Rev. 19:1-5), than for the triumph of his grace (Rev. 19:6-10) [and] it cannot be said of God that expressing his holiness in deserved retribution mars his joy."[32]

I must conclude that the doctrines of the final judgment and of hell for the impenitent are among the cardinal doctrines of the Christian faith (see *Westminster Confession of Faith*, XXXII.1; XXXIII.2) and that conscious eternal torment awaits the unrepentant sinner. These

---

[31] J. A. T. Robinson, *In the End God* (New York: Harper, 1968), 133.

[32] James I. Packer, "Is Hell Out of Vogue," *Action* (Sept.-Oct. 1989), 11.

things are spoken of clearly and plainly in the New Testament. Furthermore, if Christ bore my curse and died my death at Calvary, and if my "eternal punishment" would have been final and total annihilation, body and soul (a bizarre thing metaphysically even to contemplate), then the annihilationist must be prepared to declare that Christ experienced, body and soul, at least for a time my annihilation, that is to say, non-existence, a position far more difficult to support exegetically than the traditional view that he consciously endured the suffering and separation from God to which my sins made me liable. I would even urge, if the final state of the impenitent is non-existence, that we should stop talking about mankind's need for the work of Christ in any *urgent* sense, for if there is no hell, construed as eternal conscious torment, awaiting the impenitent, then there is no urgent need for Christ's work, the doctrines of grace, the church as the redemptive community of God in the world, and the incalculable personal sacrifices that individual Christians and Christian missionaries make to carry the gospel to the ends of the earth. But as I said above, it is just because the Apocalypse takes the fact of an eternal hell seriously that it concludes with the Spirit and the church urging any and all who are thirsty to take the free gift of the water of life (Rev. 22:17).

* * * * *

Hopefully with the same humility with which Dr. Stott presented the annihilationist case I now offer these comments in order to advance the dialogue that he requested. Obviously, I am not persuaded by his four arguments. But nothing I have said should be construed to mean that I regard him as an untrustworthy guide in *all* things Evangelical. He is far too significant a leader in modern Evangelicalism and I have learned far too much from him myself – indeed, I have learned from him even in this very book – for me to suggest that. But on this point I would urge the church not to follow him, however horrible the traditional depiction of hell is.[33] We must bear in mind that it is not the

---

[33]Since I originally wrote this article, several fine books have been published upholding the historic teaching on hell as a place of eternal conscious torment, among them being Larry Dixon's *The Other Side of the Good News: Confronting the Contemporary Challenges to Jesus' Teaching on Hell*

church or its pastors, as I have already pointed out, who authored the doctrine of hell. Rather, it is Christ and those apostles – particularly the Apostle John – whom he inspired who were the chief exponents of it. If we would be Christ's disciples, I would submit that we must teach it too.

(Fearn, UK: Christian Focus, 2002) and Robert A. Peterson's *Hell on Trial: The Case for Eternal Punishment* (Phillipsburg, N. J.: Presbyterian and Reformed, 1995).

Chapter Twenty-Two

Review of Walter C. Kaiser's *Toward an Exegetical Theology: Biblical Exegesis for Preaching and Teaching*

The author wrote this volume[1] on exegetical methodology because he is convinced that there is

> a gap…in academic preparation for the ministry. It is the gap that exists between the study of the Biblical text…and the actual delivery of messages to God's people. Very few centers of Biblical and homiletical training have even taken the time or effort to show the student how one moves from analyzing the text over to constructing a sermon that accurately reflects that same analysis and is directly dependent on it (8).

This volume he intends as a "firstfruits" offering of the (he hopes) "many similar exegetical theologies" (9).

Kaiser's book is not, in my opinion, an exegetical theology as such. Rather, it is more a "how to" manual on hermeneutics, with ample discussion and illustrations of how a pastor is to come to a biblical passage and (1) by exegesis to discover therein the one sense or meaning that the author intended (44-47), and (2) by *the process of principlization* "to state the author's propositions, arguments, narrations, and illustrations in timeless abiding truths with special focus on the application of those truths to the current needs of the Church" (152; see chap. 7).

The heart of Kaiser's book is Part II where he calls for a syntactical-theological method of exegesis composed of contextual, syntactical, verbal, theological, and homiletical analyses of the biblical text. Part III treats the special problems that arise for the preacher when he preaches from prophetic, narrative, and poetic texts. Kaiser's

---

Note: This review appeared in *Presbyterion: A Journal for the Eldership* (Spring-Fall 1983), Vol. IX, Nos. 1-2:96-8.

[1]Walter C. Kaiser, Jr., *Toward an Exegetical Theology: Biblical Exegesis for Preaching and Teaching* (Grand Rapids: Baker, 1981).

"pastor's heart," evident throughout, becomes most apparent, in my opinion, in Part IV where he admonishes the preacher always to seek to preach the Bible's message in the power of the Holy Spirit.

Kaiser is to be commended for his insistence that the task of the preacher is to discover the one intended meaning of the author in a given passage by means of sound canons of grammatical/historical hermeneutics. It is also only positive gain when he urges the preacher to "principlize" the author's meaning in timeless abiding truth to meet the contemporary church's current needs.

But the one area of his proposed methodology where I believe Kaiser will receive the most interaction from his critics (and with which I personally would plead that the Church must *not* follow Kaiser) is his insistence in many places (for example, 82, 134-40) upon what he calls "the analogy of (antecedent) Scripture." What he means by this phrase is this: in determining the author's intended meaning in a given passage, in no case is the preacher, in order to "unpack the meaning or to enhance the usability of the individual text which is the object of [his] study" (140), to use teaching from a passage written or spoken later than the biblical statement being analyzed. In arriving at the author's intended meaning, the exegete must restrict himself to a study of the passage itself and to "affirmations found in passages that have *preceded* in time the passage under study" (136, emphasis original). Kaiser's canon here grows out of his concern to give the discipline of biblical theology its just due with its vision of the progressiveness of revelation (137). To permit subsequent revelation to determine a given author's intention is to "level off" the process of revelation in a way overly favorable to the interests of systematic theology.

Aside from the vexing fact (that in itself tells against Kaiser's canon) that we just do not know for sure the chronological relationship that exists between some portions of Scripture (for example, Was Obadiah written before or after Joel? Was Psalm "x" written before or after Psalm "y"? Was Mark written before or after Matthew? Was Colossians written before or after Ephesians? Was 2 Peter written before or after Jude?) and hence we could fail to use an antecedent bit of revelation or "misappropriate" a subsequent piece of revelation for exegetical purposes, *there are passages where clearly there is no way the exegete can discern what the author or speaker intended without the benefit of subsequent revelational insight.*

For example, apart from John's later teaching in John 2:21, there is no way that the preacher can read Jesus' words: "Destroy this temple, and I will raise it up in three days" (John 2:19) and determine that it was his body to which Jesus referred. (It should be remembered that Christ's statement in John 2:19 was spoken some years before his resurrection and a good many years before John wrote his Gospel.) Another example: apart from Peter's authoritative insight in Acts 2:24-31, there is no way, I would contend, that the exegete can discern, on the grounds allowed him by Kaiser, that David was not speaking of his own (and others') resurrection when he wrote Psalm 16, but that he wrote *specifically* and *exclusively* of Messiah's resurrection. Grammatical/historical exegesis of Psalm 16 and comparison of this Psalm with previous revelation just simply do not disclose that David, "seeing what was ahead,…spoke of the resurrection of the Christ" (Acts 2:30, 31). One more example: apart from the historical facts of the Incarnation of God the Son and the special manifestation of God the Holy Spirit at Pentecost and then subsequent New Testament revelation, it is extremely doubtful that an exegete could discover all the balancing elements of the *doctrine* of the Trinity from the Old Testament alone, and yet I feel sure that Kaiser believes that these elements are there and the Old Testament intends to reveal the *fact* of the Trinity throughout (for example, Gen. 1:26; Pss. 45:6; 110, etc.). I would urge that we take seriously Warfield's (I believe, correct) insight that the Old Testament is like a room richly furnished but dimly lit. The New Testament does not bring "furniture" into the Old Testament "room" that was not there before, but it does illumine the "room" so that we can see the "furniture" that was there all the time, and that was doubtless intended to be there all along by the Old Testament writer himself.

I agree with Kaiser that there can be an undisciplined employment of the New Testament to discern the intention of the Old. But I would suggest that Kaiser, by his canon of "analogy of (antecent) Scripture," has overreacted against one abuse and fallen into the ditch on the other side of the issue. I would urge that the exegete must never conclude that he has properly understood a given Old Testament author's intended meaning *until he has taken into account the entire Scripture, especially the New Testament*. This is only urging a stance in harmony with the time-honored hermeneutical axiom: "The New is in the Old concealed; the Old is in the New revealed."

With this one caveat, I recommend this book as a helpful aid to ministers in their preparation of sermons that will communicate to today's congregations the timeless truth of God's inerrant Word.

Chapter Twenty-Three

The "Very Pernicious and Detestable" Doctrine of Inclusivism

…men, not professing the Christian religion, [cannot] be saved in any other way whatsoever, be they never so diligent to frame their lives according to the light of nature, and the laws of that religion they do profess. And, *to assert and maintain that they may, is very pernicious, and to be detested.* (*Westminster Confession of Faith*, X.4, emphasis supplied; see also *Larger Catechism*, Question 60)

There was a time in the not too distant past when evangelical leaders were in agreement regarding the eternal destiny of the unevangelized masses of mankind. Their commonly-held view was that people, devoid of personal faith in Jesus Christ, are lost. And this belief was one of the chief motives that drove the entire evangelical missionary enterprise. It was not at all uncommon to hear these leaders speak of a "lost and dying world" or an "unsaved world." Today this view is called "exclusivism" in the sense that it restricts salvation *exclusively* to those who consciously trust Christ. But increasing numbers of evangelical spokespersons today are stating either that such exclusivism simply is not biblically defensible or that the Bible is not clear about the eternal state of the adherents of other religions and are opting for what they call "inclusivism," the teaching that God's mercy is so wide that it can and does embrace many, if not all, non-Christian religionists on the globe – a doctrine, as we have just read, that the seventeenth-century framers of the *Westminster Confession of Faith* described as "very pernicious" and "detestable," a judgment that the *Confession* is not inclined often to make, particularly with the adverb "very." Before we look at this "downgrade" trend within Evangelicalism, I want to say something about this teaching within Theological Liberalism and Roman Catholicism.

Note: This article was originally published in *The Trinity Review*, Nos. 219, 220 (May-June 2003).

Theological Liberalism's Doctrine of Religious Pluralism

Theological liberalism's doctrine of religious pluralism is best represented by John Hick who first offers a too-facile, almost glib, explanation regarding how it came about that Jesus, though only a man, came to be regarded as God:

> It was natural and intelligible both that Jesus, through whom men had found a decisive encounter with God and a new and better life, should come to be hailed as son of God, and later this poetry should have hardened into prose and escalated from a metaphorical son of God to a metaphysical God the Son.[1]

He then argues that this "evolved" belief of the Christian church that Jesus is both God incarnate and the only Savior of mankind

> did little positive harm so long as Christendom was a largely autonomous civilization with only relatively marginal interaction with the rest of mankind. But with the clash between the Christian and Muslim world, and then on an ever broadening front with European colonization throughout the earth, the literal understanding of the mythological language of Christian discipleship has had a diverse effect upon the relations between that minority of human beings who live within the borders of the Christian tradition and that majority who live outside it and within other streams of religious life....
>
> If Jesus was literally God incarnate, and if it is by his death alone that men can be saved, and by their response to him alone that they can appropriate that salvation, then the only doorway to eternal life is Christian faith. It would follow from this that the large majority of the human race so far has not been saved.... Is not such an idea excessively parochial presenting God in effect as the tribal deity of the predominantly Christian West?...
>
> It seems clear that we are being called today to attain a global religious vision which is aware of the unity of all mankind before God...we must affirm God's equal love for all men and not only for Christians.... If, selecting from our Christian language, we call God-acting-towards-man the Logos, then we must say that all salvation, within all religions is the work of the Logos.... But what we cannot say is that all who are saved are saved by Jesus of Nazareth. The life of Jesus was one point at which the Logos...has acted.... From now onwards...we have to present Jesus...in

---

[1] John Hick (1977, ed.), *The Myth of God Incarnate*, Westminster, ix. My *Jesus, Divine Messiah* (Fearn, UK: Mentor, 2003), demonstrates the shallowness of such an explanation.

a way compatible with our new recognition of the validity of the other great world faiths as being also, at their best, ways of salvation. We must therefore not insist upon Jesus being always portrayed within the interpretative framework built around him by centuries of Western thought.[2]

Maurice Wiles, another religious pluralist, writes:

Where the categorical and absolute character of the religious demand as it impinges on the Christian, is tied to the historical person of Jesus in a strict metaphysical way (as in traditional incarnational doctrine), that…involves a prejudgment of the potential significance of other religious faiths…of a kind that is very hard to justify from our standpoint within one particular stream of religious and cultural development.[3]

Wiles goes on to call for the abandonment, not of Christian religious demand as such, but of the linkage of its demand "in its absoluteness" to the figure of Jesus as set forth in classic Christology.[4]

Christians, of course, should normally support *legal* tolerance toward the other great world religions, that is to say, they should actively support laws that adequately protect the rights of the individual to profess, practice, and propagate his religious views, with due allowance, of course, for the protection of the citizenry from excesses of religious fanaticism that would inflict bodily harm upon others. Christians should also cultivate in themselves and encourage in others *social* tolerance toward the other great faiths of the world, that is to say, they should respect the other great world faiths and seek to understand them and to encourage the same in others toward the Christian faith. But when it comes to *intellectual* tolerance, that is, the cultivation of a mind so broad that it can tolerate every religious view as of equal intellectual validity without ever detecting anything in any of them to reject, this "is not a virtue; it is the vice of the feeble-minded."[5] *It begs the entire question of truth.* For if Jesus is in

---

[2]Hick, *The Myth of God Incarnate*, 181-82. Ronald H. Nash provides a thorough exposition and refutation of Hick's religious pluralism in his *Is Jesus the Only Savior?* (Grand Rapids: Zondervan, 1994).

[3]Maurice Wiles (1979), *Incarnation and Myth: The Debate Continued*, ed. M. Goulder, Eerdmans, 10-11.

[4]Wiles, *Incarnation and Myth: The Debate Continued*, 11.

[5]John Stott (1985), *The Authentic Christ*, Marshalls, 70.

truth both God incarnate (Acts 20:28; Rom. 9:5; Tit. 2:13; Heb. 1:8; 2 Pet. 1:1; John 1:1, 18; 20:28; 1 John 5:20) and the only Savior of mankind, as the Bible teaches us he is, and if the Church would be governed by truth, it must continue to insist that Jesus is *unique*, finally and transcendentally so. Historically, his uniqueness resides in his birth, his sinless life and sacrificial death, his resurrection and ascension, his present session at the Father's right hand, and his return as the eschatological Judge and Savior of humankind. Theologically, his uniqueness resides in his deity, the incarnation, the atonement, and the several aspects of his exaltation. Therefore, the Church must continue to proclaim Jesus as *the only saving way* to the Father, as he said (John 14:6), his *the only saving name* among men, as Peter said (Acts 4:12), and his *the only saving mediation* between God and man, as Paul said (1 Tim. 2:5). Furthermore, the Church must declare that the goal the religious pluralist so devoutly seeks – a universal religious brotherhood binding all men everywhere joyously together in one world of common humanity – is, on his grounds, unobtainable, not only because such pluralism does not transform the human heart, but also because *only the genuinely and transcendentally unique has such universal significance that it deserves to be universally proclaimed and universally received*. Without such transcendent uniqueness and finality, there can be no universal significance or power in the pluralist's appeal, and his appeal is bound to fail. And any religious commerce, if it *is* achieved, will have to be finally imposed upon men against their will (see Rev. 13:11-17).

To abandon classic Christological teaching in favor of a religious pluralism, *if* Christ is indeed God incarnate, is tantamount to the gravest breach of the First Commandment, and it will involve one in unspeakable infidelity to Jesus Christ the Lord of Glory who, according to Holy Scripture, wears a diadem out-rivaling all the diadems of all the world's great religious and political leaders. To do so, in a word, would mean that the Church has simply ceased to be Christian at all! The Christian Church can afford to follow the modern call for intellectual religious pluralism only at the greatest cost to itself and to the world to which Christ, the King and Lord of the Church, commissioned it to go (Matt. 28:18-20; Luke 24:47; Acts 1:8). Moreover, to follow this call would be to set the Church on a course that can only lead it to religious frustration and failure, and ultimately in the end to divine judgment.

Rome's Doctrine of Inclusivism

The Church of Rome has long endorsed the inclusivist position. Karl Rahner (1904-84), a leading Roman Catholic "inclusivist," who coined the phrase, "anonymous Christian," by which he meant a non-Christian who gains salvation through faith, hope, and love by the grace of Christ that is mediated imperfectly through his or her non-Christian religion, writes in his *Theological Investigations*:

> Christianity does not simply confront the member of an extra-Christian religion as a mere non-Christian but as someone who can and must already be regarded in this or that respect as an anonymous Christian.... The proclamation of the Gospel does not simply turn someone absolutely abandoned by God and Christ into a Christian, but turns an anonymous Christian into someone who now also knows about his Christian belief in the depths of his grace-endowed being by objective reflection and in the profession which is given a social form in the Church.[6]

If Rahner was correct, the world should be seeing large numbers of these gospel-enlightened "anonymous Christians" moving out of their religions and into Christianity because of the spread of the gospel throughout the world by means of the mass media. But there is no evidence that this is happening. Indeed, according to John, far from being "already saved" when the gospel comes to them, non-Christians are "condemned already" because they do not have faith in Christ (John 3:18).

Then in paragraph 836 of its 1994 *Catechism of the Catholic Church*, the Roman Catholic Church declares: "...to [the Catholic Church], in different ways, belong or are ordered: the Catholic faithful, others who believe in Christ, and finally *all mankind*, called by God's grace to salvation" (emphasis supplied). By this pronouncement the Roman Catholic Church has irremediably defined ("deconstructed" would be the more appropriate term) its catholicity for modern and future times in such a way that it already ultimately includes everyone. By what one may regard as an ever-enlarging series of concentric circles Rome has redefined the church in order to justify this catechetical affirmation.

Not only, says the *Catechism*, are those in the church who are "joined in the visible structure...[and who are ruled] by the Roman

---

[6]Karl Rahner (1966), *Theological Investigations*, Seabury, I:131-32.

Pontiff and the bishops" (paragraph 837) but also those are in the church who "believe in Christ and have been properly baptized" even though they stand "in a certain, although imperfect, communion with the Catholic Church" (paragraph 838). Here the *Catechism* refers to all the baptized "separated brethren" throughout the world, including both the baptized members of the Greek and Russian Orthodox Churches and the baptized members of all the Protestant churches (Lutheran, Anglican, Reformed, etc.). In a word, then, the Roman Catholic Church claims that all the baptized people within professing Christendom belong to its communion. Never mind that most, at least, of these non-Catholic communions repudiate this declared association. Never mind that many, if not most, of these baptized people are simply nominal members of state churches. Never mind that many, if not most, of these baptized people never go to church. Never mind that many, if not most, of them never give a penny to the spread of the true gospel and never pray a moment for the church's health. They are, according to Rome, still related salvifically to the People of God and may go to heaven!

The *Catechism* goes on to state that even "those who have not received the Gospel are related to the People of God in several ways" (paragraph 839). Because the faith of the Jewish People – catechetically described as the "the first to hear the Word of God" – "unlike other non-Christian religions, is already a response to God's revelation in the Old Covenant" (paragraph 839),[7] because to the Jews belong all the privileges outlined in Romans 9:4-5 (paragraph 839), and because with Christians they "await the coming of the

---

[7]Theirs is indeed a response – a *negative* one – to God's revelation in the Old Covenant, for which Paul declares: "They displease God and are hostile to all men in their effort to keep us from speaking to the Gentiles so that they may be saved. In this way they always heap up their sins to the limit. The wrath of God has come upon them at last" (1 Thess. 2:15-16). Therefore, as he states in Romans 11:7-10:

What Israel sought so earnestly [that is, righteousness before God (Rom. 9:31)] it did not obtain, but the elect did. The others were hardened, as it is written:

"God gave them a spirit of stupor, eyes so that they could not see and ears so that they could not hear, to this very day."

And David says:

Messiah" (para 840), the People of God encompass the Jewish people. Never mind that the Jewish people for the most part deny the deity of Jesus Christ and thus the doctrine of the Trinity. Never mind that they for the most part rejected their Messiah, Jesus Christ, the first time he came as a misguided prophet at best and a blasphemer at worst and accordingly believe today that Christians are idolaters because we worship him whom they contend was simply a man. Never mind that they see no need for Christ's substitutionary atonement. According to Rome's teaching they are still related salvifically to the People of God and may go to heaven!

The *Catechism* then declares that because Muslims "acknowledge the Creator, ...profess to hold the faith of Abraham [they do not hold Abraham's faith, of course; they are spiritual Ishmaelites], and together with [Christians]...adore the one merciful God [Muslims and Christians

---

"May their table become a snare and a trap, a stumbling block and a retribution for them. May their eyes be darkened so that they cannot see, and their backs be bent forever."

To suggest then that the faith of Christ-rejecting Jews is even remotely a proper response to the Old Testament revelation is surely an inaccurate appraisal of the situation. Can anyone truly believe the Old Testament and not acknowledge Jesus Christ as the Messiah, Savior, and Lord revealed in it? The real truth of the matter is that no Jew who has heard of Christ and his atoning work and then rejects him believes the Old Testament revelation. Jesus expressly declared: "If you believed Moses, you would believe me, for he wrote of me" (John 5:46).

In light of the fact that the only hope of salvation for Jews resides in the provisions of the Christian gospel, it is simply gross wrong-headedness to encourage or to support them in their "Jewishness" or in their Zionist causes. Paul denounced every Jewish hope for acceptance before God that was founded on anything other than the imputed righteousness of Christ, which righteousness is received through faith alone in Christ's preceptive and penal obedience alone. And the sooner Christians realize this – that in order to win Jews to Christ they must, first, show them the futility of any and every hope for salvation that is related in any way to the fact that they have Abrahamic blood flowing in their veins (Matt. 3:9; John 1:13) or to the fact that they are circumcised (Rom. 2:25-29; Gal. 5:2-5; 6:13) or to the fact that they are practicing sons and daughters of Torah (Rom. 2:17-24; 3:9; Gal. 3:10; 4:21-5:1), and second, urge them to renounce any and every ethnic religious distinction in which they might rest their hope of salvation and to trust Christ alone – the sooner their witness to Jews will become effective.

do not "adore" the same "one merciful God"]," they too are included within the plan of salvation (paragraph 841). Never mind that the Muslims' Allah is neither the tri-personal Yahweh of the Old Testament nor the triune God of the New Testament but rather was originally a tribal deity – one in a pantheon of some three hundred and fifty false gods worshiped at Mecca – that Muhammad worshipped and "universalized" by force. Never mind that they think Christians believe their Trinity is composed of Allah, Mary, and their human offspring, Jesus. Never mind that they make Jesus' place in revelational history penultimate to Muhammad's ultimate place. Never mind that they deny both that Jesus Christ is the divine Son of God and that he died on the cross and rose again. Never mind that they believe that Christians are idolaters because we worship Christ who they contend was only a human prophet. Never mind that they see no need for Christ's substitutionary atonement. According to Rome's teaching they are still salvifically related to the People of God and may go to heaven![8]

The *Catechism* goes on to state, in fact, about all the adherents to the world's non-Christian religions, "because all stem from the one stock which God created..., and also because all share a common destiny, namely God," that God's "providence, evident goodness, and saving designs extend" to them as well (paragraph 842). Moreover, "all goodness and truth found in these religions" are "a preparation for the Gospel and given by him who enlightens all men that they may at length have life" (paragraph 843). Accordingly, Peter Kreeft, a convert from the Christian Reformed Church to Roman Catholicism, in his book, *Ecumenical Jihad* (Ignatius, 1996), without fear of any ecclesiastical reprisal, does not hesitate to describe an out-of-body experience that he alleges he had, during which he met not only Orthodox Christians, Evangelical Christians, and Jews in heaven but also Muhammad, Buddha, and Confucius.[9] Never mind that God is not the "common destiny" of all mankind, given the fact, as the Bible teaches, that every man has one of two destinies, either heaven with God or hell with the devil and his angels. Never mind that all the

---

[8]For more on Islam's errors, see Chapter 25, "What's Wrong with Islam?" which originally appeared in *Trinity Review*, Nos. 212, 213, October/November, 2002).

[9]I am indebted to Robert A. Morey, "An Open Letter to Roman Catholic Apologists," *Journal of Biblical Apologetics*, Vol. 3, No. 2 (Summer 2001): 4, for this notice of Kreeft's alleged out-of-body experience.

religions of the world with the exception of biblical Christianity are manmade, all of them being the products of fallen mankind's interaction with general revelation. And never mind that these world religions run the gamut from the crudest forms of animism, voodooism, and paganism, in which cannibalism and human sacrifice are practiced, through the multitude of world cults, to the Eastern religions of desired non-existence as in the case of Hinayana and Mahayana Buddhism. According to Rome's teaching their adherents are still related salvifically to the People of God and may go to heaven. What is this but just Christian missionary expansion with a vengeance, accomplished simply by redefining ("deconstructing" is the more accurate word) the boundaries of the church in order to include all mankind! What is this really but wholesale capitulation on Rome's part to the world's strident clamor for the Christian church to give up its alleged "triumphalist" claim to the uniqueness and finality of Jesus Christ as the only saving way to God and to acknowledge other religions as also acceptable ways to God![10]

These catechetical deliverances are but just one more expression among many others of the detestable apostasy that now grips the largest cult – the Marian cult – within professing Christendom. And what is so tragically ironic about this "very pernicious and detestable" teaching of Rome's 1994 *Catechism of the Catholic Church* is that it reasserts on the one hand the Council of Trent's medieval doctrine of justification through faith and works and on the other makes the entire Tridentine doctrine irrelevant by teaching that all sincere people may be saved, whatever their faith or lack of it. So by its catechetical deliverances everything that modern Rome teaches about the way of salvation through Christ is short-circuited. Frankly, who should care what Rome teaches about salvation if everyone may be saved simply by sincerely following the good as he conscientiously understands and does the good? Apparently, even the sincere professing atheist may be saved as long as he follows the dictates of his conscience with sincerity, for by responding to the light of conscience he is responding (without knowing it, Rome would say) in a salvific way to Christ's Church. I can only say that the modern framers of these documents had better be glad that they were not born in the sixteenth

---

[10]For more on this topic, see my *A New Systematic Theology of the Christian Faith* (Second edition; Nashville, Tenn.: Thomas Nelson, 2002), 1085-93.

century. The Romanist authorities living then would have burned them – including the present pope – at the stake for teaching such rank heresy! The New Testament predicted that false teachers would arise in the church, and if Rome is not now the purveyor of "very pernicious and detestable" false teaching, I can only say, "Please, in the name of truth, tell me what Rome would have to teach if what it presently teaches here is not false doctrine and a betrayal of Jesus Christ as the only way to God for salvation." Nevertheless, Rome's pernicious leaven appears to be leavening the lump of Christendom, for Robert Schuller stated in the *Los Angeles Herald* (9/19/97): "It's time for Protestants to go to the Shepherd [the Pope] and say, 'What do we have to do to come home?'"[11] Paul Crouch, president of Trinity Broadcasting Network, declared on PTL (10/17/89): "I'm eradicating the word 'Protestant' even out of my vocabulary…[it's] time for Catholics and non-Catholics to come together as one in the Spirit and one in the Lord." Pat Robertson declared: "My meeting with His Holiness Pope John Paul II was very warm and, through a personal letter to the Pontiff, I pledged to work for Christian unity between Evangelicals and Catholics." Charles Colson, founder of Prison Fellowship and co-author of "Evangelicals and Catholics Together," states: "We [evangelicals and Catholics] have differences, but on the ancient creeds and the core beliefs of Christianity we stand together."[12] Jack Van Impe, a former Roman Catholic and now a televangelist, has declared: "Pope John Paul II is a strong 'defender of the faith.'" And Billy Graham has affirmed more than once: "I've

---

[11]In an infamous interview between Robert Schuller and Billy Graham Schuller said: "What I hear you saying is that it's possible for Jesus Christ to come into human hearts and soul and life, even if they've been born in darkness and have never had exposure to the Bible. Is that a correct interpretation of what you're saying?" Graham responded: "Yes, it is, because I believe that I've met people…that have never seen a Bible or heard about a Bible, and never heard of Jesus, but they've believed in their hearts that there was a God, and they've tried to live a life that was quite apart from the surrounding community in which they lived." To which Schuller rejoined: "I'm so thrilled to hear you say this. There's a wideness in God's mercy." To which Graham responded: "There is. There definitely is." Such remarks, to say the least, are alarming.

[12]The problem with Colson's position is that "the ancient creeds" (Apostles' Creed, Nicene Creed, Niceno-Constantinopolitan Creed, Definition

found that my beliefs are essentially the same as those of orthodox Roman Catholics." Apparently, in spite of Rome's apostasy away from Paul's law-free gospel and the consequent apostolic anathema under which its system stands (see Galatians 1:8-9), these self-professed evangelicals are regrettably encouraging unity with Rome.

Evangelicalism's Doctrine of Inclusivism

I will now address Evangelicalism's doctrine of inclusivism. Clark H. Pinnock, a leading advocate of inclusivism, while he insists that Christ is indeed the only Savior of men, writes: "We do not need to think of the church as the ark of salvation, leaving everyone else in hell; we can rather think of it as the chosen witness to the fullness of salvation that has come into the world through Jesus."[13] In his article, "Toward an Evangelical Theology of Religions,"[14] urging what he calls the "particularity axiom" that God's saving grace comes only through Jesus Christ and the "universality axiom" that God's saving grace is for the entire race because he desires the salvation of all mankind, Pinnock embraces the notion that people of faith from other religions

---

of Chalcedon, and Athanasian Creed) are not *evangelical* creeds, that is, creeds that explicate soteric matters. They were all framed in the context of the Trinitarian debates in the fourth and fifth centuries and are underdeveloped respecting and virtually silent on matters of soteriology. Herman Bavinck, *The Doctrine of God*, translated by William Hendriksen (Grand Rapids: Baker, 1951), 285, rightly observes: "...the Reformation has brought to light that not the mere historical belief in the doctrine of the trinity, no matter how pure, is sufficient unto salvation, but only the true heart-born confidence that rests in God himself, who in Christ has revealed himself as the triune God." In short, there is *no* saving value in holding to an orthodox view of God as Trinity if one is at the same time also holding to an unorthodox view of the saving work of the Trinity. Consequently, it is simply not true, by any stretch of the imagination, that on "the core beliefs of Christianity [Roman Catholicism and Reformation theology] stand together." They differ radically on soteriological matters. By his involvement in ECT Colson betrays the entire Reformation cause, as do all of ECT's signatories!

[13]Clark H. Pinnock, "Acts 4:12 – No Other Name Under Heaven," in *Through No Fault of Their Own*, edited by William V. Crockett and James G. Sigountos (Grand Rapids: Baker, 1991), 113. He contends for this position more fully in his *A Wideness in God's Mercy* (Grand Rapids, Mich.: Zondervan, 1992).

[14]Clark H. Pinnock, "Toward an Evangelical Theology of Religions," *JETS* 33/3 (September 1990), 359-68.

will be saved by Christ even though they do not know him or believe in him.

Others, along with Pinnock, while they acknowledge that Christ is and always will be mankind's only Savior, also argue that Christ will save many who have never heard of him through the revelation of God that is available to them in nature. John Sanders, a Wesleyan thinker, supports this inclusivist hope that people who never hear about Christ can be saved by exercising trust in God as he has revealed himself in general revelation.[15] Millard Erickson even lays out what he thinks are the five essential elements of this "gospel message" in nature:

> 1) The belief in one good powerful God. 2) The belief that he (man) owes this God perfect obedience to his law. 3) The consciousness that he does not meet this standard, and therefore is guilty and condemned. 4) The realization that nothing he can offer God can compensate him (or atone) for this sin and guilt. 5) The belief that God is merciful, and will forgive and accept those who cast themselves on his mercy.[16]

"May it not be," Erickson queries, "that if a man believes and acts on this set of tenets he is redemptively related to God and receives the benefits of Christ's death, whether he consciously knows and understands the details of that provision or not?"[17]

John Stott is a spokesman for the agnostic position. He believes that all men outside of Christ are lost, but with regard to the question of the final annihilation (Stott's view of "eternal punishment") of those who have never heard of Christ he writes: "I believe the most Christian stance is to remain agnostic on this question…. The fact is that God, alongside the most solemn warnings about our responsibility to respond to the gospel, has not revealed how he will deal with those who have

---

[15] John Sanders (1992), *No Other Name: An Investigation into the Destiny of the Unevangelized*, Eerdmans.

[16] Millard Erickson, "Hope for Those Who Haven't Heard? Yes, but…," *Evangelical Missions Quarterly*, Vol. 11, No. 2 (April 1975), 124. It remains to be seen, of course, whether any unregenerate sinner can or will come to these conclusions apart from gospel proclamation. See also Evert D. Osburn, "Those Who Have Never Heard: Have They No Hope?" *JETS* 32/3 (September 1989), 367-72.

[17] Millard Erickson, "Hope for Those Who Haven't Heard? Yes, but…," 125.

never heard it."[18] Timothy Philips, Aida Besançon Spencer, and Tite Tienou likewise assume an agnostic stance here, stating that they "prefer to leave the matter in the hands of God."[19]

These are representative speakers for this growing downgrade trend within Evangelicalism, cited here for the purpose of providing a sampling of the inclusivist sentiments being urged by many at the highest levels of academic Evangelicalism. But now we must ask: Can people be saved through general revelation? Will any man, on the basis of general revelation, arrive at the set of tenets Erickson lays out? Are the Scriptures silent, as the agnostic inclusivists imply, about the eternal destiny of those who do not hear about and put their trust in Christ? I would respond in the negative to all three questions and will now give my reasons for this conviction.

General revelation universally condemns mankind; it does not and cannot save them

According to Holy Scripture, all men – Jews and Gentiles, "good" men and "bad" men, the pagans in the Far East as well as the pagans in the industrialized West – sinned in Adam and are by their own acts of sinfulness continually falling short of the glory of God (Rom. 3:23). The wages of this sin is death (Rom. 6:23). And in spite of the fact that all peoples and cultures have received general revelation and hence possess an innate awareness of God's eternal power and divine nature (Rom. 1:19-20), his moral law (Rom. 2:14-15), and the deserts of sin (Rom. 1:32), they neither glorify God as God nor are they thankful to him (Rom. 1:21), but pervert their knowledge of God in unspeakable forms of idolatry (Rom. 1:23). Far from loving God and his Christ, the peoples of this world love darkness and hate the light of Christ's gospel because their deeds are evil (John 3:19-20). Consequently, God has abandoned (*paredōken*) the world to sexual impurity, shameful lusts, and a depraved mind (Rom. 1:24, 26, 28). Far then from saving the world, general revelation serves as the ground of God's just condemnation of the world. God views the entire world as "under sin." "There is no one righteous, not even one" (Rom. 3:9-10). All are dead in trespasses and sins (Eph. 2:1). All are by nature

---

[18]John Stott (1988), *Evangelical Essentials: A Liberal-Evangelical Dialogue,* InterVarsity, 327.

[19]See *Through No Fault of Their Own,* 259, fn. 3.

children of wrath (Eph. 2:3). All are "already" under condemnation (Rom. 3:19-20). All are alienated from the life of God (Eph. 4:18), ignorant of the truth of God (Rom. 1:25), hostile to the law of God (Rom. 8:7), disobedient to the will of God (Tit. 3:3), fall short of the righteous demands of God (Rom. 3:23), and subject to the wrath of God (John 3:19).

These statements describe the peoples of the world who have never heard the gospel and who have never had a chance to accept or reject the gospel of Christ. From the biblical perspective, then, there is really no such thing as the "noble savage," Rahner's "anonymous Christian," or the "holy pagan." Such concepts exist only in the minds of unbelieving anthropologists and sociologists and certain Roman Catholic and evangelical inclusivists. In short, men are lost and under God's judgment, not only because they may have heard about and then rejected Christ at some point in their lives, but also and more primarily because they are sinners by nature and by practice, who have failed to live in accordance with the light of the law of God which they all possess. They have sinned against God's revelation without, the demands of his law written on their hearts within, and their own accusing consciences (Rom. 2:14-15).

So much for any unregenerate person ever responding to Millard Erickson's five tenets of general revelation as he set them forth. The Bible is clear that, apart from God's special wooing, he is unable to discern, to love, to choose the things that are pleasing to God, or to love God (Jer. 13:23; John 6:44, 65; 15:4-5; Rom. 8:7-8; 1 Cor. 2:14; 12:3; Jas. 3:8; Rev. 14:3).

The New Testament repudiates inclusivism

The New Testament teaches the necessity of conscious trust in Christ for salvation. Jesus Christ declared: "I am the way and the truth and the life. No one comes to the Father except through me" (John 14:6). He also taught that repentance and forgiveness of sins should be preached *in his name* to all nations (Luke 24:46-47). Peter emphatically states: "Salvation is found in no one else [not Buddha, not Muhammad, not even Moses] by which we must be saved" (Acts 4:12). John not only declares: "No one who denies the Son has the Father; whoever acknowledges the Son has the Father also" (1 John 2:23), but he also emphatically states: "He who has the Son has life; he who does not have the Son of God does not have life" (1 John

5:12). And Paul declares with equal clarity: "…there is one God and one mediator between God and man, the man Christ Jesus" (1 Tim. 2:5). He also writes in Romans 10:13-15:

> Everyone who calls on the name of the Lord [in the context, the Lord Jesus Christ] will be saved. How, then, can they call on the one they have not believed in? And how can they believe in the one of whom they have not heard? And how can they hear without someone preaching to them? And how can they preach unless they are sent?

Note here the unbreakable connection that Paul makes by this series of questions between "calling on," "believing in," "hearing about," "preaching to," and "being sent." A preacher must be sent to the unsaved, and he must *preach* about Christ to them if they are to *hear* about him, *believe* in him, and *call* on him for salvation. The clear implication of these questions is that if missionaries are not sent to preach the gospel of Christ to those who have not heard about him in order that they may *hear* about him, *believe* in him, and *call* upon his name for salvation, these unevangelized people, who are condemned already, will remain unsaved and cannot and will not be saved by any other means.

While the missionary is *nothing* in himself insofar as the success of his mission labors are concerned according to 1 Corinthians 3:5-7, his work is the *necessary* link between Christ's saving work and the salvation of men. That is to say, while the missionary in himself is of no importance, his mission work is of the *greatest* importance, for what he does, in and by God's animating and enabling, becomes a mighty weapon "to demolish the strongholds" of argumentation and every pretension that sets itself up against the knowledge of God, and "to take captive" every thought to make it obedient to Christ (2 Cor. 10:3-4).

Paul also expressly declared with regard to the destiny of men who do not trust Christ: "All who sin apart from the law will also perish apart from the law, and all who sin under the law will be judged by the law" (Rom. 2:12). In Paul's mind all of mankind may be divided into two groups: those who sin *apart from* the law and those who sin *under* the law. That is to say, some human beings sin apart from the specially revealed law of God; others sin living under the specially revealed law of God; but *all in both groups sin and thus bring upon themselves the liability of divine condemnation.* About these two groups John Murray comments:

> The contrast is...between those who were outside the pale of special revelation and those who were within [that pale].
>
> With reference to the former the apostle's teaching is to the following effect: (1) Specially revealed law is not the precondition of sin – "as many as have sinned without the law". (2) Because such are sinners they will perish. The perishing referred to can be none other than that defined in the previous verses as consisting in the infliction of God's wrath and indignation and endurance of tribulation and anguish in contrast with the glory, honor, incorruption, and peace bestowed upon the heirs of eternal life. (3) In suffering this perdition they will not be judged according to a law which they did not have, namely, specially revealed law – they "shall also perish without the law." There is, therefore, an exact correspondence between the character of their sin as "without the law" and the final destruction visited upon them as also "without the law."[20]

But take note: *Paul unequivocally declares that those who have never come within the pale of special revelation, particularly the proclamation of the gospel – will still perish!* So the Bible is not silent about the destiny of those who have never heard the gospel.

We should finally notice in this connection that the fourteen-point indictment and the juridical conviction that Paul brings against the entire human race in Romans 3:9-20 establishes that all people – both Jews and Gentiles – are under the power of sin and, unless something alters their condition, they will be speechless someday before the judgment bar of God. Therefore, in Romans 3:21-28 Paul sets forth faith in Christ's atoning death as the only solution to the universal problem of divine condemnation for sin. Faith in Christ's atoning death is not simply a way that God forgives human sin. It is the *only* basis on which God, according to Paul, justifies any sinner (Rom. 3:28).

In sum, the atoning work of Christ's doing and dying is not merely for Jews or merely for one nation or tribe or language family. It is the one and only way for anyone to come into fellowship with God. Christ's death, burial, and resurrection stand on the cutting edge of the mission message in the book of Acts, and conscious personal faith in him is everywhere declared as essential to a person's justification before God.

---

[20] John Murray (1968), *The Epistle to the Romans*, Eerdmans, 1:70.

Rebuttal of the evangelical inclusivist's arguments

Evangelical inclusivists deny that conscious faith in Jesus Christ is absolutely essential to salvation primarily for the following three reasons:

First, they contend that Jews in the Old Testament were saved apart from conscious faith in Jesus Christ, that is to say, they had only the "form" of the Christian gospel without its New Testament "content." But theirs is a false premise based upon dispensational thinking. While it is true that the elect Jews of the Old Testament would not have known myriad details about the Christ of the New Testament, such as the name of his mother and stepfather or even his human name, they did understand that the Messiah who was to come would die in their stead as their substitute and that they had to place their trust in his anticipated doing and dying for them for their salvation. The *Westminster Confession of Faith* quite correctly declares that the covenant of grace was administered in the Old Testament

> ...by promises, prophecies, sacrifices, circumcision, the paschal lamb, and other types and ordinances delivered to the people of the Jews, *all foresignifying Christ to come*; which were, for that time, sufficient and efficacious, through the operation of the Spirit, *to instruct and build up the elect in faith in the promised Messiah*, by whom they had full remission of sins, and eternal salvation. (VII.5; see also VIII.6)

I do not have time here to develop this particular rebuttal further, but I can refer you to my *A New Systematic Theology of the Christian Faith* for the fuller argument.[21]

Second, they rely upon what they view as the biblical tradition of "holy pagans" who were saved even though they held to religious faiths other than the Yahwism and Messianism of the Old Testament. They refer here specifically to Melchizedek, Job, Jethro the Midianite priest and Moses' father-in-law, Naaman the Syrian, the eastern Magi, and the Roman centurian Cornelius. But a careful reading of the biblical accounts regarding these men will demonstrate that they were hardly "holy pagans" who were saved even though they worshiped false gods. King Melchizedek was both a priest of "the most high God, owner of heaven and earth," whom Abraham identifies as Yahweh (Gen. 14:22), and *the* Old Testament type of the New Testament

---

[21]Reymond, *A New Systematic Theology of the Christian Faith*, 503-44.

Messiah's kingly priesthood (Ps. 110:4; Heb. 7–10). He was certainly a worshiper of the one living and true God and he doubtless trusted in God's saving provision for him. Job too was a worshiper of Yahweh (Job 1:21) who trusted in God's Redeemer (Job 19:25). Jethro, while he was quite likely at one time a worshiper of pagan gods, through his relationship to Moses was brought to faith in Yahweh (Exod. 18:8-12), as was Naaman as well (2 Kgs. 5:15-18). And while the eastern Magi were probably pagan astrologers before their observance in the East of Messiah's special star, from that point on they gave themselves to the task of finding the "king of the Jews" and worshiping him (Matt. 2:2, 10-12). We may be sure that the Holy Spirit instructed and directed all these people to place their faith in the future atoning work of the Messiah in their behalf.

Cornelius the Roman centurian is a special showcase for the inclusivist. Pinnock describes him as "the pagan saint *par excellence* of the New Testament,"[22] and hails him as the prime example of a man who was saved apart from faith in Christ, to whom Peter was sent only to inform him that he was already forgiven and saved. Inclusivists underscore the fact that Cornelius was a "devout and God-fearing man" (*eusebēs kai phoboumenos ton theon*) who "gave generously to those in need and who prayed to God regularly" (Acts 10:2) and that he was a "righteous and God-fearing man [*anēr dikaios kai phoboumenos ton theon*] who is respected by all the Jewish people" (Acts 10:22), about whom God declared to Peter that he was "clean" (*ekatharisen*; Acts 10:15). And they underscore that Peter plainly declares that "God does not show favoritism but accepts men in every nation who fear him and do what is right" (Acts 10:34-35).

Now it is true that Luke says all these things about Cornelius. But Luke's statements do not mean that Cornelius was a saved man prior to Peter's visit, for in fact he was not! I say this for the following two reasons: (1) Peter expressly declared later that it was by the message (*rhēmata*) that he brought to Cornelius that "everyone who believes in [Christ] receives forgiveness of sins through his name" (Acts 10:43) that Cornelius was saved (see Peter's "shall be saved," *sōthēsē*, the future indicative passive) (Acts 11:14). (2) The Jewish Christians of Jerusalem responded to Peter's explanation by saying: "Then God

---

[22]Clark H. Pinnock (1992), *A Wideness in God's Mercy*, Zondervan, 165.

has even granted the Gentiles repentance unto life" (Acts 11:18), clearly meaning that true repentance leads to eternal life and that until God grants such to people they do not have eternal life. Clearly, then, before Peter came and preached Christ to him, Cornelius was not saved, and just as clearly it was through Peter's preaching that Cornelius came to faith in Christ.

But while this is true, it needs to be said that, *prior to* Peter's coming, Cornelius was "clean" in the sense that Peter was not to view him any longer as ceremonially "taboo" but as a legitimate candidate for evangelization![23] This is plainly Peter's own interpretation of the "great sheet" vision in Acts 10:28-29 where we read: "Peter said to them: 'You are well aware that it is against our law for a Jew to associate with a Gentile or visit him. But God has shown me [by the "clean sheet" vision] that I should not call any man [ceremonially] impure or unclean [that is, an "untouchable"]. So when I was sent for, I came without raising an objection.'" It is also true that God had "accepted" (*dektos*) Cornelius before Peter spoke to him. But what does this mean? This "acceptance" by God is not the same thing as the earlier "clean" for the "clean" are all men everywhere whereas the "accepted" are said to be *in* every nation. The "accepted" *in* every nation, then, are they, in God's providence, who seek God sincerely and genuinely, as did Cornelius the "God-fearer" as he listened to the reading of the Old Testament in the Jewish synagogues, and for whom God arranges, as he did for Cornelius, that the gospel should be brought to them. Which is just to say, the "accepted" in every nation are simply God's elect. Cornelius is representative, then, not of people who can and are saved apart from faith in Christ (there are none!), but of the unsaved elect in every nation throughout the world who by the Spirit's promptings through the Word are "seeking God in an extraordinary way,"[24] that is to say, who are drawn, by God's electing love and by whatever bit of special revelation they might

---

[23]In Old Testament times God had "let the nations go their own way" (Acts 14:16) as he prepared Israel to be the repository of special revelation and the racial originator of the Messiah, and during that time he had also "overlooked the nations' ignorance" (Acts 17:23) in the sense that he had taken no direct steps to reach them savingly. But once Christ came God now commands all people everywhere to repent (Acts 17:30) and to put their trust in him.

[24]John Piper (1993), *Let the Nations be Glad*, Baker, 146.

have received, to realize (1) that they as needy sinners must meet the one living and true God someday, (2) that they are unable to answer him once in a thousand times satisfactorily, and (3) who pray day and night that God in his mercy will somehow make it possible for them to be acceptable in his sight. These, the Cornelius incident teaches us, God will save through the mission enterprise by getting the good news of the gospel to them just as he arranged for Peter to take the gospel to Cornelius.

Third (and the inclusivist's previous two reasons grow out of this more fundamental error), evangelical inclusivists believe that "people are saved by faith, not by the content of their theology."[25] Pinnock declares: "Faith in God is what saves, not possessing certain minimum information [about Christ].... A person is saved by faith, even if the content of faith is deficient.... The issue God cares about is the direction of the heart, not the content of theology."[26] In sum, according to Pinnock and inclusivists in general, it is not *what* one believes about God that counts; what counts is *that* he believes in God. Said another way, people are saved, not by the content of their faith, but by their psychic act of faith in God.

Here we have reached the nadir of inclusivist thinking. But surely saving faith must be directed not to an idolatrous and pagan substitute for God but to the one living and true God who is the Triune God and who has declared that no one can approach him except through the saving worth of his Son's saving work. And one learns this through hearing gospel preaching. Moreover, this psychic act of faith, originating as these Arminian thinkers contend it does, in man's determination and will, constitutes a sinful work that cannot save and is everywhere condemned by Holy Scripture. It bears repeating: the act of faith *per se* does not and cannot save. Faith's value depends upon its object. Speaking more precisely, it is not even faith in Jesus Christ that saves. It is Jesus Christ who saves the sinner who places his trust in him. And I must underscore again that to the degree that the evangelical inclusivist believes that people of other religions may be saved apart from a conscious knowledge of Christ, just to that same degree are they implying that the evangelical faith is irrelevant and obsolete. And that implication, regardless of the degree to which

---

[25]Clark H. Pinnock, *A Wideness in God's Mercy*, 157.
[26]Pinnock, *A Wideness in God Mercy*, 158.

one may espouse it, is a direct attack upon the uniqueness and finality of Jesus Christ, the only Savior of the world!

Conclusion

The Bible is solicitous that Christians understand that the nations are lost, unsaved, and perishing without God. They are under divine condemnation, not just because they have never heard of Christ, but more primarily because they are transgressors of God's holy law. Christians should pray that God will melt their own hearts and remove all that would blind their eyes that they may see their world as it really is – a world on a collision course with the flames of divine judgment! And they should pray that God will empower them and send them to that world with the "good news" of his redeeming love in Christ who is the only true Savior of mankind.

As I bring this paper to a close I feel compelled to ask now the following question: If you and I really believe that the world's masses must, individually and personally, consciously trust Jesus Christ's doing and dying if they would be saved from the wrath of God, what are we personally doing to bring them to that trustful faith? I would remind you that Christ, the Lord of the Church, declared: "The harvest is plentiful but the workers are few. Ask the Lord of the harvest, therefore, to send out workers into his harvest field" (Matt. 9:37; see Luke 10:2). He also stated: "Do you not say, 'Four months more and then the harvest?' I tell you, open your eyes and look at the fields! They are ripe for harvest" (John 4:35).

Let us be clear about the spiritual condition of these "fields ripe for harvest." We may not like it, we may instinctively recoil against it, but the Bible wants us to realize (and to act on this realization) that these "ripe fields" are the multitudes of lost, unsaved peoples of this world, perishing without a saving knowledge of Christ. They are under divine condemnation, not just because they have never heard about Christ, but more primarily because they are sinners by nature, by habit, and by practice. Some of you may already be doing what you can to reach them with the "good news" of the gospel and I thank God for that. But if we are Christians we must all become involved in witnessing to friends and neighbors about Christ and doing what we can to spread the gospel to the ends of the earth, for repentance and forgiveness of sins must be preached in Christ's name to all nations (Luke 24:47) since salvation is to be found in no other name under heaven than his

(Acts 4:12). We must also be more faithful in supporting with our prayers and our money – even more than we have in the past – Christ-preaching, Bible-believing missionaries on the mission fields of the world. Which is just to say, if we cannot go ourselves, we must do what we can to enable others to go.

May God raise up in our day, while divine patience still grants us time, a multitude of men and women who will boldly dare to go into this lost and dying world where no man has ever gone before with the liberating law-free gospel of God!

Chapter Twenty-Four

Why the Roman Catholic Church Is a Threat Only to Roman Catholics and a Non-Threat to Everyone Else

My monograph, *The Reformation's Conflict with Rome: Why It Must Continue*, was published in 2001.[1] I contended therein that the Roman Catholic Church, in spite of its claim that it alone possesses the four ancient attributes of the church (unity, holiness, catholicity, and apostolicity), its outward trappings of pomp and circumstance, and the awe and deference that the media pay it, is in actual fact, because of its rejection of Paul's doctrine of justification by faith alone, that is, because the marks of the true church are absent in it, an *apostate* church. Recently an intelligent Roman Catholic friend read my book and responded that while he thought its arguments were telling – they were certainly emotionally disturbing to him, he said, as I knew they would be – he had concluded after reading it that he would still remain within the Roman Catholic Church. But why, I wonder, would a Christian want to become a member of or remain within the Roman Catholic Church, given its myriad unscriptural teachings and practices?[2] Does the modern Roman Catholic really know what his

---

Note: I delivered this address at Coral Ridge Presbyterian Church, Fort Lauderdale, Florida, in its 2003 annual Conference on Evangelism.

[1]Robert L. Reymond, *The Reformation's Conflict with Rome: Why It Must Continue* (Fearn, UK: Mentor, 2001). In this article, I repeat some of the arguments found in the previous chapter and I ask the reader's forbearance in doing so.

[2]I am not addressing in this article the scandal that has recently come to light here in the United States involving homosexual pedophile priests who have preyed on Catholic youth for years with the full knowledge of their superiors who did not report their crimes to local law enforcement agencies because of church law (here is a clear case where Roman church law trumped civil and criminal law) but rather transferred these guilty priests to other parishes (where evidence indicates they continued their practice) and paid millions of dollars to the victims in return for their silence. This is another reason practicing Roman Catholics should be asking themselves hard

Church teaches? Probably not, but he should. And now he has no excuse not to know since the publication in 1994 of the *Catechism of the Catholic Church*.

Because I am concerned not only for this friend but also for other Roman Catholics like him who may read my book and for you, my present audience, I want to state more fully an argument for consideration that I only hinted at in the book. My argument here is simply this: By its dogmatic pronouncements in its Vatican II document, *Dogmatic Constitution on the Church* (1964), and its catechetical declarations in its more recent *Catechism of the Catholic Church* (1994), the Roman Catholic Church in effect (1) has made itself a threat only to those who may become or who are already Catholics and (2) has declared its own obsolescence insofar as all non-Catholics are concerned. How has the Roman Church done these two things, and what are the implications of its pronouncements?

How the Roman Church Has Done These Things

In paragraph 836 of its 1994 *Catechism*, the Roman Catholic Church declares: "...to [the Catholic Church], in different ways, belong or are ordered: the Catholic faithful, others who believe in Christ, and finally *all mankind*, called by God's grace to salvation" (emphasis supplied). By this pronouncement the Roman Catholic Church has irremediably defined ("deconstructed" would be the more appropriate term) its catholicity for modern and future times in such a way that it already ultimately includes everyone. I will elaborate.

Not only, says the *Catechism*, are those in the church who are "joined in the visible structure...[and who are ruled] by the Roman Pontiff and the bishops" (paragraph 837) but also those are in the church who "believe in Christ and have been properly baptized" even though they stand "in a certain, although imperfect, communion with the Catholic Church" (paragraph 838). Here the *Catechism* refers to all the baptized "separated brethren" throughout the world, including both the baptized members of the Greek and Russian Orthodox Churches and the baptized members of all the Protestant churches (Lutheran, Anglican, Reformed, etc.). In a word, then, the Roman Catholic Church claims that all the baptized people within professing

questions about their church and their affiliation with it, but I will not address this issue at this time.

Christendom belong to its communion. Never mind that most of these non-Catholic communions repudiate this declared association. And never mind that many, if not most, of these baptized people are simply nominal members of state churches; never mind that many, if not most, of these baptized people never go to church; never mind that many, if not most, of them never give a cent to the spread of the true gospel and never pray a moment for the church's health. They are, according to Rome, still related salvifically to the People of God and may go to heaven!

The *Catechism* goes on to state that even "those who have not received the Gospel are related to the People of God in several ways" (paragraph 839). Because the faith of the Jewish People – catechetically described as the "the first to hear the Word of God" – "unlike other non-Christian religions, is already a response to God's revelation in the Old Covenant" (paragraph 839),[3] because to the

---

[3]Theirs is indeed a response – a *negative* one – to God's revelation in both the Old and New Covenants, for which Paul declares: "They displease God and are hostile to all men in their effort to keep us from speaking to the Gentiles so that they may be saved. In this way they always heap up their sins to the limit. The wrath of God has come upon them at last" (1 Thess. 2:15-16). Therefore, as he states in Romans 11:7-10:

What Israel sought so earnestly [that is, righteousness before God (Rom. 9:31)] it did not obtain, but the elect did. The others were hardened, as it is written:

"God gave them a spirit of stupor, eyes so that they could not see and ears so that they could not hear, to this very day."

And David says:

"May their table become a snare and a trap, a stumbling block and a retribution for them. May their eyes be darkened so that they cannot see, and their backs be bent forever."

To suggest then that the faith of Christ-rejecting Jews is even remotely a proper response to the Old Testament revelation is surely an inaccurate appraisal of the situation. Can anyone truly believe the Old Testament and not acknowledge Jesus Christ as the Messiah, Savior, and Lord revealed in it? The real truth of the matter is that no Jew who has heard of Christ and his atoning work and then rejects him believes the Old Testament revelation. Jesus expressly declared: "If you believed Moses, you would believe me, for he wrote of me" (John 5:46).

Jews belong all the privileges outlined in Romans 9:4-5 (paragraph 839), and because with Christians they "await the coming of the Messiah" (para 840), the People of God encompass the Jewish people. Never mind that the Jewish people for the most part deny the deity of Jesus Christ and thus the doctrine of the Trinity; never mind that they for the most part rejected their Messiah, Jesus Christ, the first time he came as a misguided prophet at best and a blasphemer at worst and accordingly believe today that Christians are idolaters because we worship him whom they contend was simply a man; never mind that they see no need for Christ's substitutionary atonement. According to Rome's teaching they are still related salvifically to the People of God and may go to heaven!

The *Catechism* then declares that because Muslims "acknowledge the Creator, ...profess to hold the faith of Abraham [they do not hold Abraham's faith, of course; they are spiritual Ishmaelites], and together with [Christians]...adore the one merciful God [Muslims and Christians do not "adore" the same "one merciful God"]," they too are included within the plan of salvation (paragraph 841). Never mind that the Muslims' Allah is neither the tri-personal Yahweh of the Old Testament nor the triune God of the New Testament but rather was originally a tribal deity – one in a pantheon of some three hundred and fifty false gods worshiped at Mecca – that Muhammad worshipped and "universalized" by force; never mind that they think Christians believe their Trinity is composed of Allah, Mary, and their offspring, Jesus;

In light of the fact that the only hope of salvation for Jews resides in the provisions of the Christian gospel, it is simply gross wrong-headedness to encourage or to support them in their "Jewishness" or in their Zionist causes. Paul denounced every Jewish hope for acceptance before God that was founded on anything other than the imputed righteousness of Christ, which righteousness is received through faith alone in Christ's preceptive and penal obedience alone. And the sooner Christians realize this – that in order to win Jews to Christ they must, first, show them the futility of any and every hope for salvation that is related in any way to the fact that they have Abrahamic blood flowing in their veins (Matt. 3:9; John 1:13) or to the fact that they are circumcised (Rom. 2:25-29; Gal. 5:2-5; 6:13) or to the fact that they are practicing sons and daughters of Torah (Rom. 2:17-24; 3:9; Gal. 3:10; 4:21-5:1), and second, urge them to renounce any and every ethnic religious distinction in which they might rest their hope of salvation and to trust Christ alone – the sooner their witness to Jews will become effective.

never mind that they make Jesus' place in revelational history penultimate to Muhammad's ultimate place; never mind that they deny both that Jesus Christ is the divine Son of God and that he died on the cross and rose again; never mind that they believe that Christians are idolaters because we worship Christ who they contend was only a human prophet; never mind that they see no need for Christ's substitutionary atonement. According to Rome's teaching they are still salvifically related to the People of God and may go to heaven![4]

The *Catechism* goes on to state, in fact, about all the adherents to the world's non-Christian religions, "because all stem from the one stock which God created..., and also because all share a common destiny, namely God," that God's "providence, evident goodness, and saving designs extend" to them as well (paragraph 842). Moreover, "all goodness and truth found in these religions" are "a preparation for the Gospel and given by him who enlightens all men that they may at length have life" (paragraph 843). Never mind that God is not the "common destiny" of all mankind, given the fact, as the Bible teaches, that every man has one of two destinies, either heaven with God or hell with the devil and his angels. Never mind that all the religions of the world with the exception of biblical Christianity are manmade, all of them being the products of fallen mankind's interaction with general revelation. And never mind that these world religions run the gamut from the crudest forms of animism, voodooism, and paganism, in which cannibalism and human sacrifice are practiced, through the multitude of world cults, to the Eastern religions of desired non-existence as in the case of Hinayana and Mahayana Buddhism. According to Rome's teaching their adherents are still related salvifically to the People of God and may go to heaven.

What is this but just Christian missionary expansion with a vengeance, accomplished simply by defining ("deconstructing" is the more accurate word) the boundaries of the church in order to include all mankind! What is this really but wholesale capitulation on Rome's part to the world's strident clamor for the Christian church to give up its alleged "triumphalistic" claim to the uniqueness and finality of Jesus Christ as the only saving way to God and to acknowledge other religions as also acceptable ways to God![5]

---

[4]For more on Islam's errors, see Chapter 25, "What's Wrong with Islam?" which originally appeared in *Trinity Review*, Nos. 212, 213, October/November, 2002).

Jesus declared however: "If you do not believe that I am the one I claim to be, you will indeed die in your sins" (John 8:24), and also "I am the way and the truth and the life. No one comes to the Father except through me" (John 14:6). Peter emphatically stated: "Salvation is found in no one else [not Moses, not Muhammad, not Buddha], for there is no other name under heaven given to men by which we must be saved" (Acts 4:12). John, just as emphatically, stated: "No one who denies the Son has the Father [this would include Jews and Muslims]" (1 John 2:23), and also "He who has the Son has life; he who does not have the Son of God does not have life" (1 John 5:12). And with equal clarity Paul stated: "There is one God and one mediator between God and men, the man Christ Jesus" (1 Tim. 2:5).

In order to justify this position to its adherents, modern Roman Catholic apologists realized they had to deconstruct Rome's centuries-old dictum, "Outside the Church there is no salvation." So the

---

[5]Karl Rahner (1904-84), a leading Roman Catholic "inclusivist," who coined the phrase, "anonymous Christian," by which he meant a non-Christian who gains salvation through faith, hope, and love by the grace of Christ which is mediated imperfectly through his or her non-Christian religion, writes in his *Theological Investigations* (New York: Seabury, 1966), I:131, 132:

> Christianity does not simply confront the member of an extra-Christian religion as a mere non-Christian but as someone who can and must already be regarded in this or that respect as an anonymous Christian.... The proclamation of the Gospel does not simply turn someone absolutely abandoned by God and Christ into a Christian, but turns an anonymous Christian into someone who now also knows about his Christian belief in the depths of his grace-endowed being by objective reflection and in the profession which is given a social form in the Church.

If Rahner was correct, the world should be seeing large numbers of these gospel-enlightened "anonymous Christians" moving out of their religions and into Christianity because of the spread of the gospel throughout the world by means of the mass media. But there is no evidence that this is happening.

According to John, far from being "already saved" when the gospel comes to them, non-Christians are "condemned already" because they do not have faith in Christ (John 3:18). For more on this topic see my *A New Systematic Theology of the Christian Faith* (Second edition; Nashville, Tenn.: Thomas Nelson, 2002), 1085-93.

Catechism declares that this dictum "is not aimed at those who, through no fault of their own, do not know Christ and his Church" (paragraph 847), in fact, "Those who, through no fault of their own, do not know the Gospel of Christ or his Church, but who nevertheless seek God with a sincere heart, and, moved by grace, try in their actions to do his will as they know it through the dictates of their conscience – those too may achieve eternal salvation" (paragraph 847).[6] At whom then is this ancient dictum directed? Now hear me well: *It is directed only at those who, "knowing that the Catholic Church was founded as necessary by God through Christ, would refuse either to enter it or to remain in it"* (paragraph 846). That is to say, it is directed only at those who become convinced that the Roman Catholic Church is the "true church" and that they should enter its communion but refuse to do so and at those Roman Catholics who at one time believed that Catholicism was necessary but later disavowed that faith. These, the *Catechism* declares (paragraph 846), "could not be saved"! Never mind that this too is completely unbiblical! It is a case of Rome repeating the Petrine error of adding some condition for salvation beyond simple trust in Jesus Christ (see Acts 10). This is Rome's threat to Roman Catholics in its effort to keep them from "jumping ship."

The Implications of These Pronouncements

What are the implications of Rome's catechetical teaching that the peoples of the world have no absolute need to hear about Christ and his church in order to be saved and that as long as they sincerely

---

[6]Before the 1994 *Catechism* declared so, the 1964 *Dogmatic Constitution* declared:

> Those also can attain to everlasting salvation who through no fault of their own do not know the gospel of Christ or His Church, yet sincerely seek God and moved by grace, strive by their deeds to do His will as it is know to them through the dictates of conscience. (paragraph 16)!

Footnote 58 to this paragraph elaborates:

> The [Second Vatican] Council is careful to add that men unacquainted with the biblical revelation, and even those who have not arrived at explicit faith in God [even professing atheists?], may by the grace of Christ attain salvation if they sincerely follow the lights God gives them.

follow the dictates of their conscience they may be saved? It implies two things: first, that their very *ignorance* of Christ and the Roman Catholic Church is contributory to their salvation since to be told about Christ and the Roman Catholic Church is to place their souls in danger of eternal perdition if they refuse to become Catholics, or if, having become Catholics, they refuse to remain Catholics. Therefore, Roman Catholics should stop trying to convert the world to Roman Catholicism since such labor, according to their own teaching, has the potential for doing the peoples of the world more spiritual harm than good. Second, since non-Catholics, according to Rome's dogmatic declarations and catechetical instruction, may go to heaven without becoming Roman Catholics, this implies that for them the Roman Catholic Church does not need to exist. By its own statements, therefore, *the Roman communion has declared its own obsolescence and itself a modern irrelevancy to most of the peoples of the world.*

What are these catechetical deliverances but just another expression of the detestable apostasy that now grips the largest cult – the Marian cult – within professing Christendom. And should one think my words here are strident and unloving, he should read the *Westminster Confession of Faith*, X.4, that sets forth the historic position of classic Protestantism on this matter of the reputed salvation of non-elect Christians:

> [With respect to the non-elect], although they may be called by the ministry of the word, and may have some common operations of the Spirit, yet they never truly come unto Christ, and therefore cannot be saved: much less can men not professing the Christian religion be saved in any other way whatsoever, be they ever so diligent to frame their lives according to the light of nature, and the law of that religion they do profess; and to assert and maintain that they may, is very pernicious, and to be detested.

What is so tragically ironic about this "very pernicious" and "detestable" teaching of Rome's 1964 *Dogmatic Constitution on the Church*, a document of the Second Vatican Council, and its 1994 *Catechism of the Catholic Church* is that both declarations reassert on the one hand the Council of Trent's medieval doctrine of justification through faith and works and on the other make the entire Tridentine doctrine irrelevant by teaching that all sincere people may be saved, whatever their faith or lack of it. So with these confessional deliverances everything that modern Rome teaches about the way of salvation through Christ is short-circuited. Frankly, who should care what Rome teaches about salvation if everyone may be saved simply by sincerely following the good as he conscientiously understands and does the good? Apparently, even the sincere professing atheist who has not arrived at an explicit knowledge of God may be saved as long as he follows the dictates of his conscience with sincerity, for by responding to the light of conscience he is responding (without knowing it, Rome would say) in a salvific way to Christ's Church. I can only say that the modern framers of these documents had better be glad that they were not born in the sixteenth century. The Romanist authorities living then would have burned them – including the present pope – at the stake for teaching such rank heresy! The New Testament predicted that false teachers would arise in the church, and if Rome is not now the purveyor of false teaching, I can only say, "Please tell me what Rome would have to teach if what it presently teaches is not false doctrine."

The sum of the matter is this: Within the Roman Catholic Church today may be found Tridentine conservatives, crypto-Lutherans, moderate liberals, and outright syncretists, but Rome's overall drift is toward total religious pluralism and syncretism. Clearly, the Roman church has abandoned Holy Scripture's teaching with respect to the necessity of faith in Christ for salvation. Why any Roman Catholic would find Roman Catholicism necessary or even attractive now and remain in it is due to sheer spiritual blindness, which in itself indicates his lost condition. And why any Evangelical would now feel the necessity to convert from Evangelicalism to Roman Catholicism can only be traced to what Dr. Scott McKnight has called the yearning for "transcendence" that manifests itself in a longing for four things – religious certainty, a continuous place in the history of the church, ecclesiastical unity and universality, and an absolute authority – things which apparently such converts do not think they can find within Holy Scripture alone and/or within Evangelicalism because of the many interpretations that evangelicals have placed upon the Bible.[7] Of course, such converts to Rome will be gravely disappointed if they believe that the Roman church can offer them these things for two

---

[7]Scott McKnight, "From Wheaton to Rome: Why Evangelicals Become Roman Catholic," *JETS* 45/3 (September 2002), 460.

reasons: first, because that communion has multiple interpretations as well about almost everything (for such variant opinions within Catholicism just compare, for example, the Catholicism of Raymond E. Brown, J. P. Meier, Brendan Byrne, Joseph Fitzmyer, and G. Guttierez), and it has had such differing interpretations through the centuries, and second, because they will therefore still be required to choose among these opinions and draw their own conclusions about what Rome actually teaches, which *individual* decision-making, Rome itself informs them, they do not really have the authority to make. So they have not actually found religious certainty in Roman Catholicism, as they claim. Moreover, and quite paradoxically, it would appear that most, if not all, academic converts from Evangelicalism to Rome, such as Scott Hahn, Thomas Howard, and Robert Sungenis, *appeal to Scripture* to justify their move, but such an appeal reflects, in keeping with Protestantism's *sola scriptura* principle, a *private* interpretation of Scripture, that is to say, they claim they made their move to Rome having come to the truth on the basis of their *private* study of Scripture, no small claim for people who think biblical interpretation is to be done only by the church. What is truly ironic here is that these converts make their shift to Rome, they say, on the basis of their study of the Bible without really facing up to the fact that the church they are entering has over the centuries erected as church dogma a theological system which is anything but biblical but is rather a *systemic idolatry*, filled as it is with all kinds of teachings that not only have *no biblical support* at all but are also actually at odds with Scripture teaching. Theirs is truly a case of choking on gnats and swallowing camels!

And why any Roman Catholic would want to remain in such a confused communion – a communion that has betrayed Jesus Christ by making conscious faith in his atoning work completely unnecessary for salvation, a communion where its own people *never*, I repeat, *never* hear the true gospel proclaimed, a communion that is systemically idolatrous – can only be traced to abject ignorance on his part of what the Bible teaches and what his own church teaches to the contrary.

For these reasons I would urgently admonish Christian people who are concerned for biblical truth to have nothing to do with the Roman Catholic Church and if they are already in it I would urge them to repudiate its teachings, come out of it, and separate from it. I would urge that they then unite with a Reformed church where Christians are taught that the Bible is the only infallible rule of faith and practice, where the true gospel is proclaimed, and where the real spiritual and material needs of a world are addressed. And I would urge that they remember to pray that God the Holy Spirit would enlighten many others within that communion, just as he enlightened them, to follow them out of the Roman church and into a Bible-believing church.

Chapter Twenty-Five

What's Wrong with Islam?

…we [Christians] know that the Son of God has come and has given us understanding, so that we may know him who is true; and we are in him who is true; in his Son Jesus Christ. He is the true God and eternal life. Little children, keep yourselves from idols (1 John 5:20-21).

Should any Muslims read this article I would first express my appreciation to them for doing so, and I want them to know that I love them. I assure them that I have no personal animosity toward them as individuals. Rather, it is because I care very deeply for the Muslim world that I wrote this article. Second, I would respectfully urge them to examine the Qur'an and Christian theology and history to see if what I write here is true. And I would respectfully plead with them to read carefully, thoughtfully, and attentively. And to all professing Christians who read this article I would say that just because they *profess* to be Christians is no guarantee in itself that they are genuine Christians whose sins are forgiven and who are on their way to heaven. So they as well should read carefully, thoughtfully, and attentively what I write here.

Because of the destruction of the World Trade Center on September 11, 2001 by militant Muslims acting in the name of Allah, Christians in the United States of America should learn all they can about Islam and its spread in this country. A study entitled *The Mosque in America: A National Portrait*, released on April 26, 2001 by the Council on American-Islamic Relations headquartered in Washington, DC, reports that over two million Muslims were attending twelve hundred and nine mosques in the United States at the time of the study's release. What concerns me about these numbers is not so much these numbers *per se* but the fact that they represented *a three-*

Note: This article was originally published in *The Trinity Review*, Nos. 212, 213 (October-November, 2002). The reader should read Jesus' parable of the wicked farmers in either Matthew 21:33-45, Mark 12:1-12, or Luke 20:9-19 before he reads this article.

hundred-percent increase over the last six years, showing clearly that Islam is blossoming and flourishing in our country.[1]

Taking my own advice that I gave above to Muslims, for some time now, and particularly since September 11, 2001, I have been studying the Qur'an, Islam's "holy book," which is composed of one hundred and fourteen "suras" (chapters). Muslims regard the Qur'an as the infallible Word of God. Now while I am not a recognized authority on the religion of Islam I believe I can, in spite of the Qur'an's content and style,[2] read it with sufficient comprehension to understand it in the main. And I *certainly* know something about what Christianity

---

[1]Many Christians will doubtless say, "So what? They have as much right to immigrate to these shores as anyone else, don't they?" Given current immigration laws this is true enough, but let me spell out why Christians should be concerned. If Islam were to become the dominant religion in the United States, Muslims would doubtless demand, as they have already achieved in Canada, that Islamic Sharia law should govern Muslims, not our Constitution. And since Muslims worship on Friday, the Muslim citizenry would doubtless demand *and* legislate that Friday be made a day of worship. America would then either move to a four-day workweek, with Muslims worshiping on Friday, Jews worshiping on Saturday, and Christians worshiping on Sunday (think about the impact a four-day workweek would have on the US economy), or Friday would become the only worship day and Jews and Christians would have to fend for themselves as far as having a day set apart for their respective times of worship, which is the pattern followed in every Muslim country in the Middle East. Furthermore, in spite of present Constitutional protection, Christians would eventually find it more difficult to build churches, openly to buy and to read the Bible and to spread Christianity within the US, especially among Muslims. (See the short Addendum on 420 for other steps that Islamists are taking to conquer the United States by the year 2020.)

This is not to suggest that Muslims should be denied US citizenship but it is to alert Christians to the dangers that Islam is to the Christian West and to encourage the Reformed churches in America to take seriously its responsibility to evangelize American Muslims.

[2]Literary critics, subjecting the Qur'an to the same kinds of questions that the Bible has successfully faced since the nineteenth century, have rightly concluded that the Qur'an is an entirely human, fallible book with enormous errors. For a summary of this contention see Toby Lester, "What is the Koran?" *The Atlantic* (January 1999).

Thomas Carlyle's studied judgment was that the reading of the Qur'an in English is "a toilsome task," for it is "a wearisome, confused jumble, crude,

has historically and classically taught regarding Christian doctrine. And it is apparent to me from my reading of the Qur'an that it is laced with distortions concerning Christianity's doctrinal teachings. Admittedly, there are many ambiguities in Qur'anic teaching, about the meaning of which even Islamic scholars dispute, and these ambiguities may account for some of these distortions. But, in my opinion, any objective observer who knows the facts must still conclude that Muhammad, the Qur'an's author, was at best ill-informed about Christianity's core teachings and thus did not "write" infallibly when he "wrote" what he did about classic Christianity's belief system (actually he dictated his "revelations" since he could neither read nor write).

In this article I do not intend to take up the many *historical* inaccuracies in the Qur'an.[3] Nor will I address Muhammad's teaching that the husband may beat his disobedient wife (Sura 4, "Women," verse 34, or his fixation on the eternal fire awaiting the Jew and the Christian and the sensual paradise of gardens, feasting, and sexual

---

incondite; endless iterations, long-windedness, entanglement; insupportable stupidity, in short, nothing but a sense of duty could carry any European through the Koran." For Carlyle's full quotation see Philip Schaff in *History of the Christian Church* [Reprint of 1910 edition; Grand Rapids: Eerdmans, n.d.), IV, 180, who also opines that the Qur'an's passages of poetic beauty are "mixed with absurdities, bombast, unmeaning images, low sensuality. It abounds in repetitions and contradictions.... It alternately attracts and repels, and is a most wearisome book to read" (179). He concludes:

> Of all books..., the Koran is the most powerful rival of the Bible, but falls infinitely below it in contents and form.... Whatever is true in the Koran is borrowed from the Bible; what is original, is false or frivolous. The Bible is historical and embodies the noblest aspirations of the human race in all ages to the final consummation; the Koran begins and stops with Mohammed. The Bible combines endless variety with unity, universal applicability with local adaptation; the Koran is uniform and monotonous, confined to one country, one state of society, and one class of minds. The Bible is the book of the world, and is constantly traveling to the ends of the earth, carrying spiritual food to all races and to all classes of society; the Koran stays in the Orient, and is insipid to all who have once tasted the true word of the living God. (181-2)

[3]For some of the Qur'an's historical inaccuracies see Gleason L. Archer, Jr. (1994), *A Survey of Old Testament Introduction* (Third edition; Chicago:

pleasure that awaits the Muslim (Sura 36).[4] Rather, I will restrict my remarks mainly to Muhammad's misrepresentation to his followers concerning what Christians believe about God as Trinity, his misrepresentation of Christ's place in redemptive/revelational history as penultimate with his own alleged prophetic role being ultimate, his denials of Christ's deity, crucifixion and resurrection, and his denial that God requires for forgiveness Jesus' atoning sacrifice for sin. Let's look in some detail at each of these Qur'anic teachings. Technical theological language will be occasionally employed but I make no apology for the employment of this language because at times it will be necessary.

The Qur'an's Teaching on God as Trinity

I want to begin here by noting that Christianity had already enjoyed a six-hundred-year-long theological history and had already developed a carefully-thought-through theology of God by the time Muhammad (b. about AD 570), the author of the Qur'an, began to write his alleged "revelations from Allah" around AD 610. Through the efforts of the first four ecumenical councils (Nicaea, Constantinople, Ephesus, and Chalcedon) the early church fathers, listening carefully to Scripture, had worked out the church's doctrine of God as Trinity and its doctrine of the two-natured incarnate Christ. These doctrines, sometimes expressed in philosophico-theological language, were understandably sometimes quite technical and difficult for an average person to comprehend. In the course of developing its theology over these centuries the church also found it necessary to distance itself from the unscriptural views of the second-century Logos-Christologies, third-century forms of modalism, fourth-century Arianism and Apollinarianism, and fifth-century Nestorianism and Eutychianism –

Moody, 549-52; St. Clair Tisdall (n.d.), *The Source of Islam*, translated and abridged by William Muir, T & T. Clark; and Abdal Fadi (n.d.), *Is the Qur'an Infallible?* (Villach, Austria: Light of Hope). I will mention the following only to illustrate: In the distorted accounts of the Exodus Pharaoh asks *Haman* to build a tower of bricks to heaven, Pharaoh is both drowned in the Red Sea and spared, and God threatens to drop Mount Sinai on the Israelites.

[4]Islam teaches that in heaven the lowliest Muslim males will enjoy seventy-two black-eyed youthful girls (*houris*) especially created for his sexual enjoyment, with the moment of his sexual pleasure prolonged to a thousand years and his faculty of sensual enjoyment increased a hundred fold.

all views that basically had in common the denial in one way or another of the incarnation of God the Son as true man. These unscriptural heresies, however, did not die when they were rejected but rather continued to spread throughout some regions of the Middle East, and it was these heresies, especially Arianism, that spread into Arabia and to Mecca where Muhammad was born.[5]

Now a careful reading of the Qur'an will disclose that Muhammad did not have a clear grasp of what classic orthodox Christianity was teaching about the Trinity in the seventh century AD. He was hearing views that had been rejected by the learned fathers of the church such as Athanasius, Cyril of Alexandria, and Augustine. Accordingly, his consistent representation of the Trinity suggests that he conceived of the Trinity along the lines of a crude tritheism, a heresy that Christianity had consistently repudiated. In Sura 4, "Women," verse 171, the Koran declares: "The Messiah, Jesus the son of Mary, was no more than God's apostle…. So believe in God [Allah] and his apostles and do not say: 'Three.' Forbear, and it shall be better for you. God is but one God. God forbid that he should have a son!" In Sura 5, "The Table," verse 73, Muhammad teaches: "Unbelievers are those who say: 'God [Allah] is one of three.' There is but one God." Apparently Muhammad believed that in order for God to have a son he would have had to have a consort (Sura 6, "Cattle," verse 101), but since God "has taken no consort" he has "not begotten any children" (Sura 72, "The Jinn," verse 3). Then in Sura 5, verse 116, he teaches that Christians believe that God's "threeness" is composed of Allah, Jesus, whom he believed ill-informed Christians had wrongly

---

[5]Schaff, in his *History*, IV, 159, notes that the "Christians" who inhabited Arabia in the days of Muhammad

> belonged mostly to the various heretical sects which were expelled from the Roman empire during the violent doctrinal controversies of the fourth and fifth centuries. We find there traces of Arians, Sabellians, Ebionites, Nestorians, Eutychians, Monophysites, Marianites, and Collyridians or worshippers of Mary…it was a very superficial and corrupt Christianity which had found a home in those desert regions….

It was, of course, unbiblical and sinful for the imperial authorities to exile from the Roman Empire these heretics. As it was, these heresies found fruitful soil in other lands where they went unchecked and uncorrected.

deified, and his mother Mary.[6] Now whatever sub-scriptural oddities some church fathers may have espoused over the early centuries of the church about God as Trinity, I can declare categorically that not one of them ever taught that God's "threeness" included the mother of Jesus, and also that no ecumenical council ever endorsed such a notion. This is an error of massive proportions on Muhammad's part, shows his ignorance of Christian teaching, and evidences that the Qur'an contains error respecting this major doctrine in the belief system of one of its major religious contenders. It may be that he knew about the small heretical sect called the Collyridians, made up mainly of fanatical women, that had existed in the fourth century in Arabia and that had rendered divine worship to Mary by offering her cakes.[7] It may be, if he had even heard of the teaching, that Muhammad thought that the church's confessional description of Mary as *theotokos* ("God-bearer") implied that she was deity. This term, of course, was not intended to say that there was something divine about Mary; it was intended only to safeguard Jesus' full deity. Most likely, he had simply concluded that if Christians believed Jesus was the Son of God then they had to believe also that God had to have a divine consort and that his mother was this divine consort. But whatever his reasoning was behind his assertion, he was in error to conclude that Christians generally regarded Mary as a member of the Trinity.

What the church taught then and still teaches is this: that within the unity of the one living and true Godhead eternally exist three persons, God the Father, God the Son, and God the Holy Spirit, and these three are one God, the same in substance, equal in power and glory (see the church creeds here). Perhaps this definition will not satisfy Muslims but at least it takes seriously the infallible teaching of Holy Scripture and it does not misrepresent to the world what classic Christianity has taught about the Christian God, which cannot be said for the Qur'an's misrepresentation of the doctrine of the Trinity.

---

[6]Muhammad confuses Mary in Sura 3, "The Family of Imran," verses 35-45, and in Sura 66, "Prohibition," verse 12, with Miriam, the sister of Moses and Aaron. All efforts to explain this confusion on the part of Islamic apologists have proven unsatisfactory.

[7]See Epiphanius, *Adversus Haeresis*, 79.

The Qur'an's Teaching on Jesus' Secondary Place (Along With the Other Prophets) in Revelational History with Muhammad Himself Occupying the Primary Place

Islamic orthodoxy today teaches, on the one hand, that Jesus, while he was Israel's Messiah, was only one of many national prophets to Israel and that God never intended the Christianity of Jesus to become a universal religion. Islamic orthodoxy today teaches, on the other hand, that Muhammad was the only prophet sent by God to the entire world and that it is Islam alone that God intended to become a universal religion. However, if one studies the Qur'an carefully, he will discover that it seems to say the very opposite. It represents itself as a book written in Arabic for those who spoke Arabic (Sura 41, "Revelations Well Expounded," verse 3, and Sura 42, "Counsel," verse 7) and that it was intended primarily for Mecca and its environs (Sura 6, "Cattle," verse 93, and Sura 42, "Counsel," verse 7). Arthur J. Arberry surely appears to be right when he observes that the Islam of the Qur'an is fundamentally an Arabic religion, reflecting and intended for the seventh-century culture of Arabia.[8] On the other hand, the Qur'an emphatically states in Sura 3:3 and Sura 6:92 that God revealed the Mosaic Torah and the Christian Gospel *for the light and guidance of all mankind.*

But what did Muhammad teach about his relation to Jesus? Did he not see himself as superior to Jesus? Well, it is true that, according to Sura 61, "Battle Array" or "Ranks," verse 6, Muhammad does state that Jesus taught that "an apostle...will come after me whose name is Ahmad [a variation of Muhammad]." Of course, Jesus taught no such thing. He taught that *God the Holy Spirit* whom he called the Comforter (*parakletos*, John 14:16-17, 26; 15:26; 16:7-8, 13-14), whom he would send from the Father, would come after him. And he taught that the Spirit/Comforter when he came would glorify him, Jesus the Christ. Apparently, Muhammad confused the Greek word *parakletos* with the Greek word *periklytos*, meaning "famed, praised," for which the Arabic would be Ahmad (or Muhammad), and accordingly he taught that Jesus taught that he, Muhammad, was to be the last and "seal" of God's prophets.

The Gospels, however, make it clear that Jesus taught that

---

[8]Arthur J. Arberry (1970), *Religion in the Middle East*, Cambridge University Press, 7.

revelational history reached its climax and finality in him and that his chosen apostles completed God's revelatory activity (2 Tim. 3:16-17). For instance, in his parable of the wicked farmers, found in Matthew 21:33-45, Mark 12:1-12, and Luke 20:9-19, Jesus tells the story of a landowner who leased his vineyard to some farmers and then went into another country. When the time arrived for him to receive his rental fee in the form of the fruit of the vineyard he sent servant after servant to his tenants, only to have each one of them beaten or stoned or killed. *Last of all* he sent his son – Luke says his "beloved son"; Mark says "*yet one [other]*, a beloved son" – saying: "They will respect my son." But when the tenants saw the landowner's son, they said: "This is the heir; come, let's kill him and take his inheritance." This they did, throwing his body out of the vineyard. When the landowner came, he destroyed the tenants and leased his vineyard to others. The interpretative intentions of the parable, as Don Carson notes,[9] are obvious on the face of it: the landowner is God the Father, the vineyard the nation of Israel (Isa. 5:7); the farmers the nation's leaders, the servants the prophets of the theocracy (Matt. 23:37a); and the son is Jesus himself.

The central teaching of the parable is obvious – as indeed it was to its original audience (Matt. 21:45): after having sent his servants the prophets repeatedly in Old Testament times to the nation of Israel and its leaders to call the nation back to him from its sin and unbelief, only to have them rebuffed, persecuted, and often killed, God, the Owner of Israel, had in sending Jesus moved beyond merely sending another servant. Listen once again to the pertinent verses in this connection:

Matthew 21:37: "Then *last of all* he sent his son."

Mark 12:6: "...still having *one son*, his beloved, he also sent him to them *last*."

In Jesus God had *finally* (Matt 21:37: *hysteron*; Mark 12:6: *eschaton*) sent his own beloved Son, that is, his "one and only" Son, who was to be similarly rejected. The *finality* of his ministry Jesus makes clear from his teaching that the farmers' rejection of *him*, unlike the rejections of those before him, was to entail, neither a

---

[9]D. A. Carson (1984), *Matthew* in *The Expositor's Bible Commentary*, Zondervan, 451.

continuance of dealing with the recalcitrant nation on God's part nor a mere change of politico-religious administration. Rather, to reject him, he taught, would eventuate in "the complete overthrow of the theocracy, and the rearing from the foundation up of a new structure in which the Son would receive full vindication and supreme honor"[10] (Matt. 21:42-43; Mark 12:9; Luke 20:16). The Son's exalted status in the revelational economy of God is apparent from the *finality* of the messianic investiture that he owns. From Matthew's "finally" – Mark says "he had yet *one* other" and also "finally" – it is clear that Jesus represents himself as the *last*, the *final* ambassador, after whose sending none higher can come and nothing more can be done. The Lord of the vineyard has no further resources; as God's Son the Son of God is the highest messenger of God conceivable. The author of Hebrews echoes exactly this sentiment when he declares:

> God who spoke at many times and in many ways in times past to the fathers by the prophets has in these last days spoken to us by His Son whom he has appointed heir of all things, through whom also he made the worlds...[and] if the word spoken [then] proved steadfast, and every transgression and disobedience received a just recompense, how shall *we* escape if we neglect so great a salvation, which...[was] spoken by the Lord, and was confirmed to us by those [apostles] who heard him (Heb. 1:1-2; 2:2-3).

Clearly, the author of Hebrews teaches, with Jesus, the finality of God's work in Jesus Christ. Both Jesus' teaching and the uniform teaching of the entire New Testament clearly fly in the face of Muhammad's claim that Jesus taught that "an apostle named Ahmad" would come after him. Jesus' teaching here also places Muhammad in hopeless conflict with himself, for when Muhammad declares, as he does several places, that Jesus was a true prophet, it means by implication that when Jesus taught what he did in this parable about his own finality Muhammad's claim to being the last and greatest prophet is negated by the teaching of this very one whom Mohammad declares was a true prophet.

So in making himself the "Seal of the Prophets," that is, the last and the greatest of the prophets, as he does in Sura 33, "Confederate

---

[10]Geerhardus Vos, *The Self-Disclosure of Jesus* (Reprint of 1926 edition; Phillipsburg, N.J.: Presbyterian and Reformed, 1978), 162.

Tribes," verse 40, Muhammad misrepresented Christ's teaching regarding what he taught about his unique and final place in God's revelational program and thereby made himself again a *false* prophet.

The Qur'an's Teaching about Jesus' Deity

The Qur'an, it is true, affirms that Jesus was the Jewish Messiah and a true prophet of God, that he was virgin-born and performed many miracles. Therefore, Muslims believe today, because the Qur'an teaches these true and proper things about Jesus, that Christians should be lauding them and regarding them accordingly as friendly to Christianity. But the Qur'an also teaches in Sura 5, "The Table," verses 17 and 72, that it is *unbelievers* who say that Jesus is God. And in verse 116 the Qur'an teaches that Jesus denied that he thought he was deity:

> Then God says: "Jesus, son of Mary, did you ever say to mankind: 'Worship me...as god beside God?'" "Glory be to you," he answers, "I could never have claimed what I have no right to. If I had ever said so, you would have surely known it." (See also Sura 5:75)

Now think with me for a moment here. Suppose one nation's ambassador goes to another nation, presents his credentials to its leaders, and these leaders say in response to him: "We like you very much; you are a very nice person, you are kind, and your speeches are very edifying. But we simply do not believe you are who you say you are and therefore we cannot accept you in the role in which you claim to have come." Would anyone say that those leaders had really received that ambassador? Similarly, unless one accepts Jesus for who he claims to be and in the role in which he claims to have come, he has not really accepted Jesus at all regardless of the other nice things he may say about him! To be quite frank about it, Jesus is not flattered by all the kisses that unregenerate men may throw at him if at the same time they deny as false his claims to deity and his claim to sole saviorhood. This is the state in which our Muslim friends actually find themselves with their incomplete list of accolades about Jesus. They have really not accepted him regardless of the true things they say about him.

Now Jesus' self-awareness is a subject that I have given a considerable amount of my professional life assessing. I have even written a book specifically about it (see my *Jesus, Divine Messiah:*

The Biblical Witness). And I will state categorically that, based upon the teaching of the four Gospels, Jesus did in fact believe that he was God the Son incarnate, the second person of the Godhead, and that he taught others to believe so as well.

For example, look again with me at the parable I read earlier. Its high Christology – reflecting Jesus' own self-understanding of his deity – finds expression in two details in the story:[11]

A. By virtue of his sonship here, Jesus claims to possess a higher dignity and a closer relation to God than the highest and closest official status that all the prophets of the Old Testament theocracy possessed. This is underscored not only by his title "Son" but also by the highly suggestive word "beloved" that he attaches to the title "Son," applying both words to himself over against the unqualified word "servants" that he uses to describe all those who went before him.

B. The former point – that Jesus represents himself as God's beloved Son and heir over against all who went before him who were only servants – cannot be made to answer merely to a "messianic" or functional sonship, as some critical scholars would like to believe. This is apparent from two facts:

First, Jesus represents himself in the parable as God's beloved Son even *before his mission.*

Second, he represents himself as God's beloved Son *whether sent or not!* That is to say, his being sent reflects his investiture of messiahship, but *his* invested messiahship was brought about precisely by the necessity for God to send one who was the highest and dearest that the lord of the vineyard could delegate. Jesus' sonship, therefore, existed prior to his messianic mission and was *not* the result of his mission. And because he represents himself, the landowner's beloved son, as also the "heir" in all three synoptic accounts of the parable, this means that his sonship is the underlying ground of his messiahship.[12]

It is impossible, then, to avoid the strong suggestion on Jesus' part in this parable of his *eternal pre-existence* with the Father as the

---

[11]See Geerhardus Vos, *The Self-Disclosure of Jesus*, 161-3.
[12]Vos, *The Self-Disclosure of Jesus*, 162-3.

latter's "beloved Son." Here his divine station in association with his Father prior to his messianic mission in space-time history is confirmed. Thus the "beloved Son" in Jesus' parable – a self-portrait one may say with ample justification – is clearly divine.

To say the very least, then, Muhammad once again misrepresented Jesus' teaching and once again misrepresented historic Christian teaching when he denied Jesus' deity, apparently having come unwittingly under the influence of the heretical Arian teaching that had spread into Arabia. He was apparently unaware that the church had condemned Arianism at the First Ecumenical Council at Nicaea in AD 325.

The Qur'an's Teaching about
Jesus' Crucifixion and Resurrection

In his story of the wicked farmers Jesus also prophetically taught that the nation's leaders would kill him, the Son, and in his application of his story to his original auditors he taught that he would be raised from death to glory and that the destiny of all mankind would turn on their relation to him (Matt. 21:42; Mark 12:10-11; Luke 20:17-18). And two of the best-attested facts of history are his crucifixion and resurrection. But what says Muhammad about the teaching of this man whom he describes elsewhere as a "true prophet"?

Well, in Sura 4, "Women," verse 157, Muhammad denies as a "monstrous falsehood" that Jesus was crucified. He states: "[The Jews] did not kill him, nor did they crucify him, but they thought they did." According to Muslim tradition the Jews crucified a man who resembled Jesus, perhaps even Judas. Jesus himself was taken unharmed directly to heaven (see Sura 3, "The Imrans," verse 55, and Sura 4, "Women," verses 156-58).[13] This means as well, of course, that Islam denies Jesus' resurrection from the dead. With these denials Muhammad removes from Christianity's core teaching Jesus' cross and resurrection that are central to his substitutionary atonement. In Sura 5, "The Table," verse 103, Muhammad teaches that Allah does not demand sacrifices (see also Sura 6, "Cattle," verse 164), which means by implication, in opposition to New Testament teaching that apart from the shedding of Christ's blood there is no forgiveness of sin (Heb 9:22), that he did not demand Jesus' sacrificial death either.

---

[13]See J. M. Rodwell, *Koran* (Everyman's Library; New York: Dunton, 1909), footnote on Sura 3:55.

What God demands of mankind, according to Muhammad, is *absolute submission or resignation to his will*. The very word "Islam" means "submission," and "Muslim" means "one who submits" to the will of Allah.[14] But this leaves mankind in a hopeless condition, for mankind is unspeakably sinful with the corporate guilt of original sin (which

---

[14]The Arabic word translated "Islam" is etymologically related to the Hebrew word "shalom," usually translated "peace." But "peace" does not mean to most Muslim clerics in the Middle East what it means to the Westerner. To these Muslim clerics "peace" connotes "surrender" or "submission" to Allah, which means for them with respect to the non-Muslim world "placing their foot on their enemy's neck."

No Muslim scholar can truthfully deny that Muhammad taught that the faithful should "make war on the unbeliever..., and deal sternly with them" (Sura 66, "Prohibition," verse 9; see also Sura 8, "Spoils of War," verses 13-17, and Sura 9 [virtually a declaration of war against unbelievers], "Repentance," verses 5, 14, 29, 112, 123). Muhammad himself, as he sought to propagate his religion beginning with his move to Yathrib or Medina (this move is called the Hegira) in September, AD 622, waged "holy war" (*jihad*) in the name of Allah against village after village in Arabia, finally entering his birth city Mecca in AD 630 as a conqueror and cleansing its chief shrine (Kaaba) of the 350 idols worshiped there. In other words, from its beginning Islam was spread by the sword. And the first four caliphs (successors) of Muhammad – Abu Bakr, Umar, Othman, and Ali – also drew the sword and conquered one land after another through Palestine and North Africa all the way to Spain, killing multiplied thousands as they did so and also establishing a tax system (the *Dhimma*) to subjugate those they did not force to convert.

While Christianity has had its misguided Crusades, its Spanish conquistadors, and has committed other misdeeds in the name of Christ, spreading Christianity by the sword has not been its normal mode of operation and was *never* its founder's mode of operation. Yet in the last 100 years Muslim expansion still goes on apace by warfare. The Muslim Ottoman Turks slaughtered a million and a half Armenians in 1915-24 (a fact still ignored by much of the West). Today converts to Christianity are regularly executed in Saudi Arabia and tortured and murdered in Egypt. In the Sudan over two million Christians have been slaughtered and a million Christian children have been sold into slavery, all under the direction of the Islamic General Umar Bashir. In Indonesia Muslims have killed over three hundred thousand East Timorese Catholics since 1975. And Muslims in Palestine, Lebanon, Indonesia, Saudi Arabia, Iraq, etc., danced in the streets with joy while our widows and orphans mourned their dead on September 11, 2001. The late Hashemi Rafsanjani of Iran declared:

Muslims deny[15]), incapable of such submission, and unable to save itself. And mankind, because of this original sin, bears genuine guilt

Every problem in our region can be traced to this single dilemma: the occupation of [modern Palestine] by Jewish infidels or Western imperialists...The everlasting struggle between Ishmael and Isaac...cannot cease until one or the other is utterly vanquished. (Cited by George Grant, *The Blood of the Moon*, 56)

And the late Ayatollah Khomeini of Iran stated:

Until the cry *"Allah Akbar"* resounds over the whole world, there will be struggle. There will be *Ji'had*...Islam is the religion of militant individuals.... Weapons in our hands are used to realize divine and Islamic aspirations. The more people who die for our cause, the stronger our *Ji'had* shall become...The governments of the world should know that Islam cannot be defeated. Islam will be victorious in all the countries of the world, and Islam and the teachings of the Koran will prevail all over the world...We have in reality, then, no choice but to destroy those systems of government that are corrupt in themselves and also entail the corruption of others, and to overthrow all treacherous, corrupt, oppressive, and criminal regimes. This is the duty that all Muslims must fulfill, in every one of the Muslim countries first, and then throughout the infidel West, in order to achieve the triumph of our revolution and to garner the blessing of Allah. (Cited from George Grant, *The Blood of the Moon*, 72)

Nevertheless, in spite of the words of the Koran, Muhammad's own military actions, Islam's bloody history, and such declarations as the two just cited, Western political leaders are representing Islam to their people as a religion of peace and affirming that such Muslim clerics as I just cited are "radical Muslims" who have simply "hijacked this great and beautiful religion"! But Muslim authorities know very well that the Koran prescribes *jihad* as the obligation of every able-bodied male and that Islam from its inception in the seventh century to the present has sanctioned war and conquest as means of advancing Islam. The truth of the matter is that Islam is a religion of war, literally a killer religion. So in spite of what President George W. Bush, Secretary of State Colin Powell, and every major news agency asserts, the true nature of Islam is *jihad*, and the Muslim clerics in the West who say otherwise either do not understand their own faith (they are called "folk Muslims" by Middle Eastern Muslim clerics) or are purposefully attempting to conceal from the gullible Westerner the true nature of Islam.

The West cannot defeat the Muslim world by the sword. Only Reformed churches, using the *spiritual* tools God has made available to them (see 2 Cor. 10:3-4), can defeat Islam, for the real problem is one of the human heart and only Jesus Christ can change the heart of Muslims.

before God. Because of mankind's corruption and inability to please God, mankind deserves punishment, for its sin is not only real evil, morally wrong, the violation of God's law, and therefore, undesirable, odious, ugly, disgusting, filthy, and ought not to be; it is also the contradiction of God's perfection, cannot but meet with his disapproval and wrath, and *damnable* in the strongest sense of the word because it so dread-fully *dishonors* God. God must react with holy indignation. He *cannot* do otherwise. And here we come face to face, as John Murray declares,

> ...with a divine 'cannot' that bespeaks not divine weakness but everlasting strength, not reproach but inestimable glory. He cannot deny himself. To be complacent towards that which is the contradiction of his own holiness would be a denial of himself. So that wrath against sin is the correlate of his holiness. And this is just saying that the justice of God demands that sin receive its retribution. The question is not at all: How can God, being what he is, send men to hell? The question is, How can God, being what he is, save them from hell?[16]

If people are not corrupt as the Bible teaches, they have no need of the saving benefits of the cross. If people are not sinners incapable of saving themselves as the Bible teaches, they have no need of a Savior. But when by God's enabling grace they begin to understand how sinful and helpless they really are, when by God's enabling grace they begin to see themselves as God sees them – sinful and corrupt, incapable of saving themselves, and guilty before him – they will flee to the cross and begin to glory in it and will turn away from any religion that would do away with the atoning work and sacrificial death of Jesus. I know all too well – not well enough, I'm quite sure – that I am a sinner of the darkest hue and need a gracious Savior who by his death paid the price for sin and forgives sinners, something

---

[15]This is the view of Muslim orthodoxy, but the plural, not the dual, form of the verb translated "Get you all down" in Sura 2:36 refers to three or more and thus must include the unborn descendants of Adam and Eve (see also Sura 12:53 in which Joseph is quoted as admitting that his soul "incites to evil," suggesting the corruption of man's inner self). See Samuel Shahid, *The Fallen Nature of Man in Islam and Christianity* (Colorado Springs: al-Nour, 1989).

[16]John Murray, "The Nature of Sin," *Collected Writings of John Murray* (Edinburgh: Banner of Truth, 1977), 2, 81-2.

that Islam cannot and does not offer me.

In light of the above data it should be evident to all – even to Muslims – that Islam, even if it could be shown beyond dispute that it is the religion of peace that some Muslim clerics today claim it is, is still, theologically speaking, a declared enemy of biblical Christianity, misrepresenting and/or rejecting as it does the cardinal doctrines of our most holy faith. Its militant theological hostility toward Christianity is manifest in many places in the world, such as in the Muslim countries of the Middle East, in some African nations, and in Indonesia, but Islamic leaders have put on a new face in the West. According to Abdullah al-Arabi this side of Islam is

> ...usually hidden from new converts [in the West]. Major issues of life that are part of Islam, are carefully avoided, obscured, or omitted from the call of faith. Some passages of the Qur'an are inaccurately translated from the original Arabic to help lure converts.[17]

And the Islamic movement has made adaptations in order to make itself acceptable in the West. For instance, Islamic leaders abstain from mentioning

> the [Islamic] code of punishment. They stress their belief in Moses and Jesus. They no longer call Jews and Christians infidels, nor would they call them Zionists and Crusaders.[18]

They also use Christian terminology such as "Sunday school" instead of Friday Class, and their vocabulary now includes words like love, grace, salvation, justification, and sanctification. But all the while their strategy is to become accepted by the communities in which they live. This they do by becoming involved in local, state, and national political and social activities, by becoming members of local, state, and national educational committees for the purpose of changing educational programs to suit their beliefs, by writing to members of Congress in order to influence legislation, and by running for public office in order to exercise the authority of their office to make Islam more tolerable and finally acceptable to the gullible masses in the West who are living with the illusion that a lasting "cease fire" is possible with Islam. But make no mistake about it: Islam is the sworn

---

[17]Abdullah al-Arabi, *Islam Unveiled* (Fourth edition, 1994), 4.
[18]Abdullah al-Arabi, *Islam Unveiled*, 5.

enemy of the Christian faith and wants to see it finally and fully eradicated from the earth.

Conclusion

For the following two reasons I could never become a Muslim. First, as we have seen, the Qur'an misrepresents classic Christian doctrine, and to misrepresent the belief system of one's religious opposition as one makes the case for one's own belief system is, in my opinion, ignorance at best and moral obliquity at worst. Islam misleads its followers when it propagates by its Qur'anic teaching its errors concerning Christianity doctrine. This evinces (1) that Muhammad, Islam's "prophet," was at best ignorant of Christian teaching, (2) that his teachings about Christianity are generally false, and (3) that Islamic teaching, filled with such error based on the Qur'an, is hence an untrustworthy religion. Therefore, I could never become a Muslim because I could never overlook or forget the fact that my religion's so-called "holy book" propagates serious errors about Christianity's belief system and is therefore not infallible. The Qur'an itself acknowledges that if it contains any errors anywhere it did not come from God (Sura 4, "Women," verse 82). By its own standard, then, its errors about Christian doctrine mean that it is not a revelation from God in spite of all the Muslim claims to the contrary.

Second, I could never become a Muslim because of Islam's inability to address my (and mankind's) real spiritual need. If biblical Christianity is anything it is a redemptive religion. If Islam is anything it is *not* a redemptive religion but rather a religion of legalism or works-salvation. Islam demands of people *absolute submission* to Allah but it can achieve only a semblance of that required submission by legalistically legislating the lives of Muslims and threatening sanctions for disobedience. So in the end Islam teaches me (and mankind generally) that one must attempt to achieve heaven by one's good works (Sura 4, "Women," verse 124, *et al.*), which "plan of salvation" of course negates the substitutionary work of Christ's obedient life and penal death on behalf of his people, hoping that one's good works will outweigh one's bad works someday on the scales of justice of the Judge of all the earth. He who finds anything attractive in the Islamic way of salvation simply does not realize his own sinfulness and the wretched inadequacies of Islam in addressing redemptively that sinfulness. Islam leaves the world, including the Muslim world, unsaved. This is the reason my heart grows heavy and breaks with sorrow when people like Cassius Clay and John Walker Lindh convert to Islam and when I learn that Islamic strategists have determined that the black prison population in the United States is fruitful soil for converts.

I should note in passing that Islam's doctrinal hostility to biblical Christianity apparently does not bother the Roman Catholic Church, for Rome declared in its 1994 *Catechism of the Catholic Church* (para. 841) that Muslims are included within God's plan of salvation because they "acknowledge the Creator,...profess to hold the faith of Abraham,[19] and together with [Christians]...adore the one merciful God [Muslims and Christians hardly "adore" the same "one merciful God"]." Never mind that Islam's Allah is neither the triune Yahweh of the Old Testament nor the triune God of the New Testament; never mind that Muslims think our Trinity is made up of God, a human Jesus, and Mary his mother, the last two of whom we blasphemously worship along with God; never mind that they deny that Jesus Christ is the divine Son of God and that he died on a cross a sacrificial death for his people's sin and rose again for their justification; never mind that Muslims believe that Christians are idolaters because we worship Christ who they contend was simply a human Messiah and a human prophet; never mind that they see no need for Christ's substitutionary atonement or for that matter any real substitutionary atonement at all. According to Rome's teaching, in spite of their unbelief, Muslims are still salvifically related to the People of God and may go to heaven as Muslims, all of which shows how serious is Roman Catholicism's pernicious departure from the biblical faith.[20]

---

[19]Of course, Muslims do not hold to the true faith of Abraham with its messianic hope that looked directly to Christ and the gospel dispensation. Rather, Islam is the "bastard Judaism of Ishmael" (Schaff, *History*, IV. 184).

[20]This catechetical sellout of the uniqueness of Jesus Christ and the biblical faith is pervasive and constant today throughout the so-called Christian West, aided and abetted by Rome's teaching. An example of the far-reaching effect of this teaching is this excerpt from an interview between Charles Gibson and President George W. Bush on the ABC News programme *Good Morning America* on October 26, 2004:

> Gibson: "Do we worship the same God, Christian and Muslim?"
> Bush: "I think we do."
> Gibson: "Do Christians and non-Christians and Muslims go to heaven, in your mind?"
> Bush: "Yes, they do. We have different routes of getting there.... The almighty God decides who goes to heaven."

But according to Holy Scripture Jesus declared that he alone is the way to the Father and that no one comes to the Father except through him (John 14:6). Peter declared: "Salvation is in no one else, for there is no other name under heaven given among men by which we must be saved" (Acts 4:12). Paul taught that there is only one mediator between God and man, the man Christ Jesus (1 Tim. 2:6). John taught that he who has the Son has life and he who does not have the Son of God does not have life (1 John 5:12). And they all taught that one, if he would be saved, must repent of his sin of looking to his own works for salvation and must place his trust in the finished work of Jesus Christ. So I would join with their united witness and plead with all my readers to flee now in faith to Jesus and trust him for salvation, and to keep forever to him who is the true God and eternal life.

And he who, by God's doing (1 Cor. 1:30), comes to know Christ savingly will discover that only in him alone dwells all the treasures of wisdom and knowledge (Col. 2:3), that only in him alone dwells the whole fullness of deity bodily (Col. 2:9), that only in Christ does he have a divine Savior who loved him and gave himself sacrificially in death for him, paying thereby the penalty for his many sins against God, and that only in Christ can one have eternal life.

So I would respectfully but earnestly plead with Muslims to repudiate Islam, for it is a false religion that can only do eternal harm to them, even to its most submissive adherents who would martyr themselves in the cause of Allah, and turn in faith to the divine Christ who will save them.

I would also urge the Reformed church to launch a carefully planned all-out effort in the twenty-first century to evangelize the Muslim world by every appropriate means possible. The Reformed Christian mass media must increase their efforts in this regard. I single out the Reformed church here because, as Schaff observes, "if [Muslims] are to be converted it must be done by a Christianity which is free from all appearance of idolatry, more simple in worship, and more vigorous in life than that which they have so easily conquered and learned to despise."[21] The evangelization of the Muslim world –

President Bush may be a savvy politician but he is *at best* a poorly taught Christian since no well-taught, committed Christian would fly so dismissively in the face of the Bible's explicit teaching to the contraty.

[21]Schaff, *History*, IV, 154.

we are talking about over a billion, two hundred million people here[22] – will be accomplished, of course, only by the grace and power of God and at great cost to and through great dedication and sacrifice on the part of Christian missionaries because they will not be tolerated in Muslim lands. Even to speak a word against Muhammad or the Qur'an in a Muslim country, as I have done in this article, is punishable by death. (Do you remember the sentence of death that Ayatollah Khomeini of Iran passed upon Salman Rushdie because of his novel, *The Satanic Verses*?) Moreover, conversion from Islam to Christianity today can for Muslims result in disinheritance, loss of children, imprisonment, banishment from one's country, and even death because those who leave Islam are looked upon not only as traitors to their faith but also to their country if they live in a predominantly Muslim land. Nevertheless, the biblical Christ is the Muslim's only hope of heaven, and the church is under orders to evangelize the Muslim world.

But of course the same is true for everyone else as well. "Little children [and I think I am now old enough to address most readers as such: trust him and], keep yourselves from idols" (1 John 5:21).

Addendum

Anis Shorrosh, author of *Islam Revealed* is a Christian Arab-American who emigrated from Arab-controlled Jerusalem in January 1967. He is a member of the Oxford Society of Scholars, has traveled extensively, and is a lecturer and producer of TV documentaries. His forthcoming book, from which the following 20-point plan is taken, is titled *Islam: A Threat or a Challenge?*

Shorrosh suggests that Islamists have a 20-point plan to take over America by the year 2020. Here they are in an abridgement:

1. Terminate America's freedom of speech by replacing it with state-wide and nation-wide hate-crime bills.

2. Wage a war of words using black leaders like Louis Farrakhan and other visible religious personalities who will promote Islam as the religion of the African-American while insisting that

---

[22]The world Muslim population is numerically located as follows: in Asia, 911,200,000; in Africa, 324,100,000, in Europe and Russia, 37,200,000; in North America, 4,600,000; in the Caribbean and Latin America, 1,400,000; and in the Pacific region, 379,300.

Christianity is for Caucasians only. Do not tell African-Americans that it was Arab Muslims in Africa who captured them and sold them as slaves to the slave traders.

3. Engage the American public in dialogues, discussions, debates in colleges, universities, public libraries, churches, and mosques, and on the radio and TV making the case for the virtues of Islam. Proclaim how it is historically another religion, like Judaism and Christianity, that is monotheistic.

4. Nominate and place Muslim sympathizers in political office by bloc voting to bring about legislation favorable toward Islam.

5. Take control of as much of Hollywood, the press, TV, radio, and the internet as possible by buying the related corporations and the controlling stock.

6. Promote the fear of the imminent shut-off of Arab oil – the lifeblood of the American economy. America depends on oil and over 40% comes from the Middle East.

7. Yell "foul, out of context, personal interpretation, hate crime, Zionist, un-American, inaccurate translation" any and every time Islam is publicly criticized or the Qur'an is critically analyzed in the public arena.

8. Encourage Muslims to penetrate the White House, especially with Islamists who can articulate a peaceful picture of Islam. Acquire government positions and obtain membership on local school boards. Train Muslims as medical doctors to dominate the medical field, research and pharmaceutical companies. Take over the computer industry. Establish Middle Eastern restaurants throughout the USA to connect planners of Islamization in a discreet way.

9. Accelerate Islamic demographic growth via massive immigration, avoidance of birth control, marriage of Muslim men to non-Muslim women in order to Islamize them, and conversion of black prison inmates in order to turn them into Islamic militants.

10. The reading, writing, arithmetic, and research throughout the American educational system should be sprinkled with dislike of Jews, evangelical Christianity, and democracy.

11. Provide sizeable monetary Muslim grants to colleges and universities in America to establish "Centers for Islamic Studies" under the direction of Muslim directors in order to promote Islam in higher-education institutions.

12. Propagandize the entire world that the terrorists have hijacked Islam when in truth Islam has hijacked the terrorists.

13. Appeal to the historically compassionate and sympathetic Americans for sympathy and tolerance towards Muslims in America who are portrayed as mainly immigrants from oppressive countries.

14. Nullify America's sense of security by manipulating the intelligence community with misinformation and disinformation. Periodically terrorize Americans with the threat of impending attacks on bridges, tunnels, waterways, airports, apartment buildings, and malls.

15. Instigate riots and demonstrations in the prison system demanding Islamic Sharia as the way of life, not America's justice system.

16. Open numerous charities throughout the United States but use the donations to support Islamic terror organizations.

17. Raise interest in Islam on America's university and college campuses by insisting that freshmen take one course on Islam.

18. Unify the numerous Muslim lobbies in Washington, mosques, study centers, educational organizations, magazines, newspapers by use of the Internet and an annual convention to coordinate plans to propagate the faith.

19. Send intimidating messages and messengers to the out-spoken individuals who are critical of Islam and seek to neutralize them.

20. Applaud Muslims as loyal citizens of the United States by spotlighting their voting record as the highest percentage of all minority and ethnic groups in America.

If Christians are to turn back the Islamic tide comprised of *jihad*, the building of mosques throughout the world, and takeover of America they must be themselves alert to the danger Islam is to the West and educate other Christians to this dire threat to our freedoms

Subject Index

Abraham, principles of redemptive revelation in life of 88-91.
Analogy of (antecedent) Scripture:
criticism of 364-5;
Walter C. Kaiser, Jr. on 364.
Angels of God 65-75:
biblical terminology 65-6;
creation of 66;
elect angels' holy service for God 68-70;
lapsed angels' evil service for Satan 70-2;
nature of 66-8;
special question of guardian angels 72-4.
Apologetic nature of this book Preface.
Apostolic model of doing theology 14-6.
Aquinas, Thomas:
Gerstner on as a Protestant 307-18.
Arminian interpretation of Romans 9:13 106fn.

Barth, Karl 237-76:
biographical data on 237-8;
criticism of 258-63, 273-5;
his view of election 239-58;
his view of reconciliation 263-73.
Brunner, Emil 209-36:
biographical data on 209;
criticism of 231-6;
his concept of faith 228-31;
his concept of revelation 219-25;
his view of the Bible 225-8;
roots of his thought 210-18.
Bultmann, Rudolf 277-306:
biographical data on 277;
his demythologizing program 284-9;
his existentialist method 287-9;
his existential Jesus 20-2;
his false evaluation of modern science 304-5;
his form-critical method 285-7;
his modern scientific world-view 278-82;
his understanding of faith 282-4.

Children in covenant of grace 187-207:
privileges, rights, and responsibilities of

199-206.
Christology "from below" or "from above"? 18-20;
Warfield on 27.
Christ's theological method 11-13.
Covenantal nomism:
actually a covenantal legalism 157;
E. P. Sander's 147-57;
D. Moo on 150-2;
J. Neusner on 152fn.
Covenant of grace:
promises and signs of 193-4;
relation of children to 194-8;
relation of to Abrahamic covenant 189-92;
relation of to covenant of redemption 188-9.
Creation, theological significance of biblical doctrine of 53-63.

Days of Genesis:
length of 39-51;
length of seventh day 45fn;
main exegetical argument against days being literal 40-1;
Princeton Seminary's change of *Westminster Confession*'s meaning 42fn.
reasons for the "prevailing view" of as literal days 43-9;
Demythologized kerygma, Bultmann's 277-306;
criticism of 297-306;
results of 289-96.
Depravity, total for fallen man 131-5.
Dialectical encounter, Brunner's 209-36:
concept of revelation in 219-25;
criticism of 231-6;
historical roots of 210-14;
Søren Kierkegaard's influence upon 214-18.
Docetic Christ ("from above"), Käsemann's 23-6.
Documentary hypothesis 30-1

Election, Barth's doctrine of 239-58;
criticism of 258-63.
Election, unconditional:
amicus brief for 103-12;

divine election of Moses and Israel 105-10;
God arbitrary or purposive in? 111-12.
Encounter, dialectical (see Dialectical encounter).
Existential Jesus ("from below"), Bultmann's 20-2.
Exodus, salvation principles in redemptive event of 98-102.
Fallen man, natural state of 131-41:
depraved 131-35;
unable to improve his condition unto salvation 136-8;
real guilt before God 138-9;
Rome on 135fn.
Framework hypothesis 39fn, 49.

Genesis 1-11:
historical integrity of 29-37;
problems in for critics 33;
seven exegetical reasons for 34-6.
Genesis patriarchs, salvation principles governing 87-98.
God arbitrary or purposive in election? 111-12.
Great Commission, mandate to teach theology in 13-4.
Guardian angels, special question of 72-4.
Guilt, real for fallen man 138-9.

Hardening of Pharaoh's heart 103-5.
Hell, John Stott on 339-62:
criticism of his arguments for annihilation *passim*;
four arguments for annihilation 340-1;
Jesus on 345-50;
Paul on 350-3;
scriptural imagery of 356-7;
scriptural justice of 357-8;
scriptural language on 341-56;
scriptural universalism 359-60.
Inability, total for fallen man 136-8.
Inclusivism: Evangelicalism's downgrade doctrine of 377-8;
rebuttal of 379-87;
Rome's doctrine of 371-7.
Infant baptism, a justifiable deduction from three undeniable biblical truths 198.
Isaac, principles of redemptive revelation in life of 91-3.
Islam, addendum on 420;
its way of salvation 413;
reasons not to become a Muslim 417-8;
what's wrong with 401-22.

Jacob, principles of redemptive revelation in life of 93-8.
Jesus' humanity in John's Gospel 25-6.
Joseph included within Jacob's history 93fn;
his life reveals principle that exaltation follows suffering 94fn;
Judas, Barth on 255-7.
Justification by faith:
most debated topic among Paul scholars today 145-7;
Sanders/Dunn "fork in the road" concerning 145-63;
see Gerstner on Thomas Aquinas view of 307-18.

Kerygma, Bultmann's demythologized 277-306.
Kierkegaard, Søren 214-8;
his enemies 215-6;
his influence on Brunner 214;
his understanding of the Christian life 218;
his understanding of faith 217-8;
his understanding of truth 217-8.

Legalism, Judaistic:
Barrett on 156fn;
Cranfield on 146-7;
Moo on 150-2;
Ridderbos on 147;
Sanders on 147-9 (see Covenantal nomism);
Vos on 150fn.
Lord's Day observance: 165-86:
change from seventh to first day of the week 174-9, 173-7;
effects of Sabbath neglect 181-3;
effects of Sabbath observance 183-5;
intent of Colossians 2:16, Galatians 4:10, and Romans 14:5 170-1;
mankind's proper response to the Fourth Commandment 165-86;
meaning of "Lord's Day" 166-8;
proper observance of 180-1;
relationship between Lord's Day and Old Testament Sabbath institution 171-9;
special note on 185-6;
three objections addressed against universal and perpetual first-day Sabbath obligation 179-80;
Vos on change of day from seventh to first 178.

"New Perspective" on Paul's doctrine of justification, J. D. G. Dunn's 157-61.
New Testament church, activity of in doing theology 16-7.

Origin of universe:
Francis Schaeffer on 61-3;
Francis Thompson on 60-1;
vanity of modern cosmologists on 53-60.

Pentateuch, Mosaic authorship of 29-33;
critical view of 29-31;
J. B. Payne on 31;
K. Kitchen on 31-2.
Pharaoh and Egypt, divine rejection of 103-5.

Qur'an:
T. Carlyle on 402fn;
P. Schaff on 403fn;
teaching of on God as Trinity 404-6;
teaching of on Jesus' crucifixion and resurrection 412;
teaching of on Jesus' deity 410-2;
teaching of on Jesus' secondary place in revelational history 407-10.

Reasons for engaging in and doing theology 11.
Reconciliation, Barth's doctrine of 263-73;
criticism of 273-5.
Religious pluralism, Liberalism's doctrine of 368-70.
Review of Schuller's book on self-esteem 319-23.
Roman Catholicism:
a non-threat to all except Roman Catholics 389-99;
how this happened 390-5;
implications of its catechetical pronouncements 395-8.

Salvation principles governing the patriarchal age and the exodus 87-102:
in the exodus and Mosaism 98-102;
in patriarchal age, 88-98.
Satan 68fn, 70-1.
Schuller, Robert H.:
response to Reymond's review 323-6;
Reymond's reply to Schuller's response 326-38.
Self-esteem as the ground for a new reformation:
review of Schuller's book on 319-23.
Robert H. Schuller on 321-2;
Seventh day, length of 45fn.
Sin, infinite disvalue of 140
Systematic theology, department of in Reformed seminary, my vision of 113-6;
for the cultivation of students' *skills* in hermeneutics, analysis of theological treatises of church history, detection of and meaningful interaction with trends in contemporary theology, and application of scriptural theology to the world's needs 115;
for the growth and development of students' heart *attitudes* in reverence for Scripture, appreciation of their Reformed heritage, respect for the labors of systematic theologians, awe over the privilege to study God's Word, soberness, joy, meekness, and reliance upon God for all these things 115-6;
for the growth and development of students' *understanding* of the *loci* of theology, church history, the Reformed faith, and contemporary theology 114;
the department's professors as role models in these areas 116.

Theological method, Christ's 11-3.
Theology, biblical justification for engaging in 11-6.
Theology, justification of 9-28.
Trinity, doctrine of:
how we should support 117-24:
autotheotism of Son and Spirit must be upheld by any defense of 123;
caution with respect to deducing eternally continuing activities of the ontological Trinity from the Godhead's economical acts in history 118-9;
Warfield on economical activities of Trinity as reflection of terms of covenant of redemption 120.
Two modern Christologies 17-27.

Ugaritic study, contributions of to Old Testament study 77-85.
Unconditional election, *amicus* brief for 103-12.
Universalism, soteric 367-87

Westminster Trinitarianism, Nicene or

Reformed? 125-8.

Why Jesus must be God and man 129-43; Anselm on 129-30.

"Works of law" (*erga nomou*), Dunn's understanding of as Jewish "national identity markers" 158; correct meaning of 145fn.

Persons Index

al-Arabi, Abdullah   416
Albright, William F.   22, 83, 84fn.
Althaus, Paul   232
Anderson, Bernhard   31fn.
Anderson, H. George   317fn.
Anselm   129-30, 238, 358
Arberry, Arthur J.   407
Archer, Gleason L., Jr.   403fn.
Aquinas, Thomas   41fn., 140fn., 307-10, 311fn., 312-13, 316-18, 358
Athanasius   405
Augustine   41fn., 116, 119, 127, 212, 238, 307, 405

Barrett, C. K.   155fn., 156fn.
Barth, Karl   209, 213-14, 237-49, 250fn., 251-78
Bartsch, H. W.   277, 280fn.
Bashir, Umar (General)   413fn.
Bauer, Hans   78
Bavinck, Herman   116, 377fn.
Beale, G. K.   104fn.
Beasley-Murray, G. R.   20fn.
Berkhof, Louis   39, 43-4, 51, 69, 71, 72fn., 118
Berkouwer, G. C.   110fn., 238, 275, 318
Bernard of Clairvaux   212
Beza, Theodore   212
Biel, Gabriel   310fn.
Blocher, Henri   39fn.
Boettner, Loraine   127
Boice, James M.   172fn.
Bornkamm, Günther   277-8
Boyd, Jesse L., III   23fn.
Bray, Gerald   125
Bromiley, Geoffrey W.   159fn., 198fn., 239fn., 286fn.
Brown, Raymond E.   22, 24fn., 398
Bruce, F. F.   20, 25fn., 286fn.
Brunner, Emil   209-11, 213-14, 218-29, 230fn., 231-6
Buber, Martin   214
Bull, George   127
Bultmann, Rudolf   19-21, 23-4, 238-9, 277-301, 303-6
Burgess, Joseph A.   317fn.
Büschel, F   20fn.
Bush, George W.   414fn.

Buswell, J. Oliver, Jr.   28fn., 49, 127, 169fn., 175fn., 349
Byrne, B   162fn., 398

Calvin, John   28fn., 41fn., 72, 114, 116, 117fn., 119, 122fn., 123, 125, 127-8. 140fn., 162fn., 163, 201, 238, 240, 310fn., 319
Carlyle, Thomas   402fn., 403fn.
Carroll, Lewis   19
Carson, D. A.   73fn., 172fn., 185-6, 408
Casey, R. P.   22
Charles, R. H.   167fn.
Clark, Gordon Haddon   9, 217, 238, 259
Clay, Cassius   417
Cobb, John B., Jr.   209, 210fn., 212fn., 215, 221-2, 238, 255, 278, 279fn., 285fn., 289fn., 292, 296
Colson, Charles   376, 377fn.
Come, Arnold B.   238
Conzelmann, Hans   277
Cooper, Karl T.   157fn.
Cornhill, C. H.   210
Cranfield, C. E. B.   146, 147fn.
Crockett, William V.   377fn.
Crouch, Paul   376
Cyril of Alexandria   405

Dabney, Robert Lewis   44, 116
Darwin, [Charles]   210
Daube, D.   22
Davies, W. D.   22, 148fn.
Deissmann, G. Adolf   166fn.
Delitzsch, Franz   92, 344
de Margerie, Bertrand   117-18, 119fn.
Denifle, H.   310fn.
Dennison, Charles G.   185
De Witt, John R.   162fn.
Dixon, Larry   361fn.
Dodd, C. H.   12, 13fn., 22
Domitian, Emperor   166fn.
Dostoievski, Fyodor   237
Douglas, J. D.   32fn.
Downey, Roma   65fn.
Dunn, James D. G.   145-6, 148, 157-8, 161fn., 162
Dye, John   65fn.

Easton, B. S.   168-9, 170fn., 171fn., 172fn., 180fn.
Ebner, Ferdinand   214
Eckhart, Meister   212
Eddington, Sir Arthur   58
Eddy, Mary Baker   324
Edwards, David L.   339fn., 340fn., 341fn., 345fn., 349fn., 355fn., 359fn.
Edwards, Jonathan   316fn.
Eichhorn, Johann Gottfried   29
Einstein, [Albert]   55
Ellis, E. Earle   162fn.
Elwell, Walter A.   348fn., 356fn.
Epiphanius   406fn.
Erickson, Millard   378-380

Fadi, Abdal   404fn.
Farrakham, Louis   420
Fichte, Johann   210
Fitzmyer, Joseph A.   161fn., 162fn., 398
Foreman, Kenneth   311
Friedrich, Johannes   155fn.
Froehlich, Karl   317fn.
Fuller, Reginald   277
Fung, Ronald   155

Gaebelein, Frank E.   73fn.
Gaffin, Richard B., Jnr.   23fn., 185-6
Gamble, Richard C.   186
Gentry, Kenneth L., Jnr.   39fn.
Gerstner, Dr John H.   307-12, 315-18
Gibson, Charles   419
Godfrey, W. Robert   23fn.
Gordon, Cyrus   30, 77fn., 79fn., 80fn.
Goulder, M   369fn.
Graf, K. H.   29, 81, 210
Graham, Billy   376
Grant, George   414fn.
Gunkel, Hermann   277
Gunton, Colin   128
Gutbrod, W.   159fn.
Guth, Alan   56
Guthrie, Donald   339, 346, 356
Guttierez, G.   398

Hafemann, Scott J.   162fn.
Hahn, Scott   398
Hall, Rev. David W.   48
Harnack, Adolf von   237, 277
Harrison, Everett, F.   30fn., 170fn., 286fn., 341fn.
Hegel, Georg Wilhelm Friedrich   217
Heick, Otto W.   317fn.
Heidegger, Martin   278, 288-9, 296-7

Henderson, Ian   277
Hendriksen, William   377fn.
Henry, Carl F. H.   239fn., 277, 286fn, 307
Herrmann, Wilhelm   237, 277
Hick, John   368
Hodge, A. A.   116
Hodge, Charles   28fn., 41fn., 116, 117fn., 123fn. 127, 169, 172fn., 177, 184-5, 193fn., 201fn.
Howard, Thomas   398
Hume, David   212
Hunt, George   238fn.
Hupfeld, Hermann Christian Karl Friedrich   29
Husserl, Edmund   209
Hutchins, Robert Maynard   312fn.

Ibsen, Henrik   251
Ignatius, Bishop of Antioch   168

Jeans, Sir James   58
Jeremias, Joachim   196fn.
Jewett, Paul King   194fn., 209, 221fn., 229, 231-2, 233fn.
John Paul II, Pope   359, 376
Jones, Prof. David C.   11fn., 113fn.
Josephus, Flavius   153, 154fn.
Jülicher, Adolf   277
Justin Martyr   180

Kahle, P.   81
Kaiser, Walter C.   363-5
Kant, Immanuel   209-10, 214, 225
Käsemann, Ernst   23-6, 155fn., 277
Kegley, Charles W.   209, 214fn., 277, 278fn.
Keil, C. F.   87, 91
Kelly, J. N. D.   16fn.
Khomeini, Ayatollah   414fn., 419fn.
Kierkegaard, Søren   214-18, 232, 237, 251, 300
King, Henry Churchill   211
Kitchen, Kenneth A.   31-2
Kittel, Rudolf   81
Kline, Meredith G.   31fn., 39fn., 343
Klooster, Fred   238-9, 240fn., 241, 242fn., 251, 261fn., 262, 274fn., 275fn.
Knight, George W. III   16fn.
Kolb, Edward   57
Kreeft, Peter   374
Krodel, Gerhard   23fn.
Kruse, C. G   157fn.
Kuenen, Abraham   81, 210

Kuyper, Abraham   201fn.

Ladd, George E.   291fn., 297
Larue, Gerald A.   82, 83fn.
Lester, Toby   402fn.
Letham, Dr Robert   117-19, 123, 125, 127-8
Lewis, Jack P.   43fn.
Lindh, John Walker   417
Lloyd-Jones, Martyn   97, 321
Longenecker, B. W.   154fn.
Longman, Tremper   39fn.
Luther, Martin   41fn., 149, 161, 162fn., 163, 214, 227, 238, 310fn., 314fn., 317fn., 318-19
Lyell, Charles   210

Machen, J. Gresham   235
McGrath, Alister E.   309fn., 315
McKnight, Dr Scott   397
MacLeod, Donald   28fn.
McMullin, Ernan   41fn.
May, Herbert G.   31fn.
Meeter, John E.   27fn., 73fn.
Meier, J. P.   398
Metzger, Bruce M.   31fn.
Mitchell, Alex F.   126
Moo, Douglas, J.   149, 150, 151fn., 152, 155fn., 157fn., 158fn.
Montefiore, C. G.   147
Moore, G. F   147, 148fn.
Morey, Robert A.   374fn.
Morris, Henry   35fn.
Morris, Leon   25fn., 356, 359fn.
Moscati, Sabatino   77fn.
Motyer, J. A.   341, 344, 345fn.
Muir, William   404fn.
Muhammad   374, 380, 392-4, 403-7, 409-10, 412-13, 414fn., 417, 419
Müller, Karl   277
Murphy, T. Austin   317fn.
Murray, John   14, 28fn., 116, 123fn., 126-7, 139, 171-2, 173fn., 180, 185fn., 192-3, 197, 201, 382, 415

Nash, Ronald H.   369fn.
Nero, [Emperor]   167fn.
Neusner, Jacob   152fn.
Neve, J. L.   317fn.
Nicholas of Cusa   212
Nietzsche, [Friedrich]   251
Noordtzij, Arie   39fn.
Noth, Martin   30

Oberman, H. A.   317fn.
Ogden, Shubert   277
Olin, John C.   163fn.
Olson, Regina   214
Origen   360
Osburn, Evert D.   378fn.
Overbeck, Frank   237
Overbye, Dennis   56fn., 57fn.

Packer, James I.   302, 313fn., 360
Patton, Francis Landey   42fn.
Payne, D. F.   39fn.
Payne, J. Barton   31
Peale, Norman Vincent   323
Perkins, John   127
Peter of Poitiers   317
Peterson, Robert A.   362fn.
Pfeiffer, Charles F.   30fn.
Pfeiffer, Robert   81
Philips, Timothy   379
Pinnock, Clark H.   300, 301fn., 377-8, 384, 386
Piper, John   385fn.
Pöhlmann, Wolfgang   155fn.
Polman, A. D. R.   238
Powell, Colin   414fn.
Powell, Ralph E.   348
Pseudo-Dionysius   212

Rad, Gerhard von   30
Rafsanjani, Hashemi   413fn.
Rahner, Karl   371, 380, 394fn.
Ramm, Bernard   39, 213fn., 215fn., 216, 218
Ramus, Petrus   212
Rauschenbusch, Walter   211
Rayburn, Robert S.   204
Reese, Della   65fn.
Reymond, Robert L.   10fn., 117, 122fn., 323-5, 338, 383fn., 389fn.
Ridderbos, Herman N.   23, 24, 39fn., 147fn., 162fn., 277, 283, 286fn., 296fn., 298fn., 303, 350
Ritschl, Albrecht   209-10, 213
Robertson, O. Palmer   145
Robertson, Pat   376
Robinson, J. A. T.   360
Robinson, James M.   277
Rodwell, J. M.   412fn.
Root, Michael   315
Ross, Hugh   41fn.
Ross, Mark E.   39fn.
Rousseau, J. J.   251
Rushdie, Salman   419

Ryrie, C. C.   170fn., 172fn., 180fn.

Sagan, Carl   57-8
Sanders, E. P.   145-6, 148-53, 155, 156fn., 157-8, 161fn., 162
Sanders, John   378
Schaeffer, Claude F. A.   77
Schaeffer, Edith   62, 63fn.
Schaeffer, Dr Francis   54, 61, 63
Schaff, David S.   308fn.
Schaff, Philip   308fn., 310fn., 403fn., 405fn., 418fn., 419
Schelling, Friedrich W. J. von   215
Schleiermacher, Friedrich D. E.   209, 213, 251
Schnackenburg, R   24fn.
Schniewind, Julius   300
Schreiner, Thomas R.   162fn.
Schuller, Dr Robert H.   319-23, 326-36, 338, 376
Schultz, Charles   77
Seifrid, Mark A.   150fn., 154fn., 156fn.
Shahid, Samuel   415fn.
Shedd, G. T.   116
Shorrosh, Anis   420
Sigountos, James G.   377fn.
Simpson, J. P.   311-12
Smick, Elmer B.   30fn.
Smith, Gerald Birney   211
Smith, Morton H.   123fn., 127
Spencer, Aida Besançon   379
Sproul, R. C.   59, 307
Stirner, Max   251
Stott, Dr John   339-41, 345fn., 347, 349, 354-7, 359-61, 369fn., 378, 379fn.
Stuhlmacher, Peter   155fn.
Sungenis, Robert   398

Tertullian   212
Thielicke, Helmut   299
Thomas, Geoffrey   129.
Thompson, Francis   60-1

Thompson, J. A.   39fn.
Thomson, G. T   239fn
Thornwell, James Henley   116
Thurneysen, Eduard   237
Tienou, Tite   379
Tillich, Paul   282
Toplady, Augustus M.   142
Tisdall, St Clair   404fn.
Torrance, T. F.   238, 239fn.
Troeltsch, Ernst   209
Tryon, Edward P.   56
Turretin, Francis   116

Unger, Merrill F.   81, 83, 84fn.

Van Impe, Jack   376
Van Til, Cornelius   209, 238, 269
Vilenkin, Alex   56
Virolleaud, Charles   78
Vitz, Paul   322
Voetius, Gisbertus   212
Vos, Geerhardus   45fn., 87fn., 88fn., 90fn., 91fn., 92, 93fn., 94, 95fn., 97, 98fn.,108fn., 111-12, 150fn., 172fn., 178, 190fn., 351-2, 409fn., 411fn.

Warfield, Benjamin B.   27, 28fn., 41fn., 73, 74fn., 116, 118fn., 120, 121fn., 123fn., 125, 127, 201fn., 331, 365
Weber, Otto   238
Weiss, Johannes   277
Wellhausen, Julius   29, 80-1, 210, 226
Wesley, Charles   75
Westerholm, S   156fn., 160fn.
Whitcomb, John   35fn.
White, Andrew Dickson   41fn.
Wiles, Maurice   369
Wilhelm II, (Kaiser)   237

Yamauchi, Edwin M.   22
Young, Edward J.   49fn., 80
Young, G. Douglas   80
Youngblood, Ronald   39fn.

Index of Bible Characters

Aaron 80, 406fn.
Abel 35, 36, 173fn., 189
Abihu 357
Abimelech 92
Abraham 16, 34-6, 88-93, 95-8, 105-6, 149, 155, 160, 190-6, 198, 207, 313, 318, 342, 373, 383, 392, 418
Achan 357
Adam 33, 36, 40, 41fn., 45fn., 46fn., 47-8, 50, 71, 130-1, 133-4, 135fn., 172, 188-9, 263, 273-4, 276, 357, 379, 415fn.
Ahab 82
Ahaz 346
Ananias 71, 357
Apollos 14

Caiaphas 230
Cain 34-5, 173fn.
Cornelius 383-6

David 36, 71, 131-2, 222, 333, 358, 365, 372fn., 391fn.

Elihu 79
Elijah 82-3
Enoch 189
Esau 95-7, 106-8, 111
Eve 47, 50, 68, 415fn.
Ezekiel 80

Gabriel 67
Gamaliel 325, 327, 334-5

Hagar 89, 95, 106, 155

Isaac 36, 88, 90-3, 95-6, 98, 106, 191, 195, 414fn.
Isaiah 69, 352
Ishmael 89, 90, 95, 105-6, 195, 414fn., 418fn.

Jacob 36, 88, 91-8, 100, 106-8, 111, 191, 195
Japheth 190
Jehoshaphat 196
Jethro 383-4
Jezebel 82

Job 71, 383-4
Joel 197
John (apostle) 18, 21fn., 23-7, 118, 133, 166-8, 170, 180, 233, 291, 293, 354, 362, 365, 371, 380, 394, 418
John the Baptist 345
Joseph 91, 93fn., 94fn., 415fn.
Joseph, (of Arimathea) 269
Joshua 29, 32, 196
Joshua (high priest) 71
Josiah 30, 346
Judas (Iscariot) 71, 255-7, 259, 348
Jude 354

Khersonni (high priest) 81
Kish 352

Lazarus 25
Lot 342, 357
Luke 36, 293, 334, 384

Manasseh 346
Martha 25
Mary (of Bethany) 25
Mary (mother of Jesus) 191, 374, 392, 405-6, 410, 418
Matthew 233, 284, 293
Melchizedek 383
Michael 67
Miriam 406fn.
Moses 12, 29, 31-5, 41-3, 46-7, 49, 69, 71, 87, 99-101, 103-4, 108, 155, 159, 195-6, 343, 357, 373fn., 380, 383-4, 391fn., 394, 406fn., 416
Naaman 383-4
Nadab 357
Noah 34, 35fn., 36fn., 189-90, 342

Paul (apostle) 12, 14-16, 26, 58-9, 66, 71, 87-8, 95, 98, 105-12, 120, 132-3, 137, 142fn., 145, 146, 147fn., 148-50, 151fn., 152fn., 153fn., 155-63, 169-71, 191-4, 197, 200, 222, 227, 233-4, 238, 248, 274-5, 283, 289, 291, 293, 297, 301-3, 305, 309fn., 312, 313fn., 314, 318-20, 333, 336-7, 350-3, 370, 372fn., 373fn., 377, 381-2, 389, 391fn., 392fn., 394, 418

Peter (apostle) 36fn., 71, 73-4, 102, 160, 191, 197, 230, 256, 302, 354, 357, 365, 370, 380, 384-6, 394, 418
Potiphar 94fn.

Rebekah 93fn., 106

Sapphira 357
Sarah 90, 95, 106, 155fn.
Satan 68-71, 189
Shem 190
Silas 14

Solomon 131
Stephen 99, 193

Terah 91
Thomas (apostle) 21, 301
Timothy 14

Uzzah 357

Zechariah 191
Zipporah 195

Scripture Index – Old Testament

Genesis
1 40-2, 43, 44, 45fn., 46,
   48, 49, 51, 63, 68, 263
1-11 29, 33-7, 190, 226
1:1 47, 58
1:1–2:3 49
1-2 33, 35, 40, 173fn.
1:3, 6, 7 46
1:5 40, 44
1:8 40, 44
1:9, 11 46
1:13 40, 44
1:14 40fn.
1:14-15 46
1:14-18 40
1:16-18 45
1:19 40, 44
1:23 40, 44
1:24 46
1:26 46, 365
1:27 36, 46, 47
1:28 173
1:29-30 48
1:31 40, 44, 45fn. , 67-8
2 42, 43, 49, 63, 68, 174
2:1-3 46fn., 173, 174
2:2-3 44, 181, 186
2:3 172
2:4 34, 40, 42, 43fn.
2:5 40, 43
2:5-6 49, 50
2:7, 9 43
2:15 173
2:19-20 40, 50
2:22 43
2:24 36, 47, 173
3 35, 45fn., 68
3-11 36
3:1 70
3:1-5 71
3:1-7 189
3:5-6 357
3:8 298
3:15 88, 189
3:20 189
3:24 69, 298
4 35
4:3 173

4:4 189
4:7 81
4:23-4 34, 49
5 36
5:1 34
5:3 45fn.
5:22-3 189
6–9 35
6:2-4 67fn.
6:5 190
6:5-6 131
6:5-8 342
6:8-9 189
6:9 34
7:19-20 35fn.
7:24 35fn.
8:5-7 35fn.
8:10 35fn., 36fn., 173
8:12 173
8:13, 14 36fn.
8:21 36fn., 131
9:3 48
9:26-7 190
10 190
10:1 34
11 35, 36
11:1-11 190
11:10 34
11:27 34, 91
12 88
12-50 34-6
12:1-3 190
12:3 191-2
12-18 90
12:1-25:11 88
13:14-16 190
14:22 383
15:6 16, 90, 91, 193
15:7-21 190
15:12-21 89
16 89
17:1 89, 91
17:1-6 195
17:1-16 190, 193
17:7 193
17:7-9 204
17:12, 14 195
17:16 93

17:18-19 89
17:19 191
17:22 93
17:23-4 195
17:24 16
18, 19 67
18:17-19 91
18:23-32 91
18:25 355
19:16, 24 342
19:26 357
19:27-8 173, 342
20-25 90
21:1-7 89
21:9 106
21:12 95
21:17 69
22:5 90
22:15-18 91
22:16-18 190
25:3-4 195
25:5 93
25:12, 19 34
25:19-35:29 91
25:23 95
25:22-3 108
26:3-4 191, 195
26:17-22 93
28 95
28:3 89
28:13-14 195
28:13-15 191
28:15 96
28:20-1 96
30:30 96
32:1 73
32:22-32 96
32:24, 28 97
35:11 89
36:1, 9 34
37:1-50:13 93
37:2 34, 94fn.
39:2-6 94fn.
39:20-23 94fn.
41:57 94fn.
43:14 89
45:5 94fn.
45:8-9 94fn.

45:25–46:2   97
48:2   97
49:2   97
49:25   89
49:27   44fn.
50:20   94fn.

Exodus
2:11-15   100, 103fn.
2:24   191
3-14   103
3:18   101
3:19-20   100
4:17   100
4:21   104
4:22-3   100
4:23   101
4:24-6   195
5:1   101
6:3   89
6:6   99
6:13, 30   193
7-12   358
7:3   101, 104
7:6-13   104
7:14   104fn.
7:16   101
7:22   104fn.
8:1   101
8:15   104fn., 105
8:19   104fn., 105
8:20   101
8:22-3   100
8:25, 28   101
8:32   104fn.
9:1   101
9:4   100
9:7   104fn.
9:12   104fn., 105
9:13   101
9:16   105
9:25-6   100
9:34   104fn.
9:35   104fn., 105
10:1   103, 104fn.
10:1-2   101
10:3   101
10:11   101
10:20   104fn.
10:22-3   100
10:24   101
10:27   104fn.
11:7   100
11:9   101, 103

11:10   104fn.
12:12   100
12:12-13   101
12:15   45
12:21-7   101
12:37   102
13:20-2   102
14:4, 8   104fn.
14:13   99
14:17   104fn.
14:21-3   102
14:30   99
15   101, 102, 103
15:13   99
16   173
16:4   102
16:5   173
16:8, 13   44fn.
16:13-15   102
16:22-30   173
17:1-6   102
17:8-16   102
17:14   29
18:8-12   384
18:13-14   44fn.
19:5-6   99, 193
20:1-2   102
20:1-17   176
20:2   172, 174, 176
20:6   204
20:8   181
20:8-10   173
20:8-11   174
20:10   175
20:11   35, 46, 47, 176
21:1   183
23:7   313fn.
24:4   29
24:16   45
25:18   69
27:21   44fn.
31:14-15   183
31:15-17   47
31:17   35
34:25   101
34:27   29
35:2   181

Leviticus
6:20   44fn.
10:1-2   357
12:3   45
19:23   193
20:10   183

24:3   44fn.
26:14-39   358
26:41   193
26:42   191

Numbers
3:4   80
9:15, 21   44fn.
12:3   31
12:6-8   29, 43
15:30-6   175
15:32-6   183, 357
20:11   357
23:9   158
33:2   29
33:3-49   31

Deuteronomy
1:8   191
2:30   104fn.
2:34   343
3:6   343
4:32   35
5:15   172, 176
6:4-25   202
6:6-7   204
7:6   99, 193
7:6-8   100
7:8   99, 191
9:6-7   100
9:26   99
10:16   193
14:1   100
14:2   193
16:4   44fn.
18:14-21   29
18:15-19   32
28:15-68   358
28:67   44fn.
29:9-13   195
29:23   342
30:6   193
31:9   29
31:10-13   196
31:24   29
33:2   66
33:2-29   31
34   29, 31

Joshua
7:11, 25   357
8:35   196
11:20   104fn.
23:6   29

24:2   88
24:3   191
24:14   100

Judges
3:4   29

Ruth
4:18-20   36

1 Samuel
9:3, 20   352
15:22-3   147fn.
17:16   44fn.

2 Samuel
6:6-7   357
14:20   67
24:16   67, 69-70

1 Kings
6:23-32   69
8:46   131
17–19   82
17:1   82
17:6   44fn.
18:1-7   82
18:28   82
18:41-6   83
19:5-7   69
22:19   66

2 Kings
5:15-18   384
6:15-17   66
6:16   69
13:23   191
16:15   44fn.
19:35   70
20:7   78
23:10   346

1 Chronicles
1   36
16:40   44fn.
21:1   71
21:16   70
23:30   44fn.

2 Chronicles
2:4   44fn.
13:11   44fn.
20:13   196
28:3, 33   346

31:3   44fn.
36:20-1   182

Ezra
3:3   44fn.
6:3   80

Nehemiah
7:2   79
13:15-22   182

Esther
2:14   44fn.

Job
1-2   70-1
1:6   66-7
1:12   70
1:21   384
2:6   70
2:7   71
4:20   44fn.
5:1   66
19:25   384
21:26   346
24:20   346
31:33   35
38:7   66, 69

Psalms
2:7   176
5:9   132
8:5   66
10:7   133
14:1-3   131-2
14:2-3   335
16   365
19:1   234
22:9   204
22:9-10   201
29:1   66
33:6   35, 46
33:8   185
33:9   46
33:12   185
33:12-15, 18-19   185
34:7   69
36:1   133
40:6-8   147fn.
45:6   365
51:4   333, 358
51:5   131
51:16-17   147fn.
55:17   44fn.

58:3   132
68:17   66
71:6   204
73:22-3   282
80:1   69
83:5-6   106
90:2   35
90:6   44fn.
90:17   116
91:11-12   69
95:7-11   46fn.
99:1   69
102:25-27   22
103:17-18   204
103:20   67, 69
104:4   69
104:24   299
105:25   104fn.
110   13, 365
110:4   384
118:22-4   176
119:9   79
127:2   187
128:3-4   187
130:3   132
130:4   162fn.
136:5-9   35
139   79
140:3   133
143:2   132
144:15   185
145:17   299
148:2   66, 69
148:2-5   35
148:5   66

Proverbs
4:18   298
16:4   110
20:27   134

Ecclesiastes
7:20   132
7:29   130
9:3   132
11:6   44fn.
12:14   343

Isaiah
1:2-3   100
1:9   342
1:10-20   147fn.
5:7   408
5:11   44fn.

5:23   313fn.
6:1   69fn.
6:1-10   22
6:2 , 6-7   69
7:14   78, 84
8:12-13   22
14:4   68fn.
14:11   346
14:12, 16   68fn.
17:14   44fn.
29:16   109
30:33   346
37:16   69
40:25-6   35
42:5   35
43:6   100
43:27   35
44:3   204
44:24   35
45:9   109
45:12   35
45:22   22
48:13   35
49:1-6   201
51:13   35
53:4-6   189fn.
53:6   132
54:9   35
54:13   204
56:2-8   184
57:1   352
58:13   167
58:13-14   184
59:7-8   133
59:21   204
63:16   100
64:6   132
64:8   100, 109
66:22-4   343-4
66:24   346

Jeremiah
1:5   201
4:4   193
3:4   100

6:10   193
9:25   193
10:12   35
13:23   136, 380
17:9   132, 336
17:24-5   184
17:27   181
18:6   109
23:14   342
31:9   100
31:33   193
36   29
49:18   342

Lamentations
4:6   342

Ezekiel
1:26-8   69
20:13   182
22:26   182
23:8, 19, 21   100
24:18   44fn.
33:22   44fn.
35:5   106fn.
37:25   204

Daniel
7:10   66
7:13-14   13
8:16   67
8:16-17   70
9:22   70
9:21   67
10:11–11:1   71
10:13   67fn., 68
10:21   68
12:1   68
12:2   343-4

Hosea
6:7   35, 130, 189
11:1   100
12:4-5   96
12:13   101

Joel
2:16   196
2:32   22
2:28-34   197

Amos
2:6-8   147fn.
4:4-5   147fn.
4:11   342
4:13   35
5:21-4   147fn.

Micah
6:6-8   147fn.

Habakkuk
1:5-11   358
2:2-3   29

Zephaniah
2:9   342
3:3   44fn.

Zechariah
3:1   69-71
12:1   35

Malachi
1:2,3   106fn.
1:6   100
2:10   100
4:1-6   358
4:4   29

Apocrypha

Ecclesiasticus / Sirach
3:3, 14-15, 30-1   153
29:11-13   153

2 Esdras   153, 154fn.

Tobit
4:7-11   153

Scripture Index – New Testament

Matthew
1:1   191
1:18   84
1:20-1   69
1:25   84
2:2   384
2:10-12   384
3:9   198, 373fn., 392fn.
3:12   345
3:16   189fn.
4:1   189fn.
4:3   70
4:4, 7,10   28
4:11   71, 189fn.
5:1   320
5:17-18   28
5:21–6:18   147fn.
5:22   346
5:27-32   183
5:29   351
5:29-30   346
5:37   70
6:13   70
7:13   346, 351
7:18   136
7:21   22
7:22-3   359fn.
8:11   191
8:12   347
8:16   66
8:29   72, 350
9:4   28
9:34   70
9:37   387
10:15   342, 347
10:28   347
11:22, 24   347
11:25-28   22
12:3-4   175, 181
12:5   175
12:11-13   175, 181
12:24   70
12:29   70-1
12:41-2   359fn.
12:45   66
13:19   70
13:25, 28   70
13:38-9   70

13:40-3   359fn.
13:41   70
13:42   348
13:49   70
16:23   71
18:6, 8-9   348
18:10   72-3
18:20   22
19:4-5   35-6, 47
19:13-15   196
20:28   142fn.
21:33-45   401fn., 408
21:42   412
21:42-3   409
22:13   347
22:30   67
22:41-5   12
22:42   17
23:1-39   147fn.
23:33   348
23:35   35-6
23:37a   408
24:30   22
24:31   70
24:36   67
24:37-9   35-6
24:51   347, 359fn.
25:30   347
25:31-46   331
25:34   138
25:37   22
25:41   71-2, 138, 298, 306, 348
25:41-6   359fn.
25:44   22
25:46   138, 348
26:24   348
28:1   168
28:6   70
28:17   303
28:18   174
28:18-20   13, 370
28:20   17

Mark
1:24   72
2:5, 8   22
2:27-8   173fn., 174

3:22   70
5:9   72
5:29, 30   351
7:1-13   147fn.
8:33   71
9:43   346, 351
9:44, 46   351
9:47-8   346
9:48   344, 351
10:6   47
10:6-8   36
10:13-16   196
10:45   142fn.
12:1-12   401fn., 408
12:9   359fn., 409
12:10-11   412
13:32   28
14:21   340
16:2   168

Luke
1:9, 11   67
1:14   69
1:15   69, 201
1:19, 26   67
1:34-5   69
1:41-4   201
1:54-5   191
1:68-75   191
2:14   69
2:52   28
3   36
4:6   71
4:14-21   12
7:21   66
8:2   66
8:30   66
9:56   142fn
10:2   387
10:12, 14   347
10:21-2   22
11:13   132, 321
11:15   70
11:18-22   71
11:26   66
11:37-54   147fn.
11:51   35
12:5   347, 349, 351

12:8-9   70
12:47-8   349
13:10-16   175
13:11, 16   71
13:25-30   359fn.
13:27   349
14:1-6   175
15:4, 6, 8-9   352
15:10   9, 74
15:17   352
16:17   29
16:19-28   359fn.
16:22   69
16:23-4, 28   349
17:2   348
17:26-7   35
17:26-30   36fn.
17:29   342
18:13-14   333
18:15-17   196
19:10   142fn.
20:9-19   401fn., 408
20:16   409
20:17-18   412
21:36   359fn.
22:31   71
22:52-3   71
24:1   168
24:13   168
24:25-7   12
24:26   168
24:27   28
24:39   66
24:46-7   380
24:47   370, 387

John
1   263
1:1   20, 22, 370
1:1ff   244, 260
1:1-2   243
1:1-3   26
1:2-3   35
1:9   134
1:13   198, 373fn., 392fn.
1:14   20-1, 23-4, 25fn.
1:18   20, 22, 370
1:29, 36   26
1:45   25
1:47   28
2:1-11   21fn.
2:4   26
2:11   21
2:19, 21   365

2:25   28
3:1-8   189fn.
3:2   21
3:3, 5   136
3:13   22
3:16   354
3:18   138, 354, 371, 394fn.
3:19   379, 380
3:20   379
3:36   138, 332, 354
4:24   134
4:29   25
4:35   387
5:12   25
5:17   45fn., 46fn., 181
5:22-30   359fn.
5:28-9   350
5:43   32
5:46   12, 373fn., 391fn.
5:46-7   29, 32
6:36   336
6:38   22
6:42   25
6:44   136, 380
6:46, 62   22
6:65   136, 380
6:66   334
7:27   25
7:30   26
7:46   25
8:20   26
8:40   25
8:23   22
8:24   394
8:32   134
8:42   22
8:43   136
8:44   68, 70-1
8:56   191
8:56-8   196
8:58   22
9:6   25
9:11   25
9:16   21, 25
9:24   25
10:11, 15   26
10:18   189fn.
10:33   25
10:35   28-9
11:11, 14   28
11:35   25
11:45-8   21
11:47   25

12:10-12   21
12:23, 24   26
12:27   25
12:31   70
12:32   341
12:37-41   21
12:40-1   22
12:47, 48   359fn.
13:1   26
13:2   71
13:16   120
13:27   71
14:2   306
14:6   370, 380, 394, 419
14:16   118, 407
14:17   136, 407
14:26   118, 407
14:28   120
14:30   70
15:4-5   136, 380
15:6   359fn.
15:22-5   359fn.
15:26   117-18, 407
16:7   118
16:7-8   407
16:8-11   359fn.
16:11   70
16:12-15   337
16:13-14   407
16:13-15   118
17   189fn.
17:1   26
17:2   93fn., 174
17:6   22, 93fn.
17:9, 11, 12   93fn.
17:24   22, 93fn.
18:17   25
18:29   25
19:2-3   25
19:5   25
19:34   25
19:35   25fn.
19:38, 40   25
20:1   168, 171, 177
20:19   168, 177
20:22   118
20:25   21
20:25-8   303
20:26   168-9, 177
20:27   21, 301
20:28   21-2, 370
20:29   21
21:24   21

Acts
1:3   303
1:8   370
1:9   189fn.
1:11   70
2:1-4   197
2:22   21
2:23   189fn.
2:24-31   365
2:38-9   204
2:39   197
2:42   171
2:46   168
3:22   189fn.
3:25-6   191
4:10-11   176
4:12   370, 377fn., 380, 388, 394, 419
4:16   21
4:27-8   189fn., 299
5:1-10   357
5:3   71
5:19   73
5:38   325
6:7   193
7:23-9   100, 103fn.
7:35   99
7:53   69
9:2   17
9:5   301
9:22   14
10:2, 15, 22   384
10:28   158, 385
10:29   385
10:34-5   384
10:38   70
10:43   384
11:14   384
11:18   385
12:15   72, 73
12:23   70
13:10   71
13:32-3   176
13:39   159
14:16   385fn.
15:1   155
15:1-16:5   16
15:5   155
15:28-9   179
16:14-15   204
16:31   204
17:2-3   14, 17
17:17   14
17:23   385fn.

17:24-5   268
17:27   14
17:30   385fn.
17:31   359fn.
17:32-4   305
18:18, 21   171
18:28   14, 17
19:8   15
19:12   66
20:7   166, 168, 171, 177, 180
20:9-11   181
20:17-35   15
20:28   370
21:20-7   171
24:25   359fn.
25:21-6   167fn.
26:15   301
26:18   71
28:23   29

Romans
1:3   159fn.
1:4   21, 22
1:17   162, 314fn.
1:18   234, 332
1:18-32   132, 159, 182
1:19-21   134, 379
1:20-2   234
1:21-3   59
1:23-4   379
1:25   59, 134, 380
1:26, 28   379
1:32   134, 234, 359fn., 379
2:2-3   359fn.
2:5   332, 356, 359fn.
2:5-10   139
2:8   134, 332
2:8-9   352
2:12   352, 381
2:14-15   379, 380
2:15   134, 234
2:16   356
2:17   161
2:17-24   373fn., 392fn.
2:21-9   159
2:25   91
2:25-9   373fn., 392fn.
2:28-9   105
3-8   105
3:1-2   199
3:5   15, 332
3:9   15, 159, 373fn.,

392fn.
3:9-10   379
3:9-18   335
3:9-23   132
3:9-28   382
3:11   234
3:19   158fn.
3:19-20   380
3:20   146fn., 150fn.,159, 160
3:21-5   159
3:21-8   161
3:23   110fn., 379, 380
3:25   332
3:25-6   313fn.
3:27   160
3:28   146fn., 160, 162
3:28-30   159
4   312
4:1   15
4:1-5   161
4:2   146fn., 160
4:2ff   312
4:3   193
4:3-4   312
4:4-5   88, 160
4:5   162, 189fn., 308fn., 313
4:6   146fn., 313
4:8-11   313
4:11   91, 193
4:11-12   192
4:13   89, 192
4:15   333
4:16   90
4:18-24   193
4:19-21   89
4:22-4   313
4:25   255fn.
5:1   318
5:1-5   298
5:8   264
5:10   275
5:12   298
5:12ff   274
5:12-19   35, 130, 189fn., 357
5:13   333
5:14   298
5:16   359fn.
5:18   359fn.
5:20   264, 298
6:1   15
6:4   110fn.

6:6   101
6:10   193
6:15   15
6:17   16
6:17-22   101
6:21   352
6:23   298, 352, 379
7:4-6   101
7:7   15
7:7-11   333
7:23-5   101
8:2-4   101
8:7   137, 336
8:7-8   136, 380
8:11   189fn.
8:20-3   48
8:28-39   110
8:29-30   189fn.
8:31   15
8:32   255fn.
9   95, 105, 107fn.
9-11   240, 248
9:4   100, 199, 372, 392
9:5   22, 199, 370, 372, 392
9:6   105
9:7-9   106
9:10-13   198
9:11   189fn.
9:11-12   112
9:11-13   95, 106-7, 111
9:12   146fn.
9:14   15, 111
9:14-19   108
9:16-18   109
9:17   101, 105
9:18   104fn., 105
9:20-3   108-9
9:21   105
9:22   352
9:23   110fn.
9:29   342
9:30   15
9:30-32   156
9:30–10:21   156fn.
9:31   372fn., 391fn.
9:32   146fn.
10–11   249
10:2-4   156
10:4   162
10:9   16
10:9-13   22
10:13-15   381
10:14   301

10:19   29
11:2   16
11:5   16, 108, 112, 146, 157, 163
11:6   146fn., 157, 163
11:7   15
11:7-10   372fn., 391fn.
11:16-24   192
11:33   112
13:1-5   134
14   170
14:5   170-1
14:10   359fn.
14:10-12   352
15:4   87, 98

1 Corinthians
1:18   352
1:20-1   234
1:30   419
2:6-7   29
2:8   22
2:14   136, 234, 380
3:5-7   381
3:10-15   329
3:17   353
3:23   120
5:7   101
5:13   359fn.
6:3   66
7:14   197, 204
7:29-31   282-3
9:9   29
10:1-2   197
10:2-4   102
10:1-11   98
10:11   87
10:20   71
11:2   255fn.
11:3   120
11:10   69
11:20-2   180
11:23   255fn.
12:3   16, 22, 137, 280
14:26   180
15:3   255fn.
15:5-8   302
15:28   341, 359
15:51-2   189fn.
16:1   169
16:2   166, 168-71, 177, 179-80
16:22   353

2 Corinthians
4:4   70
4:5   22
5:10   353, 359fn.
5:15, 17   101
6:15   70
10:3-4   381, 414fn.
11:3   35
11:14   70
12:7   66, 71

Galatians
1:6-7   162
1:6-9   276, 323
1:8-9   163, 377
1:9   350
1:15   201
2:11-13   158
2:15-16   160
2:16   145fn., 160-2
2:20   255fn.
2:21   157, 163
3:2, 5   146fn. 160
3:8-9   192
3:10   146fn., 157, 166fn., 373fn., 392fn.
3:10-11   161-2
3:13-14   192
3:15   191
3:16-18   192
3:19a   69
3:22   133
3:26   162
3:29   192
4:4   26
4:10   170
4:21-31   106, 155
4:21-5:1   373fn., 392fn.
4:29   106
5:2   157, 163
5:2-5   373fn., 392fn.
5:3   157, 163, 166fn.
5:4   163
5:17   98
5:24   294
6:7   359fn.
6:13   373fn., 392fn.
6:16   192

Ephesians
1:1   197
1:3-6   189fn.
1:6   109fn.
1:7   109fn., 298

1:10   341, 359
1:11   299
1:12, 14   109fn.
1:19-20   189fn.
2:1   137, 234, 379
2:1-3   133, 336
2:2   70
2:3   252, 298, 332, 380
2:9   146fn.
2:16   275
3:9   35
3:9-10   122
3:10   67-8
4:6   202
4:17-19   133, 234, 336
4:18   380
5:2, 25   255fn.
6:1   197
6:1-3   205
6:4   202, 204
6:11   71
6:12   66, 71
6:13   71
6:16   70

Philippians
2:6-11   270
2:10   341, 359
2:11   22, 341, 359
3:2-3   192
3:8-9   162
3:17   171
3:19   353
4:9   171

Colossians
1:10-11   298
1:13   71
1:16   35, 66, 68
1:20   257, 275, 341, 359
1:22   275
2:3   203, 419
2:9   22, 419
2:11-12   194
2:13   137
2:15   26, 71
2:16   170
3:16   180
3:20   205
4:17   179

1 Thessalonians
1:10   332, 350
2:13   15, 29

2:15   337
2:15-16   372fn., 391fn.
2:18   70
3:5   70
4:6   359fn.
4:16   67
5:1-10   359fn.
5:3   350

2 Thessalonians
1:5-10   359fn.
1:7   67
1:7-10   22
1:9   351
2:3-12   359fn.
2:10-12   134
2:13   298
2:15   16, 255fn.
3:3   70

1 Timothy
1:15   16, 142fn.
2:4   134
2:5   370, 381, 394
2:6   418
2:13-14   35
3:1   16
3:1-7   337
3:16   16
4:8-9   16
5:15   70
5:21   67, 69
6:20   16

2 Timothy
1:9   189fn.
2:2   17, 337
2:11-13   16
2:25   134
2:26   70-1
3:15   204
3:15-16   29
3:15-17   37, 53
3:16   15, 28-30
3:16-17   408
4:1   359fn.
4:4   134

Titus
1:2   302
1:5-11   337
1:9   14, 17
2:1   17
2:13   22, 370

3:3   380
3:3-8   16
3:5   161, 193

Hebrews
1:1-2   409
1:2   35
1:3   189fn., 299
1:8   22, 370
1:10-12   22
1:14   69, 74
2:2   69
2:2-3   409
2:14   71, 189fn.
2:14-15   26
2:14-17   140
2:17   332
3:7–4:11   173fn., 174
4:3-6   46fn., 174
4:9   186
4:9-11   174
4:12, 13   359fn.
4:14   189fn.
5:5-10   189fn.
5:8   93fn.
6:2   353
6:4-8   359fn.
6:13-18   100
7-10   384
7:23-6   141
9:5   69
9:14   141
9:22   412
9:22-4   141
9:27   353
10:5-7   189fn.
10:25   165, 177, 180
10:26-31   353, 359fn.
10:29   205
11:3-4   35
11:4-5   189
11:6   301
11:7   35, 189
11:8-10   88
11:17-19   90, 93fn.
11:20   93
12:9-11   205
12:29   353
13:20   189fn.

James
2:8-11   166fn.
2:13   359fn.
2:21-3   91

3:1 337
3:8 137, 380
4:12 359fn.

1 Peter
1:2 189fn.
1:11 337
1:12 67, 74
2:7-8 359fn.
2:9 99, 102
2:11-12 102
2:23 359fn.
3:12 359fn.
3:14-15 22
3:19-20 342
3:20 35
3:20-1 197
4:17-18 359fn.
5:8 70

2 Peter
1:1 22, 370
1:16 89fn.
1:16-18 302
1:20-1 29, 37, 53
2:3-10 359fn. (check)
2:4 68
2:4-9 354
2:5 35, 342
2:6-9 342
2:11 67
3:3-7 36fn.
3:6 35
3:7 359fn.
3:10 167
3:15-16 15
3:18 298

1 John
1:1-3 21
1:8, 10 133
2:2 332
2:13-14 70
2:23 380, 394
3:1 298
3:4 297, 333
3:7-8 359fn.
3:12 35, 70
4:10 332
5:12 381, 394, 418
5:18 70
5:19 70, 133
5:20 22, 370, 401
5:21 401, 420

Jude
3 7, 16
4-6 359fn.
6 68
6-7 354
7 342
9 67-9, 71
11 35
13, 15 359fn.

Revelation
1:10 165-6, 170-1, 177
2:9 71
2:10 70
2:26, 31 94fn.
3:5 70
3:9 71
4:6-9 69
4:11 35, 189fn.
5:11 66, 69

5:11-12 74
9:11 70
10:6-7 35
11-21 359fn.
11:8 342
12:7 67-8
12:9, 10 70
12:12 70
12:17 70
13:11-17 370
14:3 380
14:7 359fn.
14:9-11 139, 354, 359fn.
14:11 70
14:13 174
14:17-20 359fn.
15:1 359fn.
16 359fn.
16:11, 21 358
19–21 189fn.
19:1-3 359fn.
19:1-5 360
19:3 354
19:6-10 360
19:20 355
20:2-3 70
20:7 70
20:10 348, 355-6
20:11-15 189fn., 359fn.
20:12-14 306
20:12-15 355
22:15 359fn.
22:17 356, 361

Other Books from
Christian Focus
by Robert L Reymond

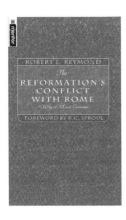

The Reformation's Conflict with Rome – Why it Must Continue

Robert L Reymond

Foreword by R.C. Sproul

Dr. Reymond clearly demonstrates in this monograph that there are several serious doctrinal differences between Roman Catholic teaching and Biblical Christianity... I am confident the reader will find this work clear, fair and accurate. I highly commend its close reading. **R.C. Sproul**

The Christian public is indebted to Dr. Reymond for producing such a lucid and incisive volume evaluating modern attempts to rejoin Protestant churches with the Roman Catholic Church... The reader will be well-informed by this decisive, but irenic, rejection of the notion that the Roman church has always embraced the biblical concept of justification by faith.
Richard L. Mayhue, The Master's Seminary

Robert Reymond is to be warmly commended for producing such a lucid book on the Reformation controversy with Rome, and why that controversy must continue even today.
Nick Needham, Highland Theological College

Written in an inoffensive yet honest way, Robert Reymond has studied the essential divisions between Roman Catholics and the Reformed church to find out the real issues and points of conflict.

Reymond looks at historical watersheds of doctrine, the development of Roman Catholic authority and contemporary attempts at rapprochement (including *'Evangelicals and Catholics Together'* and Robert Sungenis' *'Not by Faith Alone'*). In doing so he helps us understand the great truths of salvation worked out through the sacrifice of Jesus, the Messiah.

ISBN 1-85792-626-9

Jesus – Divine Messiah
The New and Old Testament Witness
Robert L. Reymond

What does the Bible REALLY say about Jesus?

'He takes great care to analyse various critical views of recent vintage and to show how they fail to give us a consistent picture of Christ. Probably not since H.P. Liddon's The Divinity of our Lord *(1867) has such a massive defence of the deity of Jesus appeared in print. Dr. Reymond worthily functions in the train of G. Vos, B.B. Warfield, and J.G. Machen.'*
Roger Nicole, Reformed Theological Seminary, Orlando

'The range of his scholarship is extensive, and there is no exegetical or theological nettle that he hesitates to grasp here. He never fudges an issue... required reading for every theological student.'
Geoffrey Grogan

'Dr. Reymond has an impressive acquaintance with the literature on the subject, and he has not shirked the difficult issues. He has rendered a service to the whole church in dealing so thoroughly with the evidence and giving his up-to-date assessment of its significance.' **Leon Morris**

'This volume displays a truly impressive breadth of scholarship, and is a consistently conservative summary of the biblical evidence as well as the critical arguments at every conceivable point of importance in the contemporary christological debate. The book is thorough, competent, and orthodox; it brings together in one volume much helpful material for the convenience of both teacher and student.'
Robert Strimple, Westminster Theological Seminary in California

'Robert Reymond has powerfully reaffirmed the biblical view that Jesus Christ is God incarnate... a superb summary of the biblical case, which will be a valuable help in defending the faith.'
Andrew T.B. McGowan, Highland Theological College

Robert Reymond is Professor of Systematic Theology at Knox Theological Seminary in Florida and is a prolific author.

ISBN 1 85792 8024

GOD-CENTERED
PREACHER
DEVELOPING A PULPIT MINISTRY APPROVED BY GOD
ROBERT L. REYMOND

The God-Centered Preacher
Developing a Pulpit Ministry Approved by God
Robert Reymond

Walk into most Christian churches in the western world today, and the chances of you hearing a biblically based and penetrating relevant message is to be polite, slim. Even churches claiming to be evangelical or reformed all too often tend towards market led, comforting talks on the one hand and impenetrable, jargon-filled theological lectures on the other. How can preachers maintain a sensible balance?

Robert Reymond has trained hundreds of pastors, and has an intimate understanding of the areas where preachers are inclined to fail. He points to 8 qualities that all Pastors should aspire to in their ministries, qualities that are all too often lacking. These include the need for a Scripturally Grounded Pulpit, the need for a Theologic-ally Articulate Pulpit and the need for an Evangelistic Pulpit.

Among the growing number of books on preaching, this one should take its place at the top echelon and be made a consistent and ready reference for reminding us that truth, passionately believed, fervently lived, and articulately presented governs the preaching task.
Tom Nettles, Southern Baptist Theological Seminary

...a very stimulating read. The first chapter alone offers immense encouragement to the preacher, buttressing confidence in the 'mere words' of Scripture to communicate the truth of God with power, and those following issue a much-needed call for robust theology, truly biblical evangelism, and genuine piety in the pulpit. ...I would heartily recommend these essays as of real value to any serious-thinking pastor, (not to mention the fact that there are gems to be plundered among the illustrative sermons at the end!)
William J U Philip, The Proclamation Trust

Robert Reymond is Professor of Systematic Theology at Knox Theological Seminary, Florida.

ISBN 1-85792-896-2

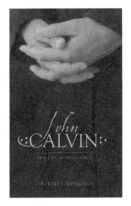

John Calvin : His Life and Influence
Robert L Reymond

"…despite his stern Calvinist upbringing" – Why is it that in the modern media the word Calvinist is always accompanied by "Stern" or "dour" or "Strict"? While most of the people who use the terms together have next to no knowledge of what Calvinism is, they have even less about who this man Calvin was. Was he some old-style reactionary? Was he some hard-line ayatollah – raging at the world without any thought? Or is there more to this man than the uninformed critics of today would have us believe?

Robert Reymond brings us John Calvin the man. The reality is quite different from the caricature often painted today. He was a man of deep spirituality, real love for he fellow man and God and with tremendous intellectual abilities. Whether the moniker "Stern Calvinist" can be applied to you or not – John Calvin's life has much to teach us.

'…tells the story of Calvin's life and thought in a compact and compelling way that will serve to acquaint readers with the warm human character of Calvin and make them want to study his writings. His description of Calvin's masterful statement at the Lausanne Disputation of 1536 is by itself worth the price of the book.'
William S. Barker, Westminster Theological Seminary, Pennsylvania

'Reymond's book is succinct and comprehensive, appreciative and probing, historical and theological, scholarly and pastoral. Especially valuable is Reymond's treatment of the burning of Servetus in which he summarizes William Cunningham's five considerations that ameliorate to some degree Calvin's involvement in the tragedy – and adds eight further points of his own.'
David Calhoun, Covenant Theological Seminary, St Louis

'…sheds new light on a famous and familiar name. His writing style is scholarly and authoritative, but at the same time anecdotal and intensely interesting reading.'
**D. James Kennedy,
Coral Ridge Presbyterian Church, Fort Lauderdale, Florida**

Robert Reymond is Professor of Systematic Theology at Knox Theological Seminary, Florida.

ISBN 1-85792-966-7

Christian Focus Publications

publishes books for all ages

Our mission statement –

STAYING FAITHFUL

In dependence upon God we seek to help make His infallible Word, the Bible, relevant. Our aim is to ensure that the Lord Jesus Christ is presented as the only hope to obtain forgiveness of sin, live a useful life and look forward to heaven with Him.

REACHING OUT

Christ's last command requires us to reach out to our world with His gospel. We seek to help fulfill that by publishing books that point people towards Jesus and help them develop a Christ-like maturity. We aim to equip all levels of readers for life, work, ministry and mission.

Books in our adult range are published in three imprints.

Christian Focus contains popular works including biographies, commentaries, basic doctrine and Christian living. Our children's books are also published in this imprint.

Mentor focuses on books written at a level suitable for Bible College and seminary students, pastors, and other serious readers. The imprint includes commentaries, doctrinal studies, examination of current issues and church history.

Christian Heritage contains classic writings from the past.

Christian Focus Publications, Ltd
Geanies House, Fearn, Tain,
Ross-shire, IV20 1TW, Scotland, United Kingdom
info@christianfocus.com

For details of our titles visit us on our website
www.christianfocus.com